Anthropology of Religion

The Unity and Diversity of Religions

ALSO AVAILABLE FROM MCGRAW-HILL BY RICHLEY H. CRAPO

CULTURAL ANTHROPOLOGY:
UNDERSTANDING OURSELVES AND OTHERS,
5TH ED. (2002)

Anthropology of Religion:

The Unity and Diversity of Religions

Richley H. Crapo
Utah State University

Boston   Burr Ridge, IL   Dubuque, IA   Madison, WI   New York
San Francisco   St. Louis   Bangkok   Bogotá   Caracas   Kuala Lumpur
Lisbon   London   Madrid   Mexico City   Milan   Montreal   New Delhi
Santiago   Seoul   Singapore   Sydney   Taipei   Toronto

McGraw-Hill Higher Education

A Division of The McGraw-Hill Companies

ANTHROPOLOGY OF RELIGION: THE UNITY AND DIVERSITY OF RELIGIONS
Published by McGraw-Hill, a business unit of The McGraw-Hill Companies, Inc., 1221 Avenue of the Americas, New York, NY, 10020. Copyright © 2003 by The McGraw-Hill Companies, Inc. All rights reserved. No part of this publication may be reproduced or distributed in any form or by any means, or stored in a database or retrieval system, without the prior written consent of The McGraw-Hill Companies, Inc., including, but not limited to, in any network or other electronic storage or transmission, or broadcast for distance learning. Some ancillaries, including electronic and print components, may not be available to customers outside the United States.

This book is printed on acid-free paper.

1 2 3 4 5 6 7 8 9 0 DOC/DOC 0 9 8 7 6 5 4 3 2

ISBN 0-07-238723-8

Publisher: *Phillip A. Butcher*
Sponsoring editor: *Kevin Witt*
Developmental editor: *Pamela Gordon*
Senior marketing manager: *Daniel M. Loch*
Media producer: *Shannon Rider*
Project manager: *Ruth Smith*
Production supervisor: *Carol Bielski*
Senior designer: *Jenny El-Shamy*
Lead supplement producer: *Marc Mattson*
Photo research coordinator: *Alexandra Ambrose*
Cover image: *©Bonnie Pelnar*
Typeface: *10/12/Palatino*
Compositor: *G&S Typesetters*
Printer: *R. R. Donnelley and Sons Company*

Library of Congress Cataloging-in-Publication Data
Crapo, Richley H.
    Anthropology of religion: the unity and diversity of religions / Richley H. Crapo.
        p. cm.
    Includes bibliographical references and index.
    ISBN 0-07-238723-8 (alk. paper)
    1. Religion.   I. Title.
BL48 .C72 2003
306.6—dc21
                                                                        2002069566

www.mhhe.com

To my beloved wife, Sharon

Brief Table of Contents

Table of Contents

7. Religious Ritual

10. Religious Adaptation and Change   250

Preface

The anthropological study of religion is as old as anthropology itself. This is quite understandable, for religion is a distinctively human phenomenon. In my view, no attempt to understand the human condition could be complete without addressing the nature of religion and the variety of its manifestations from culture to culture. This text attempts to do so in a systematic way that will introduce students to the complexities of defining what religion is, to the ways in which religion influences and is influenced by other parts of culture, and to the underlying unity within the diversity of specific religious forms. The text is meant to be used either as a stand-alone text or with the accompaniment of a reader. (The Instructor's Manual includes a correlation guide that shows how the chapters of the text coordinate with the popular anthologies about the anthropology of religion).

Overview/Approach

Despite more than 200 years of study, no consensus has been achieved even on how best to define the subject of study. Indeed, some anthropologists assert that it is futile to attempt to define religion. For instance, in the 1940s anthropologist William Howells ([1948]1986) wrote of efforts to define religion. He stated that most attempts rely on "rewording the older definitions so carefully and fulsomely that they sound as though they had been written by a lawyer. They do not satisfy, however, because religion needs a description rather than a definition." (p. 20). The sociologist Max Weber ([1922]1963) said it even more directly: "To define 'religion,' to say what it *is* is not possible at the start of a presentation. . . . Definition can be attempted, if at all, only at the conclusion of the study" (p. 1).

The intractability of religion, its unyielding refusal to be easily defined in any way that readily lends itself to useful cross-cultural application has led to an unusual state of affairs in textbooks about religion. There is a tendency to leave the very subject matter of the books undefined. Authors rely on students' ability to fall back onto their own intuitions about what religion is. This contrasts, of course, with social science texts on other institutions, in which defining the boundaries of the subject is usually the first order of business. In the study of religion, we are confronted starkly with what anthropologist Melford Spiro has characterized as "jurisdictional disputes over the phenomenon or range of phenomena which are considered to constitute legitimately the empirical referent of the term" (1966, p. 86).

Analyzing religion is like trying to unravel a mass of tangled yarn. Aside from the complexity inherent in anthropology's consistent demand for cross-cultural validity in its pronouncements about any topic, a description of even a particular religion can be a tricky business. After all, religion overlaps so much with a variety of other institutions that they are not easily teased apart. For instance, art and religion seem to go hand in hand in most societies. It is not always clear whether particular customs can be unambiguously labeled "religious" as opposed to "aesthetic." Similarly, religion and political life can often seem so intertwined that it is difficult to say for sure where one leaves off and the other begins. Other, equally problematic overlaps seem to occur between religion, abnormal psychology, social values, and cultural norms.

Nevertheless, I have always felt uneasy at the I-know-it-when-I-see-it approach to any subject of formal inquiry. Whether a subject matter is formally defined or not, the author of any text follows some criteria in selecting the material that is covered in a text, and these criteria implicitly define the topic. The definition that shapes my own thinking about religion and, therefore, the contents of this text is this one: Religion is a socially shared system of *anthropomorphic* beliefs and associated feelings that are symbolically expressed through rituals that are performed by individuals and groups to influence the universe for the benefit of human beings. Why "anthropomorphic"? Because, in my opinion, this word better captures the essence of what is really meant by the vaguer and problematic terms, "supernatural," "superempirical," or "sacred" that earlier anthropologists often used when writing about the distinctive beliefs of religious ideologies. This idea will be discussed in detail in chapter 2.

Distinctive Features

It is clear that wherever we find religion, it manifests itself in at least three contexts: the ideological, the behavioral, and the social. That is, the ideological subsystem of religion includes specific, shared beliefs and values. The behavioral subsystem includes customary—often ritualized—ways of "doing religion." The social subsystem involves various kinds of groups into which people congregate for religious purposes—each with its own distinctive religious structure and religious statuses. But there has been much debate over which of these three arenas should be given priority in our conception of what religion most fundamentally is. This text will cover each of these subsystems of religion in turn. The various ways in which anthropologists have attempted to define religions are described in chapter 1. We explore the diversity of religion in chapter 2. How religious ideology relates to the psychology of its participants is the focus of chapter 3, while religious symbolism, including myths, legends, and religious artifacts, is the subject of chapter 4. The affective component of religious ideology, along with the relationships among religion and the other institutions of expressive culture, is discussed in chapter 5. Chapter 6 highlights the relationships between religion and language, a topic that surprisingly has received scant coverage in texts on religion even though language is both a prerequisite to the very existence of religion and a central feature in religious practice. Religious ritual, the second major building block of religion, is the subject of chapter 7. The social organization of religion is treated in chapter 8. Having then covered the basic characteristics of religion, we consider how religions adjust and adapt to their social environment in chapter 9 and how they adapt to their natural environments and sometimes change in dramatic ways in chapter 10.

This text includes a number of important pedagogical elements to facilitate student learning. Each chapter begins with a chapter outline and a clear statement of the chapter's learning objectives to help students recognize where their attention should be focused. Each chapter's text begins with an extended case study that illustrates some central concepts of the chapter using examples drawn from a variety of religions from various parts of the world and from different periods of human history. The theoretical discussion of each chapter's topics is complemented with a series of boxes that provide concrete illustrations for new concepts as they are introduced. Wherever new terminology is introduced to students, the terms are given in bold where they first appear, and a running glossary is provided in the page margins to provide students with easily accessible, succinct definitions. Chapter summaries distill each chapter's main concepts and are followed by study questions to encourage students to review the primary ideas of each chapter. Each chapter also provides students with an annotated list of recommended book-length readings and an annotated list of recommended websites that deal with the topic of the chapter. An end-of-text alphabetized glossary for all terms that have been introduced in the text is also provided to make it easy for students to quickly find a useful definition of any previously learned concept.

Supplements

As a full-service publisher of quality educational products, McGraw-Hill does much more than just sell textbooks. It creates and publishes an extensive array of print, video, and digital supplements for students and instructors. *Anthropology of Religion* includes an exciting supplements package. Orders of new (versus used) textbooks help to defray the cost of developing such supplements, which is substantial. Please consult your local McGraw-Hill representative for more information on any of the supplements.

For the Student

Website to accompany ANTHROPOLOGY OF RELIGION—this free student supplement features the following helpful tools at www.mhhe.com/craporeligion1:

- Chapter summaries
- Self-quizzes (with feedback indicating why an answer is correct or incorrect)

- Key terms
- Vocabulary flashcards
- Career opportunities
- Web links
- Suggested list of films

For the Instructor

Instructor's Manual and Test Bank—this indispensable supplement features chapter overviews, lecture/discussion launchers, film suggestions, teaching suggestions, a correlation guide to popular anthropology of religion anthologies and a complete test bank.

Website to Accompany Anthropology of Religion—password-protected access to important instructor support materials and downloadable information in the instructor's manual.

Acknowledgments

I am grateful for the insightful contributions of the editorial director, Phil Butcher, and of the sponsoring editors, Carolyn Meier and Kevin Witt, and for the important efforts of the development editor, Pamela Gordon; the editorial coordinator, Julie Abodeely; the project managers, Laura Majersky and Ruth Smith; the copy editor, Joan Pendleton; the marketing manager, Dan Loch; the production supervisor, Carol Bielski; the designer, Jenny El-Shamy; the photo research coordinator, Alex Ambrose; and others at McGraw-Hill. I deeply appreciate the insightful suggestions made by the reviewers. The publisher and I wish to thank them for their constructive criticism and expert advice:

Marjorie Snipes—State University of West Georgia
David Knowlton—University of Utah
William Stuart—University of Maryland
Gerald E. Waite—Ball State University
Cynthia Mahmood—University of Maine
Jay Crain—California State University at Sacramento
Lesley Sharp—Barnard College
Webb Keane—University of Michigan
Phyllis Morrow—University of Alaska—Fairbanks
Mark Whitaker—University of South Carolina at Aiken
Gregory A. Reinhardt—University of Indianapolis
Thomas E. Durbin—California State University—Stanislaus
Robert Shanafelt—Florida State University
John Studstill—Columbus State University
David Turkon—Glendale Community College
Sean O'Neill—University of Oklahoma

About the Author

Richley H. Crapo received his PhD from the University of Utah in 1970 and is currently employed as a tenured professor of anthropology at Utah State University, where he has worked for 32 years and currently serves as chair of the Area Studies in Religion Program. He carried out his dissertation fieldwork, a study of language use by Shoshone Indians, on the Duckwater Reservation near Ely, Nevada, and subsequently published the definitive dictionary of the Big Smokey Valley dialect of Shoshone through the University of Nevada Press. His interest in Native American languages has not flagged, and he has published books on Bolivian Quechua and on cross-cultural research in human psychology. His text, *Cultural Anthropology: Understanding Ourselves and Others*, (McGraw-Hill, 2001) is now in its 5th edition. Professor Crapo's areas of expertise are symbolic anthropology (combining interests in language, personality, and religion) and gender (with an emphasis on supranumary genders and sexual identity). He has published articles in areas as diverse as Uto-Aztecan, historical linguistics, the cross-cultural characteristics of homosexuality, and Mormon studies. His hobby is gold prospecting.

CHAPTER 1

Anthropological Viewpoints about Religion

CHAPTER OUTLINE

CHAPTER OBJECTIVES

When you finish this chapter, you will be able to

1. Discuss the distinctive approach of anthropology.
2. Distinguish between scientific and humanistic approaches to explaining religion.
3. Outline the historically important insights about religion that have come from anthropology.
4. Discuss the difficulties in defining religion.
5. Discuss the differences between cognitive, social order, affective, existential, behavioral, psychological, and cultural definitions of religion.

Saying what religion *is* is no simple matter. Were all religions extremely similar, it would be much easier to achieve a consensus about its defining characteristics.

However, the world of religion is extremely diverse, and religion shares so much with other institutions such as art, play, and drama that the boundaries between it and them are sometimes quite fuzzy. For this reason, anthropologists have debated since the Victorian era how best to define religion, and even today it is perhaps an overstatement to say that we have achieved only a tenuous consensus about what ought to be considered a religion and what ought not.

The Pygmy of the Ituri Forest quite nicely illustrate the difficulty in recognizing religion. Colin Turnbull (1961) described preparations for the most important Pygmy ceremony, the *molimo,* as being carried out very casually. To prepare for the molimo, men went out to hunt for meat; women gathered mushrooms, nuts, and fruits; and children laughed and played. Turnbull pointed out that "The casual observer might have thought the youngsters were playing a game when they went around from hut to hut with a fishing line and a basket, collecting food from everyone. There was certainly nothing about the demeanor to indicate that this was an essential part of the great act of communion. And if the same observer were told that this was so, he would probably form the opinion that the molimo, whatever it was, could not mean very much if it was treated so lightly and casually" (p. 145). But for the Pygmy, neither the demeanor nor the accompanying thoughts of the participants were particularly important. The ritual need not be carried out with solemnity nor with special care or attention to the precision of its performance. For the Pygmy the forest is a personification of a benevolent deity whom they think of as being much like a caring parent. For them, the ritual simply serves as a means of communicating that everyone in the group—men, women, and children—give their deity the care, affection, and consideration that a child owes a parent. They do this by involving everyone in the collection and donation of the food that will represent their offering to the deity during the molimo. In this way, each member of the community enters a relationship with the deity in which he or she assumes that the forest will naturally reciprocate these offerings just as parents respond to their children by caring for their needs.

The centerpiece of the molimo is the food offering. The content of the "ceremony" involves nothing more than the men of the community singing together until late in the evening when, finally, the sacred molimo trumpets that are usually kept hidden in the forest are brought into the camp. Then, as the old men sing, the youth dance, and the molimo fire is fanned up. Afterward, the men hunt while the girls stay home with the women and sing together in one of the huts. After the hunt, the men stand together near the fire, resting, while the girls dance around them. In the evening, both the women and men sing the sacred molimo songs and dance. Eventually, the women's dancing becomes an effort to stamp out the molimo fire and scatter the embers with their feet, while the men do their best to retrieve the embers and return them to the fire pit and then revive the fire with erotic dances. After the men succeed in reviving the fire, an old woman symbolically ties the men together with a cord until the men—who do not resist—admit that they have been constrained by her efforts and agree on a ransom to pay her for their release. After that, the ceremony ends after some discussion about when and where to do so, since there is no fixed length for the molimo celebration.

The emphasis in all this is not on following precise and fixed forms or carefully acting out specific myths. Rather, participation is largely spontaneous, and the details might vary from one occasion to another. What is important is that the molimo ceremony allows all members of the community to participate in the web of relations that make up the community during this sacred occasion, thereby expressing and reinforcing their similar kinlike relationship with their deity. Other Pygmy religious rituals entail the same message of connectedness between human individuals and the forest as the spiritual parent and provider to its human "children." For instance, in the christening ceremony, an infant has vines tied about its ankles, wrists, and waist as a symbolic means of creating a spiritual bond between the forest and the infant. An outsider might easily mistake such Pygmy religious rituals as simply recreational activities or aesthetic expressions. Nothing in particular would make it easy for a casual observer to distinguish the Pygmies singing to the forest from a group of stoned hippies or Victorian poets grooving on Nature, with individuals perfectly free to participate or walk away, however the mood strikes them. The only way to equate this behavior with religion is to adopt a view of religion so broad that it becomes vacuous.

In this chapter, we explore the various ways in which anthropologists have attempted to define the essence of religion—the quality that distinguishes it from other parts of human life, the unity of religion within its great diversity of specific forms (of which the Ituri Forest Pygmy are but one example). Let us begin with the case of the Shoshone "water baby," a case study that illustrates the difficulty in recognizing what is or is not a religious belief in a culture different from one's own.

CASE STUDY

Water Baby, A Shoshone Religious Belief?

As part of my anthropological studies, I spent some time living among the Western Shoshone of the Duckwater Reservation in Nevada. While I was there, I worked to document social patterns in the use of the Shoshone language and to gather information about Shoshone culture. My Shoshone acquaintances sometimes told me about their traditional religious beliefs, but they also talked about the natural environment around them, including its plants and the various animals that inhabit the Great Basin desert in which they lived. Among the stories I collected were some about a creature they called paʔohmaa, *which is usually translated as "water baby" in English.*

A water baby is an unusual creature said to live in the water of springs and rivers. About the size and shape of a human baby, it also has a cry that sounds uncannily like the crying of a human baby. In addition, it has some rather gruesome habits. For instance, water babies are known for stealing human babies if they are left unattended near the water. Sometimes they will take the place of an infant and attract the mother with their cry. If a mother tries to still a water baby by letting it nurse, it will attach itself to her breast with its sharp teeth and suck the blood from her body until she dies.

My first inclination was to understand these stories about water babies as an interesting part of the traditional Shoshone religion and to classify them as something like Western folk beliefs about vampires. Although followers of mainstream Western denominations

*generally do not believe in vampires today, the existence of vampires—undead humans who
could rise from the grave and attack other human beings to drink their blood—was widely
accepted as a religious folk belief in eastern Europe during the 18th century.*

*However, classifying water babies as a Shoshone religious belief was not a simple mat-
ter. For one thing, Shoshones who told me about water babies were consistent in denying that
they were supernatural creatures. The Shoshone language has a distinctive name for religious
stories. They are called* isapaippeh nanatowente, *or Coyote stories. Although the supernatural being Coyote figures prominently in many Coyote stories, the label is applied to any
religious story, even those in which he does not appear. And Shoshones are unanimous: Stories about water babies are* not *Coyote stories. Those who told me about water babies were
insistent that they were ordinary animals such as badgers, wolves, or mountain lions.*

*The case of water babies illustrates the problem of how to recognize religious things in
another culture. Were one to write a book about the Shoshone culture, should a discussion
of water babies be included within the chapter on Shoshone religion or in a chapter on how
Shoshones classify living things in the desert habitat they occupy? In the former case, water
babies would constitute a special subset of religious beliefs, those that are not part of the
Shoshone category of "Coyote stories." In so classifying water babies, we would be asserting
that there is a category of religious ideas among the Shoshone that they themselves do not
consider to be part of their own religion. In such a case, it would certainly be incumbent on
us to demonstrate why we should classify the belief in water babies as a religious belief. If, on
the other hand, we accept at face value the Shoshone claim that water babies are ordinary animals rather than ones that belong to the realm of Coyote, we might discuss water babies as
part of Shoshone folk beliefs about the animal realm, noting that no such animal had yet been
scientifically documented.*

ANTHROPOLOGICAL APPROACHES
TO DEFINING RELIGION

Anthropologists bring a different perspective to the study of religion than do
other scholars. First, individual anthropologists base their descriptions of religions on firsthand observation by participating in the lives of those whose religious practices and beliefs they wish to understand. Second, their descriptions
and analyses of religion place each religion in its broader cultural context by discussing how it affects and is affected by such things as the economic, political,
and family life of its followers; their political values; and their family life. Finally, anthropologists who attempt to develop valid generalizations about religion and its relationship to other social institutions base their generalizations on
the broadest possible range of religions.

Anthropological Fieldwork

Anthropology also differs from other fields that study the human condition in
the methods it uses to gather information. The characteristic method of anthropology is **fieldwork,** which involves direct observation of people in the settings
in which they actually live. In **cultural anthropology,** the subdivision of the field

fieldwork
The process of
living for a pro-
longed time in a
society to docu-
ment its customs
and idealogy.
**cultural
anthropology**
The subdivision
of the field that
specializes in the
study of human
ways of life.

that specializes in the study of human ways of life, the form that fieldwork takes is known as **participant observation,** a process of participating with and observing subjects in their natural setting. Participant observation is not mere passive observation, but involves a give-and-take relationship in which anthropologists interact with those from whom they wish to learn, asking questions and seeking clarification of the ideas they formulate about how those people understand their own beliefs, feelings, and practices. Through constant clarification, anthropologists hope to achieve a more intimate and valid understanding of the insiders' ways of thinking about their own lives and customs. Although they may supplement this approach with other techniques, such as sociological questionnaires, to obtain quantifiable information, they believe that actual interaction with people for prolonged periods ultimately gives a more accurate picture of customs, beliefs, and feelings than do other approaches.

Anthropological Interpretation

Fundamental to all anthropological approaches to religion is the distinctive anthropological concept of **culture,** a learned system of beliefs, feelings, and rules for living that is shared by a group of people and that is outwardly manifested in behavior and artifacts. Anthropologists view religion as a part of any society's culture. Culture, including religious culture, is both a system of meanings that inform how people understand themselves and the world around them and a system of rules that guide how people interact with one another and adapt to the natural environment in which they live. Anthropologists who are interested in culture as a system of meanings analyze cultures much as literature is analyzed by examining the symbols of which the cultural system is composed and their meaningful relationships to one another. Anthropologists who are interested in culture as a system of rules that guide how people use their natural environments analyze the ways that cultures function in institutions such as economics, politics, and family life and the ways such institutions influence human adaptation in various natural environments.

Scientific Approaches

Anthropologists whose interests lean toward the scientific goal of explaining and predicting human behavior examine religion in the context of its interactions with other parts of culture, such as economic or political institutions, and with the natural environment. These anthropologists emphasize the practical influences of social life, human biological and psychological needs, technology, and the environment on religious practices and beliefs. Their goal is to determine what elements of religion are predictable responses to the circumstances in which human beings find themselves and to isolate the factors that give rise to the diverse religions of the world. This goal is achieved by means of **cross-cultural comparison,** the use of statistical comparisons drawn from a broad range of different cultures to test specific hypotheses about relationships among different parts of culture or between a part of culture and the natural environment.

participant observation
The form of fieldwork that uses a process of participating with and observing subjects in their natural setting.

culture
A learned system of beliefs, feelings, and rules for living shared by a group of people.

cross-cultural comparison
The use of statistical comparisons from a broad range of different cultures to test specific hypotheses about relationships among different parts of culture or between a part of culture and the natural environment.

Humanistic Approaches

Other anthropologists are more interested in studying the diversity of human religions from a humanistic perspective. Their goal is to broaden our understanding of religion as a system of meanings. In seeking to understand what religions mean to those who practice them, humanistic anthropologists have much in common with translators of foreign languages. Sometimes this work involves writing *descriptions* of particular religions that portray them in terms that their own adherents will view as a true representation of their own beliefs and practices. At other times, their effort is to *interpret* religion in an attempt to make comprehensible what might otherwise seem strange and exotic to outsiders by explaining it in terms that are familiar to the outsider's way of thinking. Humanistic interpretations of religion are typically carried out using a methodology known as **cultural relativism,** the idea that the meanings of any custom are best understood in the cultural context to which they belong. Humanistic anthropologists are careful to avoid judgmental evaluations of the religious customs and beliefs they study, because such judgments involve applying the anthropologist's own values, and this does not help outsiders understand customs and beliefs as they are understood by those in the culture being studied.

**cultural
relativism**
The approach
to interpreting
meaning that
holds that the
meanings of any
custom are most
accurately under-
stood in light of
the cultural con-
text from which
they derive.

HISTORICAL CONTRIBUTIONS TO AN ANTHROPOLOGY OF RELIGION

Anthropological interest in religion is as old as anthropology itself. After all, religion is one of the most dramatic manifestations of the human symbolic capacities that are cultural anthropology's historic preoccupation. But in spite of the long interest, the task of defining what religion is has been far from easy. Identifying exactly what to call a religion is complicated by a number of facts. First, the religions of the world are tremendously diverse. It is not enough to treat our own intuitions about religion as if they are typical characteristics of religion in general, since each of our personal perspectives has been influenced by whatever particular cultural tradition we were socialized into. So the intuitions of followers of any one religion about what the essence of religion is may be quite different from the intuitions of those who follow other religions. The anthropologist's goal is to find a way of characterizing religion that applies equally to all of the world's many religions.

However, there is a chicken-and-egg problem in determining what the essential nature of religion is. Given the great diversity of religion, it is not always clear just what should be classified as a religion before comparisons are made. At the least, we must begin with some implicit criterion for what constitutes a religion before we can make up a list of the religions of the world to be examined for common elements. Unfortunately, we cannot merely consider an institution to be a religion because its participants designate it as such. Most of the world's languages have no explicit word for religion. In most societies, religion is not segregated from other activities in a way that demands a special word to identify it. Rather it is integrated into everyday life and can therefore be difficult to separate from artistic activities, politics, or economics. It is when religious life contrasts with secular activities—for instance, when there are full-time religious specialists who monopolize the religious authority to perform group rituals and when the rituals they perform are scheduled for special, sacred days—that a word is likely to develop that refers to the sacred activities of religion. An anthropological approach to religion must surmount the problem that all languages do not have a word for religion. Again, this requires that some a priori assumptions must be made about what characteristic or characteristics may serve as a valid indicator that we are dealing with religion. Historically, the earliest anthropologists adopted the stance that religion always dealt with ideas about a **supernatural** realm, a realm of beings and powers that are believed to lie beyond the realm of natural things.

The absence of native terms for what we call religion is not an insurmountable obstacle, but it does require some clear consensus about how we, as outsiders, should decide when to call activities in another culture by our term *religion*. The question of how best to define religion must be resolved, if we want to avoid turning a text on the world's religions into a grab bag of exotica. This claim is not as extreme as it may sound. The religions of the world are diverse in part because their symbols and practices need not be rational. Individual religions may, of course, attempt to create systematic theologies that are internally self-consistent and logical, but other religions may be tolerant of diverse—even apparently contradictory or paradoxical—beliefs among their followers. For instance, the Aztec at the time of the Conquest held at least five different traditions about the origins of one of their more important deities, Quetzalcoatl, each of which attributed his birth to a different father. There is no evidence that the Aztec themselves worried much about this diversity of opinion. That religion does not necessarily subordinate its beliefs and practices to any particular guiding standard of thought, such as logic, supports symbols that are highly meaningful to members of a given religion but that may seem strange, even bizarre, to those of other religious backgrounds. Even anthropologists, who should know better, fall prey to the tendency to assume that if the nature or purpose of something is not transparent, it may be because its meaning is of an esoteric religious nature. In fact, equating religion with the bizarre has been a common enough error within the field that there is an old anthropological joke about calling any strange object from a non-Western culture a "ritual artifact of unknown religious significance." But if strangeness or lack of scientific footing is grounds for identifying a belief as religious, then is belief in UFOs, Bigfoot, or the Loch Ness Monster a religious belief? How about the childhood belief in Santa Claus? I hope you can see what a slippery slope such an approach is. It is also an approach based on subjectivity, since what is strange to one observer may not be so to another. Can "evolutionary humanism" be a "religion" as Julian Huxley (1957) claimed? Is it correct to speak of Marxism or National Socialism as someone's "religion," or is this merely a metaphor? Without a definition of *religion*, it is impossible to answer such questions with any degree of agreement.

On what basis shall we examine the belief in something strange or unscientific and determine that the thing referred to is not "natural"? If we resort to simply deciding that belief in things that are not accepted by the contemporary scientific community as "real" should be called "supernatural beliefs," then we adopt a truly ethnocentric method, one that amounts in essence to equating

supernatural
Pertaining to beings and powers that are believed to lie beyond the realm of natural things.

"supernatural" with "(scientifically) false." But at its core, the problem is thornier than that, since there is—by definition—no epistemologically acceptable way of creating an empirical definition of a supposedly superempirical thing. It is therefore not surprising that no dominant consensus exists among anthropologists about how best to define religion. Rather, scholars have developed a variety of different approaches, including those that avoid even the attempt to formalize a definition, relying instead on the audience's ability to intuit the nature of religion from the topics discussed. Although I personally regard it as important for the sake of clarity to define one's subject matter formally rather than simply to leave one's definitions implicit and unclarified, I will not attempt to impose my own preferred definition at this point in the text. Instead, in this chapter, I wish to communicate a sense of the breadth of approaches that have informed anthropological thought concerning religion during the field's nearly 150-year history.

To give a sense of the diversity of views about the nature of religion, it may help to examine the history of anthropological approaches to the subject. The earliest anthropological definitions of religion were formulated during the era of Victorian scholarship and, not unsurprisingly, these approaches cast the spotlight on the ideological component of religion and emphasized the distinctively nonscientific ways of conceiving the universe that they believed differentiated religious thinking from their own ways of understanding reality within the framework of positivist science. I will refer to the definitions of this period as "cognitive definitions" because of their focus on religious beliefs and ideas.

Cognitive Definitions: Religion as Beliefs

Sir Edward Burnett Tylor was the first scholar to hold an academic appointment as an anthropologist—at Oxford University in 1884. Tylor viewed religion through the lenses of a Victorian scholar, seeing it primarily as a system of nonscientific beliefs. He offered ([1871]1958) what he called a "minimum definition of religion" as **animism,** or the belief in spiritual beings such as souls, ghosts, demons, and gods. As a cultural evolutionist, he was particularly interested in the origin of religion among early humans, and he suggested that the belief in spiritual beings began when primitive humans were confronted with mysterious events for which they had no scientific explanation:

animism
The belief in
spiritual beings.

> A person who a few minutes ago was walking and talking, with all his senses active, goes off motionless and unconscious in a deep sleep, to wake after a while with renewed vigor. In other conditions the life ceases more entirely, when one is stunned or falls into a swoon or trance, where the beating of the heart and breathing seem to stop, and the body, lying deadly pale and insensible, cannot be awakened; this may last for minutes or hours, or even days, and yet after all the patient revives. (pp. 202–3)

soul
A spirit that
animates the
human body.

ghosts
Disembodied
human souls that
linger and do
harm to living
humans.

Early humans, Tylor believed, postulated the existence of a **soul** to explain these and other similar experiences. The coming and going of the soul explained such events as unconsciousness, dreams, and death: Dreams were memories of the soul's experiences during its nightly wanderings, and death was the result of its failure to return. From human souls, it is an easy step to the idea of **ghosts,** disembodied human souls that linger and do harm to living humans and **ancestral spirits** who continue their helpful involvement in the day-to-day earthly affairs of their descendants. According to Tylor, **gods,** spirit-beings who exercise greater-than-human power over major forces in the world or universe, arose when the spirits of important persons of the past were elevated to a higher level of power among the spirits.

According to Tylor, the religious belief in human souls led to practices such as avoiding burial places where ghosts might live or participating in **ancestor worship,** the practice of placating souls of deceased ancestors, who can be influenced to give aid to their descendants, and such religious forms eventually evolved into the worship of gods. Thus, Tylor's approach to religion used an evolutionary framework in which religious ideas and practices evolved from simple to complex.

Tylor's definition continues to be influential. For instance, Melford Spiro (1966, p. 96) offered a modified version of Tylor's definition of religion as an "institution consisting of culturally postulated interaction with culturally postulated superhuman beings."

One important criticism of Tylor's definition of religion was set forth by Robert R. Marett (1909), who regarded **animatism,** the belief in an impersonal spiritual force, as an even simpler and therefore more ancient religious idea. The idea of an unreasoning but powerful supernatural force, embodied in English words such as "sacredness" or "holiness," is probably found in all religions. However, the idea has been studied specifically in regard to the religions of Polynesia and Melanesia, where it is commonly referred to as **mana,** a term that anthropologists have adopted for the concept. The world's religions commonly portray supernatural power as residing in things and places that inspire feelings of awe, wonder, or dread, feelings that are appropriate toward the supernatural itself. Thus, unusual features of nature, such as high mountaintops, mysterious caves, and powerful waterfalls, are often regarded as mana-filled, sacred places. Even human creations, such as the awe-inspiring religious architecture of cathedrals, temples, and shrines, may be perceived as vessels of the sacredness anthropologists call *mana*.

The concept of mana is always associated with that of **taboos,** religious rules that forbid acts that bring people in contact with mana. Sacred supernatural power is both attractively awesome and potentially dangerous, and taboos prevent people both from profaning sacred things and from being harmed by the power of those sacred things. Certain acts can trigger the automatic workings of mana in ways that are harmful, and taboos are established to avoid these consequences. Among the Inuit of the North American Arctic, an important taboo forbade mixing seafoods such as seal meat with inland foods such as caribou meat. Doing so could bring on illness, not just to the person who violated the taboo but potentially to anyone in the vicinity of that individual. That it was not always the wrongdoer who was punished by the violation of the taboo meant that such infractions were antisocial acts as well as sins. So abiding by taboos is an important form of social responsibility. Even when a religion views the consequences of taboo violations as being suffered by the violator alone, such violations are still likely to be viewed as a rejection of the society itself, since religious taboos are important socially shared values within the religious community.

ancestral spirits
The souls of deceased persons who continue their helpful involvement in the day-to-day earthly affairs of their descendants.

gods
Spirit-beings who exercise greater than human power over major forces in the world or universe.

ancestor worship
The practice of placating souls of deceased ancestors who can be influenced to give aid to their descendants.

animatism
Belief in an impersonal spiritual force.

mana
Supernatural force or power.

taboos
Religious rules that forbid acts because they bring people in contact with mana.

The power of mana and the importance of taboos as protections are illustrated in the box titled "The Ark of the Covenant."

One special case of the cognitive approach focuses on the role of language as the vehicle of human thought and the lens through which religion is interpreted by its followers. Friedrich Max Müller, a German philologist with interests in comparative mythology, was interested in how linguistic processes might create religious ideas. He (1872) believed that religion developed through linguistic change as metaphors came to be thought of as actual descriptions. For instance, Müller argued that the Greek concept of a human soul developed from observation of the role of breathing in life. People lived while they breathed, and breath was like the air. The word *psyche* portrayed this relationship between air, breathing, and life. It originally meant both *breath* and *life.* The word would originally have been applied descriptively, as in "His breath has stopped"; but the second meaning, *life,* allowed an easy shift from description to metaphor to occur: "His life has gone out of him." Over time, it could be forgotten

Figure 1.1
Sacred Caves
Caves are often treated as sacred places where humans may commune with the supernatural. Shown here, Batu Caves in Kuala Lumpur, Malaysia, house several shrines and play an important role in the annual Thaipusim Festival, when fire-walking is performed in the caves.

 The Ark of the Covenant

A story in Exodus about the Ark of the Covenant offers a good illustration of the power of mana. The ark was a sacred box of acacia wood overlaid with gold. Its top was crowned with cherubim, whose outstretched wings pointed toward the center of the lid where God's visible glory was said to sometimes manifest itself. In the ark were kept the most sacred things of the Israelites: the Tables of the Law, a pot of manna (food miraculously provided to the Israelites in the wilderness), and Aaron's staff. So sacred was the ark, so full of spiritual power, that it was not to be touched by human hands. The ark was transported by authorized priests who carried it with poles that were passed through rings mounted on the sides of the ark. On one occasion when the ark was being transported on a cart, the oxen stumbled and the ark began to fall. Uzzah, a soldier, tried to prevent the ark from falling, but when his hand touched the box he died. His good intentions offered no protection from the terrible sacredness of the ark, which was taboo for good reason. His death followed his act, not as punishment for a sinful act in any moral sense, but as effect follows cause in the world of mana.

An interesting example of the ways in which language can influence what people conceive of as a compelling religious argument can be seen in a parallel between grammar and ideas that is found in the teleological argument for the existence of God. The teleological argument is an argument from design that is sometimes colloquially called the "Watchmaker argument." It asserts that where there is design, there must have been a designer and then points to the complexity and orderliness of the universe as indicative of design—thereby concluding that a Creator must have been responsible for the existence of such order and complexity.

In English, the teleological argument is sometimes pithily reduced to the succinct form, "Creation itself demands a Creator," an assertion that sounds intuitively true to the believer. However, if one examines this argument in terms of English grammar, it takes on a different significance than is intended when it is used as an argument for the existence of God. The word creation contains two meaningful elements, the root *create* and the suffix *-tion*, which was borrowed from Old French into English. This suffix means "that which has been _____-ed." In English, a noun-focused language, no declarative sentence (one that makes a contention about the nature of some part of reality) may occur without a subject that can carry out the action of the verb used. Therefore, the existence of the verb *create* (which is "demanded" by the existence of the noun *creation*) requires the existence of a noun that can serve as its subject in a declarative sentence. The noun that corresponds most closely to the verb *create* in the role of subject is the noun *creator*, which is formed of the same root and the Old French suffix *-tor*, which means "one who _____-s." Thus, what the argument "Creation itself demands a creator" really indicates is that the existence in English of a noun of the form *crea-tion* implies the existence of a verb *create*, which, in turn, requires the existence of a subject noun of the form *crea-tor*. Whether the existence of the universe, which may arbitrarily be labeled with the symbol *creation*, "demands" the existence of a preexisting deity who brought it into existence is another matter entirely. Although English speakers may be swayed by the "logic" of the sentence, this argument for the existence of God loses its impact when it is translated into many other languages.

that the "life" that departs when one dies is simply a metaphor for breath, and the word *psyche* came to be misunderstood as a concrete entity, a "soul" that had fled the body. Thus, religion to Müller was a kind of "disease" of language in which what began as metaphors eventually became concrete entities. The box titled "Creation Itself Demands a Creator" illustrates how language can play a role in how intuitively true a religious idea may seem.

The common thread of cognitive definitions is the idea that religious philosophies were always founded on some kind of belief in a supernatural realm, an idea that seemed natural to investigators whose Western culture had a long tradition of making the distinction between the natural universe and a supernatural realm. The debate among the proponents of substantive definitions long centered on which supernatural things—gods, souls, or impersonal powers—were both universal and most basic among the world's religions. Eventually, however, Irving Hallowell (1960) and Benson Saler (1977) pointed to a fundamental difficulty in all such definitions: their common reliance on the Western concept of the distinction between the "natural" and the "supernatural," a dichotomy that is not explicitly made in the majority of the world's religions. Definitions that rely on this Western folk concept are inadequate because they are culture-bound, and a strict adherence to them would, according to Werner Cohn (1967), recognize only a few of the world's many cultures as having religions.

This criticism of using the idea of the "supernatural" in definitions of religion can be expanded into *three* specific problems. First, it entails the claim that *the contrast between the supernatural and the natural realms is a product of the unique history of Western culture* and, hence, inappropriate to apply to other cultures. Second, it asserts that *the word "supernatural" implies too strong a dichotomy* to accurately reflect the ideologies of non-Western cultures. And, finally, it includes *the problem of determining when beliefs are "supernatural" rather than "natural."*

The Problem of Ethnocentrism

Some social scientists have suggested that since the use of the term *supernatural* was part of the Western theological tradition long before social science arose and since it is a word that is not part of the religious vocabulary of non-Western traditions, the use of the word by social scientists must necessarily be ethnocentric. **Ethnocentrism** is the attitude that one's own culture is superior to other cultures and that its concepts can therefore be used as the natural standard for interpreting and evaluating what goes on in other societies. Such a prejudicial approach to discussing religions that belong to other cultural traditions would not be a valid way to achieve a scientific understanding of those traditions. Nevertheless, the idea that since Western religions have long defined themselves in terms of their belief in the supernatural, it is necessarily ethnocentric to apply the concept of a supernatural realm to non-Western religions is mistaken. If a term is useful for analyzing religions in all cultures, then it is scientifically valid to use it for that purpose even if the theologians of a particular cultural tradition beat scientists to the punch in coining the term. Usefulness in helping us understand the ways in which religion functions in human societies is the sole scientific criterion of whether the term should be part of a scientific vocabulary.

However, although adopting a term from a particular cultural tradition does not, of itself, make the use of that term ethnocentric, there remain other problems with incorporating the term into the vocabulary of science. To be scientifically useful in discussing cross-cultural regularities, a term such as *the supernatural* must be definable in a way that permits the user of the term to accurately decide when to apply it in a discussion of a particular culture. As it turns out, despite the fact that the word *supernatural* is so widely used in Western cultures that its meaning seems unproblematic to most speakers of English, it has been particularly difficult to define in a way that makes it cross-culturally useful. We now examine two of the problems that social scientists have encountered in trying to incorporate this word into discussions of religion.

The Problem of Dichotomy

Is the word *supernatural* applicable to the religious ideologies of non-Western societies? When understood in the Western commonsense way to mean "beliefs concerning such things as gods, spirits, and otherworldly powers that do not seem understandable in terms of everyday folk science," then the word is useful enough. However, the word *supernatural* carries other cultural baggage that can mislead its users about the ideologies of non-Western cultures. The word arose out of the centuries of conflict between proponents of science and

ethnocentrism
The attitude that one's own culture is superior to other cultures and that its concepts can therefore be used as the natural standard for interpreting and evaluating what goes on in other societies.

proponents of religion in Western societies. This history has imparted to the word an implication that the "supernatural" or "superempirical" realm that Western theologians concern themselves with is distinctly set apart from the "natural" or "empirical" reality of interest to scientists. Understood in this way, the word *supernatural* implies too great a dichotomy to accurately reflect either the ideologies of non-Western religions or, for that matter, the religious understandings of many, if not most, lay followers of the Western religions as well.

Thus, to eliminate the Western implication that religion necessarily involves a clear-cut dichotomy between two separate and distinct realms of existence, the natural versus the supernatural, some students of religion have offered alternative terms such as *transcendent* or *sacred* as substitutes for *supernatural.*

The Problem of Identifying the Supernatural

However, none of these approaches deals with the third objection to the term *supernatural,* the impossibility of creating a scientifically useful, operational definition of the term. If the concept is justified as being scientifically useful as a cross-culturally valid category despite its not being universally present in the various religions of the world, then those who employ it must be able to specify just when a belief is a supernatural one. How do we know when a native belief pertains to something that we may properly call a supernatural realm if the native religious ideology does not include such a concept or if the believer denies that it does? It is not enough to simply define a belief as supernatural if it currently lacks scientific support. For one thing, scientific knowledge is an evolving thing. So using the current state of scientific knowledge as a criterion for what is not natural does not reliably provide consistent recognition of whether a set of beliefs is religious. More importantly, there is a problem of ethnocentrism inherent in defining religious beliefs as being scientifically false.

Various other approaches to religion have attempted to circumvent the problems associated with using the concept of a supernatural realm to define religion. These will be considered in turn.

Social Order Definitions of Religion: Religion as Congregation

Other anthropologists have emphasized religion as a social phenomenon. The social nature of religion manifests itself in two ways: All religions include group activities that involve a division of roles within the group, and all religious groups have important relationships with the other social groups and institutions of the society to which they belong. Anthropologists who have emphasized the social aspects of religion focus on how social relations play themselves out within the religious group and on the functional relations between religion and the rest of society.

Political theorist Karl Marx did not attempt to define religion, but he did develop a theory about the determinants of social life that included the relationships between religion and other institutions. Marx considered religion to be the product of changes in the mode of production—both the kinds of labor, tools, and techniques available in a society and the social relationships that determine how those resources are used and owned. Religion is thus largely an effect rather than a cause of social change; and its primary social function, according to Marx, is to inhibit change in the social order that gives rise to it. In Marx's view, where there is unequal access to wealth—as is invariably true in societies that have social classes—religion invariably serves the interests of the wealthy and powerful social classes by providing the working classes with the justification that their exploited circumstances are ordained by God.

Like Marx, the 19th-century sociologist Max Weber stressed the interaction of religion with other social institutions, such as economic institutions. Weber focused on the major religious traditions of literate societies—Confucianism, Taoism, Hinduism, and ancient Judaism. Perhaps because of this he was able to rely on his audience's common understanding of the word *religion* and did not, therefore, attempt to formulate a formal definition of the term. Nevertheless, Weber theorized about the ways religion influenced and was influenced by other institutions, and so we can say that his concept of religion emphasized its characteristic as a social institution and its important role in the history of society. Far more than Marx, Weber was willing to view religion as an active source of social change. For instance, Weber argued that the Protestant ethic embodied a value system that accounted for the political and economic changes that gave rise to capitalism, whose value system, he argued, was a special case of the more general Protestant ethic (1904).

French sociologist Emile Durkheim influenced the thinking of many anthropologists. His perspective on the nature of religion remains a major school of thought among anthropologists today. A scientific positivist by philosophy, Durkheim nevertheless believed that religion reveals what is fundamentally human about our species and argued that religion is "better adapted than any other institution . . . to show us an essential and permanent aspect of humanity" ([1912]1961, p. 13).

Durkheim argued that a science of religion must have something more substantial to study than supernatural beliefs, which cannot be directly observed or verified. What can be examined through scientific investigation, however, are the ways in which religion manifests itself as a social phenomenon. What characterizes religion, then, is not specifically the belief in things that are thought to be supernatural, but the behavior associated with those beliefs: "All known religious beliefs, whether simple or complex, present one common characteristic; they presuppose a classification of all things, real or ideal, of which men think into two classes . . . generally designated by two distinct terms which are translated well enough by the words profane and sacred" (p. 35). According to Durkheim, **sacred** things differ from the **profane** things, or the ordinary, everyday, work-a-day world; and because of the special feelings they inspire, they are set apart and forbidden. Thus, to Durkheim, religion is "a unified set of beliefs and practices relative to sacred things, that is to say, things set apart and forbidden—beliefs and practices which unite one single moral community—all those who adhere to them" (p. 37).

What distinguishes Durkheim's definition from the substantive definitions of Tylor or Marett was not his replacement of the contrast between the supernatural and the natural with the distinction between the sacred and the profane, since both oppositions perpetuate an important dichotomy between the ordinary world and the special realm of spirits and unusual powers to which reli-

sacred
The quality of things that differ from the profane, or everyday world and are set apart and forbidden because of the special feelings they inspire.

profane
The realm of ordinary, everyday experience.

gion is devoted. No, the central shift in Durkheim's conceptualization of religion is in his insistence that religious things, whether expressed as beliefs or rituals, "unite one single moral community," the community of believers. In short, Durkheim insisted that religion be understood as an essentially *social* phenomenon. In Durkheim's perspective, each religion is the product of its unique social circumstances, and its ideas symbolically embody the social categories that must be regarded as sacred if society is to survive.

To Durkheim, religion was a system of beliefs and practices concerning the sacred realm. He emphasized the importance of religious rituals as the expression of religious belief. Durkheim used descriptions of Aboriginal Australian religious beliefs and practices to illustrate his theory that religious beliefs are symbolic representations of the social order. Aboriginal Australians were foraging peoples who lived in small, seminomadic local groups. Members of each local group had relatives in other nearby groups, and these groupings of relatives formed a clan. Clan membership was socially important, since individuals were expected to marry outside their own clan, share food with fellow clan members even if they resided in other groups, and play different roles from those played by members of other clans in many other social events as well. Clan membership was also religiously important, since each clan was identified by its **totem,** a species of plant or animal, that was thought of as the spiritual ancestor of the members of that kinship group. Members of each clan were obligated by a religious taboo not to eat the type of animal or plant that was their clan's totem. However, being spiritual kin to that totem, they could perform rituals that would increase the fertility of that species or improve the ability of members of other clans to obtain it for *their* food. Thus, the religious rituals of each totemic clan were acts of social solidarity toward members of the other clans of one's local group. Respecting one's own food taboos made more of that food available to those in one's group who belonged to other clans, and each clan's rituals benefited those same others. Since the totems of the clans were both symbols of the spiritual patron of each group and of the social groups themselves, Durkheim concluded that the sacred totem of each Aboriginal Australian clan was "nothing else than the clan itself, personified and represented to the imagination under the visible form of the animal or vegetable which serves as totem" ([1895]1958, p. 236).

In more general terms, the Durkheimian model of religion sees religion as a symbolic expression of the social order. In particular, the sacred symbols of religion are representations of those social institutions and groups that must be respected by custom if a society is to function well and survive. As sacred symbols that inspire strong feelings such as reverence and awe, they inspire respect for the social order that they symbolize, thereby fostering the survival of the group and its customs.

totem
A symbolic representation of the kind of spirit believed to be shared by members of the same totemic clan.

Affective Definitions of Religion: Religion as Awe and Protection from Anxiety

The philosopher Rudolph Otto (1923) thought that the essence of religion was emotion, particularly powerful feelings such as the awe and dread experienced as the presence of holiness. The quintessential religious experience is the one recorded in Genesis 28:17, where Jacob exclaims, "How awesome is this place! This is none other than the house of God" (New Revised Standard Version [NRSV]). Similarly, Robert Lowie (1927) believed that the amazement and awe felt in experiencing unusual or strange events are at the heart of religion.

Bronislaw Malinowski (1935; [1925]1954) drew heavily on Freudian concepts that were popular among many anthropologists of the time. Freud had emphasized the similarities between religion and the psychological defense mechanisms that he observed in the neuroses of his patients. Following this perception of religion as a means of defending against psychological stresses, Malinowski viewed religion as a system of practices by which human beings cope with uncertainty. He contended, for instance, that **magic,** the use of rituals to achieve specific human ends, was something that people turned to when their scientific technologies could not be relied on to meet human needs. He noted, for instance, that the Trobriand Islanders, among whom he did fieldwork during World War I, consistently used magic when they went fishing out in the open sea, where sudden storms could be life-threatening and where their fishing with hooks and lines could not be relied on to consistently succeed, but never used magic when they fished with nets inside the sheltered lagoons. Viewed this way, magic is a "definite and practical technique which serves to bridge over the dangerous gap in every important pursuit or critical situation" (p. 90). Similarly, Malinowski contended that nonmagical religious practices have a similar effect because they reinforce social values that help society function in the way that people view as good. In functioning to perpetuate social order, religion makes life more predictable and secure. Malinowski's views have sometimes been summed up as asserting that religious practices help reduce human anxiety.

magic
Religious ritual
performed with
the intent of com-
pelling the super-
natural.

Existential Definitions of Religion: Religion as Values

The views of the theologian Paul Tillich (1948), for whom religion is equivalent to **ultimate concerns,** have influenced a number of anthropologists and sociologists. According to Tillich, religion is whatever people "take seriously without any reservation" (p. 63) and whatever therefore is the source of the meaning of life for them. This view of religion as *ultimate concerns* has been echoed by anthropologist Robert Bellah (1964), for whom religion is a "set of symbolic forms and acts which relate man to the ultimate condition of his existence." Similarly, William Lessa and Evan Vogt (1965) assert that "Religion may be described as a system of beliefs and practices directed toward the 'ultimate concern' of a society" (p. 1). By replacing the concept of the supernatural with "ultimate conditions of existence" or "ultimate concern," these definitions bypassed the Western bias of many earlier definitions.

**ultimate
concerns**
Whatever people
take seriously
without any
reservation and
which therefore
is the source of
the meaning of
life for them; a
set of symbolic
forms and acts
that relate man
to the ultimate
condition of his
existence.

Behavioral Definitions of Religion: Religion as Ritual

Anthropologists concerned themselves with religious behavior more prominently during the 1960s. Anthony F. C. Wallace (1966a) pointed out that "Ritual is religion in action; it is the cutting edge of the tool. . . . It is ritual which

Figure 1.2
Communitas
During ritual, religious congregations achieve a state of mind characterized by harmony and a sense of equality. Here, during a pilgrimage to Laguna Negra, a sacred lake in the highlands of Peru, the members of this group, including a university professor, a bricklayer, and a rural peasant woman, participate as equals in a ritual to "plant" their spirits in the lake.

accomplishes what religion sets out to do" (p. 102). Although people may recognize religion by its distinctive supernatural or sacred beliefs, humans attempt to accomplish their goals through ritual.

Religious **rituals** are stereotyped sequences of behaviors associated with particular emotions and rationalized, made meaningful, by the supernatural beliefs of the performers. Rituals are performed either to bring about desired changes—in Wallace's terminology, "transformations of state"—in humans or in nature or to prevent other, undesirable changes. When people participate in rituals for purposes such as curing illness, protecting themselves from danger, or divining the future, they are being religious in the most significant sense. Wallace concludes that ritual, having "instrumental priority," should be given priority in the definition of religion, which is best understood as "a set of rituals, rationalized by myth, which mobilizes supernatural powers for the purpose of achieving or preventing transformations of state in man and nature" (1966a, p. 107).

For Victor Turner (1969), rituals are the means by which the religious community achieves feelings of unity that he refers to as **communitas.** In communitas, members of the group embrace a sense of equality with one another that overshadows the usual hierarchical relationships that characterize their lives outside the ritual setting. The experience of communitas engendered by participation in group rituals creates strong personal bonds among the members of the group. Thus, rituals help perpetuate the community's cohesion by fostering interpersonal loyalties among its members.

Edmund Leach (1969) emphasized the role of rituals in expressing the meanings of sacred symbols in condensed form. The meaning conveyed by ritual is **multivocalic;** that is, ritual can appropriately be interpreted in a number of different ways. For instance, the sacrament of baptism by immersion practiced by some Christian denominations might be understood by one participant as an act of following in the footsteps of Jesus, who was himself baptized by John the Baptist. Another might think of it as a reminder of death and burial followed by a hoped-for resurrection. Still another might see in it the symbolism of having one's sins washed away. And a fourth might think of the ritual as a means of affirming one's commitment to Christianity or as a ceremony to celebrate the joining of a new member to an existing congregation or community of

rituals
Stereotyped sequences of behaviors associated with particular emotions and rationalized—made meaningful—by the supernatural beliefs of the performers.

communitas
Feelings of unity achieved by a religious community during the performance of sacred rituals.

multivocalic
The quality of having more than one equally appropriate meaning.

fellow believers. These different interpretations are not mutually exclusive. Rather, all are valid meanings of the ritual. This diversity of potential meaning in rituals permits the same ritual to be personally meaningful to different individuals, each of whom may experience its significance in different ways that are relevant to his or her own needs. The multiplicity of meanings inherent in ritual symbolism is one factor that lends religion a sense of "transcendent significance."

Roy Rappaport (1999) pointed out that rituals symbolically portray the conventions of a religious community (p. 130) and that participation in religious ritual is the most important means by which individuals publicly express their acceptance of the beliefs and values of their religious community:

> To say that performers participate in or become parts of the orders they are realizing is to say that transmitter-receivers become fused with the messages they are transmitting and receiving. In conforming to the orders that their performances bring into being, and that come alive in their performance, performers become indistinguishable from those orders, parts of them, for the time being. Since this is the case, for performers to reject liturgical orders being realized by their own participation in them as they are participating in them is self-contradictory, and thus impossible. Therefore, by performing a liturgical order the participants accept, and indicate to themselves and to others that they accept whatever is encoded in the canon of that order. (p. 119)

Although it is possible for a person who participates in the rituals of his group to live contrary to the values they symbolize, that ritual participation transforms mere deviance into hypocrisy, which is generally held to magnify the significance of the deviance. Although ritual participation does not guarantee conformity, Rappaport asserted that "Breach of obligation, it could be argued, is one of the few acts, if not, indeed, the only act that is always and everywhere held to be immoral" (p. 132). Thus, ritual has a binding effect that functions to increase the likelihood that people will conform to the standards of their religious community. In other words, by participating in ritual, people obligate themselves to live by the precepts expressed by those rituals.

Psychological Definitions of Religion: Religion as Projection

Although Sigmund Freud was not an anthropologist, he studied anthropological descriptions of small-scale societies and applied his psychological theories to them to explain the origins of religion. Freud ([1927]1964) asserted that religion was a symbolic expression of parent–child relations, in which childhood perceptions of the parent are unconsciously used as the basis for interpreting nature. Humans interpret the forces in nature that are too powerful for them to control by thinking about them anthropomorphically and "projecting" human qualities, especially those they experienced in powerful parental figures, onto their conceptualization of these forces. This view of the religion as an anthropocentric projection influenced the views of a number of anthropologists, including Abram Kardiner and Ralph Linton (1939, 1945) who defined religion as a projective system embodied in beliefs and rituals that provide an outlet for and resolve the tensions which the typical individual acquires as a member of society, particularly those acquired due to its child-rearing methods.

Melford E. Spiro and Roy G. D'Andrade (1958) examined concepts of god in a variety of societies and found support for the idea that characteristics of the gods were greatly influenced by the quality of parent–child relationships. In societies where parents nurtured their children and responded to their needs, the gods were similar in their responsiveness to human rituals. Similarly, in societies where parents punished children frequently, the gods were conceived of as punitive. William Lambert, Leigh Triandis, and Margery Wolf (1959) found a similar relationship between parental punitiveness and the character of the gods. In their cross-cultural sample, they determined that aggressive and malevolent gods prevailed in societies with punitive child-rearing practices.

Leslie White ([1949]1969) shifted the focus from Tylor's emphasis on the things believed in to the way in which those beliefs are created: White distinguished between *naturalistic* and *supernaturalistic* thinking. **Naturalistic thinking** is characteristic of science. It distinguishes carefully between the human experience of internal objects and events, such as headaches or dreams, and the experience of external phenomena, such as thunder. Naturalistic thinking explains internal phenomena in terms of biological processes, while considering external objects and events in the context of other external phenomena. For instance, an internal phenomenon such as a headache might be explained naturalistically as a result of tension in the muscles of the head or changes in blood pressure within the brain, while an external phenomenon such as thunder would be accounted for as being a result of the interaction of lightning with the atmosphere. In contrast, **supernaturalistic thinking** confuses the locus of an experience by discussing internal phenomena in terms of external ones or external ones as extensions of the human ego. For instance, Aboriginal Australian cultures socialized people to speak of internal processes such as dreams as if they were actually external experiences that the soul has when it leaves the human body during sleep. In many cultures, headaches are sometimes explained as being the result of magical rituals performed by someone "out there." And thunder might be thought of supernaturalistically as nature's response to "the sinful thought I just had."

Supernaturalistic thinking is not unique to religion. It is also found in artistic contexts, in the fantasy play of children, as part of the psychology of love, and in mental disorders (as will be discussed in chapter 3). However, according to White, supernaturalistic thinking is the defining characteristic of religion. In confusing internal experiences with external reality, religious thinking contrasts with the naturalistic thinking of science in which phenomena external to the human being are interpreted in terms of other external variables. In religious ideologies the external world is interpreted in terms of the human ego rather than in terms of itself. In creating religious beliefs, humans engage in projection, a psychological process through which they describe and interpret the external world in ways that reflect their own identities. In White's words, "The whole world is thus made alive and peopled with spirits who feel and behave as men do. They have desires like men, show preferences for certain foods and drink; they are susceptible to jealousy and flattery; they fight and make love. . . . The

naturalistic thinking
Thinking that distinguishes carefully between the human experience of internal objects and events and the experience of external phenomena; explains internal phenomena in terms of biological processes and external phenomena in terms of other external phenomena.

supernaturalistic thinking
Thinking that confuses the locus of an experience by treating internal phenomena as extensions or results of external ones or external objects and events as extensions of the human ego.

gods favor or oppose certain types of economic and political systems, and aid the armies of their chosen nations" (1969, pp. 64–65).

Anthropomorphism in Religion

White is not alone in viewing religious thinking as the confusion of internal experiences and external reality. Anthropologist Stewart Guthrie also argues that interpretation of the external world in a way that imputes human characteristics to it lies at the heart of religion. In religion, human beings apply humanlike models to describe and explain nonhuman parts of the universe: Lightning becomes a spear in the hands of Zeus, and natural disasters are manifestations of the anger of God. According to Guthrie (1993), "All religions do share a feature: ostensible communication with humanlike, yet nonhuman, beings through some form of symbolic action" (p. 197). This assertion is central to Guthrie's definition of religion as the systematic application of humanlike models to nonhuman in addition to human phenomena—that is, the systematic use of **anthropomorphism.** In Guthrie's view, religion, like science, is an attempt to understand the universe, but one that relies on the use of anthropomorphic models rather than mechanistic ones.

**anthropo-
morphism**
Thinking that
perceives human
qualities in the
nonhuman world.

Guthrie explains that all attempts to understand new phenomena involve the use of analogies, as, for instance, when we explain the nucleus and electrons of an atom as being similar to the sun and its orbiting planets. The religious use of the human being as a model for nonhuman things is, according to Guthrie, not surprising at all. To demonstrate why humans make quite natural and intuitively appealing models for complex phenomena, Guthrie points out that humans are (1) complex and multifaceted and therefore produce analogies for "a very wide range of phenomena" (1980, p. 187), (2) likely to be present wherever the phenomena are that they desire to explain, and (3) the psychologically most important factor in the human environment. These three facts make anthropomorphic explanations psychologically plausible. In other words, it is easy to find humanlike qualities in a wide variety of things, and humans, being important to humans, make psychologically appealing models for helping the unknown seem knowable. Thus, the choice of human models as analogies to explain unusual phenomena is common.

Nonetheless, religious anthropomorphizing does not necessarily involve visualizing supernatural beings as having human bodily form. The humanlike qualities imputed to supernatural beings can be humanlike personalities or ways of behaving. Thus, although the Shoshone foragers of the North American Great Basin used animal imagery for their gods, they still had a variety of anthropomorphic characteristics, such as cooking their food, hunting with bows and arrows, and speaking the Shoshone language. Guthrie points out that the most widespread anthropomorphic idea concerning the supernatural is that—however conceived—it responds to human symbols. Even *mana,* for instance, responds to the symbolic manipulation of rituals, and the petitioning of supernatural beings through prayer is found in all religions.

According to Guthrie, the use of language and other forms of symbolic communication to influence the nonhuman world most typifies anthropomorphism in religion. In Guthrie's view, the single most universal religious practice is probably prayer, a form of ritual that endows the supernatural "with the capacity for language" (Guthrie, 1980, p. 189).

Cultural Definitions of Religion

Anthropologist Clifford Geertz offered a broad definition of religion as a cultural system that remains quite influential. In this definition, religion is "(1) a system of symbols which acts to (2) establish powerful, pervasive, and long-lasting moods and motivations in men by (3) formulating conceptions of a general order of existence and (4) clothing these conceptions with such an aura of factuality that (5) the moods and motivations seem uniquely realistic" (1966, p. 4). Despite the daunting complexity of its formulation, this definition is quite attractive to many because it highlights the central role of symbols in religion, recognizes the important role religious systems play in stimulating emotions, recognizes the intertwining of feelings and belief in human thought, and recognizes that religious beliefs rise above the level of blasé ideas without directly using the traditional dichotomy of a supernatural versus natural (or sacred versus secular) realm.

Geertz distinguishes religion from other parts of culture such as common sense, science, and aesthetics, in which ideas are also prominent. Unlike these, religious beliefs involve the acceptance of transcendent realities. And unlike the realities of everyday life, transcendent realities cannot be acted on directly, so the belief in their existence demands faith. In this respect, religious belief also differs from scientific knowledge, since the religious belief in realms that are not directly observed contrasts fundamentally with scientific skepticism about the existing state of knowledge, a skepticism that demands the continual testing of old beliefs against new information. In contrast with the aesthetic experience, which may be recognized as stemming from perceptions that are artificial rather than real—"semblances and illusions," as he calls them—religious faith strives to convince the believer that the nonordinary experiences are based on something that is ultimately real.

Probably the greatest strength of Geertz's definition is how readily it highlights the powerful role of symbolism in human life. Religion is a system of symbols. But it is more than merely a system of symbols. It is influential. As Geertz has it, the religious system of symbols is the source of powerful moods and motivations. It is also the source of a worldview, of "conceptions of a general order of existence" to which its adherents give great credibility. That Geertz's emphasis on the cultural and symbolic nature of religion has had great appeal among cultural anthropologists is not surprising. Today, it is probably the most widely quoted definition of religion in anthropological works. Nevertheless, Geertz's definition is not without its critics. Though its breadth is one of its appeals, it is also one of its primary weaknesses. For instance, while not rejecting its usefulness, Marvin Harris has acknowledged that Geertz defines religion so broadly that it encompasses "the entire ideological sector of cultural systems" (1974, p. 546). This overstates the case, since Geertz specifically focuses on those parts of ideology that are associated with powerful moods and motivations and that are—because of that association—held to be "uniquely realistic." Yet, while he does not define religion so broadly as to encompass beliefs that are held in a matter-of-fact way, Geertz's definition does fail to distinguish between the various forms of powerful ideology that may be found in the arena of politics (such as Nazism, Fascism, or Maoism) and those that fit the more traditional understanding of religion as a spiritual institution. In highlighting the similarities between such institutions, Geertz's definition also blurs any distinction between them.

What then shall we make of all these diverse ways of conceptualizing religion? For one thing, defining religion is not an easy or straightforward proposition. A particular complication arises from the anthropological demand to define its subject matter—in this case, religion—in ways that are appropriate for any mode of life, rather than merely in a way that seems intuitively valid to members of any one society. And there is tremendous variety among the religions that anthropologists have studied throughout the world. Given this diversity, it would be wise to heed the advice of Benson Saler (1993), who has made the most thoroughgoing study of anthropological attempts to define religion:

> If we decide to define religion narrowly, we may end by excluding from our analysis of local religion various matters that relate to native conceptions and experiences, a knowledge of which would add to our understandings. On the other hand, if we conceive of religion broadly and reach out to include a diversity of social and cultural factors in our portrait, we may well raise the problem, as someone once put it, of identifying the religious element in religion. (1993, p. 73)

Because anthropologists have conceptualized religion in many different ways, they have also debated how best to characterize the common thread or threads that unify the world's many religions into a single category. One way of handling this diversity is to keep in mind the common elements, the characteristics of religion on which they agree, despite differences in opinion about which of those elements is most central to religion. Although anthropologists have not always agreed with one another about what aspect of religion to emphasize as its defining core, agreement does exist about a few particulars: A comprehensive discussion of religion must include consideration of its distinctive ideology (the *beliefs*, the *feelings* and *values* it engenders), the special *behaviors* that it motivates (particularly in rituals), and the ways it is organized *socially*.

Beliefs, Feelings, and Values

Religion involves special beliefs and feelings. Religious beliefs and ways of thinking about those beliefs differ in important ways from our most pragmatic ideas about ourselves and the world around us. The distinctive beliefs of religion differ from scientific thinking about the natural world around us. They affirm the existence of spiritual things—beings and powers that are somehow transcendent when compared with those of the ordinary, day-to-day world. The feelings that transcendent things inspire are powerful, and they are intimately connected to our most fundamental values and our ultimate concerns in life. In religious settings, people often feel powerful emotions that they may not often feel or express in other parts of their daily lives. For instance, the Christian who eats bread and drinks wine as part of the "Sacrament of the Lord's Supper" is likely to experience strong feelings that he or she does not have when eating bread and drinking wine at a picnic. Conversely, religious settings may help people inhibit the experience of otherwise unwanted feelings, such as fear or anxiety. Praying for safety before undertaking a potentially hazardous activity may leave someone confident and prepared to act, when a moment before she or he was anxious about the undertaking. The strong feelings associated with religious activities are also often expressed as generalized social values, feelings about what is good or bad and about how people ought or ought not act. By imbuing certain ways of living with value connotations of this sort, religion can motivate its adherents to abide by the conventions of their community.

Behavior

Religion always requires behavior. It is not just something we believe and have feelings about, but also something we do. The most central religious behaviors are undertaken with care and drama. They are the rituals we perform, either alone or in groups, with the intent of influencing the spiritual world. Religious rituals are highly symbolic, and they tend to portray our supernatural beliefs and intended goals. As the means by which people seek to accomplish their religious goals, rituals evoke the powerful feelings commonly associated with religious beliefs and renew our feelings of commitment to those beliefs, as well as to the community with which we participate in ritual ceremonies.

Social Organization

Finally, however personally important it may be to its individual adherents, religion is also a social phenomenon. Each religion has occasions that require the cooperation of more than one person in the performance of its rituals, and the division of labor at these times defines a particular social organization for the religious group. And no religion operates in a social vacuum. Each operates within a larger society and always has implications for its followers' roles in that broader social context. In other words, religion influences and is influenced by other institutions such as family life, community, economics, and politics.

The relative importance of these three aspects of religion—its ideology, its ritual life, and its social nature—has been at the center of anthropological debate over the definition of religion. What follows is a brief review of the various ways anthropologists have characterized religion in the past 225 years.

Chapter Summary

1. Anthropologists emphasize the concept of culture and use fieldwork as an important method for gathering information about religion in its natural cultural setting.
2. Anthropologists may approach religion from a scientific perspective that emphasizes explaining and predicting the regularities in religion and analyzing its relationships with the culture of which it is a part and the natural environment where it is found. They may also approach religion from a humanistic perspective by describing religions in terms that will seem accurate to followers and by explaining religion in ways that make it more understandable to people of other religious and cultural traditions.
3. The great diversity of religious beliefs and practices makes it difficult to determine how religion should be defined.

4. The first Victorian anthropologists who defined religion did so in cognitive terms, in terms of the kinds of beliefs it espouses. For instance, Sir Edward Tylor defined religion as the belief in spiritual beings such as spirits, ghosts, and gods.

5. Social order definitions shifted the spotlight to the social organization of religion, while behavioral definitions emphasized the importance of ritual and ceremony in religion, and cultural definitions emphasized the integration of symbols, moods and motivations, worldview, and the sense of ultimate truth that religion has for its followers.

6. Affective definitions of religion envisioned feelings such as the awe, reverence, and dread that strange and unusual phenomena can elicit as more central to religion than its beliefs.

7. Existential definitions focused on the role of religion as a mediator of values.

8. Most recently, some anthropologists have returned to the realm of religious thinking, but these cognitive definitions of religion have been framed in terms of the distinctive psychology of religious thinking rather than in terms of the substance of the beliefs that such thinking yields.

9. All religions have three fundamental elements: religious ideology (supernatural beliefs and feelings), religious ritual, and religious social organization. Any complete description of a religion or of religion in general must consider all three.

10. The supernatural beliefs of a religious ideology involve anthropomorphic thinking, which interprets nonhuman things as having humanlike characteristics. For instance, however the supernatural beings of a religion are conceived, they—like human beings—have intentions, the ability to think and reason, and the ability to feel emotions and to choose to act on the world around them. Perhaps the most universal religious idea is that the supernatural—even impersonal supernatural force—can be influenced by symbols, which are expressed in rituals and in language through prayer.

Recommended Readings

1. Duffy, Kevin. 1984. *Children of the Forest.* Prospect Heights, IL: Waveland Press. Duffy's look at the Mbuti Pygmy includes an examination of their religious beliefs.

2. Durkheim, Emile. 1961. *The Elementary Forms of the Religious Life.* Translated by Joseph Ward Swain. New York: Collier Books. (Originally published in 1912 in French and 1915 in English.) The classic examination of Aboriginal Australian religious beliefs and their relationship with Aboriginal Australian social organization.

3. Guthrie, Stewart. 1993. *Faces in the Clouds: A New Theory of Religion.* New York: Oxford University Press. A readable presentation of the argument that the essence of religion is anthropomorphism.

4. Leach, Edmund. 1969. *Genesis as Myth and Other Essays.* London: Jonathan Cape. An excellent introduction to Leach's approach to religion as a system of meanings.

5. Malinowski, Bronislaw. 1935. *Coral Gardens and Their Magic.* 2 vols. London: Allen & Unwin. Malinowski's classic analysis of Trobriand religious practices.
6. Sagan, Carl. 1996. *A Demon-Haunted World: Science as a Candle in the Dark.* New York: Random House. Sagan argues for the use of science as a valid measure for testing the truth of supernatural claims.
7. Saler, Benson. 1993. *Conceptualizing Religion: Immanent Anthropologists, Transcendent Natives, and Unbounded Categories.* New York: E. J. Brill. A comprehensive look at anthropologists' varied attempts to define religion.
8. Turner, Victor. 1969. *The Ritual Process: Structure and Anti-Structure.* Chicago: Aldine. The essential text for understanding Turner's approach to the role of symbols in religion.

Recommended Websites

1. *http://www.truman.edu/academics/ss/faculty/tamakoshil*
   Click on Field Methods for an excellent brief discussion of anthropological fieldwork methods.
2. *http://www.uwgb.edu/sar/index.htm*
   Site of the Society for the Anthropology of Religion
3. *http://www.aaanet.org/committees/ethics/ethcode.htm*
   Outlines the ethical obligations of anthropological fieldworkers.
4. *http://asnic.utexas.edu/asnic/subject/essayonreli.html*
   A summary of many of the approaches to religion taken by anthropological fieldworkers.
5. *http://www.secularhumanism.org/intro/declaration.html*
   "A Secular Humanist Declaration" by the Council for Secular Humanism.
6. *http://www.academicinfo.net/religindex.html*
   Academic links on a variety of religions.

Study Questions

1. What is the focus of scientific anthropology in the study of religion?
2. What are the goals of humanistic anthropology in the study of religion?
3. Under what circumstances are languages most likely to develop a word for "religion"?
4. What was Tylor's "minimum definition of religion"?
5. Why did Robert Marett believe that a belief in mana was more ancient than a belief in gods or spirits?
6. How are taboos related to the concept of mana?
7. What difficulties are avoided by using the concept of "anthropomorphic beliefs" instead of the concept of "supernatural beliefs" in a definition of religion?
8. How does Marvin Harris criticize Clifford Geertz's cultural definition of religion?
9. According to Wallace, why are rituals so important in religion?
10. According to Roy Rappaport what does participating in religious rituals communicate?

11. According to William Lambert, Leigh Triandis, and Margery Wolf, what kind of child-rearing practices are often associated with a religious belief in aggressive and malevolent gods?

12. In Guthrie's view, what do concepts of gods, spirits, and mana all have in common?

13. According to Leslie White, how does naturalistic thinking differ from supernaturalistic thinking?

CHAPTER 2

Diversity and Unity in the World's Religions

CHAPTER OUTLINE

CHAPTER OBJECTIVES

When you finish this chapter, you will be able to

1. List the four building blocks out of which all religions are constructed.
2. List and define some of the common religious beliefs about supernatural beings and powers.
3. Discuss the interactions between religion and feelings.
4. Illustrate the diversity and the purposes of religious rituals.
5. Explain why religion always has a social component as well as a personal one.
6. Illustrate some of the great diversity that exists among the world's religions.

Since beliefs, feelings, social organization, and rituals are *all* involved in religion, the recurring disagreements over how religion is best defined are often debates about which of these should be seen as most central to the essence of religion. What is at issue is not whether one or more of these building blocks of religion should be eliminated entirely from our understanding of what religion is and how it functions. Rather, differences exist about which of these elements most fundamentally distinguishes religion from other institutions and should therefore occupy center stage in a formal definition. For the time being, let us bypass this issue and simply examine each of these building blocks—beliefs, feelings, rituals, and social organization—in turn.

We begin with a case study, "The Navajo Origin Story," to illustrate the important point that the absence of a tradition of writing in a society is no barrier to the creation of a complex system of religious beliefs.

CASE STUDY

The Navajo Origin Story

The Navajo language is closely related to the NaDene languages, most of which are found in western Canada. Anthropologists believe that the Navajo migrated from this area while they were still primarily a foraging people and arrived in the southwestern United States around A.D. 1300. Here they adopted plant cultivation from their Pueblo neighbors and became a more sedentary people. Today, the Navajo occupy a territory in Arizona, New Mexico, Colorado, and Utah that is bounded by four sacred mountainous areas: Blanca Peak, Colorado, in the northeast; the La Plata Range in the north; Baldy Peak, Arizona, in the south; and the San Francisco peaks in the west. Their origin story, which has many similarities with that of the Pueblo Indians, is set within this territory.

According to Navajo religion, before the creation of the first human beings, the Air-Spirit people—who had the form of insects—lived in the First World. The First World was a red world that had four oceans. It was a world of mists colored white, blue, yellow, and black. Because they committed adultery, the Air-Spirit people were cast out of this world by the four Chiefs who ruled in the four cardinal directions.

When they were cast out of the First World, the Air-Spirit people flew up to the Second World, a blue world in which they met the Swallow People. At first, they got along well with the Swallow People, but on the twenty-fourth day, they took liberties with the wife of the Chief of the Swallow people. For this, they were also cast out of the Second World.

From the Second World, the Air-Spirit people flew up to the Third World. It was a yellow place where Nitchi, the Wind, lived with the Grasshopper people. This world was bounded by cliffs, and it had no plants, human occupants, or rivers. Once again, the Air-Spirit people were cast out because of their sexual immorality.

The Fourth World was a mixture of black and white. Its sky was alternately white, blue, yellow, and black. It was a large world, and it was occupied by the Kiis'áani, the People Who Live in Upright Houses, who would become the modern Pueblo Indians. These people gave the Air-Spirit people pumpkins and corn to cultivate. The Air-Spirit people resolved to mend their ways and lived with the Kiis'áani as one people.

The god named Black Body told the other gods, who are called the Holy People by the Navajo, that the Air-Spirit people were too much like beasts. So the Holy People decided to create a new people to populate their world. This new people would be intelligent and made in the image of the Holy People instead of in the image of beasts. The Holy People created Altsé Hastiin, First Man, and Altsé Asdzáá, First Woman by placing two ears of corn—a white ear for the male and a yellow one for the female—between two buckskins that were placed upon the ground atop a yellow and a white eagle feather. First Man and First Woman were animated by the White Wind, which blew between the buckskins and caused the ears of corn to move (in simulation of sexual intercourse) while the Holy People walked four times around the buckskins.

First Man and First Woman were told to live together as husband and wife. Four days later, First Woman gave birth to twins, who were hermaphrodites. Four days later, a second set of twins was born, one entirely male and the other entirely female. These two matured in another four days, and they became husband and wife. Four days later, another set of twins was born, and they married one another. Finally, a fourth set of twins was born, and they also became husband and wife. The Holy People taught them to wear masks that represented the gods and to pray for the things they needed. However, in learning to use the power of the Holy People, they also gained the ability to work witchcraft with that power. In their ceremonies, witches use masks and commit incest.

The four couples became ashamed because their relationships were incestuous, so they separated. The brothers found wives among those who were called the Mirage People. First Woman was pleased by this, because it brought the incest to an end. However, she was afraid that divorce would be too easy in the future, since marriage provides the division of labor and is therefore very important. So First Woman considered ways to strengthen marriage.

In the meantime, the children of First Man and First Woman built a great farm that had a dam and an irrigation canal. One of the hermaphrodite twins was assigned to guard the dam, and the other one guarded the lower end of the field. Since they had little else to do, the first of these twins invented pottery, and the second one invented the wicker bottle. First Woman finally came up with a plan to strengthen the marriage bond. She fashioned a penis of turquoise and a vagina of white shell and gave each a desire for the other. She gave strength to the first and endurance to the other and bestowed them on men and women so they would remain together.

Shortly thereafter, Ma'i, Coyote, and his younger brother Nahaschch'id, the Badger, were born from the union of the earth and the sky. They sprang out of the ground, and Badger descended into the hole from which people had emerged. Coyote, on the other hand, saw the people and went to visit them just as they were bestowing a penis and a vagina on a boy and girl. Coyote took some of his own beard's hair and placed it around the pair's penis and vagina to make them even more attractive. First Woman was afraid that because of this the man and woman would be too easily attracted to one another, so she told people to clothe themselves thereafter.

As the offspring of the promiscuous Sun, Coyote embodies the Sun's uncontrolled nature. Not only is he lustful, but he is impulsive in other ways as well. He constantly breaks rules. This often has dire consequences for him and others, but his impulsiveness can be a source of creativity as well. For instance, when First Man was setting the stars one by one into the sky to form the constellations, Coyote was unable to control his impatience. So he gathered up a handful of stars and threw them across the sky, forming the Milky Way. This too added to the beauty of the earth. Coyote is also a patron of human beings. For instance, just as his mother, Dawn, brings light to the world, Coyote brought fire to people, and he taught the people not to plant corn in straight rows.

For eight years, the people acted with intelligence and created no disorder. Then First Man and First Woman argued over whose work contributed more to marriage. So First Man took all the men and the hermaphrodite twins, along with all tools that had been made without the help of women, across a great river to live separately. Both groups were happy at first, but eventually some of the young women began to go down to the river where they would undress and bathe in the river, moving seductively and shouting, "Hey you men, look over here. Don't you see what you're missing!" to make sure that the men would miss them as much as they missed the men. Neither men nor women prospered without the other, and both sexes invented the practice of masturbation, a practice that caused monsters to be born. Eventually, both groups realized that they needed each other, and the men invited the women to join them.

After the women had been ferried across the river, the people discovered that three had been left behind, a mother and her two daughters. They called to be brought across, but it had grown dark, and the people told them they would have to wait where they were until morning. However, they were so anxious to be reunited with the others that they jumped into the water and began to swim across. The woman made it across and was reunited with her husband, but her two girls were seized by Tééooltsódii, the Big Water Creature, who dragged them down into the water. The people searched for them for four days. On the fourth day, the gods White Body and Blue Body signaled to the people where the girls were. The two gods opened a hole in the water so that the parents of the girls could pass through to Big Water Creature's house. As the parents passed through the passage, Coyote followed them secretly. The couple demanded the return of their children. When Big Water Creature said nothing, the couple took their daughters and left. Coyote grabbed the two infants of Big Water Creature, hid them under his robe, and followed the family back to the land.

Big Water Creature was outraged when he discovered the theft of his children, so he sent a flood to kill the people. The rising waters approached the people from all directions, so they and the animals sought higher ground by going to a nearby hill, where they planted various trees in the hope of finding a way to escape the rising waters by climbing to a higher world. However, none of the trees were high enough to provide an escape route, and the waters continued to rise. Finally, two men appeared. One was an old, gray-haired man, and the other was his young son. The son spread sacred soil and planted thirty-two reeds. The reeds grew together into a giant stalk with an opening in its eastern side that the people entered as the water approached. The people climbed until they reached the sky. Hawk scratched a tunnel through most of the sky until he saw light on the other side. Locust finished the hole and emerged into the next world. He discovered that the land of this world was surrounded by water and that there were two water birds, each of whom claimed half the land as its own.

The two water birds challenged Locust to a contest. Each bird passed an arrow into its body, through its heart, and out the other side. They flung the arrows down at Locust's feet. Locust took up the arrows and did the same, meeting their challenge, so the birds dove into the water and swam away. Then two herons came out of the water, one from the north and one from the south. They repeated the contest with Locust but were also defeated and left. This is why holes can still be seen on the sides of locusts.

Badger enlarged the hole in the sky so that the people could climb out. This stained Badger's legs black, and they remain this way even today. First Man and First Woman led the people through the hole into this, the Fifth World, just east of what is now called Single Mountain. The god Blue Body enlarged the land by throwing four stones at the cliffs that surrounded the water. Each stone caused a hole in the rock of the cliff, and the water flowed off in four directions. This formed a pathway from the island and the land. The god Smooth Wind blew on the mud to dry it, and the next day the people walked to the land.

When the people reached the mainland, they attempted to predict what would become of them. Someone threw a wooden hide scraper into the water and said, "If it sinks we will eventually die, but if it floats we shall go on living." However, Coyote quickly grabbed a stone and said, "If it floats, we will all live forever, but if it sinks, everyone will eventually die." When the stone sank, everyone was angry at Coyote and cursed him, but he cried out, "Listen! If everyone lives forever and women keep on having babies, there won't be enough room for anyone and no space to grow crops. It's better that we each live for a short while and then make room for the next generation instead of growing older until we can't plant our food, think, or speak." The people finally agreed that this was so.

The water of the flood continued to rise in the underworld, but First Man discovered the cause and returned Great Water Monster's babies, and the flood subsided. The next day, one of the twin hermaphrodites was missing. People searched until two men looked down the hole through which people had come from the underworld and saw the dead hermaphrodite below, sitting by the river. Four days later, the two who had looked also died. For this reason, people today avoid ghosts and do not look at corpses.

After the First Man and First Woman organized the world so that it has its current natural features, they made a sun and a moon, clouds, lightning, and rain. They also placed stars in the sky to beautify the nighttime. They also caused the land to be enlarged by praying to the four winds to stretch it out in each direction.

Notice how the elaborate origin story of the Navajo not only deals with the question of origins itself but also provides a grounding for social values, such as sexual morality, that were important in Navajo society. As we turn to a general discussion of religious beliefs, keep in mind that they always exist within a social context, and one of the important roles of religious beliefs, even those about past times, is to illuminate the current social lives and culture of a religion's adherents.

RELIGIOUS BELIEFS

Religious beliefs differ from the ordinary day-to-day beliefs that arise from dealing with the practical necessities of life. Religious ideologies consist of beliefs concerning spiritual beings and powers and the universe, including its human and nonhuman occupants. These beliefs can be separated into those about origins and those about the orderly structure that now prevails among existing things, both natural and supernatural.

Religious beliefs are conveyed from one generation to the next through **myths,** a religion's sacred stories about supernatural beings and powers and their roles in creating the universe and living things. **Mythology** is the collective body of a religion's myths. Among the many types and subtypes of myths, four important categories are **theogonic myths** that recount the origins of the gods or supernatural beings; **culture myths** that recount the exploits of heroes, demigods, and other supernatural beings in a time past when the human way of life was being implanted; **nature myths** that account for the origin of the phenomena of nature; and **etiological myths** that recount the origins of religious rites and social customs.

Myths recount the story of the creation of the universe, humankind, and other living things and the story of the early relations between humans and supernatural beings. Through the tales preserved in myth the beings of the religious pantheon are remembered for what they did and its lasting impact on human life. For instance, Shoshone cosmogony tells us that before the creation of humankind, there were deities with both human and animal attributes. Chief among these were Coyote and his Elder Brother, Wolf, the primary creators. In the earliest times, sex did not yet exist because the female spiritual beings had teeth in their vaginas. Coyote figured out how to change that and make sexual intercourse possible. He took his bow and arrow and went hunting for the mountain sheep. He removed the hyoid bone from his prey and used it to wear out the teeth in women's vaginas. Afterward, he procreated with a woman and her daughters, and the offspring of those unions became the first humans.

myths
A religion's sacred stories about supernatural beings and powers and their roles in creating the universe and living things.

mythology
The collective body of a religion's myths.

theogonic myths
Religious stories that recount the origins of the gods or supernatural beings.

culture myths
Religious stories that recount the exploits of heroes, demigods, and other supernatural beings in a time past when the human way of life was being implanted.

nature myths
Accounts of the origin of the phenomena of nature.

etiological myths
Stories that recount the origins of religious rites and social customs.

cosmogony
The stories in a religious ideology that describe the origin of the gods, nature and the universe, and human beings.
pantheon
The supernatural powers and beings of any cosmogony.

The **cosmogony** of a religion consists of myths that describe the origin of the gods, nature and the universe, and human beings. Cosmogonic beliefs describe the powers and beings that populate the supernatural world and recount their roles in the origin of the natural world. The supernatural powers and beings of a religion's cosmogony make up the **pantheon** of that religion. Unlike the ordinary world, the realm of supernatural beings is permeated with great and mysterious power, or *mana,* which is intrinsic to supernatural entities, who, by definition, can perform feats that humans cannot, feats that are not bound by the logic of the day-to-day world of human experience. Supernatural beings are, in other words, inherently capable of performing miraculous feats, and that ability sets them apart from human beings, although they may be otherwise quite similar in form, emotion, and mentality. Human beings may sometimes have access to mana, but only by making use of the right rituals. In contrast, supernatural beings are inherently powerful in strange and wonderful ways.

Spiritual beings are tremendously diverse and no complete catalogue of such beings is likely to include every possible type that has found its way into the world's various religions. But they may be loosely categorized based on the levels of power that they represent. The most powerful of these is a **Supreme Being,** one who is believed to have greater power than all other supernatural beings combined. These are often otiose, uninvolved in the daily lives of human beings or even human government or society at large. Often they are distant and aloof from the day-to-day affairs of even the other gods, intervening among them only when called upon by those lesser deities. Supreme deities are usually the creators or progenitors of the other high gods beneath them, but may or may not be the creator of human beings or the world that humans inhabit.

Supreme Being
A supernatural entity who is believed to have greater power than all other supernatural beings combined.

Sometimes the deity who creates the human realm is simply one of the **high gods** who are not regarded as supreme themselves, but who each exercise great power over some major force within the universe. High gods are very powerful, but their power is limited by the fact that each is specialized. Each controls something of great influence within human life, such as storms, earthquakes, warfare, or fertility. Yet, despite their great power, they may be quite human, sometimes even petty, in their other characteristics. In myths, they may compete with one another, be vain and envious of their fellow gods, and generally be as incapable of living an orderly life as are human beings. They may wage war amongst themselves, practice deceit, and even die at the hands of others.

high gods
Supernatural entities who are not regarded as supreme themselves, but who each exercise great power over some major force within the universe.
cosmology
Beliefs about the nature of and principles by which the universe is believed to operate.

Beliefs about the nature of the contemporary order of reality form the **cosmology** of a religion—its beliefs about the nature of and principles by which the universe is believed to operate. Cosmology defines the orderliness that is believed to exist in the world where human beings find themselves and among the supernatural beings and powers that also populate it. A religion's cosmology includes the ideas that explain how mana can be obtained and used in rituals and how the deities and spirits can be influenced by human beings.

Ideas about the origins of the universe are extremely diverse. We examined a brief version of the Navajo story of the creation of human beings. Let us now examine another creation story, the extended narrative example titled "The War for Kingship in Akkadian Mythology," which recounts both a conflict among the Akkadian gods and also the origin of the physical world that would later be populated by human beings.

The War for Kingship in Akkadian Mythology

The Akkadian civilization ruled Mesopotamia around 2000 B.C. Drawing upon the human experience of kingship based on military conquest, the Akkadians portrayed their gods as beings who had the same ambitions and rivalries that characterized the politics of their own day. Their creation myth was translated by E. A. Speiser and published in English by James B. Pritchard (1958). It tells the story of a great conflict among the gods in which Bel Marduk, the tutelary god of Babylon, brought order to a chaotic universe and established his right to kingship among the gods by destroying Tiamat, the great Dragon whose restless movements kept the primeval ocean in constant movement. Marduk was chosen by the younger gods as their king although Tiamat had proclaimed her consort, Kingu, as their ruler. The rebellious younger gods called upon Marduk to "Go and cut off the life of Tiamat. May the winds bear her blood to places undisclosed." As a storm god, Marduk armed himself with a bow and arrow, lightning, a net in which to capture Tiamat, a mace, and the great winds of the four cardinal directions. Then, according to the myth,

He mounted the storm-chariot irresistible [and] terrifying.
He harnessed (and) yoked to it a team-of-four,
The Killer, the Relentless, the
Trampler, the Swift.
Sharp were their teeth, bearing poison.
They were versed in ravage, in
destruction skilled.
On his right he posted the *Smiter*, fearsome in battle,
On the left the Combat, which repels all the zealous.

For a cloak he was wrapped in an armor of terror;
With his fearsome halo his head was turbaned.
The lord went forth and followed his course,
Towards the raging Tiamat he set his face. (p. 33)

Tiamat blurred the vision of Marduk and his army of gods with a spell of confusion to hide the approach of her consort, Kingu. But Marduk challenged Tiamat's right to have appointed Kingu as their ruler and demanded that she engage him in single combat.

When Tiamat heard this,
She was like one possessed; she took leave of her senses.
In fury Tiamat cried out aloud.
To the roots her legs shook both together.
She recites a charm, keeps casting her spell,
While the gods of battle sharpen their weapons.
Then joined issue Tiamat and Marduk, wisest of gods.
They strove in single combat, locked in battle.
The lord spread out his net to enfold her,
The Evil Wind, which followed behind, he let loose in her face.
When Tiamat opened her mouth to consume him,
He drove in the Evil Wind that she close not her lips.
As the fierce winds charged her belly,
Her body was distended and her mouth was wide open.
He released the arrow, it tore her belly,
It cut through her insides, splitting the heart.
Having thus subdued her, he extinguished her life.
He cast down her carcass to stand upon it. (p. 34)

Having killed Tiamat, Marduk captured Kingu and took the Tablets of Fate from him, thereby establishing his proper authority. After crushing the skull of Tiamat, Marduk cut her body open and raised half of it to form the sky, while leaving the other half to become the earth. He then set the bounds of the ocean so that its chaotic waves could not inundate the earth that he had made.

Often, the gods who are most important in the lives of human communities are less powerful than are the high gods, because their supernatural power is limited to control over things of local interest. These local, regional, and domestic gods and spirits include gods of specific mountain peaks; gods of particular communities; gods of specific religious ceremonies; spirits of waterfalls,

33

springs, or rivers. Genies, demons, and angels inhabit a slightly lower level of power and influence, although they may be even more active and involved in human lives than are those spiritual beings above them. Ancestral spirits and household and family gods are even more restricted in their sphere of influence, but they may play the same kind of role that gods do as the entities human beings can turn to as a source of aid in their endeavors. So may animal spirits, "spirit-partners," sprites, gnomes, little people, or elves, although their powers may be even less than those of local gods. Ghosts and witches are generally malevolent supernatural beings, but they too may be seen as active agents who intervene in human affairs.

legends
Stories about the early times in human existence that follow the times of mythology and whose characters, though heroic, are more like modern humans.

Closely related to myths are **legends,** stories that are usually set somewhat after the time of myth; they describe the adventures of early human heroes who embody the virtues by which people should live. The boundary between myth and legend is sometimes fuzzy, since the heroes of legend may interact with gods or other supernatural beings and are usually portrayed in larger-than-life terms. But since they are set in the times following the creation of the world and in a human social setting rather than in a supernatural world, new legends may be created spontaneously from time to time that express culturally relevant messages about contemporary events and problems. For instance, the Latter-day Saint (Mormon) subculture of the North American Great Basin region has a very active genre of "Nephite" legends that reinforce various Latter-day Saint values. The Mormon subculture includes a strong emphasis on the value of self-sufficiency, which includes such customs as home gardening, food canning, and putting aside "home storage" supplies, especially food, for use in times of need. One variety of Nephite story specifically includes the admonition to do such things to be prepared for times of adversity: In this story a mysterious hitchhiker is picked up by some kindly Mormon individual or couple. In the course of the drive, the stranger makes a point of asking the couple whether they have laid aside food storage for their future needs. When the couple looks back to answer, the stranger has mysteriously vanished from the back seat. Variants of this legend that are told word-of-mouth as real events become particularly common during times of social stress.

Both myths and legends are dynamic parts of any religion. They teach social lessons and keep society focused on the defining elements of its identity. This function is particularly evident in the religions of nonliterate societies, where myths and legends are entirely passed on by word of mouth; but even in religious traditions whose most sacred religious stories have been committed to writing and form a body of scripture, myths and legends may continue to play a role as stories to be recited or told aloud on appropriate occasions as a means of teaching important beliefs or values. Examples include the stories recounted at a Jewish Passover meal or the recitation of the Nativity story in a Christian family at Christmas time.

FEELINGS IN RELIGION

Religious feelings include both the emotions that are evoked within participants in religious settings and the distinctive values that religion instills. Religion can inspire powerful emotions. This is particularly true when people are confronted with strange and mysterious things or events. In the presence of the strange or unusual, what is unexplained may evoke feelings such as dread and awe.

Rituals also engender feelings of camaraderie and fellowship among their participants, the feeling of communitas as described in chapter 1. Victor Turner, who emphasized this role of ritual, has also examined the ways in which rituals can foster loyalty to the deeply held values of the society to which its participants belong (see discussion of the Ndembu puberty ritual in chapter 5).

The arena of religious feelings also includes **values,** combinations of rules and corresponding feelings about what ought to be or not be, what is good or evil, desirable or undesirable. Values serve as guides for behavior toward both sacred and mundane things. The emotional component of values includes feelings such as disgust toward things judged to be bad, wrong, or unacceptable and happiness about things regarded as desirable. Such feelings reinforce conformity to the value judgments about what is good and desirable or bad and to be avoided. The values of religions always include at least some **piety values,** rules that govern the behavior of people toward the supernatural itself. Piety values include both positive expectations and injunctions that forbid various acts. The former include such things as offering sacrifices and other gifts to the supernatural and participating in religious rituals. Negative piety injunctions are known as *taboos* (see chapter 1). They are rules against doing things that are believed to offend supernatural beings or to trigger the negative supernatural effects of mana. Taboos include rules against such things as "speaking the name of God in vain," eating forbidden foods, walking on sacred ground, worshiping the deities of other religions, or participating in secular activities on days sacred to a religion. The taboos of the world's religions are tremendously diverse, since the possibilities for things that can be forbidden for purely spiritual reasons are open-ended. For instance, the religion of the Apache Indians of the American Southwest included a taboo against stepping over bones, with negative spiritual consequences if it was violated. I once watched as an Apache friend "undid" his violation of such a taboo by carefully stepping backward across the bones of a dead animal that he had inadvertently walked over in the Arizona desert.

Although all religions espouse some piety values, the piety values of each religion tend to be highly distinctive. That is, piety values vary tremendously from one religion to another. For instance, among Apache Indians in the American Southwest there was a religious taboo against burning firewood that had been urinated on by a deer. Violation of this spiritual rule was believed to result in sickness. The kosher kitchens of contemporary Jews are another example of the observance of piety values. Similarly, the Mormon avoidance of alcohol, tobacco, coffee and black tea is based on the belief that God has forbidden use of these substances. The unique list of piety taboos followed in each religion gives these taboos a function in identifying the religious identity of its followers. By adhering to its piety values, members of each religious community establish themselves as full-fledged participants in their respective religious groups.

In addition to piety values, some religions—notably Judaism, Christianity, Islam, Hinduism, and Buddhism—also treat **moral values,** rules about good and bad behavior toward other human beings, as religious obligations. In these religions, acts such as murder, deceit, or theft are religiously as well as legally prohibited. Guy Swanson (1974, pp. 153–174) examined a sample of the world's religions and determined that religions tend to teach that following moral rules

values
Feelings about what ought to be or not be, what is good or evil, desirable or undesirable.

piety values
Rules that govern the behavior of people toward the supernatural itself.

moral values
Rules about good and bad behavior toward other human beings, as religious obligations.

will be supernaturally rewarded and that violating them will be supernaturally punished when social conditions make the violation of moral prohibitions most likely (see chapter 4).

RITUAL PRACTICES

rituals
Stereotyped sequences of behaviors that are associated with particular emotions and which are rationalized— that is made meaningful—by the supernatural beliefs of the performers.

One important way of looking at religion is to consider what people do when they are behaving religiously. The most distinctively religious behavior is ritual (see chapter 7). **Rituals** are stereotyped sequences of behaviors that are associated with particular emotions. No religion is without ritual, and rituals form the core of the activities that bring people together in religious congregations. Ritual may be as simple as a personal prayer or as elaborate a ceremony as mass. Rituals also contrast with habits. While both are stereotyped sequences, they differ in two fundamental ways: Habits fulfill a mundane, pragmatic function by allowing routine activities to be performed without great care, attention, or emotion, while the goal of religious ritual is to influence nonmundane forces or beings. In addition, like all rituals, religious rituals produce heightened attention and specific feelings.

The Social Settings of Rituals

Rituals are found in settings other than religion. For instance, the ceremonial swearing-in of a political official is a ritual, as is the handing out of diplomas at a school graduation event. Religious rituals do not differ from nonreligious rituals in their outward form or in their ability to elicit feelings in their participants. The difference is that rituals performed in religious settings are rationalized— that is, made meaningful—by the supernatural beliefs of the performers. Thus, religious rituals may act out or symbolize important religious beliefs and values and so function to allow participants to renew their loyalty to those beliefs and values. Religious rituals are also performed in the belief that they influence the supernatural in ways that will benefit those who perform them.

rites of passage
Rituals that celebrate status changes that members of a society normally undergo during the course of life.

Arnold Van Gennep ([1909]1960) showed that rituals are regularly practiced in all societies at those times when members of society regularly change from one status to another: at times of travel, initiation, betrothal, marriage, pregnancy, childbirth, and funerals. At birth, initiation into adulthood, and death, religious rituals are normally performed. Rituals for betrothal or marriage may also be religious. Van Gennep called these rituals that celebrate status changes **rites of passage.** It is generally accepted that rites of passage have both psychological and social benefits. Psychologically, they ease the stresses that can attend any change in status requiring individuals to abandon their old, comfortable habits and replace them with new ones. By ceremonializing the change, society reminds the individual of the importance of abandoning the old roles and conforming successfully to the community's new expectations. Because these rites are routinely practiced, the individual—who has seen numerous others undergo them—is also reassured by participating in them that others have also made the same transition in the past and that it will be possible for him or her as well. Rites of passage also function socially to facilitate the community's adjustment to the change. Such ceremonies publicize the individual's change in status so that other members will support that person in the new roles he or she will play. Thus, rites of passage facilitate the changes both psychologically and socially.

Rituals that center on pregnancy and childbirth are regularly religious in nature. For instance, the Great Basin Shoshone of North America expected husbands to hunt otters shortly before the birth of their children; since otters often playfully slide down the slippery banks of rivers into the water, eating them was believed to magically facilitate the passage of the baby through the birth canal.

Similarly, rituals concerning death and mourning typically have a religious component, since—like those of pregnancy and childbirth—they deal with life changes that humans have little or no control over. Such rituals provide psychological comfort at times fraught with anxiety. The box titled "Mourning the Dead among the Polar Eskimo" illustrates how mourning rituals may benefit their participants in times of grief.

 ## *Mourning the Dead among the Polar Eskimo*

Alfred Kroeber (1900) recorded how a Polar Eskimo named Nuktaq mourned the death of his wife after he and his wife had been brought to the American Museum of Natural History from Smith Sound, Alaska.

When his wife was dying, Nuktaq carried her out of the house to the barn. After her death, he was prepared to see her only when he had been assured that she was no longer breathing. Before going out to see her, he put on clean underclothes and dressed fully in his Eskimo attire. He also tied a cord below his hips, over his trousers.

In the barn, Nuktaq spoke to the corpse softly before approaching it. He uncovered the body and passed his hand over it from the forehead to the heart. Then he spoke to her again, telling her to remain where she was and spat on her forehead three times while telling her to wash herself. Since she had been an angakkoq, an Eskimo shaman, he reproached her for having been unable to cure herself. He then told her to appear to him in his dreams if she wanted anything, promising to satisfy her wants. However, he admonished her not to approach him at other times or trouble other persons and to remain where she would be buried. When he left the room, he walked backward.

During the ensuing five days, Nuktaq remained indoors. He sat up in bed for two nights, talking, while others in the house slept. For three days after his wife had been buried, he wore his hat only when he moved about, and he did not leave his room. When he took food, he insisted that the meat be uncooked, and he drank only water.

On the sixth day, he left the house before sunrise, wearing the cord he had worn on the day of his wife's death. He made a scratch on the porch of the house and walked twice around the house in a counterclockwise direction. On the next day, he repeated this, and on the next did so again, but walked a bit farther.

On the 10th day, Nuktaq went to see his wife's grave for the first time, as was customary among the Polar Eskimo. After this, his mourning continued, but with fewer restrictions.

Mourning customs such as these help the grieving to cope with their loss. Since the behaviors of mourning are specified by tradition, they focus the attention of the mourner on the forms that must be followed. This may help keep the mourner from dwelling constantly on his grief. Because such customs also interrupt the routine of life, they may also prevent the emotion of grief from becoming closely associated with that routine, making it easier to move back into day-to-day life when the period of mourning is over.

As indicated in chapter 1, rituals are the means by which people seek to achieve their religious ends. It is through rituals that humans believe they can influence the supernatural. This makes rituals so central to religion that at least one anthropologist, Anthony Wallace (1966b), offered a definition of religion *as* a system of rituals: "Religion is a set of rituals, rationalized by myth, which mobilizes supernatural powers for the purpose of achieving or preventing transformations of state in man and nature" (p. 107). He also suggested thirteen "minimal categories of religious behavior . . . that most observers recognize as religious" (p. 53). These are *prayer, music* (including dance), *efforts to achieve ecstatic psychological states* (through such things as drugs, sensory deprivation, pain, sleep deprivation, or deprivation of food, water, or air), *exhortation* of other human beings, *recitation of codes* (such as speaking about the myths, moral values, or other parts of the religious ideology), *simulation* (activities such as using things in rituals to represent other things that they are similar to), *use of touch* to obtain or transfer supernatural power, *taboos* (or rules that prohibit touching things filled with supernatural power), *feasts, sacrifice* (including offerings and fees), *congre-*

 ## *Dreams and Ceremonies of the Iroquois*

In many ways Iroquois ideas about the human psyche paralleled those of Freudian psychology and included the belief that a subconscious part of the psyche might communicate its needs to the conscious self through dreams. Iroquois beliefs also paralleled Freud's ideas in asserting that unconscious needs could be transformed into psychosomatic illnesses if they were not dealt with. However, unlike Freudian psychology, these Iroquois beliefs were part of a shared religious system that quite naturally provided therapeutic relief for unconscious needs through the community practice of religious rituals.

Anthony Wallace (1958) described how the dreams of individuals influenced the practice of ceremonies among the seventeenth-century Iroquois of North America. Dreams could be both the cause for a community to practice a ceremony and the creative source of new rituals. He explained that

The annual festival at Midwinter not merely permitted but required the guessing and fulfillment of the dreams of the whole community. There were probably several dozen special feasts, dances, or ceremonies which might be called for at any time during the year by a sick dreamer: the *andacwander* ceremony, requiring sexual intercourse

between partners who were not husband and wife; the *ohgiwe* ceremony, to relieve someone from persistent and troubling dreams about a dead relative or friend; the dream guessing ritual, in which the dreamer accumulated many gifts from unsuccessful guessers; the Striking Stick Dance, the Ghost Dance, and many other feasts, dances, and even games. The repertoire could at any time be extended by a new ritual, if the dreamer saw a new ritual in a dream, or if his clairvoyant divined that such a ritual was called for. Even normally social dances became curative when performed for someone at the instigation of a dream. Some rituals were the property of "secret" medicine societies, membership in which was obtained by having received the ministrations of the society upon dream-diagnosis of its need. Visions of false faces called for the rituals of the False Face Society; visions of dwarf spirits indicated a need for the "dark dance" of the Little People's Society; dreams of bloody birds were properly diagnosed as wishes for membership in the Eagle Society; dreams of illness or physical violence and injury were evidence of need for the Medicine Men's Society Rite or for the Little Water Society. The relationship of dreams to ritual was such that the repertoire of any one community might differ from that of the next because of the accidents of dreams and visions and any element might at any time be abstracted from the annual calendar of community rituals and performed for the benefit of an individual. (p. 254) *gation* (or coming together in processions, meetings, and convocations), *inspiration* (that is, recognizing divine intervention in human affairs), and *symbolism* (manufacturing and using objects that represent religious ideas). Such behaviors serve as the basic building blocks for rituals and ceremonies.

Ceremonies

Rituals may be highly specialized events that occur in specific contexts, such as saying grace before a meal or making the sign of the cross after a frightening event, but a number of rituals can also be organized into a more complex sequence of rituals called a **ceremony.** Individual rituals are often performed privately, even when a person is alone, but ceremonies are less specialized than single rituals and also typically bring a number of people together into a congregation that shares the ceremony as a group. The box titled "Dreams and Ceremonies of the Iroquois" illustrates the way in which religious ceremonies may consist of various rituals that serve a common purpose.

ceremony
A complex sequence of rituals.

THE SOCIAL ORGANIZATION OF RELIGION

In common language, North Americans sometimes distinguish between being "personally religious" and participating in an "organized religion." Although this distinction may be a useful characterization of individuals who have disengaged from or do not participate in the group ceremonies of the religious tradition in which their primary religious beliefs or personal practices are rooted, all religious traditions do include a variety of rituals that are sometimes participated in by groups. Although religion may be very important to its adherents even in their private lives, it is also a social phenomenon, and anthropologists have never discovered a religion that was unique to a single individual. True, the beliefs and rituals that form a new religion may be born in the mind of an individual. But it must achieve at least a small following of other persons who accept those beliefs and practices to achieve the status of an actual religion, since in all societies individuals who espouse beliefs and engage in rituals that no one else finds comprehensible are typically regarded as insane rather than religious.

Anthropologists use various typologies for characterizing the different ways that religions are socially organized, and religious social organization will be discussed in greater detail in chapter 8. At this point, it will be enough to emphasize that groups perform rituals that are understood in terms of the same religious beliefs and values that inform the personal rituals of individuals. These groups may be families or members of a local community or neighborhood that share the same religion. Sometimes these group rituals are organized by the family or local group, as when, for instance, a Christian family gathers together on Christmas Eve to read the story of Jesus' birth from Christian scriptures or when a Jewish family holds a Seder meal as a celebration of Passover. At other times, group rituals are organized by part-time religious specialists, as for instance, when an individual seeks out the services of a faith healer or a fortune-teller who works with individual clients. Finally, some group religious rituals are presided over by religious specialists who conduct rituals in scheduled ceremonies that bring more or less the same group of individuals together as a congregation. In this final case, the religious specialists may be economically supported by their congregations as full-time religious specialists, and religions that have this kind of organization may develop complex bureaucratic religious hierarchies.

The religious institution also exists as part of a larger society, and it influences and is influenced by institutions such as the economic system, the political life of society, and the gender-role norms of that broader society. These will be examined in detail in chapter 9.

THE DIVERSITY OF RELIGIOUS BELIEF AND PRACTICE

Part of the intrigue in studying the religions of the world is the tremendous diversity that exists in religious belief and practice. What is mundane in one society may be sacred in another. For instance, in the 19th century, the priests of the Toda people of the Deccan Plateau of India were dairymen, and their dairies were temples. But the diversity of religion goes far beyond what outsiders might merely find unexpected. Indeed, behavior that is shocking or forbidden in one society may be required in the religious practices of another. For instance, the Aztec gods demanded human sacrifice in return for their work of sustaining the world, and those who were killed to feed the gods were rewarded with the promise of becoming gods themselves. Among the Kwakiutl Indians of British Columbia, the most sacred religious organization was the Cannibal Society, and although the Kwakiutl themselves considered cannibalism to be disgusting, eating a small amount of human flesh was required of those who wanted to join. In India, just a century ago, and in much of the ancient Middle East, the ecstasy of unity with the divine was achieved through sexual intercourse with a sacred prostitute. Among many of the tribal peoples of Siberia, religious curers indicated their special connection with sacred powers by cross-dressing; and among many Native North American Indian societies, same-sex marriage was expected of the religious practitioners who played important roles in christening children, curing fertility, or organizing funeral rituals. Anthropologists have described many religious rituals in which hallucinogenic drugs are a central ingredient. In the ancient Egyptian and Andean civilizations, the rulers were regarded as gods on earth, and the royal lineages were perpetuated by brother–sister marriages, since they united members of the sacred royal line. The great diversity of religious forms is one reason anthropologists have difficulty agreeing on a simple definition for religion that is still broad enough to encompass all varieties of religious behavior. Compare the approach described in the box titled "The Devadasi Priestesses of India" with the approach of many Western religions, which contrast human sexuality with the realm of the sacred.

Every culture includes customs and institutions that help people survive. All societies have routine ways for people to get food, find shelter, or protect themselves. The pragmatic emphasis of institutions that specialize in the routine use of human skills places certain natural constraints on the form of these customs. For instance, human beings the world around must make tools that work effectively. Since the laws of physics place constraints on the forms that various tools must have, adzes, hoes, or canoe paddles are recognizable for what they are despite some differences in the particulars of the substances from

Frédèrique Apffel-Marglin (1985) described the historical Hindu temple-dancer complex that lasted until recent times in southern India. In earlier times, girls in some parts of India were sometimes dedicated to a goddess or god. After the dedication ceremony, a symbolic marriage to a deity, the girl embodied the sovereignty of the female consort of that god. She served the deity as a priestess or servant to the god, a counterpart to the male temple servants. Her dedication to the deity withdrew her from the world of human lineages, and she could not marry and add to the children of an earthly family. However, she was not required to remain chaste. She was permitted to have lovers, but was required to remain unattached to them. Having renounced all attachment to worldly things, her active sexual-ity ensured the fertility of the land, the coming of rains, and prosperity to the kingdom. Since she partook of the sovereignty of the goddess she represented, her most appropriate sexual partners were others who also shared in divine sovereignty, the male temple servants who represented the god to whom she was married and the ruler of the kingdom in which she resided. Her temple duties included dancing and singing before the ritual offerings of food to the god or goddess of the temple to which she was dedicated. Through the erotic dance of the *devadasi*, the food offerings were made spiritually nourishing to the gods. Symbolically, the devadasi transformed women's generative life force into food for the gods, in return for which the gods granted fertility and food for humans.

Asha Ramesh and H. P. Philomena (1984) have described the changes that took place in the status of the devadasi in this century. Originally, the devadasis were supported by the temple. More recently, each dancer had a patron, usually a landlord, merchant, or some other man of high standing, who paid for her dedication and had the privilege of spending the first night with her after the ceremony. This relationship could continue for a longer period for a fixed sum of money, but it did not bar the devadasi from relationships with other men when the patron was not visiting her. Today, the system of patronage has been replaced by the practice of commercial prostitution, and "after the dedication the girl is usually sent to urban centres like Bombay—to become a member of the prostitute population of big cities" (1984, p. 85).

Figure 2.1
Erotic Religious Art
This frieze from the Devi Dagadamba temple of Khajuraaho, India, shows couples in a variety of sexual poses. Erotic imagery was part of the sacred symbolism of Hinduism in western India from the 10th through 13th centuries and in Nepal today.

which they are made, their exact form, or how they may be decorated. Though they too may vary according to circumstances, economic and political institutions have recognizable similarities throughout the world—again, because practicality requires that they have certain characteristics if their functions are to be effectively fulfilled.

Religion is unlike these other institutions in one important respect. Although those who participate in religious activities may also have some instrumental purposes in mind, they do not routinely rely on their own skills to achieve them. Rather, religious purposes are mediated by supernatural beings and powers that are brought into action by the religious activities. Humans do not control the success or failure of the purposes for which those religious activities are performed. This less direct connection between religious actors and their intended purposes allows the forms of religious practice—and the beliefs that grow up around them—to take on a multitude of diverse forms, forms that need only in some way be symbolically compatible with those ultimate goals. Although aesthetics may give some symbols an edge—say, the use of wine rather than water to represent blood or the use of water rather than sand to represent cleansing—it is nevertheless the nature of symbols that, in principle, anything can be used as a symbol to stand for virtually anything else. Thus, religious symbolism has tremendous play, allowing great diversity in form not possible in those institutions that rely on human actions for achieving specific results. In short, religions are less constrained by practical considerations in how they set about to achieve their ends than are many other institutions and customs of human life.

Chapter Summary

1. All religious ideologies include a cosmogony that explains the origins of supernatural beings and powers, the universe, and human beings. Stories about the origin of supernatural beings and powers form a religion's mythology. The supernatural beings in those stories make up the pantheon of the religion.
2. Religion inspires strong positive emotions, especially emotions that provide cathartic release from the stresses of life. Religious feelings are often expressed in rituals.
3. All religions include piety values, rules concerning good and bad behavior toward the supernatural realm. Moral values concerning the treatment of other human beings are found in some religions.
4. All religions involve ritual behaviors. Rituals are the instrumental part of religion, the means by which humans attempt to influence the supernatural realm. Rituals are performed both privately and in groups. By participating in the public ceremonies of religion, individuals proclaim their acceptance of the beliefs and values that they symbolize. Thus, participation in religious rituals can have a stabilizing influence on members of the religious community.
5. All religions sometimes involve group activities, so religions can be described in terms of the social settings in which religious rituals are practiced and the ways in which religious groups are organized.
6. Religious beliefs and practices are tremendously diverse. This diversity arises because religion uses symbolic action that aims at influencing nonhuman beings and powers to achieve desired ends and because religion is less constrained by issues of practicality than are many of the nonreligious customs of a society.

Recommended Readings

1. Brady, Margaret K. 1984. *"Some Kind of Power": Navajo Children's Skinwalker Narratives*. Salt Lake City: University of Utah Press. A documentation of the active skinwalker folklore among Navajo children.
2. Child, A. B., and I. L. Child. 1993. *Religion and Magic in the Life of Traditional Peoples*. Englewood Cliffs, NJ: Prentice-Hall. Examines the characteristics of traditional religions throughout the world.
3. Fernandez, James W. 1982. *Bwiti: An Ethnography of Religious Imagination in Africa*. Princeton: Princeton University Press. A scholarly analysis of the Bwiti religion of the Fang people of Gabon.
4. Fuller, Christopher John. 1992. *The Camphor Flame: Popular Religion and Society in India*. New Jersey: Princeton University Press. An exceptional analysis of Hinduism and Indian social life.
5. Lehmann, A. C., and J. E. Myers. 1985. *Magic, Witchcraft, and Religion: An Anthropological Study of the Supernatural*. Palo Alto: Mayfield. A collection of articles emphasizing a broad range of topics concerning the world's diverse religions.
6. Lessa, W. A., and E. Z. Vogt, eds. 1979. *Reader in Comparative Religion: An Anthropological Approach*. 4th ed. New York: Harper & Row. A collection of classic theoretical and descriptive articles concerning the main issues in the anthropology of religion.
7. Reed, A. W. 1999. *Aboriginal Myths, Legends and Fables*. Sydney: Reed New Holland. Portrays the religious world of Aboriginal Australian sacred tales.
8. Vecsey, C., ed. 1990. *Religion in Native North America*. Moscow, ID: University of Idaho Press. A collection of articles on American Indian religions.

Recommended Websites

1. *http://www.metalist.com/links/shamanic.htm*
   A site with many links about ethno-shamanism.
2. *http://www.adherents.com/*
   A growing collection of over 44,000 adherent statistics and religious geography citations for more than 4,000 religions and religious bodies.
3. *http://www.hinduwebsite.com/hinduindex.htm*
   An excellent resource on the diversity of Hindu traditions.
4. *http://www.al-islam.org/*
   A useful beginning-level resource on Islam.
5. *http://www.accesstoinsight.org/*
   Resources on Theravada Buddhism.
6. *http://www.americanwicca.com/university/*
   Information on the history, beliefs, and practices of American Wicca.
7. *http://www.mun.ca/rels/native/micmac/micmac1.html*
   Religious traditions of the Micmac of Newfoundland, Canada.

Study Questions

1. In Navajo mythology, how were First Man and First Woman created?
2. Why are moral values less diverse in the world's cultures than are piety values?

3. Compare and contrast the characteristics of myths and legends.
4. Why are piety values more fundamental to religion than are moral values?
5. Under what circumstances are religions likely to teach that the supernatural punishes immoral behavior?
6. Why are rituals so important in religion?
7. What are the psychological and social effects of rites of passage?
8. How do religious rituals differ from simple habits and from nonreligious rituals?
9. What were the main activities of Iroquois religious ceremonies?
10. Why must religion be understood as being more than a purely personal system of beliefs and practices?
11. Using examples you have learned, illustrate that the religions of the world are extremely diverse.

The Psychology of Religion

CHAPTER OUTLINE

CHAPTER OBJECTIVES
When you finish this chapter, you will be able to

1. Discuss the intellectual, affective, and attitudinal functions of religion.
2. Discuss the relationships between religiosity and mental health.
3. Compare religious curing ceremonies with Western psychotherapy.
4. Explain how religion functions to help people cope with stress.
5. Explain the role of catharsis in religious settings.
6. Discuss the psychology of trance.

Religion has sometimes been viewed as a "projective system," a system of meanings that reveal its followers' psychological preoccupations and stresses. While this is likely true, religion also fulfills numerous other psychological functions for human beings, such as providing relief from the stresses that are common in each society, providing intellectual answers to existential questions, and providing psychological stability. One question religion sometimes addresses is what it means to be human. In the following case study, "The Sherpa Temple as a Model of the Human Psyche," the way in which one religion views human psychology and its place within the larger reality of the sacred universe is examined.

CASE STUDY

The Sherpa Temple as a Model of the Human Psyche

Anthropologist Robert A. Paul (1975) has illustrated how religion may portray ideas about the human psyche and the nature of reality through analysis of a Sherpa temple in north-eastern Nepal. Sherpa cosmology is based on a threefold division of the universe into matter, speech, and mind. These three categories are fundamental to makeup of the human psyche and the universe itself. Matter is the realm of the bodily senses. Speech is the realm of words and language and is the basis of culture. And mind is the realm of religion and perfection. This threefold division of reality is also manifest as the "three jewels" of Sherpa Buddhism: the priestly community, which represents the material embodiment of Buddhism; the Dharma, or teachings, that make up what is spoken about in the religion of Buddhism; and the Buddha, who is the unmanifest perfection of mind.

Paul described the main temple of the Shorung valley in northeastern Nepal to demonstrate how the architecture of the Sherpa temple is a model of the Sherpa threefold division of reality. Entering the temple represents turning one's consciousness inward to explore what lies within the human psyche beneath the conscious mind and, in so doing, discovering the divine that lies hidden within. Only men are permitted to enter the temple; and just as those who join the priestly community renounce the world, devotees may enter the temple only when they are ritually unpolluted. Their avoidance of material things that are classified as spiritually polluting stands for the destruction of the blinding influences of the mundane senses.

The porch of the temple is guarded by the four gods of the cardinal directions who prevent evil influences from entering the temple. At the door itself are two gods who stand in threatening poses, indicating that the spiritual journey into the temple will be threatening until the pilgrim gives up his attachments to the world, his own ego, and even to life. According to Paul, the main chamber of the temple represents the material world of the human senses. On the inner wall of the door is a mural that portrays six dancing goddesses, each of whom represents one of the human senses. One holds a piece of cloth, representing the sense of touch. The second carries a pair of cymbals to represent hearing. The third holds a mirror for sight. The fourth represents taste by holding a sacrificial dough cake. The fifth holds an incense burner, symbolic of smell. And the last holds a prayer book to represent mind. The other walls and ceiling of the main chamber are decorated with murals in bright primary colors, but it is illuminated only by the dim light of butter lamps. The murals are filled with chaotic images, forms, and colors reminiscent of dreams or psychotic hallucinations. The scenes impart the message that the world of the senses is chaotic and untrustworthy.

On the wall to the left of the entrance is a mural dominated by the terrible god Dorje Zhinup, the Unyielding Youth. He has three faces, each with frowning eyes of dark blue (the Sherpa color that stands for unchangingness or indestructability). His great fangs drip grease and spittle, and he wears necklaces of human skulls and the skins of flayed animals and men. He is dancing, and people are portrayed as crushed beneath his feet. Some of his many hands brandish weapons. Others hold skulls filled with soup made from human brains, hearts, and other organs. He clutches his blue female consort to his bosom in a sexual embrace. His entourage is a court of ferocious attendants. This is the god of the human senses and of the human passions born of them. The mural reveals that those who immerse themselves in the world of the senses and the passions that arise from them are binding themselves to a world of chaos.

On the right wall of the main chamber are several murals. In one, the central figure is Buddha Heruka, a frightening manifestation of the god who is described as the unyielding mind-hero. It also features the five "sky-going-female-ones" through whom the divine is said to be experienced by those who practice Tantric yoga. These represent the quest for the divine that requires transcendence of the senses. The most important mural on this wall portrays the union of the All-Perfect-Ones. Its central deity is the Guru Rimpoche, the divine manifestation of the eighth-century founder of Tibetan Buddhism and the most important deity in the Sherpa pantheon.

On the floor of the chamber three imposing statues are greater than life size. These three statues represent the three levels of existence and the order of the creation of the world. The right-hand figure is the Guru Rimpoche portrayed as the one who subdues demons. The left-hand figure is Dhyani-Boddhisattva Pawa Cherenzi, the merciful aspect of the central figure, Ongpame, the religion body of Buddhahood. Because Guru Rimpoche is the teacher and savior of the world his statue represents the creation of the material level of reality and the means of transcending it. Dhyani-Boddhisattva Pawa Cherenzi is a benevolent deity portrayed in a meditative pose holding a rosary that he uses to count the prayers and good deeds that are offered to him. He represents the creator of this universe. The Ongpame statue stands in the center and is larger than the other two. Ongpame is the Dhyani-Buddha of Boundless Light who stands for the highest order of reality, the "religion body," that was produced by the meditations of the Adi-Buddha, the otiose supreme and absolute godhead who is all good, omniscient, unmovable, and beyond comprehension.

The statue of Ongpame is so large that its head projects into the second floor of the temple. According to Paul, the second story of the temple is dominated by the head of Ongpame, "his eyes half closed in meditation, but possessing also the third eye of wisdom in the form of a protuberance on the forehead" (p. 139). Perched atop the pinnacle of the topknot of the statue is an eagle devouring two snakes, representing "the triumph of the upper world, the sky, or spirit, over the underworld, earth, or matter" (p. 140). While the first floor represents the world of matter and the senses, the second floor represents the world of mind. In contrast with the chaos of the first floor, the second floor is filled with symbolism of the orderliness of the teachings of Buddhism. All of the gods portrayed here are benevolent. On the left wall Guotama meditates against a field of a thousand smaller Buddhas. There is an *image of Zhembi Yang, god of knowledge, and another of Drolma, savioress of devotees. The walls are adorned with a neat grid that forms bookshelves for the hundreds of volumes of the sacred Tibetan scriptures, the Kanjur and Tanjur, that are believed to contain all knowledge. According to Paul, the message of this floor is that books are holier than idols. They are never discarded or destroyed, and mice are considered to be the worst of all demons.*

Entry into the second floor is a privilege that requires self-discipline and renunciation of worldly things. Only men may enter the second floor, and those who tread here must obey 253 moral rules that include the prohibition of lying, alcohol, sex, and laziness. This floor celebrates the triumph of reason over the senses, but reason is a harsh taskmaster. As Paul puts it, "Sweet reason, it now appears, is not so sweet after all, but obeys a demanding and jealous god. . . . Control and mastery are won, but at a heavy price, namely renunciations and extreme discipline" (p. 141).

The triumph of the order of reason over the chaos of the senses represents the second level of reality. The final level, which stands for mind, or the incomprehensible and absolute realm of the immutable godhead, is represented in the Sherpa temple by two chapels, one on either side of the main chamber of the second floor. The first houses sacred relics, idols of Guru Rimpoche, and a small golden model of "a sacred reliquary mound, which is supposed to date from the time of the Guru Rimpoche" (p. 142). The second chapel is a room "guarded by pictures of dancing and grinning skeletons, weapons of all sorts, and flayed animal skins." In the chapel, "the walls are painted black, the room is dark and dank, lit only by a single butter lamp. A fearful chill cannot help but creep up the spine" (p. 142). The god of reason who aids the devotee in overcoming his passions is, it seems, even more terrible than the ones of the senses. The chapel of the Srungma, the god of reason and protector of religion, is dominated by images of terror and death. The walls are black and decorated with murals of cemeteries. The idols in the chapel are smaller than life size, painted in the dark-blue color that represents unchangingness, and locked in sexual embrace with their consorts. "The Srungma drinks from a skull and is adorned in human skins, organs, and bones. . . . The room that houses him is black, and the horrifying murals of cemeteries and other gruesome scenes are executed in white paint with occasional red touches, creating a nightmarish and ghoulish atmosphere" (p. 142).

According to Paul, in return for his gift of triumph of reason, the Srungma "demands absolute submission, renunciation, and purity from those he protects. The closer one gets to him, the purer one must be in order not to be destroyed, because his adamantine power destroys all that is not itself adamantine, that is, everything human except the soul" (p. 142). The Srungma promises that which is eternal, "but as the grinning skeletons remind us, there is nothing eternal in our lives except death, the tomb, the bones which remain when the flesh has rotted" (p. 142). Like the Freudian superego, the Srungma, who raises his devotees above the passions, is an authoritarian god. Reason imposes order on chaos, giving us an orderly comprehension of the world, only by imposing "logic, structure, rules, abstractions, concepts, symbols, in short, things which make the world stand still, which reify the Heracleitian flow into concrete things." However, "when does a thing stand still forever? Only when it is dead" (p. 143). This unpleasant truth introduces the final goal of Tibetan Buddhism, the annihilation of the ego, a goal that requires the devotee to overcome the Srungma as well as the passions. As Paul puts it, "The last remnants of narcissism, ego attachment, and reason itself are therefore overthrown in a series of mystical initiations through which the adamantine power of the Srungma is transmitted in small doses from a fully initiated guru to his disciple. In the course of these (theoretically), the ego is overthrown and in a series of meditations partially based on earlier, pre-Buddhist religious symbolism, the disciple witnesses his own death and experiences his body being torn apart and eaten by hosts of cannibalistic demons" (p. 143). The intent of these higher meditations is to experience a consciousness that is not tied to the ego, thereby learning that consciousness is not synonymous with the ego, "that the knower is not identical with the ego, and that the destruction of one does not necessitate the death of the other" (p. 144).

The final and highest symbolism is the highest mural in the temple, the mural that decorates the ceiling of the temple. Here is a depiction of the Adi-Buddha, the absolute godhead that the Sherpas refer to as Kuntu-Zangbu, the Perfectly Good One, from whose meditation all reality was created. He is portrayed as a benign, seated deity, and his color is the adamantine blue that represents his unchangingness. As he meditates he holds a pure white female consort in a sexual embrace, indicating his fertility as the Creator, the highest embodiment of the Buddha nature with which all devotees seek union.

THE PSYCHOLOGICAL FUNCTIONS OF RELIGION

Religion has **psychological functions,** effects on the psychological states of its individual participants. The psychological functions of religion may be viewed as falling into three general categories: (1) intellectual effects, (2) affective effects, and (3) attitudinal effects. In its intellectual functions, religion provides answers to questions that are unavailable from other sources. Religion's affective functions are its various effects on feelings such as fear, anxiety, and confidence. The attitudinal functions are its effects on how individuals participate in society at large.

psychological functions
Effects of customs on the psychological states of their individual participants.

Intellectual Functions of Religion

Sir Edward Burnett Tylor (1873), the first anthropologist to attempt to define religion, emphasized religion's intellectual functions. He stressed the role of religion in providing answers to important questions such as why things exist, what causes death, and what happens to human consciousness at death as well as questions about how the world works that cannot be explained in utilitarian or scientific ways.

More recent theorists who maintain a Tylorian interest in religion's intellectual or cognitive functions focus especially on how religious ideology influences people's perception of the world and how it works and how humans must, therefore, adjust to the world around them. Religion, in their view, helps people make sense out of the world in which they live. Anthropologist Robin Horton explains that by positing the existence of supernatural beings with humanlike qualities, religion extends "the field of people's social relationships beyond the confines of purely human society" (1960). Religious thought, he argues (1967), is an effort to reduce the complexity of the world around us to a simpler system of comprehensible ideas, much as scientists attempt to reduce the world's complexity to a few simple laws. Religion's equivalent of scientific laws may be anthropomorphic beings who are thought to control the diverse and otherwise chaotic forces around us; like scientific reason, religious thought functions to reduce the ambiguity of our experiences.

The viewpoint that religion is a system of thought that replaces chaos and complexity with order and simplicity has another implication. Religious

The "Dreamtime" of Aboriginal Australian Religion

In the mythology of the Aboriginal Australian religions, the creation of the world occurred in a timeless supernatural past called the "Dreamtime." Dreamtime stories, which vary in their details from one part of Australia to another, tell of the creation of the Australian landscape, the plants and animals that cover the land, and the spirit ancestors of the Aboriginal peoples.

W. Lloyd Warner (1958, pp. 240–49) recounted the Australian Dreamtime creation story of the Murngin people of Arnhemland: Two sisters of the ancient Dreamtime left their home in the southern central interior of Australia and walked toward the sea. As they traveled, they named the various plants and animals that they encountered. The older sister carried her child, a son, and the younger was pregnant and gave birth to a son on the way. While gathering bark to make a bed for her younger sister, the older sister profaned the sacred pool of their brother Yurlunggur, the Python, when her menstrual blood fell into the pool. In anger, Yurlunggur rose from the bottom of the pool, causing water to flood the earth. He called the first cloud into existence with his hiss, and the rain fell. Taking this storm to be a bad omen, the sisters sang and danced to try to stop the rain. But Yurlunggur's magic caused them to fall into a deep sleep, and he swallowed them both as well as their two children. Water covered the entire earth until Yurlunggur let it abate. After this, Yurlunggur regurgitated the sisters and—in some versions of the myth—their

children. Nevertheless, Yurlunggur swallowed them again, intent on keeping them down this time. Meanwhile, two men from the sisters' homeland heard the thunder, the voice of the Python, and feared that the sisters had been killed. So they tracked them and found blood from the two women and collected it in two baskets that they took to a dance ground where they slept. While they slept, the spirits of the sisters appeared to them in a dream and taught them the ceremonial songs and dances that were the source of their power and admonished them to perform the ceremonies forever.

The Murngin myth of the two sisters is not merely recited. It is danced and sung in ceremonies that reenact the events of the myth. By participating in the ceremonies, men reenter the eternal Dreamtime, which does not merely belong to the past but also remains an active part of the ceremonial experience of the Murngin today.

By reenacting their creation myths, the Murngin and other Aboriginal Australians keep the Dreamtime alive. Thus, the Dreamtime is not merely the name of past, supernatural events, but represents a state of mind for living participants as well. The Murngin do not distinguish between the supernatural and natural realms as two separate divisions of reality. Rather, their lives are intertwined with the beings and events of their creation stories as they enter and reenter the Dreamtime world as active participants.

worldviews, like the perspective of science, offer guidelines for coping with the world around us. That these guidelines are conveyed in an anthropomorphic terminology makes them no less potentially useful. If we are advised to stay indoors because thunderstorms are the effects of an angry god, the advice provides as much protection from lightning strikes as it would were it phrased in nonreligious terms. Similarly, if relationships among the members of religious pantheons are modeled after human relationships in society, as Horton suggests, the ways the spirits and gods interact are likely to provide valid models of how to successfully conduct one's affairs with other human members of one's own society. If, for instance, the king of the gods is portrayed as quick to anger, it is a reminder that one would do well to speak diplomatically to human rulers as well.

Even though the guidelines are not produced with the self-conscious intent that may guide scientific research, religious guidelines for coping with the human and nonhuman world around us tend to survive in the long run because they work, while maladaptive religious guidelines do not survive as long because groups that follow them are more prone to becoming extinct. The adaptive benefits that religion-based guidelines often have will be explored in more detail in chapter 9, but a few examples here will illustrate this point briefly. Using religious means such as divination for making otherwise politically divisive decisions can defuse the potential internal conflict that such questions may have within a community, since the decision is ascribed to supernatural authority. Even personal decision making that would involve no social conflicts can be helped by religious guidelines. For instance, divination can help individuals overcome indecisiveness, thereby promoting efficiency in the accomplishing of tasks.

The box titled "The 'Dreamtime' of Aboriginal Australian Religion" illustrates how religious beliefs provide a worldview that helps people understand the world around them and their own current customs as orderly and meaningful.

Affective Functions of Religion

Religion has effects on human feelings as well as on thought. Religion's psychological effects on the emotional life of human individuals include increased confidence and enhanced feelings of security. Individuals confronted with dangerous or otherwise daunting tasks may be more willing and able to undertake them because their religious beliefs promise safety or rewards in the next life.

Magic and the Control of Anxiety

The simple act of ritual may be enough to allow people to feel happy and secure in circumstances that might otherwise leave them feeling unhappy or worried. Bronislaw Malinowski (1935) placed great emphasis on the fact that religious rituals, particularly magical rituals, may play a role in helping people function in dangerous situations where fear might otherwise undermine the effectiveness of their behavior and in circumstances where people have insufficient control over the success of their enterprises. For instance, in his study of the magic of Trobriand Islanders (see chapter 1), he illustrated how magic was customarily practiced when fishing was least likely to be successful and when fishing took place in the less secure setting of the open ocean.

George Gmelch (1978) performed an interesting test of Malinowski's insight that magic is associated with circumstances in which people feel less certain of success than they would like to. He examined the use of "superstitious" rituals by members of baseball teams. Such rituals are legend in many sports. For instance, some players insist on eating certain foods before important games or wearing particular "lucky" articles of clothing during them. Gmelch cites an interesting example that indicates how complex such "superstitious" rituals can be: "On each pitching day for the first three months of a winning season, Dennis Grossini, a pitcher on a Detroit Tiger farm team, arose from bed at exactly 10 A.M. At 1 P.M. he went to the nearest restaurant for two glasses of iced tea and a tuna fish sandwich. Although the afternoon was free, he changed into the sweat shirt and supporter he wore during his last winning game, and one hour before the game he chewed a wad of Beech-Nut chewing tobacco. During the game he touched his letters (the team name on his uniform) after each pitch and straightened his cap after each ball. Before the start of each inning he replaced the pitcher's rosin bag next to the spot where it was the inning before. And after every inning in which he gave up a run he would wash his hands" (p. 39). Asked about his rituals, he said, "You can't really tell what's most important so it all becomes important. I'd be afraid to change anything. As long as I'm winning, I do everything the same" (p. 39). Gmelch found that such rituals were particularly common among pitchers (who are least able to control the results of their own efforts), while outfielders (who have the greatest control over their own success or failure) rarely performed them. Since the success of pitchers is partly beyond their own control, being influenced by the skill of the batter facing them, they face an uncertainty of success—regardless of how practiced they may be—that outfielders do not. The success or failure of outfielders is much more under their own control, and practiced skill and confidence are more directly related for them than for pitchers, who may worry about whether the skill of a batter will outmatch their own. Thus, it is no surprise that outfielders were unlikely to feel the need for the support that rituals provide.

The role of religion in helping people cope with fear and anxiety has been commented on so often and for so long that the idea has almost become a commonplace that overshadows the similar role of religion in helping people cope with other unpleasant emotions, such as anger, grief, or shame.

The affective influences of religion can be unpleasant as well as pleasant. For instance, religious rituals such as prayers for safety before a journey may remind us that freeway driving in heavy traffic can be dangerous, thereby *raising* our anxieties, but anxiety can be a source of greater alertness and carefulness.

Attitudinal Functions of Religion

Religion also functions to motivate individuals to cooperate with other members of the religious community and to participate in customs of society that they might otherwise not support. Not all the cooperative work of society benefits everyone equally. If self-interest or simple cost–benefit analyses guided each person's decisions about whether to participate in the undertakings of his or her community, many projects that promote the common welfare would be understaffed and unsuccessful. Religion-based feelings of guilt or shame can inhibit the violation of social norms, and religion can also provide positive incentives that motivate altruistic behavior and behavior that benefits others more than self. Again, the long-term survival of the entire community may be fostered by the motivational guidelines that religion provides to individuals. For instance, Aztec warriors knew that going to battle might mean death on the battlefield at the hands of an opponent of superior skill or death on the sacrificial altar if they were taken prisoner. But Aztec religion promised a glorious afterlife for those who died in defense of the state and threatened disastrous consequences should prisoners not be brought home from war to be sacrificed to the gods. The sun god would refuse to carry the sun across the sky each day if he were not fed with the hearts of sacrificial victims, and all life would end. Thus, despite some fears

New religious ideologies (see chapter 10) typically develop when religious innovators who have been preoccupied with their own personal difficulties and with the social problems around them reorganize their own worldview. Such reorganization may happen during a hallucinatory experience that is commonly perceived as a divine revelation or, if it is not accompanied by a visionary experience, simply as acquisition of new insights through a process of intense thought and study. According to Wallace, "Nonhallucinatory formulations usually are found in politically oriented movements" (p. 160), while it is very easy and natural for those that involve hallucinatory imagery to be understood as coming from a supernatural source.

However, the contrast between insights gained during a single episode of vivid visual imagery and those achieved without it must not be overdrawn. There is no inflexible necessity that the formulator of a new code must perceive the process as a religious revelation or merely a personal grappling with ideas that culminates in a new insight. For instance, prior life history may predispose the formulator of a new code to perceive his or her insights as inspired rather than merely thought out, even in the absence of a visionary episode. The three following examples are intended to illustrate this fact.

Deardorff (1951) and Parker (1913) described how a new religious movement was founded among the Iroquois Indians of New York State in 1799. As summarized by Anthony Wallace (1966b),

The prophet of the new religion was Handsome Lake, a Seneca chief who had fallen upon evil days and become a drunkard. Handsome Lake's personal difficulties mirrored the tribulations of Iroquois society. In two generations the Iroquois had fallen from high estate to low. With the British victory in the French and Indian War they had lost the respect of the two groups of white men between whom they had for years been able to hold a balance of power. They had seen their towns burned, their people dispersed, and, after the American Revolution, their statesmen and warriors made to seem contemptible because they had supported the losing side. They had lost their lands and were confined to a sprinkling of tiny reservations, slums in the wilderness, lonely settlements. They faced a moral crisis: they wanted still to be men and

women of dignity, but they knew only the old ways, which no longer led to honor but only to poverty and despair; to abandon these old ways meant undertaking customs that were strange, in some matters repugnant, and in any case uncertain of success. And so the Iroquois stagnated, bartering their self-respect for trivial concessions from the Americans, drinking heavily when they had the chance, and quarreling themselves.

Into this moral chaos, Handsome Lake's revelations of the word of God sped like a golden arrow, dispelling darkness and gloom. Heavenly messengers, he said, had told him that unless he and his fellows became new men, they were doomed to be destroyed in an apocalyptic world destruction. They must cease drinking, quarreling, and witchcraft, and henceforth lead pure and upright lives. Handsome Lake went on, in detailed vision after vision, to describe the sins that afflicted the Iroquois of 1799 and to prescribe the new way of life that would avert the fiery judgment. Some of his instructions were directed toward theological and ritual matters, but the bulk of his code was directed toward the resolution of moral issues presented by the new social and economic situation of the reservation Iroquois. He told the Iroquois to adopt the white man's mode of agriculture, which included a man's working the fields (hitherto a woman's role); he advised that some learn to read and write English; he counseled them to emphasize the integrity of the married couple and its household, rather than the old maternal lineage. In sum, his code was a blueprint of a culture that would be socially and technologically more effective in the new circumstances of reservation life than the old culture could ever have been. (pp. 31–32)

Like Handsome Lake, Joseph Smith Jr., the founder of the Church of Jesus Christ of Latter-day Saints (commonly known as the Mormon church), fits the classic pattern of a visionary prophet who founds a new religious movement. Joseph Smith was born in 1805, and his early life, including daily Bible reading by his family, predisposed him to a religious worldview. The transformation of his religious beliefs began with a single dramatic event that Mormons refer to as his "First Vision." His experience makes an interesting case study, since he recorded his own account of it on several occasions during his life.

In conformity with Wallace's and Silverman's models in which the cognitive resynthesis of a

(box continues)

(box continued)

visionary leader is a response to psychological stress, Joseph Smith recounts that his early life was a difficult one. In the earliest recorded account of his vision, he explained that his family was indigent and had a difficult time providing for its nine children. The necessity of working hard from an early age meant that he was unable to obtain a formal education beyond learning from his family to read, write, and do basic arithmetic. He recounted that by the age of 12, he was already "seriously impressed with regard to all important concerns for the welfare of my immortal Soul" (1832 handwritten account recorded by Frederick G. Williams). His religious concerns were magnified by the occurrence of a wave of religious revivalism that swept through New York during this period of his life, but he reported that the competing religious views of the preachers of different denominations merely added to his confusion and "this was a grief to my Soul . . . [and] my mind bec[a]me exceedingly distressed . . . and I felt to mourn for my own Sins and for the Sins of the world" (Williams, 1832). His own religious confusion was compounded by the fact that his own family was divided in its denominational loyalties.

In his 15th year, Joseph Smith attempted to resolve his religious concerns by appealing directly to God in prayer. In his own words, "Being wrought up in my mind respecting the subject of Religion, . . . I knew not who was right or who was wrong, but considered it of the first importance to me that I should be right, in matters of so much moment, matter involving eternal consequences" (1835 account recorded by Warren A. Cowdery). "Being this perplexed in mind," he went to an isolated spot near his home and prayed for wisdom. He reported that his first attempts to pray were thwarted by what seemed to him to be an unseen force, but finally he was able to pray successfully, and this was followed by a dramatic vision: "A pillar of fire appeared above my head; which presently rested down upon me, and filled me with unspeakable joy" (Cowdery, 1835). In this vision, he saw both angels and Jesus, who assured him that his sins were forgiven and admonished him not to join any existing denomination but to await further inspiration directly from God.

During the years that followed his original visionary experience, Joseph Smith cultivated his ability to obtain information about God's will through a variety of methods, including the use of divining rods and "seer stones" and eventually by simply speaking while in a revelatory state of mind. In 1829, he published the Book of Mormon, a story of Israelites who journeyed to the Americas in ancient times that he claimed to have translated by inspiration. In the next year he formally organized a church to proclaim the doctrines that he had come to teach.

The story of Mary Baker Eddy, founder of Christian Science, illustrates that the formulation of a new religious code need not be accompanied by hallucinatory visions to be understood as coming from a supernatural source. She was born on a farm in Bow, New Hampshire, in 1821; reared in a home with Puritan values, she learned to participate in daily Bible reading. Her childhood was spent in ill health, and her poor health continued until her 45th year of life. Her health problems were a significant enough impairment that she spent years searching for a cure through various forms of treatment, but none were successful. Her frail health preoccupied her throughout her life.

Mary Baker Eddy was married twice and was widowed twice. Her second husband was a practicing healer, and some of his views about healing may have influenced or set the stage for her own final understanding of the nature of divine healing. In 1866, after the death of her second husband, she was severely injured by a fall on the ice. While reading one of the biblical accounts of Jesus' healing a sick person, she felt dramatic relief from the injury. Along with this relief came the insights informing the religious perspective that became the foundation of Christian Science. Though her healing was not accompanied by a visionary experience, she was convinced that it had a divine source, and the experience catalyzed her future understanding of the Bible.

Reading the Bible over the next several years in light of her healing experience, Mary Baker Eddy formulated a new understanding of the human condition, health, and healing. In 1875, she published *Science and Health with Key to the Scriptures*, which set forth her insights about the nature of God and human well-being. Its central claim was that God, being totally good, could not be the creator of evil. Everything that God created must also

(box continues)

be good. Therefore, all evil, including such things as illness, must not be real parts of God's creation. Rather, they are illusions, not reality; and when humans come to truly be in tune with this fact, the illusion of illness can be overcome. In 1879 Mary Baker Eddy founded the Church of Christ, Scientist, and a new religious movement had its formal birth.

Since her new insights were not acquired in a single, visionary experience, the new religious worldview that she set forth in *Science and Health with Key to the Scriptures* is referred to by followers of Christian Science as a "discovery" rather than as a "revelation." The use of the secular terms "science" and "scientist" in references to the church also reflects this difference in her pivotal experience from the classic religious vision in which the new worldview is formulated during a single otherworldly vision. Nevertheless, religion was an important element of Mary Baker Eddy's life, and her cure and the insights that followed were achieved during the course of her daily study of the Bible. So it was quite natural that she understood her insights to be religious, with a divine source, even though they did not involve a single epiphany during a hallucinatory vision.

(such as the fear of death by sacrifice) that were comforted by religion and because of others (such as the fear that the world might end if prisoners of war were not brought home for sacrifice) that religion aroused, individuals could find the motivation to serve the state as warriors.

RELIGION AND MENTAL HEALTH

Anthropologists have long noted that those religious rituals used in curing are not limited to the treatment of physical illnesses. Many non-Western religions include practices that are analogous to those of Western mental health practitioners. In this section, we consider how mental disorders and religious innovation are both responses to life stresses and how different religious practices may be responses to the particular stresses that are prominent within various mental disorders.

Religion and Mental Disorders

Mental disorders clearly involve an interplay of biology and culture. We know, for instance, that a predisposition toward certain mental disorders can be genetically inherited but that particular stressors experienced in life also play a role in the onset of the symptoms of mental disorders. The relationship between biology and culture can be conceptualized as one in which biological factors set the thresholds of an individual's ability to function effectively in the presence of various stresses, while culture and social life determine which stresses and what level of stress individual members of a society must cope with. When a particular life stress exceeds an individual's threshold of coping for that particular stress, the individual's behavior will begin to show symptoms associated with particular mental disorders. Implicit in this formulation is the idea that the psychological processes involved in mental disorders are not unique to persons who are diagnosed as having a mental disorder. Rather, they are the normal human means of responding to stress.

55

**mazeway
resynthesis**
A psychological
process in which
individuals reor-
ganize their sys-
tem of values and
their understand-
ing of their own
identity, the na-
ture of human so-
ciety, and the na-
ture of the natural
environment.

The Psychology of Religious Innovators

Anthony Wallace (1966b) noted that founders of new religions who claim to
have obtained their insights through divine revelations do so during a period of
personal stress that culminates in a hallucinatory trance (pp. 152–53). During
this revelatory experience, in a process he called **mazeway resynthesis,** they reorganize their system of values and their understanding of their own identity,
the nature of human society, and the nature of the natural environment. In the
process, they formulate a new religious code that can guide their functioning
within the world as they now understand it. This new religious code, if accepted
by others, becomes the guiding principles of a new religion.

Julian Silverman (1967) elaborated the process that culminates in cognitive
reorganization in individuals who experience hallucinatory revelations of the
type discussed by Wallace. He asserted that the predisposing conditions for cognitive reorganization are fear, guilt, and feelings of impotence and failure that
arise because of "inadequate or incompetent behaviors in life situations that are
culturally acknowledged as crucially important" (pp. 23–24). However competent, this individual faces circumstances in which "one perceives oneself as being unable (a) to attain what are culturally acknowledged as the basic satisfac-
tions or (b) to solve the culturally defined basic problems of existence" (p. 25).
In other words, individuals who undergo mazeway resynthesis are socially
marginal because their level of coping skills—even if they are superior to those
of the average member of society—are inadequate to cope with their life circumstances. Such adverse circumstances lead to a period of preoccupation with
one's situation, isolation, and estrangement, followed by a stage of narrowed attention and self-initiated sensory deprivation. Persons who undergo this kind
of life-changing experience become so intent on their own difficult situation and
the intense feelings they are experiencing that "they are carried, as it were, into
another world." For these individuals, "this experience comes about in an
abrupt and obscure manner. Often, the experience is activated by various omens,
such as participating in or seeing a certain event take place, having a dream,
finding an object of some peculiar form, etc." (p. 26). Periods of this kind of self-
absorption may increase in frequency and duration, and this process may make
success in ordinary social life even more difficult.

The culmination of the self-absorbed preoccupation that precedes mazeway
resynthesis is a psychological state dominated by dreamlike imagery and reverie in which "the world comes to be experienced as filled with superpowerful
forces and profound but unimaginable meanings" (p. 24). In this revelatory
state, the individual constructs new values and understandings that portray reality in a new way. Silverman noted that the same sequence of events has been
noted in the psychotic experience known as acute (or reactive) schizophrenia,
although psychotics differ from those who go on to become accepted as inspired
religious leaders in their failure to achieve a successful cognitive reorganization
that is acceptable to others in their social environment.

The box titled "Three American Religious Innovators" illustrates how social
stresses can be resolved through mazeway resynthesis in a religious innovator
who formulates a new worldview and how that worldview may be perceived
either as the result of a vision or simply as inspired insights.

To say that mental disorders and religious innovation may both involve the same normal psychological response to stress should not be understood as saying that there are no differences between the two processes. Individuals are seen as suffering from a mental disorder because, in responding to the stresses of life, they fail to achieve a new, more adaptive outlook and practices that allow them to cope with their stresses successfully enough to function effectively in their social setting. In contrast, religious innovators achieve a new way of looking at the stresses of life and create adaptive rituals for responding to them. In fact, their resolutions of the problems they encounter in their social environments are so successful that they appeal to other members of society for whom those same problems are sources of stress. Thus, the response of religious innovators to social stresses attracts converts. Those with mental disorders fail to cope with the stresses of life and in so doing generally isolate themselves from others.

If the new religious movements that are the creations of religious innovators are seen as successful adaptations to social stresses, then one might expect to find a correspondence between various types of religious practices and the kinds of social stresses that are common where each type of religious practice is common. This is, indeed, the case. For instance, Anthony Wallace (1966b) described close parallels between the **mystical experience**—an ecstatic psychological state of feeling oneself merged with the divine—and the mental disorder called depression. Individuals who suffer from depression perceive themselves as worthless and behave in ways that invite nurturing behavior from others. Similarly, the motivation to strive for mystical unity with the divine is, as Wallace described it "a profound sense of dissatisfaction with one's secular identity, a feeling of anxiety or fear, a desperate sense of the need to be saved before being damned by some final disaster" (p. 152). In effect, the mystical approach to religious practice offers its followers a religious means for overcoming their own perceived worthlessness. During the mystical experience individuals experience what Ruth Underhill (1955) referred to as their "own finiteness and imperfection" (p. 169) as being overcome when they experience the ecstasy of merging their own identities with that of God, who is absolute and perfect.

mystical experience
An ecstatic psychological state of feeling oneself merged with the divine.

What Freud called *hysteria*, a set of psychological disorders that are today referred to as *dissociative disorders,* are more common in certain kinds of cultures. Seymour Parker (1962) has summarized the traits that are typically found in these cultures as including (1) early socialization that is not severe and in which there is a high level of need gratification, (2) a corresponding emphasis on communal values and expectations of mutual aid, and (3) a markedly low ranking of female roles compared with male roles. When the needs of individuals, especially those of low social rank who are not permitted to meet their own needs through self-reliant assertiveness, are occasionally not met by others, those individuals are likely to manifest the symptoms of a dissociative disorder—anxiety about unmet needs that expresses itself as dependent or manipulative behavior that seeks need gratification from others. These are the same circumstances in which religions often offer their followers the opportunity to engage in the dissociative trances of spirit-possession rituals (see discussions of spirit-possession rituals in chapter 7 and of women's cults in chapter 9).

In contrast with the dissociative disorders, *anxiety disorders*—in which individuals experience high levels of anxiety that interfere with their ability to behave in self-reliant ways—are more common in societies in which there are high expectations for individuals to function autonomously and to be socially dominant over others without relying on emotional support from others. In these societies, the religious practice of *visionary trances* and *spirit-travel trances* (see chapter 7) are much more common. In these religious practices, persons undergoing the trance become quiescent, their bodies sometimes being cared for by others, while they experience vivid hallucinatory imagery that they believe to be out-of-the-body experiences of their souls. These religious practices can be thought of as therapeutic outlets for the psychological need to have dependency needs met by others rather than, as is usually demanded, by one's own independent efforts.

RELIGION AND PSYCHOTHERAPY

Sigmund Freud (1907, 1928) saw religion as a psychopathology, an obsessive neurosis by which people attempt to cope with frustration and remorse. He felt that like other neuroses, religion prevents people from viewing the world realistically, and he therefore hoped that humankind would eventually outgrow the psychological need for religion. Paul Radin (1937), adopting Freud's viewpoint, argued that "the fundamental trait of all [inspired religious curers] and medicine men everywhere . . . [is that] they must be disoriented" (p. 107). A similarly negative view was shared by many social scientists in the first half of the 20th century even before Freud became popular, and they often saw religious experience and religious status in terms of deviance. For instance, Waldemar Borgoras's (1907) classic study of Chuckchee charismatic religious specialists portrayed such individuals as socially withdrawn, listless, and prone to falling into trances. They were, in other words, social deviants. William Howells ([1948] 1986) echoed this viewpoint when, in discussing native diviners in South Africa, he wrote, "As elsewhere, the profession automatically picks out people of a high-strung temperament" (p. 137), although he acknowledged that their religious calling "appears to give them social satisfaction and psychiatric help" (p. 137).

Such a jaundiced view of religion and its practitioners is no longer characteristic of scholars in either the psychological or social sciences. Larson et. al. (1992) found that there was a "positive relationship between religious commitment and mental health" in a large majority of the psychiatric articles published between 1978 and 1989, and Judd (1999) found the same for articles published between 1985 and 1995. In general, recent research tends to support the claim that religious persons in Western cultures do tend to have a higher likelihood of dogmatism and prejudice toward social groups other than their own, but tend to experience more subjective well-being and marital and family stability and less delinquency, depression, anxiety, and substance abuse than do less religious people. Overall, religiosity tends to correlate positively with good mental health.

Some of the conditions treated by traditional religious curing would be classified as psychological or psychosomatic disorders by Western practitioners. Religious curing and Western psychotherapies also have a number of interesting similarities. Since one acknowledged function of religion is providing relief from psychological distress, it is not surprising that significant parallels are found between some religious rituals and some forms of secular psychotherapy. These parallels are most notable in the case of traditional religious curing practices and those of Western psychotherapists. For instance, both religious curers and psychotherapists may use a specialized jargon for discussing the conditions of their patients. Both carry out their therapeutic work in special settings. Their skill at their work is attested to by diplomas on the wall in one case and by the common knowledge of the community in the other. Both communicate to their clients that they have empathy for their problems and desire to help them feel better. Such things inspire in clients a confidence that recovery from their problems is possible and probably do, in fact, increase the likelihood that the patients will feel that they benefitted from having consulted and worked with these specialists.

E. Fuller Torrey (1986), who studied African religious healing practices, believes that successful healing both by religious healers and by Western psychologists and medical practitioners involves a number of similar factors: the naming process, the personality of the doctor, the patients' expectations, and certain techniques for curing. By having a name for the illness, the doctor or religious curer inspires the patient's confidence in his or her ability to cure the condition. Successful practitioners are those whom patients perceive as empathetic. They show nonpossessive warmth and a sincere interest in the patient's recovery. Patients' expectations of a successful cure are heightened by such factors as evidence of the healer's special skills, indicated by such things as the impressive setting in which they work, the unusual tools they use, and the high fees they charge. Similarly, the longer the pilgrimage to the doctor's place of practice, the greater will be the patient's expectation of a successful cure. Finally, practitioners throughout the world have used techniques such as drugs, shock treatment, or conditioning that are impressive and influence the patient's faith in the success of the process.

The use of hypnotic states as a means of helping patients process unconscious mental processes is relatively recent within Western psychotherapy, but the induction of trance states has long been practiced in religious curing therapies throughout the world. Psychiatrist Robert Bergman (1973) described an experience with Navajo curers at a training school in Rough Rock, Arizona, that highlighted the role trance states play for their curers and diagnosticians:

> Another high point for me was demonstrating hypnosis. The group ordinarily looks half asleep—as seems to be the custom with medicine men in meetings. This was unnerving at first, until I found out from their questions and comments that they had been paying very close attention. When hypnosis was demonstrated, however, they were obviously wide awake, although at times I wondered if they were breathing. Working with a carefully prepared subject (I was unwilling to face failure before this audience), I demonstrated a number

of depth tests, somnambulism, age regression, positive and negative hallucinations, and some posthypnotic suggestions. When I was done, one of the faculty members said, "I'm 82 years old, and I've seen white people all my life, but this is the first time that one of them has ever surprised me. I'm not surprised to see something like this happen because we do things like this, but I am surprised that a white man should know anything so worthwhile." They also pointed out the resemblance of hypnosis to hand trembling, a diagnostic procedure in which the [curer] goes into a trance and his hand moves automatically and indicates the answers to important questions. (p. 666)

While Navajo diagnosticians use trance to facilitate their ability to recognize the nature of a patient's illness, patients too may benefit from hypnotic suggestions given them during religious curing ceremonies. Hypnosis is used both in some forms of Western psychotherapy and in Navajo curing ceremonies. Hypnosis may function to communicate to patients that their condition will improve. Psychiatrist Donald Sandner (1979) has discussed the way such suggestions are communicated during Navajo curing ceremonies, using images of healing drawn from Navajo mythology. One important medium through which these images are introduced in Navajo curing is the *dry painting.* Commonly—though incorrectly—called "sand paintings," these complex images made of various ground minerals such as charcoal, gypsum, yellow ocher and sandstone portray stories of healing from important mythological tales. These designs are prepared on the ground where the patient will be seated. Sandner explains that "When the painting is finished the floor becomes a holy altar upon which 'the gods come and go.' The patient is then allowed to enter and sees the completed painting all at once" (1979, p. 71). Seated on the dry painting, the patient is surrounded by mythological images of healing. Under these conditions, the patient is very receptive to the influences of the messages about health and healing and psychologically may feel much improved.

Anthropologist Simon Messing (1958) described the role of the *zar* cult in Ethiopia as a system of therapy for a variety of psychological disturbances. *Zar* is a general term for problems of living "ranging from frustrated status ambition to actual mental illness" (1958, p. 1126). Zar is thought of as a form of spirit possession in Ethiopia. People are diagnosed as suffering from possession by zar spirits when they are prone to accidents, are sterile, experience convulsive seizures, or show extreme apathy. Patients are questioned by a zar doctor who "will lure his own zar into possessing him in a trance, and through his intercession try to lure the unknown zar of the patient . . . into public possession" (p. 1120). If this is successful, the spirit is led to identify itself and to agree to accept specific offerings in return for no longer subjecting the patient to unwanted possession. The patient is then enrolled into a zar society "of fellow-sufferers, renting, as it were, his temporary freedom from relapse through regular donations and by means of participation in the worship of the spirit" (pp. 1120–21). According to Messing, "Most patients treated for *zar* possession are married women who feel neglected in a man's world in which they serve as hewers of wood and haulers of water, and where even the Coptic Abyssinian Church discriminates against females by closing the church building to them" (p. 1121). People are thought to be chosen by zar spirits "for their melancholy natures or weak personalities (e.g., alcoholics)" (p. 1122), but some are chosen "for unusually attractive qualities, e.g., the beauty of a woman or the changing voice of a chorister" (p. 1122). Zar doctors also become possessed by zar spirits, but they maintain control over when and for how long this happens. Messing describes a typical curing ceremony:

> At nightfall the patient is conducted to the house of the zar doctor. The scene inside is warm with illumination, burning incense, and the assembled membership of devotees, all chronic cases themselves. A relative hands an entry gift, called "incense money," to a disciple who passes it quietly to the doctor behind a screened platform. The doctor ignores the new arrival until the spirit has taken full possession. Only then does the doctor emerge, her eyes bright and curious, her gestures commanding, for the spirit is now using the doctor as a medium. She greets her flock and orders drinks for everyone. The male reader-composer of liturgy of the zar cult intones old or new hymns of praise to the zar, accompanied by the rhythmic hand clapping of the worshipers." (p. 1124)

The goal of such rituals is not to eliminate possession by zars but to transform zar spirits from adversaries to allies who will protect rather than harm. Zar cults may also help individuals overcome stresses related to status deprivation. The cults mix patients from all social classes. This gives low-status patients opportunities for upward social mobility that they otherwise lack in a society in which members of different classes otherwise do not interact. According to Messing, the cults also function as a form of group therapy in which members have a close-knit social network that provides them with security and acceptance.

Problems thought of as caused by spirit possession occur in many other parts of the world. In northern India the idea that people can be possessed by ghosts or godlings is used to categorize behavioral disorders that might be called *anxiety disorders*. Stanley and Ruth Freed studied possession in the village of Shanti Nagar. They found that both men and women might be possessed. The affliction typically happened to people who were experiencing "difficulties and tension with close relatives" (p. 153), and "it often [affected] persons whose expectations of aid and support [were] low" (p. 153). For instance, young brides who are separated from their own parental homes when they take up residence with their husband's family may experience stress from the demands placed on them by the unfamiliar family. After a period of stress, an attack of possession is brought on by a trigger such as the sexual demands of the husband. The attack of spirit possession makes the victim the center of attention by the family, who show their concern and attempt to help the afflicted person. The attack may have other benefits to the patient. For instance, a young bride who has difficulty adjusting to having sex may not be visited by the husband while she is suffering. Thus, there can be psychological benefits from undergoing spirit possession.

According to the Freeds, "A typical attack in Shanti Nagar involves loss of consciousness, trance, and conversion symptoms" (p. 171) such as paralysis. In some other villages it may also include aggression or actual physical violence to others. Relatives may attempt to exorcize the spirit by means of punishment, such as putting hookah water in the eyes of the possessed persons, squeezing rock salt between their fingers, or using other such home remedies. Repeated attacks may lead the family to hire a religious curer who may call upon a spirit under his own control to catch the offending ghost so that it can be forced to bargain with the curer. The healer may try to get the ghost to agree to accept a ritual offering in return for leaving the victim, or he might use spells to drive the spirit out or to transfer it to someone else—often a religious specialist—who can control it. Or, like the home remedies, various forms of shock treatment may be used to drive out the spirit. The caring and concern demonstrated by a family's willingness to pay for the services of a healer and the patient's belief in the efficacy of the religious healing rituals may, in fact, result in a return of the patient to normal functioning.

RELIGION, STRESS, AND CATHARSIS

Religion has psychological functions, effects on the psychological states of its individual participants. In this chapter, we examine various psychological functions of religion in reducing stress and helping individuals cope more effectively with their emotions. The role of trance states in religion and the relationship between religion and mental health are also considered.

Ecstatic States and the Psychology of Catharsis

catharsis
The sudden discharge of a distressful emotion.

The paradoxical coexistence of attraction and dread associated with sacred things that Otto emphasized (see chapter 1) involves the combination of opposing feelings that Freud described as present in the cathartic experience. In **catharsis,** the sudden discharge of a distressful emotion, one experiences a wavering between two contrasting emotions, fear or guilt and security, grief or shame and joy, or anger and security or joy. This is because cathartic release from the tension of a distressful emotion occurs in situations that evoke that emotion strongly enough for it to seem real, but not so strongly that it feels overwhelming. In other words, catharsis occurs when a distressful emotion is experienced at a level that seems both real and yet "safe." For instance, the fear evoked on a roller-coaster ride results in exhilaration rather than distress, because the rider is able to remember that "it's only a ride" and thousands of others have ridden it without harm.

Distress and Emotion

stress
The physiological changes by which the body begins to mobilize its energies to ward off disease or to cope with social or psychological problems.

Distress

Whenever we are confronted with a problem, our bodies undergo changes in respiration, circulation, digestion, and muscle tension. These physiological responses were first discussed by Hans Selye (1976), a medical doctor who noticed that the early symptoms of all illnesses have the same general characteristics. He called the physiological changes by which the body begins to mobilize its energies to ward off disease **stress.** Although his interests were medical, the same stress response occurs when we are confronted with social and psychological difficulties as when we face organic illnesses.

Depending on the pattern of the physiological changes, we can experience the stress process in a number of different ways. In some cases, our psychological response to feeling stress is unpleasant, in which case we speak of **distress.** Distress may manifest itself in various ways. For instance, stress may be experienced as a generalized unpleasant physiological state, called **anxiety,** or it may take on a number of specific patterns that we experience as various distressful emotions. For instance, in dangerous situations, we begin to hyperventilate, our heart rate increases, our normal digestive processes are interrupted, and our extensor muscles—ones that open hinges such as the elbow—become tense, producing an "open" body posture and tremor. These are the physiological responses that we experience as "fear." The other common distressful emotions—guilt, shame, grief, and anger—each have their own distinctive pattern of physiological responses (see Table 3.1).

distress
Psychological response of experiencing stress as subjectively unpleasant.

anxiety
Stress experienced as a generalized unpleasant physiological state.

Emotion

Emotion is more than just a feeling. Each **emotion** is a combination of the (1) feeling associated with a particular pattern of stress and (2) thoughts about the nature of the situation in which the feeling occurs. How we think about our bodily feelings is more important than the physiological states themselves in determining whether we experience the feelings as distressful or exhilarating. For instance, we feel fear when we think we are in danger, guilt when we believe we have harmed someone, grief when we perceive a loss or rejection, or shame when we believe our incompetence has been noticed. In all of these cases, the subjective experience is one of distress.

emotion
A combination of the (1) feeling associated with a particular pattern of stress and (2) thoughts about the nature of the situation in which the feeling occurs.

Under the right conditions, the same stress processes that normally produce distress can seem pleasant instead of distressful. The thrill of a roller-coaster ride is "fun" and exhilarating because it is simultaneously frightening but believed to be safe. When it is voluntarily induced or understood as not really having negative consequences, the energy embodied in any of the distressful emotions can be vitalizing—an example of what Hans Selye (1976) called **eustress.**

The cognitive component of emotion, or the thought processes that accompany feelings, mediates between our feelings and our social experience. Theodor Kemper (1978) suggests that there is an intimate connection between human social organization and emotion. The various positions that each individual holds within society or the kinds of relationships that he or she enters into because of those positions are each characterized by expectations about how much power the individual should exercise and how much honor they should show that they expect to receive from others within each of those relationships. When individuals play their roles adequately by exercising the culturally approved amount of power and by calling for an appropriate show of respect from others, then the social relationships they are participating in function well, and the individuals experience emotional satisfaction. Conversely, inadequate role playing is both socially and psychologically distressful.

eustress
The experience of stress as vitalizing rather than distressful.

The distressful emotions of human life result from inadequate handling of power and honor when we interact with others. When we fail to behave powerfully enough to play our expected roles properly, we are likely to experience **fear** at the harm we may not be able to defend ourselves from; and when we

fear
The emotion experienced when we fail to behave powerfully enough to play our expected roles properly or when we are not able to defend ourselves from harm.

63

TABLE 3.1 Emotional Responses to Inadequate Role-Playing

Problem (context of stress)	Individual's Interpretation of the Role-Playing Difficulty	Individual's Physiological and Behavioral Responses to Tension State**	Individual's Subjective Feeling
Unknown danger, nonspecific	"I need to act but I don't know what to do. I cannot cope with this."	Generalized visceral tension, hyperventilation, breathlessness, tightness of chest, stomach spasms, diarrhea or constipation, rapid heartbeat, respiratory distress, fainting, nausea, sweating, tremor, and agitation	Anxiety (includes frenzy, helplessness, inner conflict, worrying, feelings of loss of control)
Known danger	"I have too little power."	*Facial pallor, coldness of hands and feet, rapid and shallow breathing, rapid heartbeat, immobilization or retreat	Fear (includes terror, apprehension)
Harm to another	"I have used too much power."	Head lowered (lower than in shame), gaze averted with only quick glances at other people, avoidance of eye contact, wringing of hands, face takes on "heavy" look with tightness around eyes, dryness of mouth, tightness of sphincter muscles, preoccupation with concepts of fault and wrongdoing	Guilt (includes self-reproach, remorse)
Rejection, loss, isolation	"I have too little esteem; I am worthless."	*Sadness with or without tears, headaches, nasal congestion, swelling of eyes, feelings of hopelessness	Grief (includes loneliness, sadness, sorrow, pensiveness)
Loss of face	"I have claimed too much esteem and others know it."	*Blushing, lowering or covering of face, gaze averted down and to one side, confusion; body curved inward on itself, curled up to make self look smaller, eyes closed	Shame (includes shyness, embarrassment, mortification contriteness, sheepishness)
Frustration	"Someone/something stands in my way."	*Violence of movement or speech, repetitiveness	Anger (includes hate, rage, annoyance)

In a given situation, when we fail to play our social roles appropriately, we experience emotional distress.

*Source of these responses is "The Distancing of Emotion in Ritual," by T. J. Scheff, 1977, *Current Anthropology*, 18(3), 483–506.
** Alternatively, any of these may be realized as emotionless and/or distraction.
Note: Ideas about power and honor (esteem) adapted from T. D. Kemper, *A Social Interactional Theory of Emotions* (New York: Wiley, 1978). From Richley H. Crapo, *Cultural Anthropology: Understanding Ourselves and Others*, 5th ed., (New York: McGraw-Hill, 2001), p. 134. Reprinted by permission of The McGraw-Hill Companies.

recognize that we have used more power than we are entitled to, we feel **guilt** for the harm we have done. When we demand more respect from others than we think we are deserving of, we are likely to feel the emotion of **shame** or worry about the shame we will feel when we are caught out. And when we play our roles in a way that brings less honor than we believe those in the same kind of relationships normally receive, we are apt to feel **grief,** the longing for comfort from others that comes when they show us love, respect, and esteem. These are the four basic categories of distressful emotions that we experience when we believe that our relationships with others are not what they should be because of our own failure to play our socially prescribed roles adequately. **Anger,** another emotion we feel when we are distressed about the outcomes of our interactions with others, replaces fear, guilt, shame, or grief when we perceive the problem as being the fault of the other person instead of ourselves.

Distress and Catharsis

Ritual and Emotional Catharsis

Psychiatrist Thomas Scheff (1977) drew upon Freud's concept of catharsis as an important way of understanding how religious rituals help their participants overcome the distressful emotions that they experience in life. Scheff argues that when rituals evoke distressful emotions at a level that allows participants to experience them as simultaneously real yet safe, they enable the participants to discharge, through catharsis, the stress that those emotions normally cause when they are repressed. The psychology of catharsis will be explored in more detail in the next section. At this point, we simply point out that the cathartic experience is a component of all of the institutions of expressive culture. Scheff clarified Freud's concept of catharsis by distinguishing between the distressful-tension states of emotions and emotion as discharge of stress. For instance, fear experienced as a tension state is manifested by pallor, chill, and panting, while shivering and cold sweating occur during the discharge of fear—when its tension is released. Similarly, the swelling of nasal membranes, watering of the eyes, and sighing that signal the tension of grief contrast with the tears and sobbing that come when people "let go" of their grief and discharge its tension. Scheff defines catharsis as the spontaneous discharge of emotional tension that occurs in settings that permit a person to feel the emotion while feeling safe to do so. Scheff explains that catharsis is expressed "by convulsive, involuntary bodily processes whose external manifestations are weeping, for grief, shivering and cold sweat, for fear, spontaneous laughter, for embarrassment or anger, and 'storming' (rapid forceful movement and vocalization) with hot sweat, also for anger" (p. 485).

In Scheff's view, catharsis is not triggered, as Freud believed, when the memory of a traumatic experience and its accompanying distressful emotion is evoked and put into words. Rather, it is triggered in settings such as rituals or drama that evoke the feeling to a degree that makes it real and involving, but not so intensely that it overwhelms. Scheff refers to the state of mind in which a distressful emotion is experienced in this balanced, real-but-safe way as

guilt
The emotion experienced when we recognize that we have used more power than we are entitled to and have done harm to someone else.

shame
The emotion experienced when we demand more respect from others than we think we are deserving of.

grief
The emotion experienced when we play our roles in a way that brings less honor than we believe those in the same kind of relationships normally receive; the longing for comfort from others that comes when they show us love, respect, and esteem.

anger
The emotion we feel when we are distressed about the outcomes of our interactions with others and perceive the problem as being the fault of the other person instead of ourselves.

aesthetic distance and asserts that rituals are effective at producing catharsis—emotional release from the tensions of distressful emotions—when they successfully evoke those emotions at aesthetic distance.

Scheff (1977) suggested that ritual can play a dramatic role in alleviating the experience of distressful emotions. According to Scheff, catharsis occurs when the distressful emotion is reawakened enough to both participate in it and observe it dispassionately—that is, when the distressful feeling is evoked at a level that is not overwhelming. In the language of drama criticism, experiences that evoke emotions so powerfully that they overwhelm are said to be **underdistanced.** Those that fail to evoke emotions at all are referred to as **overdistanced.** In Scheff's application of this terminology to the psychology of emotions, "Overdistancing corresponds to repression, underdistancing to the return of repressed emotion" (p. 486). Experiences that evoke emotions enough to involve the audience but not so much as to overwhelm them are said to have aesthetic distance. As Scheff puts it, "At esthetic distance, there is a balance of thought and feeling. There is deep emotional resonance, but the person is in control. If a repressed emotion such as grief is restimulated at esthetic distance, the crying that results is not unpleasant: it is not draining or tiring—the person feels refreshed when it is over. The same is true with fear, anger, and embarrassment" (p. 486). It is at the level of esthetic distance that distressful emotions can be experienced safely enough to discharge them. In the process of catharsis, the distress of those emotions is replaced with a subjective sense of relief and feelings of security, happiness, or both.

aesthetic distance
The state of mind in which a distressful emotion is experienced in a balanced, real-but-safe way, in which it is felt strongly enough to be involving yet not so intensely as to overwhelm.

underdistanced
Adjective describing experiences that evoke emotions so powerfully that they overwhelm.

overdistanced
Adjective describing experiences that fail to evoke emotions at all.

Religion and Catharsis

According to Scheff, in its psychological function ritual provides a dramatic frame within which distressful feelings that are normally repressed are evoked at aesthetic distance, thereby allowing participants in the drama of the ritual to achieve cathartic release from distress. In other words, rituals help their participants experience distressful emotions at aesthetic distance and experience psychological and physiological relief.

Scheff (1977, p. 489) illustrates the role of ritual in eliciting emotion at aesthetic distance in a discussion of rituals of mourning in classical and preliterate societies:

> It would seem that myth and ritual provided a framework for catharsis. Weeping was encouraged and accepted. In the case of the Quechan, a California Indian tribe, "crying is expected of one. Only by allowing yourself to let go of your emotions do they know how badly you feel for the family. . . . The room is filled with tears, men and women joining together paying their respects. This begins four days of mourning" (Swift Arrow 1974:24). Many traditional societies have a special place marked off, as well as a definite period, for weeping. In the Bara culture, of Madagascar, callers are received in a hut called the "house of many tears": "The closest kinswomen begin to cry and the others gradually join in, the most recently arrived mourners joining earliest and most vehemently. As they wail the women cover their heads and faces, put their hands on one another's backs" (Huntington 1973:67). It would appear that public mourning was common in classic Greek society, in connection both with funeral rites and tragic

---

drama (Lucas 1968:273): "Since pity, especially in tragedy, is often pity for the dead or the bereaved, it is akin to the shared or public lamentation which is part of life in small closely knit communities. . . . [There is a suggestion] that the audience luxuriated in community sorrow, "surrendering itself' to lamentation and taking part in the mourning along with actors and chorus."

People can be overwhelmed by grief or other emotions, but expression of these emotions in the setting of religious ritual can make them easier to experience because it is the nature of ritual to communicate a sense of control and structure. Participation in ritual can make it easier to express potentially threatening distressful emotions and achieve the aesthetic distance from them that permits catharsis to occur, leaving participants feeling better than when the distressful emotion is totally avoided.

In some cases, instead of feeling stress as an unpleasant emotion, individuals experience no emotion at all, a response to stress that is called **affectlessness**. Affectlessness is a common response to extreme stresses such as the prolonged dangers experienced in warfare and is, for instance, a symptom of post-traumatic stress disorder. For individuals who manifest stress as affectlessness, religious ritual can be a safe setting where they can experience the emotions that they normally do not.

Figure 3.1
Iroquois False-Face Curing
The ceremonial curing rituals of the Iroquois emphasize high drama. Religious curers wearing grotesque masks that represent spirits who control various diseases raise the emotional tension of the patient, who then experiences cathartic release from those tensions.

affectlessness
A state of experiencing no emotion at all during situations that evoke stress.

Cultural Diversity and Religion as Stress Reduction

The psychological processes involved in stress reduction are universal, but the specific stresses that are commonly shared by members of a religious community vary from society to society. Robin Horton (1960) makes the point that the needs that religion fulfills for people depend on the kind of needs that their society does not fulfill for them. To Horton, religion is patterned on the kinds of human relationships that people experience in society, relationships that are projected into a sacred or supernatural realm. When human relationships fail to meet people's needs within society, they seek to have them met by turning to the transcendent relationships found in their religion. Religions differ because unmet human needs vary from one society to another. For instance, technologically simple societies that are composed of small, face-to-face, local communities are generally good at fostering friendships that meet people's needs for intimacy through close human bonds and mutual support. However, their limited technologies make them less effective at controlling their environment and predicting things people need to know to function effectively within it. In contrast, technologically complex societies have a better scientific ability to predict and control their environment. They are, for instance, better able to produce large amounts of food and build durable shelter. However, their large-scale communities lead to problems of isolation, alienation, and loneliness for many. It is to be expected then, that in small-scale societies, people are more likely to turn to religion to control the world around them, using magic to influence the weather, increase the fertility of the animals they hunt, and cure illness, while members of large-scale societies turn to their gods for love, nurturing, and personal support. Figure 3.2 illustrates relationships among problems, stress, and ritual.

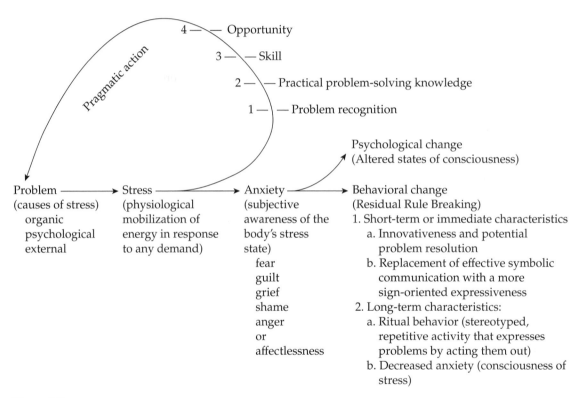

Figure 3.2
The Stress Process
Humans generally attempt to solve problems that cause stress by directly attacking them. However, direct pragmatic action to solve problems may not be possible if (1) we fail to recognize what the problem is, (2) we have not learned how to solve the problem, (3) we lack the necessary skill to deal with the problem, or (4) we lack the opportunity for dealing with it. When we cannot solve problems directly, we experience anxiety; and anxiety may lead us to experience altered states of consciousness that may be interpreted as evidence of contact with the supernatural. Anxiety also increases our likelihood of either spontaneously creating rituals that express our feelings about our problems or, alternatively, of participating in established religious rituals that we have previously learned.

Social stresses can also vary within a society. In large-scale societies, the types of stresses with which people must cope from day to day tend to vary from one economic class to another and from one geographical region to another. These differences are relevant for understanding differences in the religious symbolism of the various religions found in societies such as contemporary nation-states. In turn, these differences of religious symbolism contribute to an understanding of why particular religions may recruit their members more successfully from one economic class or another. For instance, in the United States and Canada, denominations that emphasize a fundamentalist theology tend to recruit and maintain members most effectively from persons of laboring-class backgrounds, particularly those whose social standing has declined or who feel that they are not achieving the success that their skills and training have led them to expect. Upper-middle-class plus upper-class people are most likely to affiliate with the so-called "mainstream denominations" that emphasize "civil religion" values such as being good neighbors and being responsible citizens.

Religion and Social Class

Social class influences religious ideology and practice, and differences in the theological orientation of the various denominations reflect the values that are typical of the social classes that predominate among their followers. Worldwide, members of oppressed social groups tend to follow religions whose doctrines offer the hope of a rewarding afterlife that will make up for the oppression experienced in life; and members of the upper classes of society, being more highly educated, tend to participate in religions that teach nonliteralist theologies. Thus, membership in particular denominations within a religious tradition tends to reflect the social standing of religious followers. For instance, in the United States, although they have adherents in every social class, Episcopalians and Jews are somewhat overrepresented among Americans with higher incomes. Lutheran and Roman Catholic congregations fall in the middle, having a somewhat greater representation of members with incomes in the middle range. In contrast, Evangelicals and Baptists are overrepresented among Americans with lower incomes, and members of Pentecostal and Holiness churches tend to belong to the lowest economic classes. As might be expected, changes in social standing influence religious preferences. For instance, in the United States an upwardly mobile person may also change to a higher-status denomination that is more representative of the new social circles he or she has entered.

Religion as a Source of Stress

Religion may not only provide emotional benefits, but it may also raise uncomfortable questions, stimulate anxiety, and be a source of alienation from the larger social environment. For instance, religion may stimulate feelings of guilt for wrongs done to others or shame about the violation of piety norms. Such feelings can, in turn, motivate individuals to set things right. On the other hand, they may simply become habitual feelings associated with depression and a generalized sense of "sinfulness" or personal unworthiness.

Religious beliefs can be a source of anxiety. For instance, the belief in witchcraft, sorcery, ghosts, demons, or other evil supernatural beings can be a source of recurring fears and anxieties. Beliefs that humans may use supernatural power to harm their enemies can validate mistrust of other members of a community and so are sometimes associated with the perpetuation of social tensions. The witchcraft trials of colonial Salem, Massachusetts, illustrate this role of religious belief in arousing anxieties and magnifying interpersonal tensions. In 1692 the daughter and niece of Reverend Samuel Parris became ill with what were called "fits," convulsions accompanied by speaking gibberish. These fits began shortly after the girls had engaged in a forbidden practice, trying to foretell whom they would marry by staring into a cup of water into which they had dropped the white of an egg. The convulsions failed to respond to treatment, and the village doctor suggested that witchcraft was the cause of the affliction. Soon, similar behavior spread to at least eight other neighbors, including some adults. Then the girls began making accusations. Those first accused were marginal members of the community: Tituba, a Caribbean slave; Sarah Good, a beggar; and Sarah Osborne, a bedridden old woman. The accusations escalated into hanging 19 women and men, crushing one man to death, and imprisoning 150 people from Salem and surrounding areas, 17 of whom died while being held in prison.

Religious rituals may also stimulate distressful emotions. For instance, a ritual such as a family prayer for safety on a trip may stimulate anxiety about the drive that might otherwise remain unconscious. The stimulated concern may then function as a reminder that will stimulate greater-than-usual care and alertness. Religious rituals that function to improve the social solidarity of their participants can also be used to unify them against other groups considered to be enemies. In this case, the rituals promote aggression and preparation for hostility against those enemies as well as promoting solidarity among compatriots. For instance, al-Qaeda's training of terrorists, including those who crashed airliners into the World Trade Center in New York and the Pentagon in Washington, D.C., in 2001 made powerful use of religious instruction as motivation.

THE PSYCHOLOGY OF TRANCE STATES IN RELIGION

Trance states occur in many contexts; religion is merely one. However, they are a prominent experience in religious settings and are often elicited during religious rituals. In this section, we explore the nature of trance and its role in religion.

Trance

trance states (altered states of consciousness) Psychological states in which a person loses his or her usual sense of separateness from the world and engages in supernaturalistic thinking.

Normally we experience ourselves as observers of the world around us, which seems to be a thing separate from us and governed by cause and effect. In **trance states,** or **altered states of consciousness,** as they are also commonly called, we lose our usual sense of separateness from the world and experience a blurring of the distinction between self and not-self in which our body boundaries may seem subjectively to be less distinct and things that we usually regard as outside ourselves may feel like extensions of our own ego. Leslie White saw this aspect of trance states as the central characteristic of religious ideation, which he referred to as *supernaturalistic thinking* (see chapter 1). During trances, time may seem to pass more rapidly or slowly than usual or may seem to stop altogether. Cause and effect may seem irrelevant to what is happening, and we may be able to entertain contradictory beliefs simultaneously. The meanings that things usually have for us can change dramatically during a trance. Things may seem more or less meaningful than they usually do, and much of the trance experience may seem difficult or even impossible to put into words afterward. In simple terms, reality seems to have a dreamlike quality during trance states.

Nonetheless, trances are not necessarily strange and exotic conditions. In fact, every normal person experiences trance states every day. For instance, the common experience called "daydreaming" is a mild trance state during the waking state. That twilight period of half-wakefulness that we all pass through while falling asleep is an altered state of consciousness. Most people can remember that during this transitional state they seem to hear voices, although they are usually indistinct and distant, as if heard from a separate room, and the sentences are typically disjointed or not fully coherent in their meanings. Similar brief trance states in which members of a congregation feel particularly in tune with the presence of the divine are common during religious ceremonies.

Trance states are more likely to occur when we are tired or experiencing stress. For instance, they can be induced by sensory and/or motor overload that may result from repetitive physical activity, loud sounds, and bright lights. Prolonged sensory deprivation or decreased mental alertness, as might be experienced during meditation, can also bring on trance states. So can prolonged efforts to remain alert, a kind of trance that is common enough in situations such as driving monotonous stretches of highway late at night that it has its own name—"highway hypnosis." Trances may also be the result of changes in brain chemistry, whether from taking drugs or alcohol or from hyperventilating, or even as a side effect of being ill. In short, trances are a response of the brain to stress, which interrupts the brain's usual ways of interpreting sense experiences.

Trance States and Religion

Trance states occur in religious settings. They are often experienced by participants during ritual performances. Five common elements of rituals seem to be involved in the induction of trance states:

1. Prolonged praying.
2. Repetitive moving and dancing.
3. Repetitive rhythm and singing.
4. Repetitive verbal praises.
5. Monotonous background noise.

All of these common elements of ritual are ways of inducing physiological stress, and trance is a common response to stress.

Erika Bourguignon (1979) found that trances induced by religious rituals could be classified into two general types: **spirit-possession trances** and

spirit-possession trances
Trances that are subjectively experienced as a giving up of or losing personal control over one's actions while control is assumed by a spirit that has entered one's body.

Figure 3.3
Repetitive Movement and Verbal Praise to Achieve Religious Trance
These Mevlevi dervishes from Turkey use a prolonged whirling dance and the repetition of a short exclamation in praise of God to achieve a state of trance that they view as a state of religious ecstasy.

**visionary
(or spirit-travel)
trances**
Trances involving
visionary experiences that may
seem like "out of
the body" experiences in which
the ego seems to
leave the body
and is able to
move about the
environment or
even enter a usually unseen spiritual realm while
the body remains
behind.

visionary (or spirit-travel) trances (which Bourguignon simply calls "trance"). In the former, the trance is subjectively experienced as giving up or losing personal control over one's actions, while control is assumed by a spirit that has entered one's body. The latter kind of trance involves visionary experiences which—though not necessarily—may even seem like an "out of the body" experience, one in which the ego seems to leave the body and is able to move about the environment or even enter a usually unseen spiritual realm while the body remains behind. The frequency of these two kinds of trance appears to be related to the kinds of stresses that are most common in the societies where they are found.

Possession Trance

According to Bourguignon, religions with possession-trance rituals are more likely to be found in societies with agriculture and other forms of food production than in foraging societies. This may be, at least in part, because spirit possession is statistically more common in societies with prominent distinctions in status, such as social stratification or slavery, both of which are more often found in societies that are able to produce food surpluses. Gender ranking may also be a factor in the rise of spirit-possession practices, since women tend to be prominent in possession trance (while the possessing spirits are often thought to be powerful male figures). In at least some cases, women may predominate because participation in spirit-possession rituals allows them to play socially dominant and powerful roles that are not available to them outside the religious setting (see the box titled "Korean Possession Trance as Catharsis"). The induction of spirit-possession trances often involves the use of music, singing, and dancing; and the possessed person remains physically active during the trance, but may have no memory of what she or he did or said while possessed.

Socialization of children that stresses various forms of compliance—such as obedience, reliability, and nurturing—is prominent in societies that have possession-trance rituals. Again, these traits are often particularly stressed in the rearing of daughters more than in the rearing of sons. The trances tend to occur in group settings sponsored by cult groups rather than being practiced by lone individuals. Membership in these possession cults may be acquired as part of the cure of an undesired, spontaneous possession by an unfriendly spirit.

 ## *Korean Possession Trance as Catharsis*

In Korea religious healers who participate in spirit-possession rituals are predominantly women. Brian Wilson (1980) has described the psychological effects of such rituals for a woman curer he called Mansinim in a society in which women never have authority over men outside this religious setting:

Earlier Mansinim had told me that as a child she had been a tomboy, a troublemaker, beating up boys in the village. Her mother called her *son mosum* ("tomboy"). She said that she had "always wanted to be a man," and that when she dies she hopes to be "a great general" in the spirit world. She complained that her husband is "quiet and mild and never behaves like a man." Since Mansinim cannot become a general in real life she becomes a general in *kut*. And since she rejects the subordinate role that a wife is expected to play to a husband, she reverses that role by being ritually transformed into the husband's mother who, as parent and departed ancestor, commands the husband's respect. What is interesting about this situation is that it is not just a bit of craziness—this "acting out" of spiritual roles expresses a keen insight into the reality that is presented by the dynamics of interaction in this family. For in fact Mansinim *is* the dominant member of the family by virtue of a personality and character that are much more aggressive, assertive, forceful, "masculine" (by Korean standards) than her husband's. Therefore the ritual role reversal is simply a way of recognizing and even utilizing what is already a fact in the power structure of this family. Once Mansinim is released from the necessity of playing the subordinate role of submis-

sive wife she can, in *kut,* unfurl her "real self" . . . and play this 'self' with gusto. Which she does. When she dons the red robe of the *Changgun* with the gold breastplate and metal helmet you'd better *believe* that she is a general! Her entire manner and bearing changes from her normal circumspect mode of behavior, and she stomps heavily around with her sword almost daring anyone to challenge her. (pp. 6–7)

Wilson described a dramatic recollection of Mansinim that encapsulates his view of how her religious role provided an alternative outlet for ambitions that were denied her within Korean secular life:

I vividly recall . . . Mansinim, standing on a mountainside dressed in the red and green costume of *San Sin,* the Mountain God, weeping and crying out as her husband knelt at her feet, "If I had been born a man, I would have been a great general." In many subsequent conversations Mansinim expressed her dissatisfaction over the limitations and restrictions placed upon her simply because she was a woman. And yet in her life she had resolved contradictions that appear to baffle behavioral scientists: While passionately resenting her circumscribed lot as a woman she nevertheless had learned to cope successfully with the demanding and sometimes conflicting role of wife, mother, and ritual specialist. I measure "success" domestically in terms of the obvious affection and respect that passed between Mansinim and her husband, children and grandchildren, and professionally by the heavy demand for her services. (p. 3)

Visionary Trance

Visionary trances are often solitary experiences that occur during periods of isolation and fasting or drug use by an individual who is seeking a vision. The individual is physically quiescent during the trance, but retains very vivid memories of what he or she experienced during the trance. These trances are more often sought by men than women. They are more common in societies whose economy is based on foraging for wild foods or on hunting and simple gardening than in agricultural societies. They are more common in egalitarian societies than in those with social classes and in societies in which the genders are not stratified. Societies in which visionary trance is prominent also differ in qualities of socialization from societies in which possession trance predominates. They tend to be societies whose child rearing emphasizes the importance of assertiveness, independence, self-reliance and personal achievement rather than compliance. Like spirit-possession trances, visionary trances may involve an element of socially approved divergence from the usual role expectations of the participant; the usually self-reliant individual becomes quiescent during the trance and may be taken care of by the ministrations of others.

Figure 3.4
A Tapirapé Vision Trance
This Tapirapé religious specialist from Brazil is in a tobacco-induced trance and is being helped to walk by two other men.

Dreams as Religious Experiences

Visionary trances have similarities to dreaming. As Bourguignon (1979, p. 253) put it:

> The similarity between trance states and dreams, both of which are private, internal experiences, is great, and in cultural terms, they are often either interchangeable or used together in some way. For example, the Diegueño Indians of California used the drug *toloache (Datura Stramonium)* in the initiation of their "dream doctors." . . . As one of them explained: "*Toloache* puts you into a kind of dream state of mind that stays with you the rest of your life, and you never forget what you have learned. It helps you to keep on learning and gives you real power in everything. Without it you aren't a real doctor." (Toffelmeier and Luaomala 1936:201).

However, dreams may play a role as a supernatural source of knowledge without being tied specifically to the status of religious specialist. Anthropologist Roy D'Andrade (1961) examined the use of dreams as a means to obtain or control supernatural powers. Such uses of dreams are unsurprisingly more common where visionary trances are also practiced, but they may also occur inde-

The Iroquois had a theory of dreams that was quite similar to those developed by Sigmund Freud early in this century. According to Anthony Wallace (1967), the Iroquois believed that when the soul had unfulfilled needs, it could communicate them to the conscious mind through the imagery of dreams. If these desires of the soul remained unfulfilled, a person might become physically or psychologically ill. Some dreams were understood to be the communication of a supernatural being, but the implications were the same: Either the mandate of the dream would be fulfilled, or great harm might result—in the case of such a dream, not just on the dreamer, but on the community or nation as a whole.

Once a year at Midwinter or when someone was ill, the Iroquois held dream-guessing rituals to discover and fulfill the *Ondinonc,* or "secret desire of the soul," of individuals who expressed their dreams through riddles. According to Wallace, "someone will say, 'What I desire and what I am seeking is that which bears a lake within itself'; and by this is intended a pumpkin or calabash. Another will say, 'What I ask for is seen in my eyes—it will be marked with various colors'; and because the same Huron word that signifies 'eye' also signifies 'glass bead,' this is a clue to divine what he desires—namely, some kinds of beads of this material and of different colors" (p. 178). Dreams of sexual desire were particularly expressed at an *Andacwander* feast that involved sexual license and that Wallace characterized as a "therapeutic orgy."

During the yearly *Ononharoia* festival, the "Feast of Fools," "men and women ran madly from cabin to cabin, acting out their dreams in charades and demanding the dream be guessed and satisfied" (p. 180). Even dreams that involved overt harm to the dreamer required action, although the harm was minimized when it involved members of the same community by acting out the violence symbolically. For instance, Wallace, citing a case recounted by a Jesuit priest, Father Lalemant, in 1642, explains

Nightmares of torture and personal loss were apparently not uncommon among warriors. In 1642 a Huron man dreamed that non-Huron Iroquois had taken him and burned him as a captive. As soon as he awoke, a council

was held. "The ill fortune of such a Dream," said the chiefs, "must be averted." At once twelve or thirteen fires were lighted in the cabin where captives were burned, and torturers seized fir brands. When the dreamer was burned; "he shrieked like a madman."

When he avoided one fire he at once fell into another. Naked, he stumbled around the fires three times, singed by one torch after another, while his friends repeated compassionately, "courage, my Brother, it is thus that we have pity on thee." Finally he darted out of the ring, seized a dog held for him there, and paraded through the cabins with this dog on his shoulders, publicly offering it as a consecrated victim to the demon of war, "begging him to accept this semblance instead of the reality of his Dream." The dog was finally killed with a club, roasted in the flames, and eaten at a public feast, "in the same manner as they usually eat their captives" (Father Lalemant, Relation of 1642, in Kenton 1927, 2:42, as quoted in Wallace, 1967, p. 179).

Iroquois culture mandated—as a moral obligation—that people attempt to fulfill the dreams of others, on the grounds that the failure to do so would make them responsible for the sickness or death that would befall the dreamer if the secret desire of his soul was not fulfilled.

Unlike the culture of Europe in Freud's time, in which distressing dream images—particularly those of a sexual nature—represented impulses that were unthinkable to act upon and should be suppressed when they became conscious through dreams, the culture of the Iroquois permitted individuals to obtain relief from the tension of pent-up desires that became conscious. Where European culture stigmatized individuals who became aware of their unacceptable inner impulses and expected them to struggle against such tensions alone, Iroquois custom provided a form of therapeutic relief in which the dreamer was shown care and support by the community. As Wallace put it, "The culture of dreams may be regarded as a useful escapevalve in Iroquois life. In their daily affairs, Iroquois men were brave, active, self-reliant, and autonomous; they cringed to no one and begged for nothing. But no man can balance forever on such a pinnacle of masculinity, where asking and being given are unknown. Iroquois men dreamt; and, without shame, they received the fruits of their dreams and their souls were satisfied" (p. 190).

pendently. D'Andrade found that societies that used dreams to seek and control supernatural powers are more likely to be (1) those in which sons leave their own parental home, local group, or village when they marry instead of remaining with the familiar support network where they were reared and (2) those in which the socialization of children strongly stresses the importance of independence and self-reliance. D'Andrade interpreted these correlates of the use of dreams as indicating that this religious practice arises from anxiety about having to be alone, independent, and reliant on one's own skills to survive. The box titled "Iroquois Dream Therapy" illustrates the parallels that systems of religious curing can have with Western secular psychotherapies by comparing Iroquois ideas about the psychology of illness and curing with those of Sigmund Freud.

Brain Processes During Mystical Religious Experiences

Recent studies in brain functioning have found that two distinctive changes in brain activity occur during certain religious practices and during spontaneous mystical experiences. D'Aquili and Newberg (1999) found that a form of brain monitoring called single positron emission computed tomography showed a sharp decrease of neural activity in an area of the parietal lobe during meditation by Buddhist monks and prayer by Franciscan nuns. This area, called the *posterior superior parietal lobe,* normally functions as a kind of "orientation area" that monitors input from all of a person's senses and defines the boundary between the self and external reality. In effect, it is the part of the brain that is responsible for distinguishing between things in the outside world that are experienced through the external senses, such as vision or hearing, and those things, such as thinking in words or experiencing a pain in one's stomach, that are part of one's own, internal "self." During the religious activities of meditation or intense prayer when individuals perceive themselves as experiencing oneness with a transcendent or spiritual reality, the parietal lobe's "orientation area" becomes quiescent. It stops accepting input from the external senses and is unable to do its usual work of establishing the boundary between the self and the not-self. When this brain area becomes quiescent, individuals experience their "self" as becoming boundless or at one with a higher spiritual reality. It is noteworthy that this corresponds to what Leslie White (see chapter 1) believed to be the defining element of religion—thinking that involves what he called a confusion of self with no-self.

Medical researcher Karl L. R. Jansen (1997) found that changes in the functioning of another region of the brain correspond to so-called out-of-the-body experiences such as those referred to as *visionary trances* and *spirit-travel trances* (see chapter 7) in anthropology and in what are commonly referred to as "near-death experiences" in popular culture. Near-death experiences occur spontaneously when a brain structure called the *hippocampus* stops receiving external input from other parts of the brain. The hippocampus normally functions as a "memory gate." It is the part of the brain that helps us form memories, especially memories of discrete skills when we learn them. It also plays a role in the learning of new skills by monitoring data from the external world while we are interacting with it and retrieves memories of skills that we learned in the past that may be useful in the current situation. In effect, the hippocampus helps us learn to handle new current situations by reminding us that we have already learned various skills that may be helpful. However, the hippocampus's normal role of monitoring our current interaction with the external world can be interrupted by events, such as a stroke or brain trauma from an accident, that interrupt the flow of oxygen to the brain. While interruption of oxygen to the parietal area causes the sensation of having left the body during the oxygen deprivation, the hippocampus adds another element to the experience of being outside one's own body. When the hippocampus becomes cut off from the external input it normally receives, it may continue to draw upon its reservoir of stored memories of specific actions and use these memories as building blocks to generate internal images of interacting with other beings, including deceased relatives or religious figures, such as Jesus, the Buddha, or God, that are part of one's own religious background.

Chapter Summary

1. The psychological functions of religion include helping people to (1) make sense out of parts of their environment that they cannot explain in nonreligious terms, (2) overcome indecisiveness and emotional distress, and (3) be motivated to cooperate with others when the nonreligious rewards for doing so are not great enough to have the same effect.
2. Research indicates that in Western cultures religious people as a group are somewhat more likely to be dogmatic and to show prejudice against other groups than are nonreligious people. Otherwise, religiosity correlates positively with a variety of measures of good mental health and positive social functioning.
3. Some of the conditions treated in religious curing ceremonies would be classified as mental disorders by Western psychiatrists, and religious curing practices have some similarities with Western psychotherapies.
4. Religious innovators often experience a hallucinatory trance following a period of social and personal stress. During this trance state, they formulate a new worldview that accounts for the problems of their society. This hallucinatory experience has similarities with the reactive schizophrenic process; the difference is that religious innovators formulate new worldviews that are meaningful to others within their own societies, while the new ideas of reactive schizophrenics are not likely to seem meaningful to others.
5. Different social conditions cause different stresses to be typically experienced by members of each society. One reason for the diversity of religious forms is that religions have characteristics that help their followers cope with the stresses that they commonly experience. So religions tend to differ in different societies and among members of different parts of the same society.
6. The feelings aroused by sacred things paradoxically involve both attraction and fear or dread. This allows the religious experience to be a source of psychological catharsis for its participants. Catharsis allows people to discharge the tensions associated with the distressful emotions of fear, guilt, grief, shame, and anger and to replace this distress with a positive emotional experience.

7. Trance states are a psychological response to stress. They also play a role in religious rituals. There are two types of religious trances—spirit-possession trances and visionary (or spirit-travel) trances. Spirit-possession trances are more common in socially stratified than in egalitarian societies. They are also more likely to employ female than male practitioners. In addition, they are also more common in societies in which child socialization stresses the importance of compliance. Visionary trances are more common in non-stratified societies, especially those with foraging, hunting, and simple gardening economies. They are more often practiced by men and in societies in which child rearing stresses self-reliance.

8. Dreams, like visionary trances, are sometimes used as a source of spiritual knowledge.

Recommended Readings

1. Bourguignon, Erika, ed. 1973. *Religion, Altered States of Consciousness, and Social Change.* Columbus: Ohio State University Press. Studies in the social roles of trances.

2. Crapanzano, Vincent, and V. Garrison, eds. 1977. *Case Studies in Spirit Possession.* New York: Wiley. Cross-cultural studies of the varieties of spirit possession.

3. Hood, R. W. Jr., B. Spilka, B. Hunsberger, and R. Gorsuch. 1996. *The Psychology of Religion: An Empirical Approach.* New York: Guilford. A careful examination of psychological research on religion.

4. Kalweit, Holger. 1988. *Dreamtime and Inner Space: The World of the Shaman.* Translated by Werner Wunsche. Boston: Shambala. Examines the inner world, rituals, and healing techniques of the religious curer.

5. Lewis, I. M. 1996. *Religion in Context: Cults and Charisma.* 2nd ed. Cambridge: Cambridge University Press. Discusses the relationships between power, gender, and the psychology of religious practices, such as spirit possession, witchcraft, and shamanism.

6. Moore, S. F., and B. G. Meyerhoff, eds. 1978. *Secular Ritual.* Atlantic Highlands, NJ: Humanities Press. This collection examines the role of ritual in a variety of nonreligious contexts, including politics, recreation, sport, and theater.

7. Obeyesekere, Gananath. 1984. *Medusa's Hair: An Essay on Personal Symbols and Religious Experience.* Chicago: University of Chicago Press. A neo-Freudian look at the symbolism of hair in a Sinhalese Buddhist ascetic.

8. Spiro, Melford. E. 1971. *Buddhism and Society. A Great Tradition and Its Burmese Vicissitudes.* London: Unwin. Documents Burmese Buddhism at the level of folk practice.

Recommended Websites

1. *http://www.digiserve.com/mystic/*
   A site on mysticism in world religions.

2. *http://www.psywww.com/psyrelig/index.htm*
   Contains a variety of resources on the psychology of religion.

3. *http://bhidalgo.tripod.com/litreview.htm*
   A discussion of the neuropsychology of religious experiences.
4. *http://www.gnosis.org/welcome.html*
   A fine resource on gnosticism, past and present.
5. *http://www.saybrook.edu/app/lg/cr3080.asp*
   A discussion of the psychology of religious curing practices.

Study Questions

1. Explain how the imagery of the Sherpa temple might be seen as a model of the human psyche.
2. What are three psychological functions of religion?
3. How did Mary Baker Eddy's revitalization experience differ from those of Joseph Smith Jr. and Handsome Lake?
4. In what ways are religious curing and Western psychotherapy similar?
5. What is the role of the dry painting in Navajo curing ceremonies?
6. What are the circumstances under which catharsis is likely to be experienced?
7. What evidence can you give that distressful emotions are influenced by social circumstances?
8. Illustrate the existence of social-class differences in religious preferences.
9. Discuss the possibility that rituals might be classifiable in terms of the kinds of distressful emotions they help people obtain catharsis for. Provide some specific examples.
10. What did Gmelch discover about the likelihood of rituals among baseball players?

CHAPTER 4

Religious Myths
and Symbols

CHAPTER OUTLINE

Case Study: The Aztec Creation Myth

Symbolism

Religious Worldview
 Cosmology
 Myths
 Box: Coyote and Wolf
 Legends

The Origin and Variability of Symbols
 The Limits of Variability in Religious Symbolism
 Religion and Society
 Box: Navajo "Witches"

Artifacts as Symbols
 Religious Technology as Symbols of Religious Status
 Box: Keris Knives in Malaysia
 Religious Technology as Ritual Implements
 Box: Balinese Masks

CHAPTER OBJECTIVES

When you have read this chapter, you will be able to

1. Discuss the nature of symbolism and distinguish among the various kinds of symbols.
2. Describe the structure of religious ideologies.
3. Analyze the differences in a variety of religious cosmologies and interpret the meanings of the dominant symbols of their mythologies.
4. Explain the functions of myth.
5. Distinguish between the story-line meaning, the mythic symbols, and the structural meanings of myths.
6. Explain why myths draw on different symbols in different kinds of societies.

7. Analyze relationships between religious symbols and a society's natural environment, subsistence technology, and social organization.
8. Identify symbolic dualism in myths.
9. Identify the *mythemes* of a myth.
10. Demonstrate that religious beliefs are influenced by the organization of the society in which they are found.
11. Define *legend* and explain how legends depict important societal values.
12. Explain how religious taboos function to maintain the apparent orderliness of a religion's ideology and worldview.
13. Explain the social functions of religious technology.

Religion is the archetypical realm of symbolism. Its symbols are imbued with tremendous emotion, because they represent answers to life's most fundamental questions of meaning and existence: Where did I come from? Why am I here? Will I cease to exist when I die? All religions provide their believers with answers to these and other existential questions. The answers take the form of cosmology, myths, and legends. We begin with a case study, the Aztec origin myth, which illustrates several ways in which religious symbolism functions within a religion's sacred stories. Look especially for recurring symbolism, and consider the possible messages that this symbolism may communicate apart from the story line itself.

CASE STUDY

The Aztec Creation Myth

The Aztec civilization began with the founding of the capital, Tenochtitlán, in the Valley of Mexico in A.D. 1325 and lasted until its conquest by Hernan Cortés in 1519. In the year of its conquest, Tenochtitlán had a population of about 300,000, five times that of London in the same year. Aztec society, like that of other civilizations, had social classes and a multitude of occupational specialists, including scribes. Because the Aztec had a tradition of writing and because the Spanish friars developed a system for writing the Aztec language—called Nahuatl—using a Latin alphabet, we have much information about Aztec history and religion that might otherwise have been lost.

The Aztec, like many other American Indian societies, viewed the world in which they lived as the most recent of a series of worlds, or creations. The Aztec referred to our current world as the Fifth Sun, because it was preceded by four other creations. But before even the first world was created, the gods occupied a spiritual realm. The primal deity was a divine couple called Ometecutli ("Lord of Duality") and Omeçihuatl ("Lady of Duality"). This couple produced the next generation of gods, four of whom were sons who represented the four cardinal directions and who were centrally important in other parts of Aztec mythology: Xipe (also called Red Tezcatlipoca), whose realm was the East; Tezcatlipoca (the Black Tezcatlipoca), who ruled the North; Quetzalcoatl (the White Tezcatlipoca) of the West; and Huitzilopochtli (the Blue Tezcatlipoca), who was associated with the South.

The second of the four divine sons, the northern Tezcatlipoca whose symbol was the night sky, created the First Sun (or First Age), which was called "Four Jaguar," the Aztec name for the year in their calendar in which it was eventually destroyed. Tezcatlipoca populated his world with giants who practiced no agriculture but who subsisted on acorns and fruits. He himself sustained this world by carrying the sun across the sky each day until, after 676 years (thirteen cycles of the Aztec calendar), his world was cataclysmically destroyed by his rival Quetzalcoatl, who sent a plague of great jaguars that devoured the giants.

Quetzalcoatl, god of the wind, created the second world, which was called Four Wind. He peopled it with men who subsisted on pine nuts, and he served as the Sun Carrier of this world. Quetzalcoatl's world lasted for 676 years and came to an end in the year for which it was named in the Aztec calendar. The destruction of Quetzalcoatl's world occurred when Tezcatlipoca sent a devastating hurricane that killed all of the men who lived in it except for a few survivors who were transformed into monkeys.

Tezcatlipoca created the Third Sun, a world that he populated with men who survived by eating seeds. Instead of carrying the sun himself this time, Tezcatlipoca appointed another god, Tlaloc, to that role. Tlaloc was the Aztec patron of agriculture because he was the god of the rain and storms that were so necessary for farming in the high Mexican desert. Tlaloc's world was known as Four Rain because it was destroyed by Quetzalcoatl on a year with that name in the Aztec calendar after it had existed for only 364 years. The destruction of this world was brought about by a rain of fire—that is, by lightning. Only a few of the men of the Fourth Sun survived, and they were transformed into birds.

The Fourth Sun was created by Quetzalcoatl. He populated it with men who subsisted on primitive corn and appointed Tlaloc's wife, Chalchiutlique, the goddess of water, as its Sun Bearer. This world was called Four Water. It lasted for 312 years, when Tezcatlipoca sent a great flood that lasted for 52 years and drowned all of its inhabitants except some who were transformed into fish. Because the flood destroyed the sun, the world was in darkness. So to create the fifth world, the gods gathered together in the city called Teotihuacán to choose a Sun Bearer. Two gods volunteered for this role. The first was Tecçiztecatl, a proud and haughty god who hoped to gain praise from the other gods. He made offerings of expensive copal, which is also called liquid amber, and used stingray spines to pierce himself to make an offering of blood. The second volunteer, named Nanautzin, was a poor deity whose body was ugly and covered with scabs and who could only afford to use pine pitch as his incense and maguey spines to let his own blood. To become the Sun Bearer, one of these gods had to offer his own life by leaping into a great bonfire. The high-status deity was given the honor of attempting this feat first. He tried four times to jump into the fire, but he was too afraid. Then Nanautzin was given the opportunity, and he jumped into the blaze immediately. Tecçiztecatl, having been put to shame by Nanautzin's bravery, jumped in after him.

The gods waited expectantly to see from which part of the horizon the new sun would arise. Finally, they saw the sky begin to lighten in the east, and the sun appeared and began to rise into the sky. Then a second sun appeared, the transformed Tecçiztecatl. Angered by his audacity, one of the gods struck him in the face with a rabbit. This dimmed his light and transformed him into the moon.

However, the newly risen Sun Bearer demanded that the gods feed him in return for his labor of carrying the sun across the sky. Although they fled to avoid being sacrificed, the new sun god chased them down and sacrificed them one by one to satisfy his thirst for blood. The last of the gods to be caught and sacrificed was the god of the Evening Star, Xolotl, the twin brother of Quetzalcoatl, who was identified with the Morning Star.

To create the humans who would populate the new world, Quetzalcoatl descended to the underworld and negotiated with Mictlantecutli, the Lord of the Land of the Dead, for the bones of the people of the previous world. Quetzalcoatl bled himself and mixed the blood of this auto-sacrifice with the bones and ashes and formed human beings from the mixture. Since the gods themselves were sacrificed in order to create this world, create the sun, and feed the Sun Carrier for his labor, it has been the duty of humans ever since to perform sacrifice to feed the gods. If they were to stop, the sun would stop crossing the sky each day, and the world would come to an end.

The name of the Fifth Sun was Four Earthquake, which foretold its own destiny of being one day destroyed by a great earthquake. In the Aztec calendar this date recurs every fifty-two years. Because the arrival of the Spaniards in 1519 coincided with the Aztec year Four Earthquake, the Aztec emperor was hesitant to respond too aggressively to the strange invaders, a hesitation that quite possibly made the Spanish victory over the Aztec much more likely than it otherwise might have been.

SYMBOLISM

Symbolism is the expression of meaning through the use of signs and symbols. Religion is a part of culture in which symbolism is very important and often greatly elaborated. Religious symbolism can take many forms. It may be embodied in myths and other religious stories that communicate important ideas and values, in rituals that act out beliefs and values, or in concrete objects such as sacred religious artifacts.

All animals, including humans, communicate by using **signs,** objects or actions that have a natural meaning based on (1) a similarity between them and what they stand for, (2) a consistent co-occurrence in nature of signs and their referents, or (3) a connection between the two that is determined by biology. Signs in human communication include such things as posture, eye contact, tone of voice, emphasis, or volume of speech. These signs naturally and unconsciously express the emotional state of the speaker, communicating important details about his or her level of interest in the topic, the situation, or the listener. The "naturalness" of the meanings conveyed by signs can be illustrated by the way an angry speaker's volume increases as his or her anger grows. Using signs, it is possible to communicate wants and needs quite effectively. For instance, my dog picks up its food bowl and drops it repeatedly when I fail to feed it at the usual time. The message this communicates is so naturally linked to the need that I have no trouble recognizing its meaning.

Human communication adds to the very natural, pan-animal use of signs. We humans also use **symbols,** objects or events like the words of language, that stand for something only because we humans have established a consensus about what they mean. There is, for instance, no inherent connection between a peacock and the goddess Hera beyond the fact that ancient Greeks agreed that the peacock would be one of her symbols. The arbitrariness of the agreed-upon relationship between a symbol and what it stands for can readily be illustrated by the symbols of language—words. They need not sound like or be in any way similar to the things they stand for. A long word like *microorganism* may stand for something very small, while a short word like *whale* may stand for something quite large.

The fact that meaning is assigned to symbols has two results. It makes language very effective at communicating about anything that can be conceived of.

symbolism
The expression of meaning through the use of symbols.

signs
Objects or actions that have a natural meaning based on the similarity between them and what they stand for, the consistent co-occurrence in nature of them and the things they stand for, or a connection between the two that is determined by biology.

symbols
Objects or events that stand for something else only because humans have established a consensus about what they mean.

key symbols
Symbols that
inspire strong
positive or nega-
tive feelings and
are regarded as
very important
by those in whose
culture they are
found, are sur-
rounded by rules
such as taboos,
are found in
many different
contexts, and are
surrounded by
cultural elabora-
tion such as hav-
ing many words
to refer to them.
summarizing
symbols
Key symbols that
represent what
a system means
to the partici-
pants generically.
elaborating
metaphors
Key symbols that
provide more
detailed informa-
tion about a com-
plex system to
make it more
comprehensible.
root metaphors
Symbols that
order conceptual
experience by
serving as points
of reference for it.
key scenarios
Symbolic por-
trayals of means–
ends relation-
ships that order
action by sym-
bolizing ways
to appropriately
act out those
relationships.

If no word already exists for that new idea, one may be invented and its mean-ing explained to others. Language is therefore very useful at making finer and finer distinctions and communicating subtle differences and complex ideas. But because of this open-ended ability to discuss new ideas and more subtle dis-tinctions, things communicated through the symbols of language are always po-tentially ambiguous as well as insightful, for any statement may be qualified even further. This fact raises the specter of a possibly unspoken qualification behind any assertion made by one human to another in the ordinary use of lan-guage. In short, the human use of symbolic communication opens up new av-enues of understanding, but it simultaneously brings with it the problem of am-biguity and the capacity to lie.

Sherry Ortner (1973) has pointed out that in any culture some symbols are more important and influential than others. Inspiring strong positive or nega-tive feelings, these **key symbols** are regarded as very important by those in whose culture they are found, are surrounded by rules such as taboos, are found in many different contexts, and are surrounded by cultural elaboration such as having many words to refer to them. Their emphasis reveals some of the cen-tral concerns and preoccupations of the people to whose culture they belong. Ortner distinguishes two types of key symbols, those whose function is sum-marizing and those whose function is elaborating. **Summarizing symbols** rep-resent what a system means to the participants generically the way a national flag symbolizes a country or a cross represents Christianity. **Elaborating meta-phors** are key symbols that provide more detailed information about a complex system to make it more comprehensible. They are of two types: **root metaphors,** symbols that order conceptual experience by serving as points of reference for conceptual experience, and **key scenarios,** symbolic narrative portrayals of means–ends relationships that order action by symbolizing ways to appropri-ately act out those relationships. Cattle are a root metaphor for the East African Dinka people. As symbols they give meaning to many aspects of the external world. For instance, the colors of various things are referred to by terms for the various shades of cattle. The Jewish story of Abraham's eager offer of hospital-ity to three strangers by giving them food and a place to rest from their journey (and the resulting covenant blessing of Abraham) serves as a key scenario in Judaism of the importance of hospitality and treating others with kindness and mercy.

RELIGIOUS WORLDVIEW

All religions have concepts about the nature of reality, what kinds of rules it fol-lows, how it came to be the way it is, and what supernatural beings and powers were involved in its origins. Such beliefs form the **worldview** of each religion.

Cosmology

Religious worldview, or cosmology, consists of beliefs about the nature of the supernatural and its relationship to human beings. It provides answers to ques-tions about the nature of life and death, the reasons for the creation of the universe, and how human society originated. Cosmology can take many forms. For instance, in one version of the Navajo creation story the first people emerged to the surface of this world through a cluster of reeds after a journey from four successive previous worlds. In the earlier worlds, the first people had the forms of animals, insects, and the masked spirits that are still portrayed in Navajo ceremonies. The first people were led to this world by First Man, who was created in the east by the union of white and black clouds, and First Woman, who was created in the west from the joining of yellow and blue clouds. After arriving on the surface of this earth, the first people built a sweat lodge and then the first hogan according to the instructions of Talking God. The Navajo gods, called the Holy People, created the natural features of the land and placed the sacred mountains in their locations to mark the boundaries of the people's territory. They then placed the sun, the moon, and the stars in the sky. The people spread out and named the features of the land, including the four sacred mountains. The world was inhabited by monsters who plagued the people and killed many of them, but Changing Woman—who embodies the seasons of the world and the centrality of change in human experience—was impregnated by the Sun and gave birth to two sons named "Monster Slayer" and "Child Born to Water." These twins were great heroes who killed the monsters that plagued the people. The remains of these monsters were transformed into rock and form some of the natural features of the land that can still be seen. After the world had been made safe, the ancestral clans of the modern Navajo were created. One of the problems that arose was whether the people who had been created should live forever like the Holy People. Wolf originally wanted people to live forever. So he took a piece of wood intending to cast it into the water, saying "If this floats, people will not die," but his younger brother Coyote quickly grabbed a stone and threw it into the water first, saying, "If this sinks, people will die." At first Wolf berated Coyote for doing this; but Coyote explained that his way was better, since if people lived forever they would simply grow older and more decrepit, and there would eventually not be enough room for their descendants. Thus, death is a necessary thing.

In Gnostic theology, the Absolute Godhead was beyond human ability to describe and had no attributes that humans are capable of understanding. The universe as we know it arose in two stages. Originally, the universe arose as "emanations" from the Godhead much as light and heat radiate from fire. The first of these emanations was manifest as the deity people know as "God," who is also incomprehensible. From God proceeded new emanations, or Aeons, lesser beings created in pairs as male and female. Each of these successive pairs differed more and more from the incomprehensible, divine nature from which they were created, being therefore less perfect—although less incomprehensible too. After thirty emanations had been produced, the divine world was complete. The last of the Aeons was Sophia, or Wisdom, whose sin was wishing to comprehend the Godhead, who is unknowable. For this she was exiled from the divine world. One of the Aeons, called the Demiurge, sought to supplant God as the center of the divine world and also fell from grace. It was he who created the baser world of matter and its human occupants as an act of spite because of his exile. Human nature combines elements of the duality between the perfection of the Absolute Godhead and the imperfect Demiurge. Humans

worldview
Beliefs about the nature of reality, what kinds of rules it follows, how it came to be the way it is, and what supernatural beings and powers were involved in its origins.

contain a perishable element in their physiology and psyches that came from the false creator as well as a "divine spark," a fragment of the essence of the divine Godhead.

Most people are unaware of the divine essence within them, and it is the goal of the Demiurge (or "Half Maker") and his minions, the Archons (or "Rulers"), to keep humans in ignorance of it. Being ignorant, most people mistake the Demiurge for the true Godhead. At death, the divine spark is freed from confinement within baser matter but is usually returned to the slavery of another body and returned to the confinement of mortal life. Salvation and the ability of one's divine essence to join with the Absolute Godhead comes only when people are freed from the ignorance of spiritual realities that is imposed by the Demiurge. This ignorance is dispelled through Gnosis ("knowledge"), the saving awareness of spiritual realities that dispels ignorance. Gnosis, however, cannot be attained by purely individual effort. The imperfect parts of human nature make this impossible. So Gnosis must be revealed through divine Messengers of Light from the Godhead itself and dispensed to individuals by them or their appointed teachers. Gnosis is passed to followers of Gnosticism in the form of revealed knowledge and sacramental rituals in which that knowledge is imparted.

Order Within Diversity

It is clear from the two contrasting views just described that ideas about the world in which we live and humankind's place within it can be extremely diverse. However, the diversity in human cosmologies is not random. Cosmologies do not arise in a vacuum but within existing social circumstances, and these circumstances influence the forms that cosmologies tend to take. According to Clyde Kluckhohn (1942, pp. 78–79), mythology rationalizes the fundamental needs of a society. That is, it portrays a people's ways of thinking about such things as their economic, biological, social, and sexual needs. Because of the relationship between religious beliefs and factors such as these, there are some general patterns in how such ideas are formed. For instance, in foraging societies where each local community is small and politically autonomous, the gods who were most active in the creation of the world and its early history are often zoomorphic beings who combine animal characteristics with human behavior. These creator deities tend to be otiose and uninvolved in contemporary human life. The supernatural beings who are most active in day-to-day human life are likely to be localized supernatural beings such as ghosts, spirits, dwarves, or other beings whose influence is limited to the local area. In contrast with foraging societies, sedentary horticultural and agricultural societies are more likely to have gods who make the sun shine, rains fall, and the crops grow. Just as these societies have economic specialists, their cosmologies tend to be polytheistic, with gods who specialize in controlling particular forces of nature and who are actively involved in the affairs of human beings. The pantheons include gods of agriculture, animal fertility, war, weather, and the various parts of nature with which sedentary agriculturalists must cope. Those agricultural societies that have powerful governments tend to have gods whose roles as authority figures are stressed.

Myths

Myths are a religion's sacred stories about supernatural beings and powers and their roles in creating the universe and living things. They include stories about the origins of the first humans, the institution of human society, and the roles of early heroes who interacted with the gods. The mythology of a religion is the collective body of its myths. Although the words *myth* and *mythology* have taken on a negative meaning in modern usage, with connotations of falsehood, these words as used by students of religion in the social sciences have no such implication. In referring to a story as a *myth,* we mean only that it is a religious story about the origin of things, and the word *mythology* may be applied to *any* religion's collective myths.

Myths provide validation for religious beliefs as well as for the values that guide contemporary life, thereby giving support to the rules that guide human custom—especially customs regarding relations with fellow human beings in the contemporary world. In effect, myths give vitality to the contemporary values concerning human relations. For this reason myth has been referred to as the "sacred charter" of a society.

Myths can be told in story form, but they are often acted out ceremonially in song and dance, rituals, and drama. In this chapter, we focus on myth as portrayed in language, either written or oral. Through myths people learn that there is order in their universe and gain a sense of the human place within that order. As Claude Lévi-Strauss put it (1978), myths represent a desire to understand the world as orderly and, "if this represents a basic need for order in the human mind and since, after all, the human mind is only part of the universe, the need probably exists because there is some order in the universe and the universe is not chaos" (p. 13). The meanings of myths that communicate order and help human beings find a personal relatedness to the world around them are encoded into myth at several different levels. At the most superficial level, every myth has a **mythic story line,** the sequence of events in a myth forming the tale that accounts for the orderliness of the universe and that validates the customs and values of the society to which the myth belongs. Within the story are important individual **mythic symbols,** objects or events that each stand for or represent some important element of the supernatural realm, the order of nature, the human role within creation, or relationships between these. A different kind of meaning is also communicated by the relationships among the mythic symbols of the story, relationships that form what Lévi-Strauss (1969, 1973, 1978) called the structural meaning of the myth.

Meaning as Story Line

According to Bronislaw Malinowski ([1925]1954), "Myth fulfills in primitive culture an indispensable function; it expresses, enhances, and codifies belief; it safeguards and enforces morality; it vouches for the efficiency of ritual and contains practical rules for the guidance of man. Myth is thus a vital ingredient of human civilization; it is not an idle tale, but a hard-worked active force; it is not an intellectual explanation or an artistic imagery, but a pragmatic charter of primitive faith and moral wisdom" (p. 101). The role of myth in explaining and validating the contemporary values of society is illustrated by the Yanomamö of

mythic story line The sequence of events in a myth forming the tale that accounts for the orderliness of the universe and that validates the customs and values of the society to which it belongs.

mythic symbols Objects or events in a myth or legend that each stand for or represent some important element of the supernatural realm, the order of nature, the human role within creation, or relationships between these.

Coyote and Wolf

The Great Basin Shoshone made their living by wandering the desert valleys and foothills of the mountains in search of wild foods. Their major deities were animallike beings, among whom Coyote and his brother, Wolf, played major roles. Wolf was the elder and wiser brother of the pair, the creator of the world in which the Shoshone lived. Coyote was the embodiment of unsocialized impulse and creativity. His actions sometimes had positive effects, but they were more often harmful to himself or others. Either way, they were always acts of impulse. He was the creator of human beings, a womanizer, and an inveterate gambler.

The most common Shoshone myths were tales of Coyote and his foolishness that were told both for amusement and for teaching children about the impulsiveness they should learn to control, since Coyote regularly violated the rules of common

sense and decency that guided Shoshone life. One important story was about Coyote's role in human mortality:

A long time ago people never used to die. Coyote's brother, Wolf, said, "When people die they will get up after two days." Coyote didn't like that. Coyote said, "When we die, we should die forever." Wolf didn't like that. Coyote kept on asking his brother why the dead should get up. He didn't like that, he wanted them to die forever. After that Wolf wished that Coyote's son would die. Coyote had Magpie for his son. After Coyote's son died, Coyote went to his brother's place and said to him, "Raise my son to life after two days." Wolf didn't answer for a long time. Then he said, "You, Coyote, said that people should die forever." Wolf told him to burn all his clothing, and cut off his hair and burn it. Wolf told him that dying forever was what Coyote wanted in the first place. If it weren't for Coyote there would be too many people now (Smith, 1993, p. 3).

Venezuela and Brazil, a horticultural society in which aggression was so common and valued that the Yąnomamö called themselves "the fierce people." Wife beating was common and public. Aggression and fearlessness were highly valued, and Napoleon Chagnon (1992, p. 205) estimated that about 25 percent of Yąnomamö men died violently. These characteristics were legitimized by the Yąnomamö creation story in which men sprang from the blood of the Periboriwa, the Moon, after he was shot in the stomach by Suhirina, another of the Spirit People (see the box titled "'Moonblood,' a Yąnomamö Origin Myth" in chapter 6). By acting out the aggression so characteristic of Yąnomamö life, the gods demonstrate that aggression is fundamental to existence itself, and the myth provides a rationale for the warlike nature of the Yąnomamö and their neighbors; for, after all, men themselves sprang from the blood of an act of violence.

The box titled "Coyote and Wolf" describes an aspect of Shoshone myth.

Mythic Symbols

Myths are filled with individual symbols that evoke important concepts. Mythic symbols are objects or events in a myth or legend that each stand for or represent some important element of the supernatural realm, the order of nature, the human role within creation, or relationships between these. Mythic symbols elaborate and embellish individual elements of the story line of myths and legends with archetypal images. For instance, in European portrayals of death as the "grim reaper," death's skeletal form points to his power as the angel of death; the hourglass that he carries communicates that each mortal life runs its course and ends; and the scythe he carries represents his power to bring an end to life and "harvest" human souls. The presence of such individual symbols adds to the multivocality (see chapter 1) of myths and legends, packing them with more details of meaning than an unadorned, bare-bones story line would otherwise have. The role of individual mythic symbols in adding meaningful detail to a story line is particularly noticeable in visual portrayals of myths and legends.

Structural Meaning in Myth

Lévi-Strauss argued that the way a myth is organized encodes important information that he called the **structural meaning.** By structure Lévi-Strauss refers to a recurring relation between symbols considered as minimal units, the constant relations between elements of a myth's system of symbols regardless of what the set in question is. He believes that the constancy of symbolic relations in myths reflects the organization of the human mind.

Lévi-Strauss noted that the important symbols of myths, legends, and folktales are typically organized into dichotomous pairs that stand in binary opposition to one another. For instance, Cinderella's father was loving but powerless to protect her, while her stepmother was active and unloving. Cinderella was lovely, but her stepsisters were ugly. The magical slippers that Cinderella wore were made of fragile glass, yet they were the strongest of the magical gifts she was given and survived the stroke of midnight. Similarly, Lévi-Strauss points out that the human conflict in such stories is often mediated by a supernatural character whose special status is symbolized by the coexistence of opposing qualities—such as animal and human characteristics—that make it ambiguous and unclassifiable. Alexander Alland (1977) illustrated the roles of binary opposition and of ambiguous supernatural figures in myths with the following story from the Abron people of the Ivory Coast about how human beings acquired sores:

structural meaning Meaning that is encoded into the way a story is organized: the relationships among the mythic symbols of myths and legends that form the underlying structure of the story and that convey a message concerning the tensions or conflicts in a society's ideology.

> Once long ago a spider was wandering through the forest when it heard a woman singing. The song pleased the spider very much and it began to look for the woman. The spider followed the sound until it came upon her. After greeting the woman, the spider said: "I like your song very much." "Would you like to learn it?" asked the woman. "Yes," replied the spider. "Then you must do what I do and repeat the song as I sing it," said the woman. The woman danced and sang her song. The spider imitated her movements and sang along with her. As it did so, the sores which covered the woman's body began to heal and little by little they appeared on the spider's body and legs. When her sores had completely healed, the woman stopped singing and dancing, but the spider could not stop for it was crying and dancing in pain. The woman went back into the forest, and the spider continued on its way. Soon it came to a village of men. When they heard the spider's song, the people of the village came out to greet it. After they had exchanged greetings, the spider asked the villagers if they would like to learn its song. "Yes," replied the villagers. "It is very beautiful." "Then you must all do what I do and repeat the song as I sing it," said the spider. The spider danced and sang its song. The villagers imitated the spider's movements and sang along with it. As they did so the sores on the spider's body and legs began to heal and little by little they appeared on the bodies and legs of the villagers. When the transformation was complete the spider said, "Thank you," and disappeared into the forest. This is how man got sores. (pp. 75–76)

Alland pointed out that not only is the story composed of various dichotomies—such as the paradoxical coexistence of pain and dancing, the single woman whose home was the wild forest, a place of nature, versus the multiple men who occupied a village, a place of custom and order—but the entire story also divides in half, the second part mirroring the first. In the first half of the story, illness comes from nature to the ambiguous, supernatural character, the talking spider. The spider is the mediator of illness from the female in the dangerous and untamed forest to the civilized village of men.

Figure 4.1
Mythic Symbols.
The eyes of the Buddha below the roof of this *Stupa,* a Buddhist monument that represents enlightened body, speech, and mind, in Kathmandu, Nepal, symbolize the all-seeing omniscience of the Buddha.

Lévi-Strauss (1955) argues that the relationships between the recurring mythic symbols of a story encode a level of meaning separate from and, in his opinion, more important than that of a myth's story line. In his view, the structured relationships between the important symbols of a myth form a model that reconciles contradictions that exist within a culture. He points out that over time, the same story may evolve into a number of different versions where specific elements of the story line may differ. The unity of the story, what makes all of its differing versions recognizable as variants of the same story, is the unchanging structural relationships between its important binary oppositions. Lévi-Strauss's approach to discovering the structure of a myth is to reduce it to its simplest form by recasting it into the shortest possible sentences. These, he claims, represent the basic units of meaning, the **mythemes,** of the story out of which the structure is built. Mythemes, according to Lévi-Strauss, reveal the basic concerns of humanity, and they tend to be found in all cultures. By arranging the recurring mythemes of the story into categories, the fundamental structure of the myth can be uncovered. The pattern of these categories represents the fundamental conflicts within a culture that the myth resolves.

Lévi-Strauss's classic illustration of how the structure of a specific myth may be analyzed is his examination of the Greek myth of Oedipus. Table 4.1 represents Lévi-Strauss's arrangement of its mythemes; each column represents a category of meaningfully similar mythemes. Lévi-Strauss identifies the common element of meaning in each of the successive columns as (A) being more involved with kin than permitted by higher authority, (B) being less loyal to kin than required by custom, (C) rejection of earth-monster symbolism, and (D) affirmation of earth-origins symbolism. These last two columns need some elaboration to make their meanings clearer. According to Lévi-Strauss, in mythologies where humans are created by coming forth from the earth—sometimes

mythemes
The basic relationships that are predicated in myths, that constitute a myth's smallest units of meaning, and that are the building blocks of the myth's underlying structure.

TABLE 4.1. Lévi-Strauss's Arrangement of the Mythemes of the Oedipus Myth

A	B	C	D
Kadmos seeks his sister Europa who was ravaged by Zeus			
		Kadmos kills the dragon	
	The Spartoi kill each other		
			Labdacos (Laios's father) = lame (?)
	Oedipus kills his father Laios		
			Laios (Oedipus's father) = left-sided (?)
		Oedipus kills the Sphinx	
Oedipus marries his mother Jocasta			
	Eteocles kills his brother Polynices		
			Oedipus = swollen-foot (?)
Antigone buries her brother Polynices despite prohibition			

emerging from a cave, sometimes by being molded out of clay—humans are typically portrayed as incomplete or imperfect. For instance, the first humans may be unable to walk, to see, or to speak. The names of Oedipus, his father Laios, and his grandfather Labdacos all seem to refer to such an impediment. Thus, Lévi-Strauss takes their common theme to be an affirmation of the earth origin of human beings. This sets column four in binary opposition to column three, the common elements of which are the slaying of an earth symbol. Lévi-Strauss takes this to be the fundamental conflict in the Greek worldview. According to Greek mythology humans were created by Prometheus, who molded them from a mixture of earth and water and who later overcame their inferiority to animals by giving them fire, which he had stolen from the sun. Yet the Greeks also recognized that human individuals were born as a result of sexual intercourse:

> The myth has to do with the inability, for a culture which holds the belief that mankind is autochthonous, . . . to find a satisfactory transition between this theory and the knowledge that human beings are actually born from the union of man and woman. Although the problem obviously cannot be solved, the Oedipus myth provides a kind of logical tool which, to phrase it coarsely, replaces the original problem: born from one or born from two? born from different or born from same? (p. 435)

The myth of the creation of humans from the clay of the earth symbolizes the dilemma of "born from one" in another way. Being of the same origin, were the first man and woman like brother and sister? If so, the sexual union that continued the human line was an incestuous one. The issue of incest is, of course, central to the story of Oedipus as well. The first two columns mirror the dilemmas of an earth origin versus a sexual origin and of an incestuous origin versus a nonincestuous one, but in so doing they provide a resolution to the problem:

> By a correlation of this type, the overrating of blood relations is to the under-rating of blood relations as the attempt to escape autochthony is to the impossibility to succeed in it. Although experience contradicts theory, social life verifies the cosmology by its similar structure. Hence cosmology is true. (p. 435)

In other words, the structure of the Oedipus myth is a kind of algebraic statement of the form A:B::C:D in which the dilemma of Greek cosmology (the earth origin versus sexual origin of humankind) is counterposed to a similar contradiction in human social life—that people can be both overinvolved and underinvolved in their relationships with kin. Through counterposition, the subliminal message resolves the logical dilemma in Greek mythology by suggesting that opposing facts can, in fact, both be true, as confirmed by real-life human experience.

The major problem with Lévi-Strauss's method for decoding the message of a particular myth is the subjectivity involved in determining what constitutes the shortest possible sentences, or mythemes, into which a myth can be condensed. Nevertheless, the idea that there are structures within the story lines of myths is plausible and given some credence by the fact that various types of myth are not unique to specific cultures. In other words, it does seem to be possible to classify myths based on different structures that are found in many of the world's cultures. For instance, folklorist Anna Rooth (1957) examined three hundred creation myths found among North American Indian cultures and found that most of them could be placed into one of eight types:

- Earth-diver myths in which land is created by some being diving to the bottom of the ocean to bring sand or mud to the surface to make the land.
- World-parent myths in which a Sky-father deity and an Earth-mother deity procreate and the goddess of the earth gives birth to the important features of the world.
- Emergence myths in which humans and other living things emerge from a world below this one through an opening in its sky.
- Spider-creator myths in which Spider weaves a foundation for the earth or fastens together the vegetation that will become this earth.
- Struggle or robbery creation myths in which the creator shapes the world by theft of the sun, fire, or water or by struggling with "giants" who are keepers of fish or of weather.
- Ymir creation myths in which the world is fashioned from the body of a dead being such as a giant, a man, or a woman.
- Two-creator myths in which the world is created by two companions such as two brothers, two sisters, or a father and son.
- Blind brother myths in which two brothers compete rather than cooperate in creating human beings, one of the two being blinded by the trickery of the other and being banished along with the less perfect humans he has created.

All but the last of these eight categories are also found in the myths of Eurasia.

Clyde Kluckhohn (1959) pointed out that myths about witchcraft always include the three themes of (1) *were*-animals that can travel at miraculous speed and that gather in sabbaths to work evil, (2) illness, emaciation, and death that results from the magical introduction of noxious substances into the bodies of victims, and (3) a connection between incest and witchcraft. On a more general level, he also found certain themes that were particularly common in myths throughout the world: (1) catastrophic destruction by floods, fires, earthquakes, plagues, or famines that were often portrayed as punishments, (2) incest stories (although the specific type seems to vary in different societies), especially including a theme in which the first parents of humanity engaged in incest, (3) sibling rivalry, especially among brothers, that often ends in fratricide, (4) symbolic castration themes, sometimes—especially in native North America—expressed in the vagina dentata motif that couples fear of sexual intercourse with castration anxiety.

Another important approach to study of systems of religious symbols is that of Mary Douglas, who was also interested in the structure of myths and other symbolic systems such as taboos and rituals. She differed from Lévi-Strauss in that she saw social structure—the relationships between human members of society—rather than the psychobiological organization of the human mind as the universal referent of symbolic structures. Douglas (1966) examined the food taboos of Leviticus in terms of their meaningfulness at the structural level. Leviticus outlines various food taboos that, if violated, result in a state of impurity. Douglas argued that taboos and the defilement associated with their violation are always part of a system for ordering ideas and can only be understood in the context of that system. Failure to recognize this has led people to see the forbidden foods of Leviticus as a hodgepodge of unrelated animals with no rhyme or reason for being lumped together as unclean: "Why should the camel, the hare and the rock badger be unclean? Why should some locusts, but not all, be unclean? Why should the frog be clean and the mouse and the hippopotamus unclean? What have chameleons, moles and crocodiles got in common that they should be listed together?" (p. 41). Viewing the list of forbidden animals apart from the Hebrew system of ideas about animals and nature makes the list seem arbitrary and senseless.

Leviticus as a whole deals with two concepts: holiness and abomination. Holiness, or *qadesh,* is from the Hebrew root meaning "set apart" or "separateness." It is an attribute of God and is the opposite of abomination, or *toevah,* which means "ritual impurity" or "confusion." Holiness encompasses the concepts of justice, moral goodness, and piety, but it also includes the ideas of wholeness and completeness. For instance, physical imperfections barred men from serving as priests and animals from serving as sacrifices to God. Thus, holy things, like God, are perfect examples of the category to which they belong. In contrast, abominations, or "confusions," mix the characteristics of different categories. So hybrids are abominations and, therefore, condemned. For instance, Leviticus 19:19 forbids the breeding of hybrid cattle, sowing fields with two kinds of grain, or wearing clothing of cloth made of two different kinds of fiber, and Leviticus 18:23 forbids matings between humans and animals.

Douglas explained that holiness also implies completeness. The categories of creation that God had established and pronounced good should not be confused. For instance, in Genesis God commanded each kind of creature to reproduce "each after its own kind." Therefore, individuals who fail to conform to the class to which they belong must be abominations. According to Douglas, "The dietary rules merely develop the metaphor of holiness on the same lines" (p. 51). To illustrate this, Douglas begins with Hebrew livestock. Those that were eaten—herds of cattle, sheep, and goats—were the archetypical "clean" animals. What defined them as a group was that they were all cud-chewing animals with cloven hoofs. So any wild animal with these two traits—such as antelope, wild goats, and wild sheep—belonged to the category of edible and therefore "clean" animals. In contrast, animals of mixed or "confused" characteristics were toevah, abominations. Pigs were not rejected because they were dirty scavengers, but—exactly as Leviticus says—because they have cloven hooves yet fail to chew the cud. Having mixed characteristics, they are "confusions" and not to be eaten.

Douglas showed that the other animals forbidden as foods also fail to conform to the defining characteristics of their class. For instance, according to Genesis, God created three categories of nature: the sky or firmament; the waters; and the land. After creating each, he pronounced it good. Then he filled each of these categories of nature with living things appropriate to it: birds for the sky, fish for the water, and animals for the land. He pronounced each order of living thing good and ordered each to reproduce "after its own kind." Douglas notes that each of these categories of animals can be characterized by distinctive physical characteristics and modes of locomotion. Birds have two legs and fly with wings; ordinary fish have scales and swim with fins; and animals have four legs and either hop, jump, or walk. "Unclean" animals in Leviticus are those in any class that have the wrong form of locomotion: water creatures that have no fins or scales (Leviticus 11:10–12); four-footed animals that fly instead of hopping, jumping, or walking on the earth (Leviticus 11:20–26); animals that go on all four but have forelegs with hands like humans instead of feet like proper animals (Leviticus 11:27); and land animals that creep, crawl, or swarm instead of using the "normal" forms of locomotion (Leviticus 11:41–44).

As Douglas pointed out, understanding that "uncleanness" in Leviticus is a matter of nonconformity to the system by which the various categories of living things are defined explains what otherwise appear to be arbitrary distinctions. Viewed in this way, the hare and the rock badger, the mouse and the hippopotamus do have something in common that sets them apart from animals such as the frog, the antelope, and the sheep. They fail to have all of the characteristics that define any of the normal categories of living things that constitute the Hebrew taxonomy of animals. Recognizing that symbolic defilement is a matter of deviation from the folk taxonomies of a culture even accounts for the most arbitrary-seeming of distinctions in Leviticus—the fact that some varieties of locust are "clean," while others are "unclean." From a structuralist point of view, the answer is simple: Having more than two legs meant that locusts belonged to the earth rather than the sky. Those that walked on the earth conformed to their proper order of creation and were edible, while those that flew in the air like birds were anomalies and, therefore, toevah.

Legends

Legends are stories about the early times in human existence that follow the times of mythology and whose characters, though heroic, are more like modern humans. Although legends are thought of as more-or-less historical, they may include supernatural elements as well. Like myths, legends portray messages about the human values and goals of the culture to which they belong, but the focus of legends is more clearly human life and custom than is that of myth.

Although they may be written down, legends and myths are fundamentally a form of **oral literature,** tales told by word of mouth for pleasure and edification. They consist of the tales told by people and passed down, generation after generation, about the great events and individuals of their past. Although they are told as stories held to be true, they typically entail remarkable events that frequently involve potentially supernatural forces at work and characters of heroic proportion. As oral literature, the story line of legends includes information about the values and aspirations of people at the grassroots level of a religious community. The heroic characters of legend embody qualities that their audiences view as admirable and to be emulated or unacceptable and to be avoided. When they are incorporated into explicitly religious narratives—as are the stories about the great exploits of the Patriarchs that follow the creation myths of Genesis—religious legends function to bridge the gap between the otherworldly and potentially alien world of the supernatural and the mundane world of their audience. In this role, the focus on human events, dilemmas, and characters who—despite their remarkable qualities—can be readily accepted as historic attests to the audience that the supernatural world with which the characters of legend interact is also real. Thus, religious legends lend authenticity to the myths that they embellish.

legends
Stories about the early times in human existence that follow the times of mythology and whose characters, though heroic, are more like modern humans.
oral literature
Tales told by word of mouth for pleasure and edification.

THE ORIGIN AND VARIABILITY OF SYMBOLS

The symbols out of which myths, legends, and other religious beliefs are constructed are drawn from the life experience of the people who use them. For instance, Leslie White (1959) has noted that foragers emphasize zoomorphic deities, while food producers, who live in socially more complex groups, portray their gods in anthropomorphic terms. That supernatural imagery is drawn from social experience is not a new idea. Aristotle wrote that "all people say that the gods also had a king because they themselves had kings formerly or now; for men create gods after their own image, not only with regard to form; but also with regard to their manner of life" (Haught, 1996, p. 17–18).

The Limits of Variability in Religious Symbolism

Like the other institutions of expressive culture, such as art, the ideologies of religion are not directly constrained by the limitations imposed on people's understanding of how to make a useful tool, their strategies for fulfilling biological needs such as hunger, or their ideas about how an economic system must be organized. Religion is free to posit the existence of supernatural powers that defy the laws of physics to which toolmaking must conform. It may proclaim an uncountable number of diverse gods who "live" yet do so eternally, unlike humans and animals, for whom life processes eventually culminate in death. Religion may even recommend use of limited funds that no human economist would acknowledge as cost-effective or sustainable from a mundane point of view—proposing, for instance, that religious donations will leave the giver better off than will spending the same funds on his or her own material needs.

Nevertheless, the fact that religious ideology is less immediately constrained by the practicalities of daily life does not mean that there are no constraints at all. Although religion is less tied to the world of practical knowledge than are ideas concerning toolmaking, food production, or the politics of daily life, the beliefs and values of any religion must somehow speak to those who follow it. Religion must remain within the realm of what seems plausible to those followers despite its contradiction of some of their "commonsense," pragmatic understandings about the world around them. If a religious ideology fails to "make sense" in the context of the lives of people, they will simply not accept it.

To be sufficiently attractive to maintain a following, a religion's beliefs and values must be seen by those who espouse them as supporting the secular knowledge that informs their daily lives. In short, a viable religious ideology must be compatible with the nonreligious culture of its adherents. This is the main limitation on the form of religious belief and custom. The necessary compatibility of religion with the nonreligious culture of its own followers is at the root of Emile Durkheim's ([1912]1961) insight that religion tends to be built out of symbolism that reflects the important institutions of human social life. Others, such as Roy Rappaport and Marvin Harris, have pointed out that religion may also play a dynamic role in the regulation of a society's adaptation to its natural environment (see chapter 10).

The role of religion in a society's ecological adaptation is nicely illustrated by J. Stephen Lansing's (1991) analysis of the role of Balinese temples in the regulation of irrigation water. Water temples were found throughout Bali, from mountain lakes to the seacoast. The temples organized important rituals, such as making food offerings to local deities in which local farmers were expected to participate. The ritual calendars followed by the temples also controlled when irrigation water was to be used in each local area within a region. This system of religious control optimized the use of water in the rice paddies. The arrival of the Green Revolution brought an end to this efficient system of cultivation. Hoping to increase productivity, the Indonesian government introduced a new brand of "miracle rice," pesticides, and new fertilizers and encouraged farmers to individually replant their fields as often as possible instead of following the religiously regulated system in which neighboring farmers replanted less often and at the same time. Initially, this new approach to "modern agriculture" led to some increase in productivity. However, this increase was short-lived. As more farmers turned to the new system, the increased yields from the new techniques were outweighed by the loss of several benefits that the system of religious regulation had maintained. The first of these costs was an increase in water shortages, since water use was no longer staggered from one area to another. The second cost was an increase in vermin that attacked the crops. Under the old system of staggered water allocation, the rice paddies of entire regions would lie fallow between their own turns at irrigation water. This made it more difficult for rice pests—including rats, insects, and insect-borne diseases—to become established in a region. Eventually, the Indonesian government recognized the superiority of the old system and the Balinese were permitted to return to their traditional religious system of controlling irrigation.

Religion and Society

Emile Durkheim ([1912]1961) originated the idea that religious symbolism sanctifies those institutions of human social life that human beings must be loyal to if society is to survive. Thus, according to Durkheim, the realm of religious symbolism is bounded because each religion's symbolism is derived from the social life of a particular society. Guy Swanson (1974) has investigated Durkheim's thesis that religious symbols reflect the important institutions of the society of which they are a part. Using a sample of 50 societies, he tested specific predictions concerning the relationships between various social characteristics and religious beliefs in monotheism, polytheism, ancestral spirits, reincarnation, the human soul, supernatural sanctions for violations of moral rules, and sorcery and witchcraft. His findings for each of these will be outlined in turn.

In Swanson's usage, **monotheism** is the belief in a high deity who maintains order within the universe as a whole and who is supreme over all other supernatural beings. It should be noted that this definition does not preclude the case in which other supernatural beings are also gods or deities—that is, supernatural beings who control major forces within the universe, such as storms, plant or animal fertility, or warfare. The crucial element of this definition is not the number of gods believed in but supremacy of one god over all other gods or lesser supernatural beings that may exist within a religion. Thus, the classical Greek or Roman pantheons would be monotheistic religions in Swanson's sense, because Zeus and Jupiter were not just "first among equals" but—at least according to some authorities—supreme with respect to the other gods. In this context, the concept of supremacy implies the ability to promote or demote other supernatural beings, so supremacy entails the existence of at least three levels of power or authority—that of the supreme deity at the top of the hierarchy with at least two levels of supernatural beings beneath it.

monotheism
The belief in a high deity who maintains order within the universe as a whole and who is supreme over all other supernatural beings.

Following the Durkheimian thesis that religious symbolism is a model of important societal institutions, Swanson suggested that such a religious hierarchy would be most likely to be developed in societies in which the decision-making hierarchy had three or more levels of groups that exercise original and independent jurisdiction in some area of decision making. These included groups such as families, lineages, and clans, in kin-based societies, and governmental specialists in nonkinship societies. Such "sovereign groups," as he called them, would be natural models for supernatural beings who also make and implement decisions; and a hierarchy of at least three levels would provide a good model from which the religious concept of a supreme supernatural being could be based. His cross-cultural sample supported this generalization. The belief in a supreme being was found in only 11 percent of societies with only one or two levels of sovereign groups, in 78 percent of those with three levels, and in 91 percent of those with four or more such levels.

Some supreme deities are active in the lives of human beings and in the histories of their societies. Others are aloof and distant, being unconcerned about human affairs. The most common case of a supreme being who is otiose is that of a creator who brought the universe and lesser gods into existence and who may be responsible for its continuation, but who does not intervene in human affairs. People may believe that such a deity exists; but being uninvolved in human affairs, he is not likely to be an object of worship or placation. When Swanson looked at what kinds of societies viewed the supreme being as active in human affairs, he found that the number of levels of sovereign groups was not a strong predictor of whether gods were active in human affairs or aloof from them. He considered the possibility that involvement of gods in the daily life of people might reflect how involved sovereign groups were in people's daily lives. As a measure of this, Swanson examined the number of decision-making groups that were appendages of the sovereign groups. These "communal groups," as he called them, included groups that provide community services such as education, medical care, or military protection, but which are not sovereign groups because their authority is delegated from a higher sovereign body. When this measure was considered, Swanson found that 80 percent of societies in his sample that had two or more such service groups also viewed their high god as active in human affairs, while those with only one such communal group or none at all viewed the supreme deity as otiose.

polytheism
A belief in many
gods, none
of whom are
supreme.

Polytheism is a belief in many gods, none of whom is supreme over the others. Although they neither created nor maintain order within the universe as a whole, they are superior to other supernatural beings, such as angels, demons, ghosts or spirits of local sacred places. Their sphere of influence is limited or restricted to a single place, as with the spirit of a particular waterfall or the ghost that haunts a particular graveyard or even the patron spirit of an entire village. As gods, polytheistic supernatural beings have more general authority than do spirits. They control major forces within the world that have a wide influence on human life, such as the ocean, storms, the growth of crops, animal and human fertility, warfare, or trade. Swanson referred to such nonsupreme deities as "superior gods" to indicate that they did exercise power that was greater and more generally influential than that of spirits—such as genies, sprites, demons, or other supernatural beings who are tied to specific functions or places or to a single, limited human group.

Since superior gods differ from one another because each specializes in controlling a particular force or process of concern to human beings, Swanson hypothesized that a natural societal model for their existence would be the number of different communal specialists that exist within human groups. In the simplest of human societies, age and gender are the only basis for dividing up the work of life. Within each gender or age group, people are generalists. For instance, among foragers, all women are expected to have the skill to recognize and find the various plant foods that must be gathered for human consumption and to make the tools, such as digging sticks, net bags, and baskets, that are necessary for obtaining, transporting, and processing those foods. In societies that have domesticated their food supply, specialists may arise so that the lives of all members of a community are not so similar; some may be potters or farmers, while others are warriors or traders.

Swanson compared the number of different specialists with the presence or absence of superior gods and found that the number of superior gods is positively correlated with the number of specializations in human social life—particularly with the number of those specialties compatible with the purposes of the group in which they function.

Spirits are supernatural beings whose power and influence is tied to a particular location or human group and whose power and influence is less than that of gods. Spirits may take on innumerable forms; these include ghosts, genies, sprites, and spirits of specific features of the environment, such as springs, waterfalls, or whirlwinds. In some religions, the most important spirits are **ancestral spirits,** believed to be the spirits of deceased members of one's family who return and continue to help the family achieve its goals. Ancestral spirits, rather than other kinds, tend to dominate the religious ideologies of societies that have sovereign groups based on kinship—groups such as lineages and clans. These are societies in which ancestry is traced through parents of only one sex, and all those descended from the same ancestor form a corporate group with economic and political decision-making authority. Unlike nuclear families, these ancestry-based kinship organizations last beyond a single generation, so their economic and political goals and purposes are passed on from one generation to the next. Under such circumstances, the symbolic belief that ancestors who were guided by those goals and purposes in earlier generations might continue to work in their support after death by returning to aid or instruct their descendants is an intuitively appropriate statement about the continuity of family purpose. Whereas the religions of about half of the societies in Swanson's sample with no sovereign kinship groups other than the nuclear family had an ancestral spirit doctrine, about 90 percent of those that possessed lineages or larger sovereign kinship organizations did.

A variant of the idea of ancestral spirit involvement in society is the belief in **reincarnation,** the idea that spirits may be reborn, usually into the same group, after a period of existence in the spirit world. The symbolism of active ancestral spirits emphasizes the continuity of purpose within family organizations that transcends many generations by portraying the spirits of ancestors as remaining active in the affairs of their descendants. In contrast, reincarnated spirits actually return to the realm of mortality, bringing their own, individual personalities and purposes with them. The continuity of purpose symbolized is that of an individual rather than a group of kin. Socially, the best predictor of a belief in reincarnation is not sovereign kinship groups that last for many generations, but small residential groups, face-to-face communities that may be made up of nonrelatives who, by virtue of being neighbors, share common interests, work efforts, and decision-making authority.

Swanson found that reincarnation was most common where "the pattern of settlement is by small hamlets, compounds of extended families, small nomadic bands, scattered rural neighborhoods, or other units smaller than a village" (p. 113). Reincarnation was a religious belief in slightly over half of the societies in his sample that had such residential groups. They were absent when the ultimate sovereign group was simply a single nuclear household and occurred in fewer than 15 percent of societies with larger settlement groups such as villages and towns or cities.

spirits
Supernatural beings whose power and influence is tied to a particular location or human group and whose power and influence is less than that of gods.

ancestral spirits
Spirits believed to be those of deceased members of one's family who return to the family and continue to help the family achieve its goals.

reincarnation
The idea that spirits may be reborn, usually each into its own group, after a period of existence in the spirit world.

Swanson also found an inverse relationship between ancestral-spirit and reincarnation beliefs. Even when society was organized into small, autonomous residential units of the kind most associated with reincarnation beliefs, such beliefs remained unlikely if the ultimate sovereign groups were not these small residential units but the kind of kinship groups that were associated with the belief in ancestral spirits. Where the spirits of ancestors remain active as spirits in the lives of members of their descent groups, then reincarnation beliefs are inhibited even when the residential units are the small kinds that otherwise stimulate the rise of reincarnation beliefs.

In societies on the lower end of the residential spectrum, those in which the nuclear family household is the entire local group, the conditions that foster ancestral spirit beliefs and reincarnation beliefs are not present, and neither of these religious beliefs is likely to be found. In societies with larger settlement groups such as villages and cities, another factor comes into play. Such larger residential groups usually do not share reincarnation beliefs. However, under certain circumstances they may. India is a good example of the coupling of reincarnation beliefs with larger settlements such as villages, towns, and cities. Here, the larger residential groups are not themselves sovereign, decision-making bodies, but are subdivided into smaller residential segments based on caste divisions within the community, and these smaller residential units share common goals and purposes as sovereign residential groups like those in which reincarnation beliefs are most common. They differ from hamlets and other such groups only in that their isolation from others is not geographical but social. The functional effect is apparently the same, in that the major autonomous residential group is both larger than an isolated nuclear family yet smaller than a village.

soul
A spirit that is believed to animate the human body.

The concept of a human **soul,** a spirit that is believed to animate the human body, can take two different forms. In one form, each individual has a personal soul that maintains his or her personality and life memories after death. In the other form, a single spiritual essence vitalizes members of the entire human community. Unlike the first form, where each individual possesses a spirit that is completely lodged within his or her body, the second form of animating spirit transcends the body of each individual, and its central locus is external to the individual. At death, the animating part of this transcendent spirit simply withdraws from the body to return to the great common sea of spirit.

The first of these two portrayals of the human soul symbolically emphasizes the individuality of each separate person, while the second, in which all individuals share a common spirit essence, expresses the idea that individuals are simply parts of the greater social whole.

Swanson investigated this idea by comparing those societies in which the individuality of each person is established with those organized in ways that emphasize the common group identity shared by all members of the community. He identified four potential indicators of individuality versus commonality. His first measure was the number of distinct groups to which each individual must belong. Swanson reasoned that members of society would be most likely to perceive themselves as individuals when they were on their own to accomplish their life goals, while membership in sovereign social groups as a means of achieving goals would deemphasize the individuality of each person.

He also argued that when the number of sovereign groups to which each person belonged was large, the more parts of a person's life skills would be identified with their roles in different social groups; as a result, they would be more likely to perceive the vital essence of their souls as transcendent and lodged outside of their individual bodies. Swanson's second measure of individual social differences was the presence or absence of what he called "unlegitimated contacts," situations in which individuals must interact closely with one another to achieve common ends even though their cooperation is either without the consent of all involved or no mechanisms exist for resolving conflicts in their individual objectives. Again, Swanson argued that the larger the number of such unlegitimated contacts, the more likely individuals would be to perceive their own goals, intentions, and motives as highly personal. Swanson's third measure of individuality was the presence of small settlement units, which he expected to be less likely to submerge individual identity than would larger settlement groups. His final measure was the presence of sovereign kinship groups, which Swanson expected would emphasize the common group identity of all its members rather than their individuality.

Using the four measures, Swanson was able to assign each society in his sample a combined score of individualism versus group orientation. He then compared this composite score for each society with its type of soul concept. His findings supported the expectation that when societies are organized in ways that create a sense of individuality, there is a greater likelihood of espousing the religious belief that each individual has a unique individual soul.

All religions include piety values and rules that require conformity to them. For instance, taboos forbid acts that are unacceptable simply because they are believed to have dangerous supernatural consequences. Thus, taboos may be imposed to prevent a person from coming into contact with things that are filled with mana, whose power may be dangerous in the same way electricity can be to someone who touches a bare electrical line. Taboos may also forbid acts that might offend supernatural beings, who may retaliate against those violators. Such piety rules are found in all religions. However, not all religions also include taboos against violating moral rules, rules that forbid violating the rights of other human beings. The religious belief that there are **supernatural sanctions for violation of moral rules,** supernatural punishment for violating moral rules, Swanson determined, is most likely to be found in societies where the stability of the social order is particularly threatened by the likelihood of moral violations. For instance, social classes, interpersonal differences in wealth, debts, and the rule of primogeniture in inheritance are positively correlated with such beliefs. In societies where it is customary to share surplus goods with others, there is little reason to steal from others, but theft is more likely where wealth differences are the norm. Similarly, where debt exists, lenders know that they might not be repaid because debtors may fail to repay their debt. Under such circumstances, religion functions to support the stability of society by teaching that the violation of human obligations has harmful supernatural consequences while conformity to moral norms will result in supernatural rewards. Likewise, **primogeniture,** the inheritance of property by the eldest child, can be a source of conflict among siblings and their families. Where it is the norm in inheritance, religion once again helps to prevent interpersonal conflict through

supernatural sanctions for violation of moral rules
Supernatural punishments for violating moral rules or rewards for obeying them.

primogeniture
The inheritance of property by the eldest child.

matrifamilies
Families in which
mothers and their
relatives have
authority over
the husband and
his children.

sorcery
The use of magi-
cal rituals to
harm other hu-
man beings.

witchcraft
The use of an
innate, spiritual
power to harm
others.

the idea that those who violate the law may be supernaturally punished. Societies that are socially stratified into social classes tend to have all three of these
traits, so the presence of social classes is very strongly correlated with the belief
in supernatural sanctions for moral transgressions. Swanson also found that in
societies with **matrifamilies,** families in which maternal relatives have authority over the husband and his children, the obligation of men to show deference
to the authority of their in-laws tends to be supported by supernatural sanctions
for the violation of moral rules. Again, such sanctions function to reduce the
likelihood that a man whose economic contributions to the family may be important will act on his resentment that he must subordinate himself to the authority of his wife and her kin.

The religious belief in **sorcery,** the use of magical rituals to harm other human beings, and in **witchcraft,** the use of an innate, spiritual power to harm others, is found in many but not all societies. Swanson argued that sorcery symbolizes the hostility felt toward others when individuals found it necessary to
interact with them but society lacked the means of regulating those relationships: "The widespread use of black magic suggests a serious lack of legitimate
means of social control and moral bonds. It implies that people need to control
one another in a situation where such control is not provided by means which
have public approval" (p. 146). He found that there was a positive statistical correlation between sorcery and societies where "people must interact with one
another on important matters in the absence of legitimated social controls and
arrangements" (p. 151).

John Whiting and I. L. Childe (1953) also examined the role of sorcery as a
religious equivalent to secular means of enforcing legal obligations. They compared societies that had political mechanisms for the enforcement of law with
those that lacked such mechanisms and found that sorcery was much more
likely to be present in the latter.

Although neither of these studies looked specifically at witchcraft, it too
may be seen as a functional equivalent of law enforcement. Although sorcery is
an antisocial act in the sense that black magic harms others, Swanson's and
Whiting and Childe's studies indicate it fulfills an important prosocial function—the punishment of offenders who violate the rights of others in societies
that have no effective secular means of protecting those rights.

The belief in or actual practice of sorcery is to be expected when people experience anger and hostility over the violation of their rights, yet must continue
to be involved in the same kind of unprotected relationships in which those violations are likely to occur. The actual use of black magic is both an outlet for that
anger and a means of punishing wrongdoers or, in some cases, coercing them to
relent in their wrongs. Sorcery may result in a restitution of the sorcerer's rights
if the wrongdoer is informed that the victim has used harmful magic that will
be undone only if appropriate restitution is made. Believing that the malicious
sorcery of others is the cause of one's own misfortunes is a natural by-product
of the existence of actual sorcery practices and serves as an explanation for
accidents, illness, and death among one's own group. Thus sorcery has an ambivalent quality. Its practice may be prosocial in intent, but its practice by others will be thought of as antisocial as well.

Despite its antisocial side, specialists who acknowledge that they practice sorcery may nevertheless be tolerated within societies that lack effective legal enforcement mechanisms because wronged persons may find their services useful as a means to coerce or punish wrongdoers. Witchcraft, in contrast, tends to be seen as purely antisocial. In fact, since witches are believed to have an *innate* power to harm that ordinary people lack, they are likely to be seen as the antithesis of human beings. They are commonly described in terms that invert ordinary human ideals. For instance, witches typically love the night, while true humans may fear the dark. Humans travel slowly, on foot, while witches may have the power to fly at great speeds. Witches are associated with death and the dead, and they are often thought to engage in sexual practices, such as incest, that are forbidden by human society. While sorcerers may be tolerated, those believed to be witches are likely to be put to death. Thus, witchcraft tends to take the form of accusations made against those suspected of being dangerous unhuman beings rather than to be an avocation of self-acknowledged practitioners.

Since one is endangered when others become convinced that one is a witch, witchcraft accusations may function as a powerful threat to cease and desist from whatever behavior leads to the suspicion of witchcraft. Thus, witchcraft accusations, like the practice of sorcery, may operate as a judicial order to conform to societal norms. When individuals deviate enough from a society's ideals of normal behavior, their deviance inspires suspicion and gossip that they might be witches. When such deviants learn that they are suspected of being witches, they can be powerfully motivated to demonstrate their good standing as upright members of the group. For instance, among the Hopi, those suspected of being witches, or two-hearts, included those who were self-seeking and ambitious. Those who sought positions of power, who won too frequently in competitive situations, and who became wealthy risked being thought of as witches. Since those suspected of witchcraft might be killed if public sentiment became too strong, a potential Hopi witch was under powerful pressure to demonstrate that the suspicions were in error. Officeholders were well-advised to use the power of their positions for the benefit of the community at large rather than for personal gain, and the wealthy could undermine the strength of witchcraft accusations by expending their wealth in hosting public festivities. In both cases, conformity to public ideals was enforced by the dangers associated with suspicion of witchcraft.

One form of witchcraft belief that is common in many cultures around the world is the **evil eye,** the belief that some individuals have the power, intentionally or unintentionally, to harm others whom they envy. Helmut Schoeck (1955) quoted a college student of Italian descent from West Virginia who described her beliefs about the evil eye in this way:

> There is a certain spell you cast on people. In Italian they call it the "malukes" [apparently an Americanized version of Italian *malocchio,* evil eye]. A person may get the "malukes" from bad eyes of someone *who is envious of that person.* The effect may be mild and yet people have been known to almost die of this evil spell. You feel very tired and restless. Many people get very sleepy and don't eat. Some become so ill that a doctor can't help them. The only thing that

evil eye
The belief that some individuals have the power, intentionally or unintentionally, to harm others whom they envy.

will take the spell away is prayers of a certain type. You must take an article of clothing with you when you are having the spell taken away. Usually a woman takes her brassiere. They also say salt drives away evil spirits. You may also hold your fingers in a certain way. You usually have them horned. *I have seen some of these things work.* I don't know if it's true or not, but I guess if you have faith in something it will work. (p. 153)

According to Schoeck, belief in the evil eye was particularly powerful in rural southern Italy, Spain, Portugal, and Latin America, especially Brazil. The most probable suspects for practicing the evil eye were individuals likely to be envious of those whose lives were more fulfilled in respect to things valued in their culture. For instance, in many European cultures where the belief is prevalent, the envy of single persons, especially widows, may unintentionally harm the married; mothers may avoid barren women for fear that their children might be endangered by their envy; and strangers are considered more likely to be sources of evil-eye afflictions than are acquaintances, family, and friends. Schoeck illustrates the effects of evil-eye beliefs by citing the fear that mothers have of barren women: "Italians never feel sure whether or not some *jettatore* [someone who may cause harm by the evil eye] is present, and rarely mention the subject. But whenever a friendly gathering of mothers with children, in Italy,

---

 ## Navajo "Witches"

Not all religions make a neat distinction between witches and sorcerers. The Navajo religion is a case in point. It includes the belief in *yenaldloshi,* a term that literally means "evil walking animal-like." In English, these evil beings are often referred to as skinwalkers or as "Navajo witches." But yenaldloshi represent something of a mixed case, having some characteristics that fit this text's definition of sorcerers and others that come closer to that of witches. Like sorcerers, yenaldloshi begin life as ordinary humans, and their evil is done by means of magical rituals. In other words, people learn to become yenaldloshi. Nevertheless, yenaldloshi have many witchlike characteristics. They are seen as the apotheosis of evil, as having the ability to transform themselves into animal form, and as being so antihuman in their practices and dangerousness that a suspected yenaldloshi might be put to death.

Folklorist Barry Toelken describes yenaldloshi this way:

To the Navajos, witches are those who intend to do evil to others, usually by inflicting physical or psychological

harm upon them. They are described as independent, competitive, acquisitive. If a Navajo becomes wealthy and does not share the goods, he or she may be suspected of witchcraft. Witches are characterized as having unbridled appetites for sex, and they can inflict psychological damage on others by the use of ointments, herbal magic, and the "shooting" of magical agents through the air. They are thought to be often in contact with death: They dig up graves in order to get old jewelry and body parts to use in their ceremonies. They consort with animals, almost exclusively with predators. They are most often, though not always, men, and the most feared of all are those who in their daily lives are medicine men ("singers"). They are aggressive and they come looking for their victims, doing their reconnaissance at night when most Navajos are at home with their families. They put on animal skins (wolf, coyote, or dog) by passing through ritual hoops (analogous to the hoops used by singers to rid people of disease), and since they wander about at night in the form of predators, they are called yenaldloshi (literally "evil walking animal-like," but usually phrased as a noun in English: "skinwalker"). (1987, p. 396)

Latin America, or an Italian neighborhood in this country suddenly breaks up as soon as a childless woman joins the group, the wise observer knows what has happened. The frightened mothers just take it for granted that the barren woman must envy their happiness and therefore cannot help casting the evil eye" (p. 159).

The contrast between sorcery and witchcraft can be useful, particularly in those societies that distinguish between the two categories. Nevertheless, among the many varieties of religious ideas about harmful use of spiritual power are mixed cases that do not lend themselves to easy classification. For instance, among the Navajo, individuals traditionally called "witches" in English are thought of as human beings—rather than as beings who merely look human—who have learned to use sorcery in antisocial ways. Yet they are not simply sorcerers, since they also have acquired a number of rather "witchlike" characteristics, such as the ability to transform themselves into animal forms. The box titled "Navajo 'Witches'" explores this example of a mixed case in more detail.

ARTIFACTS AS SYMBOLS

Symbols that play a role in religion may also take more concrete form. Human artifacts such as sacred masks, religious paintings, and other objects used in ritual settings may communicate important religious meanings. Such objects that function as religious symbols rather than as objects of utilitarian use may be referred to as **religious technology.** In forms such as paintings and sculpture, they may portray important mythological events or religious characters. They may also symbolize the status of religious specialists. For instance, clerical collars indicate that the wearer is a Christian pastor, a mitre represents the office of a Roman Catholic bishop, and a tambourine and dress decorated with mirrors identify a Siberian religious curer.

religious technology
Objects that function as religious symbols rather than as objects of utilitarian use.

Religious Technology as Symbols of Religious Status

Many objects used as accouterments distinguish one religion from another. One common religious object is the fetish, a mana-filled object that protects its bearer from adverse spiritual influences. In Christianity, crucifixes, images of saints, and the Bible itself sometimes play this role. Many Native Americans carry medicine bundles, small bags containing objects sacred to the bearer, and participants in New Age movements may wear crystal pendants for their healing or protective power. The box titled "Keris Knives in Malaysia" discusses an interesting example of artifacts as important religious symbols.

Objects that communicate the special status of religious specialists are not limited to societies in which the status of religious specialist is a full-time occupation, but they are particularly common when such full-time statuses exist. In Christianity, clerical collars reveal the wearers' religious profession; and in denominations that have a complex religious hierarchy, the dress of those at different levels in the hierarchy may differ markedly. For instance, the formal dress of Catholic bishops differs from the simple clerical collar and black vested suit

Every adult Malay man is expected to own a *keris* knife. Keris are pattern-welded damast (damascene) blades that come in different sizes and shapes, and their surfaces have hundreds of different patterns. Their defining characteristics include a distinctive shape of the blade near the hilt. One side of the blade is relatively straight, while the other side flares broadly near the hilt and has decorative irregularities that support the flare's function as a guard. Between the blade and the hilt is a separate piece of metal called the Ganjah that represents the feminine aspect of the universe. The shaft of the blade that passes through a hole in this piece represents the masculine, so that the union of these two pieces symbolizes the spiritual union of the masculine and feminine aspects of the universe, symbolism that endows the blade with great power. Blades may be straight or curved, and curved blades always have an odd number of "waves." The damascene blades are composed of many layers—traditionally at least 64—that alternate between iron and nickel-iron surrounding a steel bar. How these layers are treated during the welding process can result in many different patterns formed by the darker iron and silver-colored nickel-iron. Each pattern has a traditional spiritual significance. For instance, one common pattern called Beras Wutah ("Scattered Rice Grains") is said to bring prosperity, since only the wealthy can afford to scatter rice. A blade should be carefully matched to the characteristics of its owner. For instance a keris of the pattern called Butel Mayit ("Death Shroud") should be owned only by a man of power or war, since its power might bring harm to other men.

The keris is considered to be a magical weapon with protective power. For instance, many Malays keep one tied to the roof beams of the house because it is believed that it will rattle a warning if an enemy should try to enter the home. Ideally each year a ceremonial cleaning of each blade is carried out in the Muslim month of Muharram. This is the first month of the Muslim year and therefore appropriate for a ceremony of renewal. This cleaning is a ritual in which the spiritual power of the blade is also renewed. Blades that are to be cleaned and renewed are carried into the appointed place in a ritual procession. Each of the cleaners is blessed. Then any rust is removed from each blade by a gentle washing and by using each blade to pierce a lime or other acidic fruit. After this the blade is soaked in a trough of lime juice and arsenic. The arsenic turns the iron black but leaves any visible nickel silver. This process brings out the smokelike pattern on each blade and is also thought to cause the spirit of the blade to rise to its surface. Each blade is then cleaned again with a mildly acidic solution to remove any arsenic. Finally, each blade is washed with water and scented with sandalwood oil or another fragrant oil. By tradition, sheaths should ideally be made of wood, which is thought of as dampening the spiritual power of the blade when it is not unsheathed.

of the priest in particulars such as miters and croziers or pastoral staffs that indicate the bishop's distinctive position of religious responsibilities—the staff for his role as a spiritual shepherd and the flame-shaped mitre (symbolizing the Holy Spirit) for his role in leading worship. Similarly, when a boy enters the life of a Buddhist monk, his head is shaved and he is given a robe to wear.

Religious Technology as Ritual Implements

Other religious artifacts function as aids to religious practices. No religion is without such artifacts, so the list of possible examples would be endless. One well-known example is the rosary, used in both Buddhism and Christianity

Figure 4.2
A Ndebele Shaman
This South African shaman of the Ndebele tribe communicates his status as a diviner by wearing a porcupine quill headdress, animal hides, rattles on his feet, and a special whisk he waves while calling spirits.

to help people keep track of where they are in a long series of prayers. In Judaism skullcaps called yarmulkes are worn by men in worship services and special shawls called *talaysim* may be worn during prayer. Prayer wheels help the Tibetan Buddhist meditate and increase their spiritual merit. Among New Age Americans, crystals and incense play a similar role.

Two fundamentally important artifacts in Wiccan religion are the chalice and the athame, which are used to celebrate the Great Rite that symbolizes the union of the male and female principles of the universe from which life arises. The chalice is a cup that represents the feminine principle of water, and it is the symbolic womb of the Goddess. It is an important feature of Wiccan altars. The athame is a knife. It is often black-handled, although this is not a necessary characteristic. It is a masculine symbol that is associated with the East as a cardinal direction as well as with the center of the cardinal directions. The athame has been dedicated to the use of "cutting" symbolic forms such as pentagrams in the circle which surrounds participants in certain rituals. As an extension of the wielder's will and intuition, it is also used for evoking spirits or banishing unwanted spirits from Wiccan ritual circles. The use of an athame for mundane purposes such as cutting food or even self-defense destroys its ability to be used for spiritual purposes.

Masks are a special case of religious aids used for impersonating spirit-beings. In ceremonial settings, the wearer may be thought of as becoming or embodying the deity whose mask he or she wears. One well-known contemporary example is the wearing of kachina masks in the sacred ceremonies of the Pueblo Indians of the southwestern United States. The Hopi occupy a number of villages on and near three mesas in northern Arizona. One village, Old Oraibi, was first settled about A.D. 1050 and is the oldest continuously occupied community in North America. The gods of the Hopi people are called *kachinas*. During most of the year, the Hopi kachinas live in the San Francisco Peaks, northwest of Flagstaff, Arizona. However, during half of the year when the Hopi are very involved in performing sacred rituals, the kachinas come to the Hopi communities so that the people may interact with them. On these ceremonial occa-

Balinese Masks

Masks play an important role in the reenactment of the myths of many different religions. In Bali, for instance, the story of the titanic conflict between the beneficent Lord of the Forest, a dragon-like character named Barong, and the evil witch Rangda, the Queen of Death, is acted out by dancers who wear masks carved from wood to indicate which character in the story each dancer represents. During the epic battle between these two adversaries, the outcome is never certain. At some times Barong seems to have the upper hand, but at others Rangda seems about to win. Finally, as Rangda's victory seems to occur, men rush onto the dance floor with blades that Rangda forces them to wield against their own bodies. Dancing in a state of trance, these men threaten to stab their own chests with their knives, but finally they are saved by Barong, although Rangda is not clearly defeated—implying that the conflict between the forces of good and evil will continue.

Art is an important element of life in Bali, as is religion, and the two are intimately intertwined. Girls are taught the intricacies of Balinese dance from an early age, and boys are expected to master the arts of carving and playing the sacred instrument of Bali called the gamelan. Carved masks play an important role in the sacred dances that reenact Balinese mythology. As boys grow in age and skill, they learn to carve masks of increasing intricacy.

sions, the kachina visitors are portrayed by Hopi men who wear kachina masks. While they wear the masks, they become embodiments of the gods.

In Bali, masks are also used in the danced reenactment of the myths of religion that are accompanied by music from sacred xylophonelike *gamelans.* Masks representing the Balinese god Barong, the all-good lord of the jungle, and the witch Rangda are particularly important, for their conflict represents the cosmic battle between good and evil. Their masks are preserved in special temple sanctuaries. When dancers don masks, whether those of gods or lesser supernatural beings such as demons, they give themselves over to the personality of the spirits that the masks embody. In dance, they do not simply reenact a story, but also live the story through dance. Thus, the line between art and religion blurs in the Balinese sacred dances. For instance, the figures of Barong and Rangda may engage in spontaneous slapstick that elicits laughter from the audience, but this is not the laughter of mere entertainment, since laughter is a form of beauty and is pleasing to the gods. The ritual use of masks in Bali is discussed in the box titled "Balinese Masks."

Chapter Summary

1. Religion is a realm of emotionally powerful symbolism. Religious ideology has three important components: cosmology, myths, and legends.
2. Religious worldview, or cosmology, consists of beliefs about the nature of the supernatural and its relationship to human beings. It provides answers to questions about the nature of life and death, the reasons for the creation of the universe, and the way human society originated.
3. Myths are a religion's sacred stories about supernatural beings and powers and their roles in creating the universe and living things. They include sto-

ries about the origins of the first humans, the institution of human society, and the roles of early heroes who interacted with the gods.

4. Meaning can be found at different levels in myths. On the surface, meaning has the form of a story line. Within the story there are powerful, individual mythic symbols. Finally, the structure of the myth may also convey meanings.

5. Legends are stories about the early times in human existence that follow the times of mythology and whose characters, though heroic, are more like modern humans than are the characters of myth.

6. Religious ideology is less immediately constrained by the practicalities of daily life than are other parts of ideology. Yet, its variability is not without some limits. The beliefs and values of any religion must remain within the realm of what seems plausible to its followers despite its contradiction of their "commonsense" understandings about the world around them.

7. Many specific religious beliefs are conditioned by particular characteristics of the social organization of the society where they are found. For instance, belief in monotheism, polytheism, ancestral spirits, reincarnation, the individual human soul, sorcery and witchcraft, and supernatural punishments for the violation of moral rules are each more likely to be found in societies whose social organizations have particular characteristics.

8. Religious taboos function to maintain the apparent orderliness of religious ideologies and worldviews by forbidding acts that might make their inconsistencies more readily noticed.

9. Religious technology may function to communicate information about religious statuses such as one's religious affiliation or the positions of religious responsibility one may hold. Religious technology may also play an important role in the rituals and ceremonies of religion.

Recommended Readings

1. Buck, Christopher. 1999. *Paradise and Paradigm: Key Symbols in Persian Christianity and the Baha'i Faith.* Albany, NY: State University of New York. Buck applies Ortner's concepts of key scenarios and root metaphors in the analysis of Iranian Christianity and the Baha'i religion.

2. Douglas, Mary. 1966. *Purity and Danger: An Analysis of the Concepts of Pollution and Taboo.* London: Routledge & Kegan Paul. Discusses the nature of the relationships among symbolic pollution, taboos, and the symbolic order in worldviews.

3. Iwasaka, Michiko, and Barre Toelken. 1994. *Ghosts and the Japanese: Cultural Experience in Japanese Death Legends.* Logan: Utah State University Press. Japanese death customs and ghost legends in their historical context.

4. Lévi-Strauss, Claude. 1966. *The Raw and the Cooked: Introduction to a Science of Mythology.* Baltimore: Penguin. Lévi-Strauss's seminal work on the structural analysis of myths.

5. Needham, Rodney. 1979. *Symbolic Classification.* Santa Monica: Goodyear. A British anthropologist's view of the role of symbols in human life.

6. Sullivan, Lawrence E. 1988. *Icanchu's Drum: An Orientation to Meaning in South American Religions*. New York: Macmillan. A readable compendium of the mythology of the native religions of South America.

7. Swanson, Guy. 1974. *The Birth of the Gods: The Origin of Primitive Beliefs*. Ann Arbor: University of Michigan Press. A clear demonstration of relationships between various social characteristics and religious symbols from a student of Emile Durkheim.

8. Turner, Victor. 1967. *The Forest of Symbols: Aspects of Ndembu Ritual*. Ithaca: Cornell University Press. A collection of essays on symbolism and ritual among the Zambian Ndembu of Central Africa.

Recommended Websites

1. *http://www.pibburns.com/myth.htm*
   A useful site on myths and legends.
2. *http://library.thinkquest.org/29064/main.html*
   The Genesis Project site about Creation Myths.
3. *http://members.bellatlantic.net/~vze33gpz/myth.html*
   An excellent resource on myths and legends.
4. *http://www.julen.net/ancient/Mythology_and_Religion/*
   Mythology links.
5. *http://www.bartleby.com/196/*
   An online edition of Sir James Frazer's classic work on comparative mythology.
6. *http://classiclit.about.com/cs/assyrobabmyths/*
   A very useful set of links to websites about Assyrian and Babylonian mythology.

Study Questions

1. According to Gnostic belief, how did the world originate?
2. Explain what Lévi-Strauss means by the "structural meaning of myth."
3. According to Malinowski, what indispensable function does myth fulfill?
4. What recurring themes did Clyde Kluckhohn find in myths?
5. What kind of information about a society or culture does oral literature often reveal?
6. What kind of subsistence system is likely to be associated with zoomorphic deities?
7. What did the Shoshone deity Coyote symbolize?
8. In the view of Emile Durkheim, how do religious beliefs arise?
9. What social characteristics are common in societies where the belief in sorcery is prominent?
10. What are two functions of religious technology?

CHAPTER 5

Religion as Expressive Culture

CHAPTER OUTLINE

CHAPTER OBJECTIVES

When you finish this chapter, you will be able to

1. Explain the relationships among the various institutions of expressive culture.
2. Discuss the relationships between ritual and feelings.
3. Explain the role of feelings such as awe, reverence, and dread in the experience of the sacred.
4. Discuss the functions of religion as a source of values.
5. Explain the concept of religion as "ultimate concern."
6. Discuss the various ways in which nature and the human body are drawn upon for sacred symbolism.
7. Explain the role of pilgrimage in religion.

Religion is closely associated with other social institutions in which the expression of feelings is important. In this chapter, we focus on the role of sacred feelings in religion. To do so we examine the relationships between religion and play, courtship love, art, and mental disorders. We discuss the roles of feelings and values in religious settings and explore how religion draws upon both nature and the human body as a source of powerful symbolism. To illustrate the importance of the expression of feelings and values in religious rituals, we first examine the integration of religious ritual into family life in the case study "Passover Seder—An Important Jewish Folk Practice."

CASE STUDY

Passover Seder—An Important Jewish Folk Practice

Although the Day of Atonement is the most sacred religious observance of Judaism, the Seder meal of Passover is thought of by many, perhaps most, Jewish families as the most important folk practice or family custom of religious significance. The Seder is a collection of many kinds of Jewish traditions drawn together into a book called the Haggadah, or "Telling," that is used as a guide for what to do and say during the important Seder meal of Passover. The Passover Seder is a ceremonial meal that commemorates the exodus of Jewish slaves from Egypt about 3,400 years ago and on a deeper level celebrates of the fact that God has kept the Jewish people alive as a people despite 2,000 years of being scattered throughout the world. The ritual of the meal unifies the family in remembering how God saved the Jewish people from bondage and in dedicating themselves to renewed commitment to honor God by living in accordance with His will. The Seder meal is held after sunset at the beginning of Pesach, or Passover Day, since days in the Jewish calendar are measured from one evening until the next. The meal is divided into fourteen parts.

The centerpiece of every Seder table is a "Seder plate," often a special plate that may have been in the family for some time and can therefore be an important symbol of the family's continuity and heritage. The various foods arranged on it symbolize the life of bondage in Egypt and will be tasted at different points in the ritual. These symbolic foods are carpas *(vegetable appetizers that will be dipped in salt water symbolizing the importance of a whetted appetite to the enjoyment of a meal and the importance of the desire for freedom from oppression to the true enjoyment of freedom),* maror *and* chazeret *(bitter herbs that represent the bitterness of slavery and oppression),* charoset *(a mixture of chopped apple, nuts, cinnamon, and wine that symbolizes the mortar that Jewish slaves used when they were forced to build the cities of the Egyptian king),* zaroa *(a shank bone from a sheep that represents the sacrificial lamb that was once a part of the meal), and* beitzah *(a hard-boiled or baked or roasted egg that is burnt on one end to represent the burnt offerings in the Temple).*

The first act of the Seder meal is the Kiddush *or prayer of sanctification of Pesach. The Kiddush blessing is made over red wine that symbolizes the blood of the sacrificial lamb that was eaten on the day of Passover until the destruction of the Second Temple. Four cups of wine will be drunk at four times during the Seder. Each represents one of the four ways in which God has redeemed the Jewish people as stated in Exodus 6:6–7: "Therefore say to the children of Israel, 'I am God and I will* take you out *from under the toils of Egypt, and I will* deliver you *from their labors, and I will redeem you with an outstretched arm and with great judgements. And I will take you to Me as a people, and I will be to you God.'" The first three cups are drunk in thanks for God having delivered His people out of bondage in Egypt and for all that He has provided them with since then. The fourth gives thanks specifically for God's gift of the Torah, which gives the Jewish people meaning and purpose in life. The wine is drunk on each of the four occasions while leaning to the left. This leaning, or "reclining" as it is sometimes called, may be done by resting against a pillow. It is reminiscent of the practice in Hellenistic times of eating while reclining instead of seated on chairs, and it symbolizes the aspiration for a day of relaxation and freedom from the oppressions of the past.*

The second act of the Seder is Urchatz, *the washing of hands in preparation for the meal. Then comes* Carpas, *the serving of an appetizer of a green vegetable or a potato dipped in salt water. This is accompanied by a blessing, "Borei Pri Ho' adomah," a standard blessing before eating any vegetable. This is done so that the children at the Seder may ask, "Why do we dip the vegetable?" The answer to this question fulfills one of the purposes of the Seder, to explain why the Jews had to experience slavery. The children are told that the appetizer is a reminder that just as one cannot really enjoy food unless a hearty appetite has been stimulated, one cannot truly enjoy freedom before one has experienced slavery.*

The fourth ritual of the meal is the Yachatz, *breaking in half the middle* matzoh *of three that rest on a plate on the table. Matzoh are large wafers of unleavened bread that symbolize the bread that had to be made in haste—without the use of leavening that takes time to make the bread rise—when the Jewish slaves of Egypt were preparing for their exodus from Egypt. The larger half of the broken matzoh is wrapped in a napkin and saved to be eaten later at the end of the Seder, while the smaller half is left on the table for the meal itself.*

Next comes the Maggid, *the telling of the Passover story, the story of the Exodus from Egypt. The Maggid is based on the injunction in Exodus 13:8, "And you shall tell your children on this day, that because of this did God take me out of Egypt." The Maggid is introduced by a series of questions, sometimes asked by the youngest child or sometimes by all the children together. The questions are introduced by the query, "Why is this night different than all other nights?" and then go on to inquire about various symbols in the Seder meal. In answering these questions, the Exodus story is explained. At the end of the telling of the story of the Exodus, the second cup of wine is drunk, leaning to the left. This is followed by the* Rochtza, *a washing of the hands accompanied by another blessing.*

The seventh part of the Seder is the Motzei matzoh, *two blessings spoken over the matzoh. After these blessings, the matzoh is eaten, leaning to the left. Then the* maror, *bitter herbs such as romaine lettuce or grated horseradish, are eaten from the Seder plate. The symbolism of the bitter herbs is a reminder that slavery was bitter for the Jews in Egypt. Then comes the eighth part of the Seder,* Korech, *the eating of a sandwich of matzoh with bitter herbs, while leaning to the left. This symbolizes the experience of both freedom and slavery, the original meal having been eaten at the moment before freedom. Thereafter comes the* Shulchan Orech, *a meal consisting of the family's favorite traditional delicacies.*

After the meal comes the Tzafun, *or dessert, in which the matzoh that was set aside previously is eaten while—in some families—everyone is standing. Some families make a game of hiding this portion of matzoh and having the children hunt for it or having the children hide it and the father look for it. The Tzafun is an important event in the Seder, since the matzoh represents the lamb that God commanded to be eaten on Pesach. The matzoh was substituted for the lamb after the destruction of the Second Temple, because from that time there was nowhere for the Pesach lamb to be sacrificed appropriately for use in the Seder meal. After the Tzafun, the third cup of wine is poured, the prayer of Grace after Meals is recited, and the wine is drunk, leaning to the left.*

At this point, the fourth cup of wine is poured along with an extra cup that is poured and placed at the center of the table for Elijah the Prophet. The door is opened to permit Elijah to enter the home. Elijah is the prophet of redemption, and he visits every home during the Seder. It is believed that one day he will do so, announcing the coming of the Messiah and the redemption of God's people.

Next comes the Hallal, *the recitation of psalms in gratitude of God, and the fourth cup of wine is drunk, leaning to the left. The Seder ends with the* Nirtzah, *which means "It should be accepted." The Nirtzah is a service in which all present express their joy at having performed the Seder and hope for redemption. A highlight of the Nirtzah is the song "Chad Gadya" in which a kid is eaten by a cat, which is eaten by a dog, which is hit with a stick, which is burned in a fire, which is put out by water that is drunk by a cow, that is killed by a man, who is struck down by the Angel of Death, who is vanquished by God. The message of the song is a statement about the nature of the world: Each thing exercises power over something else but is, itself, dominated by yet another thing; however, all are ultimately subordinate to God. This message was important for the Jews to remember through most of their history, during which they were dominated by one nation or another. It reminds them that nations come and go, that only God is eternal, and that God has kept them as a people despite the exile that they endured for millennia.*

As a folk practice perpetuated at the level of the family, the Seder is characterized by great vitality and adaptability in its ability to adjust to changing circumstances and to incorporate the current concerns of different Jewish communities throughout the world. For instance, the number of glasses of wine has been adjusted by some families to five rather than four—at one time, the fifth glass was dedicated to Soviet Jews who were experiencing terrible persecution and at another time dedicated to Ethiopian Jewry. Haggadah books that outline the practices of the Seder have been written to accommodate the values of Jewish feminists and other groups with special concerns. Thus the Seder has remained a vital celebration of both the changing concerns of Jews throughout the world while still proclaiming an important message about the continuity of Judaism and its hopeful view of a future in which the oppressions of the past will be replaced by freedom and social justice.

EXPRESSIVE CULTURE

expressive culture
The part of culture most involved with organizing and expressing feelings.

Religion is a part of what anthropologists refer to as **expressive culture,** the customs and institutions of a culture that are most involved with organizing and expressing feelings, often by means of meaningful individual rituals or group ceremonies, games, and festivals. The phrase "expressive culture" is commonly equated with the various arts, including folk performance such as storytelling and professional art. For the purpose of placing religion in the broader context of human affective expression, I wish to use the phrase somewhat more broadly to include the related phenomena of fantasy-play, art, courtship love, and mental disorders. In some of these, like religion, the existential function of attempting to overcome anxiety and to feel good about ourselves and our place within the universe and the supernaturalistic assumption that there are forces at work beyond our immediate perception are explicitly accepted. Theologians, for instance, may devote volumes to the existential functions of religion or to defining the nature of the supernatural, its beings, and its forces. In other cases, these functions may not be explicitly acknowledged. However, their role in all forms of expressive culture accounts for the difficulty in distinguishing religion from these other forms. This underlying similarity between religion and the other types of expressive culture is illuminated in this chapter.

Science and the Problem of Expressive Culture

Much more has been written about expressive culture from the perspectives of the arts and the humanities than from the perspective of science. The edges of the psychological processes involved in spirituality and artistic creativity are fuzzy, and they seem to overlap or grade into each other. This overlap can make it difficult to define clearly whether a given behavior is best seen as part of one expressive institution or another. For instance, there is no obvious way of distinguishing between the religious "inspiration" that produces a new worldview and the artistic "inspiration" that gives rise to a fictional story set in a fantasy environment other than the assertion in the former case that the vision came from a source other than the mind of the religious innovator and that his or her vision represents a true portrayal of some reality that differs from the current world of human experience. Furthermore, elements of expressive culture such as visual art, music, dance, and folk narrative are often incorporated into explicitly religious settings to enhance the religious experience or give it meaningful form. The frequent sharing of the same settings can further blur the distinction between religion and other forms of aesthetic experience. Because of the fuzzy boundaries and the overlap among the various kinds of expressive culture, they have all been difficult to define. Texts that deal with them often simply rely on the common sense or intuition of their readers and avoid any attempt to provide a precise definition of the sort usually found in texts about institutions outside the domain of expressive culture, such as politics or economics.

Figure 5.1
Graceful Buddhas
Art and religion are both parts of expressive culture, and art often plays a role in religious ritual and in communicating religious messages. These graceful Buddhas decorate the courtyard of a temple in Luang Prabang, Laos.

The Characteristics of Expressive Culture

All forms of expressive culture, religious and nonreligious, involve at least occasional use of the repetitive behaviors of *ritual* (see chapter 7) and *trances* (see chapter 3). *Religion* involves the otherworldly experiences of trance states like inspiration, revelation, and spirit possession. The rituals of religion are based in supernaturalistic beliefs and are understood in terms of those beliefs. Similarly, the other categories of expressive culture also involve trance and ritual. Let us now

projection
The treatment of
internal images
and ideas as if
they were exter-
nally real.

briefly consider the similarities and differences between religion and each of the other types of expressive culture.

Fantasy play also involves both trance and ritual. Children engage in fantasy play long before they develop language and the so-called normal state of consciousness that it entails. The role of **projection**—the treatment of internal images and ideas as if they were externally real—has long been recognized by psychologists as an important part of fantasy play. Like other forms of super-naturalistic thinking, fantasy play involves a child's treating internal mental im-agery as if it were part of an external setting in which the play occurs. For in-stance, during fantasy play pushing a toy car may become "driving," a broom may become a "horse," or a shadowed corner of the room may become filled with "monsters" that the child responds to with real fear. Like the predictable and repetitive elements of religious ritual, fantasy play in children can become quite stereotyped and repetitive, yet engrossing to the children who participate in it.

The production of *art* may involve a trance state that has been referred to as a "creative reverie" experienced by artists when they are engaged in intensive artistic work, and many kinds of art—in particular, the performance forms of art—can have much in common with the rituals of religious performance. Con-sider, for instance, the similarities of highly structured classical Greek plays with elements as commentaries on the action of the play provided to the audi-ence by a chorus of nonactors and the ceremonial liturgies of religion with their ritual interplay between priest and congregation. The functions of religion and art are so compatible that music, dance, poetry, and visual arts are often incor-porated into religious ceremonies to enhance their effect on those who partici-pate in them. Art performances vary in the degree to which they incorporate highly predictable sequences, but anyone who has watched a Greek play, read haiku, or appreciated the blues will be aware that the rules that govern some ele-ments of the arts can be seen as defining rituallike sequences.

Courtship love, too, can involve altered states of consciousness in which the object of one's affection is perceived in highly unrealistic ways as more an em-bodiment of one's own subjective ideals of beauty than others perceive. In many cultures, the practices of courtship have been organized into highly predictable sequences of events, including negotiations between families, formal periods of engagement, and, finally, wedding ceremonies. Courtship is more spontaneous in North American culture today than it once was when books of etiquette pre-scribed the detailed norms that participants were expected to follow, but it still contains rather stable elements—pickup lines, small talk, soft lights, wine, and music—that clearly signal the nature of the situation and the romantic intent of the participants.

Finally, *mental disorders* may also be seen as belonging to the arena of ex-pressive culture, although they are a consistently stigmatized form. Neverthe-less, as with the socially more acceptable types of expressive culture, mental disorders include ritualized behavior, altered states of consciousness (such as hallucinations and less dramatic distortions of reality such as delusions and projection), and supernaturalistic beliefs such as the belief that one is be-ing influenced by forces beyond one's own control. Behaviorally, the outward symptoms of mental disorders have a repetitive and predictable quality that, like the rituals of religion, can express quite dramatically the kinds of stresses that the participant is attempting to cope with in life.

What then distinguishes each form of expressive culture from the others? It is neither the role of trances (or the beliefs that arise from them) nor the practice of rituals that distinguishes one from the other. Rather, the different manifestations of expressive culture differ most clearly in the arena of social organization and in how each type of expressive culture is valued within the societies in which it is found. Religion always includes shared supernaturalistic beliefs and the practice of shared rituals in group settings. It is never a purely private system of rituals and supernaturalistic beliefs such as those of mental disorders or those of fantasy play which can also be a purely solitary activity. While religion and mental disorders both typically involve a strong commitment to the "ultimate reality" of its supernaturalistic beliefs, children seem normally able to distinguish the fantasy images that accompany play from ordinary reality readily enough when they talk about them, although on occasion—especially when they are associated with fear, as are images of "monsters" or "ghosts"—they may act as if they represent real, external dangers. Nevertheless, the motivation to participate in fantasy play is not a commitment to the objective reality it portrays, as is commonly true of religion. Ideological commitment to the objective reality of its supernaturalistic beliefs also tends to distinguish religion from art, whose symbols are usually accepted both by their creators and their audiences as metaphors valued for their expressive effect rather than their literal truth. Finally, religion can be distinguished from courtship love in the larger number of participants who share feelings of communitas for one another during its group rituals.

Whereas religious rituals are participated in by groups of people who cooperate to deal with concerns that they share, the rituals that are symptomatic of mental disorders represent the piecemeal and spontaneous responses of individuals to the particular stresses of their own lives. Religion and mental disorders also differ in effectiveness: The ritual lives and nonnaturalistic beliefs of religions generally successfully provide their participants with psychological relief from stress, while the ritualistic symptoms of mental disorders are typically experienced as involuntary behaviors, appear to provide less successful relief, and may even become sources of distress themselves for those who perform them. In contrast, members of religious bodies perceive themselves as participating voluntarily and report greater life satisfaction as a result. Despite these differences, the occasional example of collective religious behavior—such as the group suicides committed by members of Jim Jones's People's Temple and members of the Heaven's Gate community—demonstrates that the difference between religion and mental disorders is not simply a matter of one being *necessarily* adaptive and the other maladaptive.

Although the various institutions of expressive culture differ in important ways, these differences form fuzzy boundaries rather than clear-cut ones, and the institutions of expressive culture sometimes grade into one another in a way that makes it impossible to say when one becomes another. This is more than merely a matter of shared circumstances, such as the common use of art to enhance religious ceremony. Indeed, the boundaries of these institutions are fuzzy and grade into one another in ways that make it difficult, perhaps impossible, to define a clear line of demarcation between them. For instance, author Alex Haley grew up in a society that tended to marginalize Blacks, yet achieved great skill as a writer. He struggled to recover the cultural heritage of his ancestors that defined an important part of his identity as a Black American. In an interview with journalist Joan Wixen (1976), Haley described how, during a period of suicidal depression and doubt about his ability to finish his work, *Roots,* he had the cathartic experience of hearing the voices of his ancestors encouraging him to continue his effort to complete their story. Haley explained that he experienced a period of writer's block while trying to portray his ancestor Kunta Kinte's experience on a slave ship. Haley decided that he needed a greater personal sense of what the voyage might have been like, so he booked passage on a freighter from Liberia to Florida and spent each night, stripped to his underwear, lying on a plank in the darkness of the hold of the ship and imagining the plight of black slaves who had been chained in even worse conditions. After five nights, Haley thought seriously of simply jumping overboard to end his problems. He had spent all his money trying to write his book; he was recently divorced; and he was well past the deadline that his publisher had set for his book. Haley described what happened in the midst of this turmoil: "And you know, at that point I experienced one of the most psychic experiences I have ever had in my life. I began to hear voices. No big frantic thing. Just voices as if I were in a dream" (p. B12). These "voices," which he identified as those of his aunt, his grandmother, Kunta Kinte, and other ancestors, all encouraged him not to kill himself but to finish his chronicle of their lives. Acting on this encouragement, he went on to write his widely acclaimed account of his family's history. Haley's story illustrates the fuzzy boundaries between the various forms of expressive culture in that it might equally be interpreted in the context of the psychology of stress, the nature of the artistic process, or even a "religious" experience.

The cores of religion and art might be distinguishable by the fact that while both religious rituals and artistic presentations may be done in large part to communicate or stimulate feelings or ideas in an audience, the participants in religious rituals normally consider their meanings to be "ultimately true," as Rappaport, Geertz, and others have characterized it, while the impact of art *is* its essence. Religious rituals are received as statements of truths in their own right, while artistic meanings are generally perceived as metaphors to ponder. Yet, at their edges, distinctions such as this blur. Consider, for instance, this description of religious trance by a Navajo shamanic diagnostician, or *"hand trembler."* One Navajo method of diagnosing the cause of illness and the appropriate ceremonial cure was by interpreting the meaning of how a diagnostician's hand trembled during a trance-induced state in a diagnostic ceremony. Gregorio, a widely respected Navajo diagnostician, explained how he acquired his gift in a way that is metaphorical yet also expresses the *real* presence of spiritual power:

> I wasn't feeling very good. You know some days you act like you are going to sleep, want to lie down. I felt that way. I was lying down . . . and I went to sleep for a little while. When I woke up my legs and feet and whole body felt all large, just like when you sit down and your legs go to sleep. I felt like that all over

my body. And I could feel something through my arms there, as if it was running through my hands and out the end of my fingers. After that my hands started shaking. This happened right in the middle of the afternoon. My hands trembled all afternoon till toward sundown, then I stopped for a little while and started again after dark. . . . It was dark night, but I thought the sun was shining on me. I felt like the sunshine was coming in the door. The sun was shining bright like today in a little spot where I was sitting (quoted in Leighton and Leighton, 1949, p. 20).

Notice how Gregorio alternates between describing what he experienced with words such as "as if" and "like" and describing it with words that speak of his internal, subjective experience of "sunshine" as actually "shining on me." His description involves poetic simile yet simultaneously asserts that more than mere simile is involved. He describes his shamanic trance as feeling "like lightning or sunbeams coming down from Heaven" into the room and explains that "Everything is white and bright.

Figure 5.2
Korean Shaman Performing a Rite
Korean women who become shamans enter trances so the gods may speak through them. This female shaman is performing a kut, or exorcism ritual, at Samjak, Seoul, South Korea.

Nobody could see that but you. You don't see that yourself, but you are having thoughts like that. The light doesn't stay long, then your hand starts shaking" (1949, p. 20).

FEELINGS IN RELIGION

Some philosophers and anthropologists, including Friedrich Schliermacher, Rudolf Otto, and Mircea Eliade, have considered the feelings that sacred things evoke to be central to religion. There is no distinctively *religious* emotion, no emotion that has only a religious significance. However, religious settings and activities do tend to be charged with stronger feelings than do those that are mundane. For instance, the philosopher Rudolf Otto focused on powerful feelings such as the reverence, dread, and awe that one might feel in the presence of something sacred. In recent times, anthropologists who emphasize feelings have tended to do so in conjunction with a discussion of motivations and values, especially motivations evoked during rituals and the social values that rituals support.

Ritual and Feelings

It is typical for rituals to stimulate emotion. Rappaport (1999; p. 49) points out that emotion in ritual settings may be strong and persuasive and suggests that this is the source of the power that rituals have for human beings. In fact, some consider the stimulation of emotion to be one defining feature of ritual. Both anthropologists and psychologists have discussed relationships between ritual and emotion, some emphasizing the adaptive benefits to society that the stimulation of emotions may have and others emphasizing the psychological benefits that the emotional experience may have for participants in the rituals.

Any of the human emotions may be linked to religious rituals, and those feelings and attitudes that are seen as appropriate in one religious tradition may not be appropriate during the rituals of a different religious tradition. The solemnity and reverence common in rituals of the Judeo-Christian tradition are not necessarily the preferred feelings in religious rituals everywhere. For instance, sacred clowns play an important role in Hopi rituals. The clowns are one of the many different kachinas, Hopi gods who are portrayed by members of the community during sacred ceremonies. The clowns represent youth, impetuousness, vigor, and hypersexuality; and their buffoonery, which is expected to draw laughter from onlookers, is necessary if the rains are to come and the crops are to grow abundantly. Don Talayesva, a Sun Chief at Oraibi, Arizona tells how:

> Once on a dance day the fun-making Katcina ran into the plaza stark-naked. A clown caught him and asked him what he was doing. He replied, "I am chasing my penis and can't overtake it; it is always a little ahead of me. I think a person would die if he ever overtook it." The people laughed. The clowns frequently captured women and imitated the sexual act in the open plaza to entertain the people. On some occasions they fasten long gourd necks in front of them and pursued the women. Aunts would also chase their nephews and jokingly pretend to have intercourse with them. (Simmons, 1942, p. 76)

He also recounted how he reproached the white school principal for his disapproving looks when the clowns engaged in sexual clowning:

> I walked up to him, shook hands, and said in Hopi, "Well, white man, you want to see what goes on, don't you? You have spoiled our prayers, and it may not rain. You think this business is vulgar, but it means something sacred to us. . . . If this were evil, we would not be doing it. You are supposed to be an educated man, but you had better go back to school and learn something more about Hopi life." (p. 190)

The emotions of ritual life differ from one culture to another. But the emotions that are universally important to those who participate in rituals are those that are relevant to their lives and social experiences outside the ritual setting. For instance, anthropologist Clifford Geertz (1973) has discussed the important role of emotion in Navajo curing ceremonies, called *sings*, and the way the feelings expressed in the ceremonies can help make illness more endurable:

> The sustaining effect of the sing (and since the commonest disease is tuberculosis, it can in most cases be only sustaining), rests ultimately on its ability to give the stricken patient a vocabulary in terms of which to grasp the nature of his

distress and relate it to the wider world. Like a calvary, a recitation of Buddha's emergence from his father's palace, or a performance of *Oedipus Tyrannos* in other religious traditions, a sing is mainly concerned with the presentation of a specific and concrete image of truly human, and so endurable, suffering powerful enough to resist the challenge of emotional meaninglessness raised by the existence of intense and unremovable brute pain." (1973, p. 105)

The problems people commonly confront and the ideal responses differ from culture to culture. The religious rituals of each culture provide a model of the problems and of appropriate responses to them, and they also hold out hope that the responses will bring success. As Geertz summarizes the Navajo case, "The sort of counterpoint between style of life and fundamental reality which the sacred symbols formulate varies from culture to culture. For the Navaho, an ethic prizing calm deliberateness, untiring persistence, and dignified caution complements an image of nature as tremendously powerful, mechanically regular and highly dangerous" (1973, p. 130).

Sociologist Emile Durkheim ([1912]1961) examined the ways in which the feelings stimulated by religious rituals function to perpetuate the stability of society. Durkheim contrasted the realm of *sacred things*, which inspire feelings of awe, respect, or reverence because they are set apart or forbidden, with the world of the *profane*, the ordinary, routine, and taken-for-granted world of day-to-day life (see chapter 1). According to Durkheim, the sacred things that people attempt to influence by means of rituals and that are portrayed in those rituals are symbolic representations—that is, metaphors—for the parts of society that must be respected by members of society if society is to survive. Rituals elicit and perpetuate the feelings that inspire conformity to the norms of the group. By doing so, they help maintain the stability of society.

Durkheim illustrated his belief that religion is, in effect, the worship of the social order of the religious community by analyzing the sacred symbols of the Aboriginal Australians of central Australia; this group of people survived by foraging for wild plants and animals and lived in local groups whose members were divided into a number of different clans. Each clan was named for a particular totem (see chapter 1), usually a species of plant or animal that was part of the native diet, but sometimes for an inanimate object such as the boomerang or a mythological being or force of nature. This plant, animal, or object was the totem of its human clan, identifying the kind of spirit that members of each clan were believed to have. Thus, members of one clan might be *kangaroo people* who were believed to have been born when the spirit of a kangaroo entered the womb of a woman, causing her to become pregnant. Others might be *wallaby people, witchetty grub people,* or *crow people.*

Members of the same totemic clan would regularly come together from diverse local groups of Aboriginal Australians and cooperate to perform rituals that were intended to influence their sacred totem in ways that would benefit everyone. For instance, *kangaroo people* would perform rituals that would insure the fertility of the kangaroo, which was an important food resource for Aboriginal Australians. Participation in the ritual reinforced the common social bond of members of the totemic clan who resided in many different locations. Thus, rituals that were believed to influence the clan's sacred totem had an effect on the profane life of the people. Since the rituals involved cooperation between members of the clan who did not reside in the same community, participation in the rituals reinforced the solidarity of the clan and helped perpetuate peaceful relations between members of neighboring communities.

Durkheim did not consider the Aboriginal Australians as unique in the way their religious symbols for sacred things were also symbols for parts of their social order. Rather, he believed that sacred symbols stood for the basic institutions of social life in all religions and that because of this relationship, religion everywhere functions to maintain the stability of the social order of which it is a part.

Rappaport (1999) explains that "Intensification of emotion is an aspect of consciousness alteration, and it almost goes without saying that the significata of ritual representations—the general points of the ritual—are capable of arousing strong emotions, thus altering consciousness" (pp. 258–59). Art may also play a role in stimulating and directing emotion during rituals, and Rappaport notes that "These emotions, as well as being powerful, sometimes seem rather specific: sadness, joy, solemnity, certainty. Much subtler and more complex but nameless and even unnamable feelings may be evoked. The particular feelings experienced may, of course be as much a function of the ritual context as of the aesthetic qualities of the object itself. That they are at a funeral may suggest to those present that what they feel while listening to the dirge is grief, but what each of them feels may well be different" (p. 387). What is important is not that everyone who participates in a particular ritual experience the same emotion but simply that some emotion be experienced so that it can be associated with meanings that the art or other symbols of the ritual convey. Religious symbolism may, for instance, portray the importance of submissiveness or cooperation. Rappaport contends that the meanings communicated in ritual transform whatever emotions participants experience in religious rituals into "socially approved attitudes" (p. 387) that are shared by members of the religious community.

Anthropologist Victor Turner finds that there are two contrasting types of symbol in rituals that function to create loyalty to society; these are *sensory symbols* and *ideological symbols.* The meanings of **sensory symbols** relate to physiological facts and processes such as mother's milk, blood, menstruation, birth, semen, genitalia, sexual intercourse, urine, feces, and death. These symbols produce strong feelings in participants in a ritual that uses them. **Ideological symbols**—such as Judaism's seven-branched candelabra called the *menorah,* the Christian cross that often adorns church buildings, or a Native American "sweat lodge" in which people seek spiritual purification—express allegiance to the religious community and its customs, social values, and morality. Strengthened by feelings of *communitas* (see chapter 1)—feelings of fellowship, equality, and unity—and the powerful feelings induced by the physiologically stimulating parts of a ritual, such as drinking, feasting, singing, and dancing, the emotions evoked by the use of various sensory symbols is transferred to the values expressed by the ritual's ideological symbols. Thus, ritual stimulates loyalty to society, motivation to support its customs and values, conformity to its customs and laws, and acceptance of the established relationships between the individuals and groups that make up society. In this way rituals reinforce those things that give the community its cohesion and continuity by fostering feelings of commitment to the societal obligations of its members.

sensory symbols Those conventional signs whose meanings relate to physiological facts and processes (such as mother's milk, blood, menstruation, birth, semen, genitalia, sexual intercourse, excreta, and death); they produce strong feelings in participants in ritual that use them.

ideological symbols Those conventional signs used in rituals to express allegiance to society and its social values and morality, conformity to its customs and laws, and acceptance of the established relationships between the individuals and groups that make up society.

Turner (1967) made important contributions to understanding the relationships between ritual and feelings in his analysis of Ndembu rituals. The Ndembu of northwestern Zambia are a matrilineal society who trace ancestry through mothers. Their Milk Tree ritual is a puberty ritual held to initiate young women into adulthood. In this ritual, ideological symbols include symbols of gender, marriage, and village, while the dominant sensory symbol is milk. At puberty when a girl's breasts have begun to grow but before she has begun to menstruate, she is wrapped in a blanket and laid at the base of a *mudyi* tree sapling. The mudyi tree "is conspicuous for its white latex, which exudes in milky beads if the thin bark is scratched" (p. 21). Because of this, the Ndembu say it symbolizes human breast milk and the breasts from which it comes. They also refer to it as "the tree of a mother and her child" (p. 21). The puberty ritual is not a fertility ritual that draws on the symbolism of menstruation, which has not yet occurred. Rather, according to Turner, the main theme of the puberty ritual "is indeed the tie of nurturing between mother and child, not the bond of birth" (pp. 20–21). Nurturing is further emphasized by ritual acts that symbolize feeding and other symbols of foods. In addition to the bond between a specific mother and her child, the tree also stands for the continuity of Ndembu society and culture and the groups of relatives, matrilineages, that are united by their common descent from the same woman. Yet, the behavior required by the Milk Tree ritual is not entirely harmonious, as one might expect in a ritual concerning the continuity of society and its values. Women and men are segregated from one another during the ritual, and the women show hostility toward the men. Women are also divided into competing categories: married women versus unmarried women, women of one matrilineage versus others, and women of one village versus women of another. According to Turner, these competing groups symbolize the fact that although Ndembu society's succession and inheritance are matrilineal—passing down a line of women—its marriage custom requires patrilocal residence for married couples, and women have to leave their own matrilineal household to live in their husbands' villages among women of other matrilineages when they marry. Thus, Ndembu society is organized around two contradictory principles, matrilineality (which governs inheritance and group identity) and patrilocality (which governs where a married woman resides). Thus, the Milk Tree ritual symbolizes the harmony and unity of Ndembu society, but it also expresses the tensions that its customs create among its members.

The Experience of "The Holy"

Rudolf Otto (1923) pointed out that the word *holy*, which denotes an attribute of the supernatural, means more than simply "the good" or even "the absolute good"; it also denotes a quality of experience that he called the **numinous,** a feeling of one's own dependence, "the emotion of a creature, submerged and overwhelmed by its own nothingness in contrast to that which is supreme above all creatures" (10). The holy is not simply something that is talked about with words, but an overpowering and energetic majesty of which we stand in dreadful awe. Its essence is better captured in the feelings of the experience than in any other way. Any understanding of the supernatural that ignores the centrality

numinous
Pertaining to a feeling of the dependence of one's own existence; the emotion of a creature; the feeling of being submerged and overwhelmed by one's own nothingness in contrast to that which is supreme above all creatures.

of feelings to the religious experience, especially feelings associated with the holy, cannot be considered complete.

Otto (1923) argued that supernatural things are experienced as a sense of the uncanny, the eerie combination of feelings such as awe, reverence, and dread that are inspired by mysterious things. The essence of sacred things is the ambivalence we feel toward them. They fascinate and draw us toward them, while simultaneously repelling us in fear. They are the experience of Jacob at Bethel: "And Jacob awaked out of his sleep, and he said, Surely the LORD is in this place; and I knew it not. And he was afraid, and said, How dreadful is this place! this is none other but the house of God, and his is the gate of heaven" (Genesis 28:16–17).

The uncanny emotions of religious experience are perceived as apprehension of a presence that is simultaneously real and ineffable, a presence separate from the self that can be neither proved nor refuted, but nevertheless felt. This presence has been variously referred to as the holy, the numinous, or the sacred. Its apprehension is experienced as what Otto calls "creature-consciousness," a feeling of being submerged and overwhelmed by one's own nothingness in contrast with the holy, a feeling of absolute dependence that paradoxically combines the contrasting emotions of both attraction to the holy and dread of its presence. Coleridge captured some of what Wallace (1966a) called the "ambivalent glamor" of the experience of the sacred in his description of a shaman:

> Beware! Beware!
> His flashing eyes, his floating hair!
> Weave a circle round him thrice,
> And shut thine eyes in holy dread,
> For he on honey dew hath fed,
> And drunk the milk of paradise.

The power of the sacred is attractive, yet it is simultaneously a source of danger.

Mana

The sacredness of holy things is sometimes conceived of as an impersonal supernatural force called *mana* (see chapter 1). Some form of the concept of mana can be found in all of the world's many religions; and although the specific ideas associated with it vary, the symbolism of mana always carries with it the potential for evoking feelings, since mana is not just ordinary power or energy, but *sacred* or *supernatural* power. Mana-filled things are both attractive and threatening; as the Zuñi put it, they are both *tso'ya* (beautiful) and *attanni* (dangerous). Barbara Tedlock (1992) makes this paradoxical contrast the leitmotif of her reminiscences of the Zuñi. Two examples illustrate the sense of eerie beauty associated with supernaturally powerful things:

> The kids took the antlers back outside. But then one of them suddenly burst in the door, proclaiming excitedly, "Hish attanni/ *Very dangerous!* Run outside, Kyamme, Tsilu, and you'll see something AMAZING!
> A pale-greenish airglow hung in the center of the northern horizon as white rays, tinged magenta and lime green, flashed across the black sky, broke up, and reformed into undulating luminous sheets. Phantomlike translucent light flickered across the celestial arch, melted into a choppy river of fire, and

was extinguished. Tiny greenish points of light were all that was left behind, glimmering along the edge of the horizon.

"Kwap uhsi?/*What's that?*" asked Hapiya.

"Aurora borealis, the northern lights. You never see them this far south," Dennis said. "They're caused by solar radiation. . . ." Neither of us could think of the whole explanation, and it didn't seem to explain anything anyway. (pp. 154–55).

In describing the decoration of a wall for the weeklong Shalako (masked dance) celebration, Tedlock recounts that "Tola appeared in the doorway, cradling in her arms the enormous pelt of a cinnamon-colored bear, sacred hunter of the west. As she made her entrance she called out in a low gravelly voice, 'Attannnniiii,' meaning *dark, muffled, shaggy, old, fearful, dangerous*" (pp. 234–35). The pelt was to become part of the beautifully decorated Shalako wall. The process of decorating such a wall is called *teshkuna* (literally, "shrine construction"), which Tedlock explains is "a verb formed from the root 'tesh,' meaning 'shrine, sacred, taboo, forbidden'" (p. 233). Tedlock explains that "it is in the meeting and interplay between these two aesthetics that Zuñi Pueblo articulates its own mythopoetic religious core" (pp. 236–37).

People or things imbued with mana are often set apart from mundane things because their power is seen as simultaneously attractive and dangerous. For instance, E. E. Evans-Pritchard (1974) described the aura of power embodied in the Nuer leopard-skin priest:

It is said that a leopard-skin priest . . . will not approach people when they are making pots lest the pots crack; and in this sense he may be said to respect . . . the earth. If anything goes wrong with the standing crops he may be asked to anoint . . . the earth with butter. He may also be asked to anoint seed and digging-sticks with butter before sowing. When a [leopard-skin] priest is buried, his corpse, so that it will not be in contact with the earth, is placed between hides on a light platform in the grave. (p. 291)

This idea of mana-filled persons as awesomely powerful is not unique to non-Western religions. For instance, Christian scriptures include the same concept in the story of how a woman was cured of an illness by merely touching Jesus' clothing:

As [Jesus] went, the crowds pressed in on him. Now there was a woman who had been suffering from hemorrhages for twelve years; and though she had spent all she had on physicians, no one could cure her. She came up behind him and touched the fringe of his clothes, and immediately her hemorrhage stopped. Then Jesus asked, "Who touched me?" When all denied it, Peter said, "Master, the crowds surround you and press in on you." But Jesus said, "Someone touched me; for I noticed that *power* had gone out from me." (Luke 8:42b–46, italics added)

The italicized word *power* in this story is the Greek word *dunamis*, meaning *strength, power,* or *ability.* In the context of a miraculous cure, when the power was transferred by simple contact, the word *power* could aptly be translated as *mana.*

Mysticism

The role of ecstatic feelings is particularly important in the form of religious experience called **mysticism,** a sense of timeless and spaceless union or oneness

mysticism
A sense of timeless and spaceless union, or oneness, with the divine that is accompanied by profoundly positive feelings.

Renunciation of worldly life, or at least some form of asceticism, is found in all of the ecclesiastical religions. Christian, Hindu, and Buddhist monks form ascetic communities in monasteries where they can dedicate themselves to spiritual pursuits. Typically, the ascetic life involves some combination of poverty, fasting, sexual abstinence, and seclusion. In Hinduism, an ascetic life is an ideal for all devotees during their final years.

Hindu life is guided by the dharma ("duty, law, morality, conduct"), the rules that govern life. This guide to right conduct emphasizes the virtues of truth, nonviolence, sacrifice, purity, and renunciation or detachment.

In the Hindu view of human life, the life cycle is divided into four successive stages called the asramas: the student, the householder, the anchorite, and the sannyasin. The first stage is one of preparation and probation, devoted to study and discipline. The second is one of carrying out responsibilities to society by raising and supporting families and by taking an active part in the affairs of community and state. The third is a period of withdrawal from life, a time of meditation and study. Finally, the sannyasin stage is one of complete renunciation of all possessions and attachments and possible entry into the wandering life

of the ascetic. Renunciation and nonattachment to material objects is the highest of values, so the ascetic has reached the apex of spiritual life on earth.

Millions of Hindus go on pilgrimage each year, visiting holy sites for a few days or weeks; although few actually take up the full-time status of the wandering ascetic, those who do spend the final years of their lives on a perpetual pilgrimage traveling from one holy place to another, living off the charity of the temples they visit in each place.

The sannyasin who renounce all worldly attachments and become lifetime pilgrims are called *Sadhu*. They may spend years visiting the thousands of shrines dedicated to different gods that are scattered throughout India. At these shrines they can usually find free lodging and food that is shared by others as an act of charity. Early each morning they participate in the Puja—the devotional service for the deity of the shrine. These services may involve chanting, singing, or prayer, depending on the local custom of each shrine. At other times in the day, Sadhus may meditate alone at the shrine. After a day or so, they may choose to walk to another shrine a few miles down the road. Traveling in this way they may visit many parts of India and neighboring countries over the years.

Figure 5.4
An Ascetic Renunciate
This Hindu Sadhu, or wandering ascetic, is sitting at the foot of the steps at Tsurphu Monastery, seat of the Kagyu lineage of Tibetan Buddhism.

with the divine that is accompanied by profoundly positive feelings. The mystical experience is typically described as *ineffable;* that is, one who experiences it cannot find words to adequately describe it. The mystical sense of union with the divine typically includes a simultaneous sense of oneness with all reality; and during this state, the usual symbolic categories into which experiences are

126

Figure 5.3
Meditation
Meditation is one technique by which members of many religions seek mystical union with the Divine. This woman is meditating under a pyramid, a New Age symbol of supernatural power, near Boulder, Colorado.

normally divided merge into one another, and the sense of boundaries between self and other are dissolved. The very sense of self may seem to dissolve as well. Thus, any attempt to talk about the experience is likely to seem not only inadequate but also paradoxical to the mystic. It is the kind of experience that "words just don't do justice to"—and "you have to experience yourself to understand it."

R. W. I. Hood's research (1977, 1978) demonstrated that individuals were likely to experience feelings of mystical transcendence in situations where they succeed at activities that were more stressful than they had anticipated at the outset of their effort. For instance, river runners successfully negotiating a river that was more difficult than they expected are likely to feel mystical elation or transcendent "oneness" with the environment, while the same feelings are not likely to be experienced by those who expected the river run to be difficult. The search for mystical "oneness" with the Absolute is described in the box titled "Hindu Renunciation as Expressive Culture."

Values in Religion

Judgments that involve feelings concerning good and bad are expressed as mandates for human behavior. Such judgments, or *values* (see chapter 2), are the "shoulds" and "should nots" of religion. All religions include values concerning behavior that is judged good or bad because of its spiritual consequences. Such piety values include *taboos* (see chapter 1)—rules against various acts—as well as rules that *require* behavior believed to bring benefits from the supernatural. Piety rules are extremely diverse from one religion to the next, and the practical consequences of piety rules are often far from evident. Their lack of obvious practical rationale can make them seem quite arbitrary or even strange to outsiders. For instance, Apache religious values include taboos against stepping over the bones of dead animals and against burning wood that has been urinated on by a deer. Doing these things is believed to result in illness or other harm. The Jewish kosher rules that define mutton as an acceptable food but rabbit as unacceptable, fish with fins and scales as acceptable but shellfish or squid as unacceptable, and chicken as acceptable but chicken hawks as unacceptable do not appear to have any simple unifying principle beyond divine mandate. Although Mary Douglas (1966) argued that the original Levitical food taboos were meaningful in terms of the ancient Hebrew worldview, the distinctions between acceptable and unacceptable foods do not seem to follow any logical principle to most Jews today. Even the great twelfth-century Jewish Sage Maimonides concluded that "those who trouble themselves to find a cause for any of these detailed rules are in my eyes devoid of sense" (Maimonides, Guide to the Perplexed).

Although all religions have rules of piety, *moral values* (see chapter 2)—values that govern the human treatment of other humans—are often not a religious matter. For instance, David Aberle (1966) wrote concerning the Navajo:

> The traditional Navaho fears error in his rituals and particularly error in the fixed prayers which chanter and patient must repeat in the course of a ceremony. Error may not only render the ceremony ineffectual but may cause illness to the patient years later. . . . Navaho supernatural power is likely to harm man when man breaches various taboos, but these taboos have almost nothing to do with the moral order. If a man were to commit murder, he might have ghost trouble—but so might he if he worked in a hospital or happened to burn wood from a hogan where someone had died. His ghost trouble stems from ritual contamination, not God's curse or the ghost's vengeance. Theft, adultery, deceit, assault and rape have no supernatural sanctions. . . . True, ceremonies are impaired if the singer becomes angry or if there is quarreling at the ceremony. In this sense there are supernatural sanctions against misbehavior—but only while the ceremony continues. On the other hand, the Navaho must fear the consequences of many accidental breaches of taboos. (p. 196)

In contrast with the great diversity of piety values in the world's religions, religious support for moral values is more predictable. As you will recall from chapter 4, Guy Swanson (1974) suggested that the supernatural is likely to reward moral behavior and punish immoral behavior between human individuals in societies where there are important relationships that are fraught with hostility, envy, jealousy, and other feelings that increase the temptation to violate the moral rules that society expects to govern important relationships.

Religion as "Ultimate Concern"

For theologian Paul Tillich (1963), "Religion is the state of being grasped by an ultimate concern, a concern which qualifies all other concerns as preliminary and which itself contains the answer to the question of the meaning of our life. Therefore this concern is unconditionally serious and shows a willingness to sacrifice any finite concern which is in conflict with it" (p. 6). This view of religion as an expression of *ultimate concerns*—what in a secular sense might be translated as an individual's or group's "highest priority values," the values that are used as the ultimate reasons for things—had an impact in some sociological and anthropological circles. For instance, anthropologists William Lessa and Evan Vogt (1965) wrote, "Religion may be described as a system of beliefs and practices directed toward the 'ultimate concern' of a society or social group. 'Ultimate concern,' a concept used by Paul Tillich, has two aspects—meaning and power. It has meaning in the sense that the central values of a society are meaningful, and it has power in the sense of ultimate, sacred, or supernatural power which stands behind those values" (p. 1). From this perspective, religion embodies the most fundamental value orientations of a society and functions as the most authoritative source of their validation for members of society. "Because our religion says so" is, in effect, the ultimate answer to questions about why societal values should be accepted.

Although some sociologists and anthropologists have gone so far as to define religion as whatever constitutes a group's ultimate concern, whatever they consider of overriding importance, this definition merges what most people generally have in mind when they think of "religion" with other institutions that may also function as a people's "ultimate concern." By *defining* religion as a people's ultimate concern rather than simply treating it as one of several institutions in which an ultimate concern may be expressed, scholars make it possible for various secular institutions to be unnecessarily confused with religion. Following such a definition, National Socialism might be said to have been the "religion" of Nazis, football the "religion" of Green Bay, Wisconsin, and the Playboy lifestyle "religion" of some hedonists. That such secular entities may have social effects that are *similar* to those of religion as sources of the guiding values of one group or another—that is, that they may be what anthropologists call **functional equivalents** of religion in the traditional sense of the word—is certainly true. But while it is useful to notice such similarities between these institutions and the **functions** of religion, the effects it has on the stability of a society and on how its customs are carried out, it is also useful to be able to contrast religion with the other institutions that may share some of its social functions. Thus, religion should be understood as being one important social institution that normally instills respect for a society's ultimate concern, but not necessarily the only institution that may play such a role.

NATURAL SYMBOLS

Van Gennep (1960) noted that the symbolism of certain rituals involved a similarity between the physical act and its desired effect. Such symbols of ritual follow Sir James Frazer's (1911) Law of Similarity. As signlike symbols, their meaning still involves specific culturally defined conventions that would be lost on an outsider, but they also express a variety of compatible meanings that can be interpreted correctly across cultural boundaries. For instance, a person with no knowledge of the history of Christianity would not be reminded of Jesus' baptism by a contemporary baptismal ceremony. Nevertheless, the use of water as a symbol of purification in the ritual *is* likely to be appreciated throughout the human world. This unusual quality of the signlike symbols found in religious rituals gives those rituals a sense of greater or transcendent meaning than they might otherwise have, allowing them to arouse stronger feelings than do ordinary symbols. The rituals of all forms of expressive culture tend to use these signlike symbols. Mary Douglas (1970) called such symbols **natural symbols,** objects or acts at least some of whose possible meanings are derived from their perceived attributes or normal human uses—for example, water for cleansing, blood for life or death, or eating for unity.

The Human Body as a Source of Natural Symbols

The human body itself is a fertile source of natural symbols. Freud ([1940]1949; [1900]1950) founded the field of psychoanalysis on the claim that the dream content and neurotic preoccupations of his patients were often highly symbolic

functional equivalents
Institutions or customs that have a similar effect on the stability of a society.
functions
The effects that part of a culture has on the stability of a society and on how its customs are carried out.

natural symbols
Objects or acts at least some of whose possible meanings are derived from their perceived attributes or normal human uses; they play prominent roles in religious symbolism throughout the world.

of the human body and bodily processes, particularly those related to toilet training and sexuality. According to Rodney Needham (1972),

> there is one specific kind of natural resemblance among men that all human beings recognize, and which permits effective comparison across the divides of culture and language. The locus of this resemblance is provided by the human body, the one thing in nature that is internally experienced, the only object of which we have subjective knowledge. (p. 139)

Mary Douglas (1966) argued that "the organic system provides an analogy of the social system which, other things being equal, is used in the same way and understood in the same way all over the world" (1970:12). She has also indicated that

> the body is a model which can stand for any bounded system. Its boundaries can represent any boundaries which are threatened or precarious. The body is a complex structure. The functions of its different parts and their relation afford a source of symbols for other complex structures. We cannot possibly interpret rituals concerning excreta, breast milk, saliva and the rest unless we are prepared to see in the body a symbol of society, and to see the powers and dangers credited to social structure reproduced in small on the human body. (p. 115)

Stanley Tambiah (1973) and James Fernandez (1974) have discussed the use of the human body as a material metaphor in the performance of ritual. Fernandez notes that this use often involves the identification of the human body with a variety of "primordial symbols"—such as those that express the contrast between human and animal, culture and nature—and that through this use of metaphor, statements are made about the nature of human identity and human relationships. He cites, for instance, the expression of social dominance and submission in the games of children in northern Spain when one child, usually a younger one, becomes a *caballos* and is "ridden" by another in the role of a "hunter" of wolves. As religious examples of metaphoric transformation of the human body, he cites the identification of dancers with animals, who themselves stand for ancestral spirits, in the ancestral cult of the Mitsogo of western equatorial Africa:

> Among . . . the Mitsogo, the ancestral cult of bwiti climaxes at a vertiginous moment in which the men, having danced for hours at an increasing pace, begin to exit one by one from the cult house. They dance out in the forest and shortly return bedecked with skins, feathers, and fronds representing various animals: pythons, leopards, elephants, and various birds. While it is said that the powers of bwiti are demonstrated in its capacity to charm the animals (who have an identification with the dead) out of the woods so that they can take part in cult life—take up human attributes—the essential fact is that cult members have taken the role of animals. Throughout equatorial Africa, leopard societies showed men in that role. (p. 121)

Similarly, the Christian mass involves the progressive metaphoric identification of participants as sinful and isolated individuals, as applicants for family membership, as participants in dialogue, as witnesses of divine sacrifice, and as members of the family of God through symbolism of the "stained body," the "sacrificial lamb," the "bread and wine," the "lamb of God," and the "living body." Ritual, by implication, is not simply an acting out of roles, but a meta-

Figure 5.5
Natural Symbols
The host and the wine, two natural symbols, that represent the flesh and blood of
Christ in the holy sacrament of Communion. This Polish priest is performing the sacra-
ment of the body of Christ at an outdoor mass in Todos Santos, Baja California, Mexico.

phoric participation in primordial symbols that sanctifies societal truths about
human identity and relationships.

Eating, Defecation, and Urination

The human body is commonly treated as a metaphorical microcosm of the
social body, and symbolism derived from the human body expresses how society is understood. In particular, symbolism concerning body orifices is a method
of communicating the way body boundaries are defined and maintained; such
symbols play a role in defining the boundaries of society and the importance of
the unity of society. So rituals that involve the communal sharing of food often
play a role in ceremonies where new individuals are incorporated into the social group. Thus, First Communion celebrates a young person's full entry into a
Catholic religious congregation, and participation in the sacrament of the Lord's
Supper typically requires membership in the local congregation or at least acceptance of one's status as a fellow Christian in Protestant denominations.

In symbolic contrast with eating, symbols derived from things such as spit,
excrement, or urine that leave the body through its orifices often symbolize expulsion from the group, defilement, loss, and death. Conversely, taboos that forbid certain foods as "unclean" function to perpetuate the separateness of the
societies that follow them from other societies that do not. For instance, as recorded in 2 Maccabees 6:18–28, when the Greek king Antiochus attempted to

unify the countries he had conquered, he outlawed the Jewish taboo against eating pork that perpetuated the separateness of the Jews from his other subjects.

Similarly, when symbols of breath, menstrual blood, sexual intercourse, semen, and excrement are incorporated into social rituals and taboos, they too take on a social significance. For instance, as recorded in the Mishnah (in Tractate Middoth), during Second Temple times, if a priest who was serving in the Temple had a nocturnal emission, he was required to leave the dormitory and purify himself in a ritual bath, or mikvah, that was located outside the holy ground of the Temple before he could be reunited with the priestly community. Thus, his bodily pollution symbolically removed him from the social body, and bodily cleansing readmitted him into the social group. This symbolism paralleled the earlier symbolism of Leviticus in which soldiers of Israel were required to leave the camp when they responded to a call of nature at night and could not return to the ranks of the military community until they underwent a ritual bath (Deuteronomy 23:13).

The Levitical and Second Temple examples are by no means unusual. As Douglas noted (1966) in her book *Purity and Danger*, excrement and other products that leave the body are often used as symbols of not belonging to the social body. For instance, among the Navajo, witches—who embody all things that are in opposition to Navajo concepts of humanness—are believed to make use of excrement.

Sexuality

Ritual orgies, or periods of sexual license, involve a temporary elimination of the ordinary sexual taboos by which orderly interpersonal relationships are normally perpetuated in a community. As symbols, rituals of sexual license are most common at times in which the social order is viewed as under threat of dissolution. Thus, for instance, they may be incorporated into New Year's rituals when the end of the year is viewed as a time in which the world and society may come to an end. Eliade (1959, pp. 146–47) interprets the sexual license of the Roman Saturnalia in this way, the ritual orgies symbolizing a regression to the chaotic time that preceded the creation of the world and the ordering of society. In contrast to sexual orgies as symbols of societal chaos, the rite of *hieros gamos* (sacred marriage) and procreation between the king and priestess in some early Mesopotamian societies at the time of transition from one year to the next symbolized the survival of society at the time of transition and the return of fertility to the land and the agricultural fields that were society's source of survival. Samuel Noah Kramer (1981) analyzed the union between the king and the priestess of Inanna, which was celebrated on the Mesopotamian New Year's Day that marked the beginning of spring and a return of fertility to the land, in these terms. Through this act of symbolic renewal of the land's fertility, the king also validated his authority to rule the nation. So the renewal of nature and the renewal of the political order were both symbolized by the same rite.

Hair

Hair is also a powerful source of religious symbolism that often represents the vital power of the human individual in various forms such as sensuality, fertility, or strength. The Greek Gorgon Medusa illustrates the power of hair symbolism. Her power to turn to stone those who looked upon her was symbolized by writhing snakes that covered her head instead of hair. The phallic quality of the snakes-as-hair symbol also introduced a paradoxical quality to the imagery, making it even more powerful. The aura of her dreadful power was magnified in Greek mythology by the transformation of her hair into a living mass of snakes.

In various religious traditions, priests are expected to shave their heads to symbolize their chastity and renunciation of worldly pursuits. As is common with symbols that embody powerful feelings, the same symbolism may be manifest in opposite ways. Thus, the Nazarites were Israelites who symbolized their vow of dedication to God by *not* cutting their hair. So the cutting of the Nazarite Sampson's hair can be seen as a symbolic castration in which the loss of his hair deprived him of the strength it represented.

Matted hair is another way of calling attention to hair symbolism. Classical Aztec priests neither cut nor washed their hair. Because of their roles in the ritual sacrifice of human beings, the hair of Aztec priests became matted with the blood of sacrificial victims, a powerful reminder of the role played by priests in feeding the gods with the blood of sacrifices. Gananath Obeyesekere (1984) discusses the symbolism of the matted hair of female Sri Lankan Hindu ascetics as a symbol of chastity, celibacy, and penance based on the destruction of the sensual qualities of the hair through neglect rather than shearing.

Left and Right

Another source of natural symbols is the contrast between left and right. Human beings are bilaterally symmetrical, but not perfectly so. Generally, the right side of the human body is slightly larger than the left, and most humans— about 85 percent—are right-handed. For most of us, both because of its size advantage and the advantages that come with greater use, the muscles of the right side of the body tend to be stronger than the corresponding ones of the left.

Robert Hertz (1973) noted that the distinctions between left and right are elaborated in most societies in ways that associate positive connotations with the right and negative ones with the left. For instance, in Latin "left" was *sinister*, a word that combined the meanings of both direction and danger. This combination of meanings was expressed in the social ritual in which guests at banquets were reminded to cross the threshold of the building with their right foot, thereby leaving the sinister qualities of the left side of the body outside. Around the world, the left is typically used as a natural symbol that is associated with concepts such as dark, weak, down, cold, wet, and feminine, while the right is commonly used for the opposite meanings of light, strong, up, warm, dry, and masculine.

Nature as a Source of Natural Symbols

The human body is not the only source of natural symbols. Nature also provides them. Those features of nature that human beings experience in similar ways throughout the world are an apt source of natural symbolism.

The Cardinal Directions

The cardinal directions, particularly the symbolism of east and west, have symbolic significance across many cultures. The sun rises in the east and sets in the west, and many cultures have fastened on this fact of nature as a source of natural symbolism. Consistently, the direction of the sun's rising is associated with light, beginnings, birth, and renewal; while the west is associated with darkness, death, and the afterlife. For instance, among the !Kung San foragers of the Kalahari Desert of southern Africa, there are two gods. The creator, ≠Gao!na, who resides in the east, looks like a man, although he is taller than a human and has long hair. He is acknowledged as the creator of all things, including the water holes, plants, and animals that are so important to the San. ≠Gao!na also created human beings, and when they die he collects their souls and hangs them in a great tree where he lives. He dries them with the smoke of a magical medicine that he burns beneath them and transforms them into servants who do his bidding. But for the most part he is otiose, aloof from human affairs, so the San have no major rituals to placate him, although they do pray to him to alleviate their hunger or illnesses or to protect them from death. ≠Gao!na sometimes sends the souls of the dead to bring either good or bad fortune, including illness, to human beings. The San also recognize a second, lesser god, one who is more active in human affairs. //Gauwa, as he is called, resides in the west and is associated with the souls of the dead. According to the San, when humans die, their souls wander in the veldt until they are found by //Gauwa. He hangs the souls that he collects in his camp to dry, then smokes them much like tobacco is smoked by human beings. Sometimes he sends the souls of humans to cause illness among the living. In healing ceremonies, //Gauwa may be addressed spitefully, called a bringer of illness, a bad one, and a liar, and told to go away so that the sick may recover.

The center of the world, or *axis mundi*, often plays an important role in mythology. It particularly tends to symbolize connections between this world and the supernatural world.

Trees

The tree has been used in numerous cultures to symbolize the axis mundi and the connection between the underworld, the earth, and heaven. For instance, Yggdrasil, the world tree (an ash) of Norse mythology has roots in the various worlds of Norse mythology, although the list varies by source: one in Asgaard, one in the world of the Frost Giants, and one in Niflheim or one in Hel's realm, one in the giant's realm, and one in Midgaard. The world tree is also a symbol of nurturing, since trees are a place of refuge for various animals and a source of food for both animals and humans. For instance, Yggdrasil provides honeydew and berries that are beneficial to pregnant women. During the destruction of Ragnarok, Lif and Leifthrasir will hide themselves in Yggdrasil and survive on honeydew until they can go and repopulate the world.

According to Alfred Tozzer (1907, pp. 154–56) some of the Maya of Yucatán believed that the universe consisted of seven levels, each of which was formed by the branches of a great ceiba. Michael Coe (1975, p. 102) explained that this Maya world tree was rooted in the underworld. Each level was governed by its own supernatural being. For instance, the fourth level was that of the Master of Animals. Souls could move from one level to another on a ladder made of vines.

The tree of life is another variation on the theme of the world tree. It is a central symbol in the Jewish creation story, where it has its place in Eden, the primeval garden in which the first human pair were placed. In Aztec mythology, the tree of life was portrayed as the maize plant that nourishes humanity, but its image was sometimes also formed from the flow of blood that spurts from the open chest of a human sacrificial victim. By paradoxically combining images of food—maize for humanity and blood for the gods—the Aztec tree of life symbolized the reciprocal relationship between the gods and humans. In Aztec cosmology, humans were created by an act of self-sacrifice by the gods, and human beings were duty-bound to offer their blood to feed the gods in return, thereby forestalling the end of the world, which would follow if the gods were not fed. The Christian symbol of the cross has, at times, been assimilated with that of the world tree.

The tree can also be a symbol of wisdom. In this form, it too is found in the Hebrew myth of Eden, where its fruit was said to be the source of the knowledge of good and evil, the godlike moral capacity that shifted the primal parents of humanity from a state of innocence to a state of knowledge, rendering them true moral agents capable of sin. The Bodhi-tree of Buddhism is also a symbol of wisdom. It was the tree under which Gautama was meditating when he achieved enlightenment and became the Buddha.

Heavenly Bodies

The sun is the most visibly powerful of the heavenly bodies. It moves from horizon to horizon each day, warming the earth. It is therefore an apt symbol of masculine strength and warriorhood, a role it has fulfilled in numerous cultures. For the Aztec, the Sun Carrier god sustained the world by his labor, and he was fed on the blood of human sacrifices so that he would not stop carrying the sun across the sky each day, lest the world end. For the Greeks, the sun was Helios, who drove his bright chariot across the sky each day. Among the Navajo, the sun god Jóhonaa'éí was a great warrior and a symbol of sexual virility. It was he who impregnated Asdzą́ą́ nádleehé, or Changing Woman, who bore the Hero Twins, who ridded the world of the monsters who plagued humankind.

In contrast with the sun, the moon is typically—though not inevitably—a feminine symbol, since its monthly cycle corresponds with the female menstrual cycle. It is commonly associated with love and human fertility. Other heavenly phenomena, such as stars, planets, comets, and shooting stars, have long been thought of as supernaturally meaningful. In the classic civilizations where a tradition of writing existed, ideas about the meanings of celestial phenomena were systemized into various forms of astrology. For instance, in the ancient Near East, the stars were conceived of as deities; and the planets, or "wandering stars," were regarded as particularly potent gods. In most Near Eastern countries Jupiter represented the king of the gods, Saturn the ancient and otiose father of the other gods, and Venus the torchbearer of the sun. The 12 major constellations of the particularly bright stars were each associated with a particular nation, and the apparent passing of one or more of the planets through a constellation indicated that the god of the planet was actively influencing the affairs of that nation.

The Natural Elements

Nature has often been seen as consisting of four basic elements—air, water, earth, and fire—and these four are a ready source of religious symbolism. The invisibility, but palpable vitality and power of the wind, allows it to be easily associated with supernatural beings. For instance, concepts of various kinds of "winds" are central to Navajo theology, in which winds were intimately involved in the creation of the first humans, fingerprints whirls were associated with the moving patterns of the wind, and the human soul is called one's "indwelling little wind." In their desert environment, where the winds frequently whip up the dry surface dirt into visible whirlwinds, this dual manifestation of air and earth is referred to as wǝǝ tso'appeh, or "cylindrical ghost," an idea not unlike the Celtic idea that whirlwinds were traveling "little people."

Perhaps particularly in agricultural societies, the earth has been often personified as "Mother Earth" who gave birth to the other gods or the first humans. This association is not limited to early societies. For instance, one Wiccan source, Starhawk (1989) emphasizes the identification of Wiccans with the earth-as-goddess:

> The Goddess is first of all earth, the dark, nurturing mother who brings forth all life. She is the power of fertility and generation; the womb, and also the receptive tomb, the power of death. All proceeds from her; all returns to Her. As earth, She is also plant life; trees, herbs and grains that sustain life. She is the body, and the body is sacred. Womb, breast, belly, mouth, vagina, penis, bone, and blood—no part of the body is unclean, no aspect of the life process is stained by any concept of sin. (p. 89)

Water has almost universally been drawn on as a symbol of spiritual purity and cleansing. For instance, after Pomo Indian shamans of northern California suck a "disease object" from the body of a patient, this source of spiritual and physical harm is typically placed in a bowl of water, which is believed to have the power to dissolve the evil-causing agent. Christian baptism and the Jewish mikvah both use water as the symbol of spiritual cleansing. And colonial Americans sometimes tested those accused of witchcraft by dunking them in a river, believing that a witch would float, on the principle that water, being pure, would accept an innocent person but reject an evil witch.

Fire is a particularly powerful source of imagery for spiritual power and supernatural beings. Its heat suggests power, and its constant movement and ability to consume the things it burns make it easy to personify as a living being.

Animals and Plants

The vitality of animals and plants has made them a common source of religious symbolism. For instance, the serpent has often played a role in mythology, sometimes even being raised to the level of a divinity. Other times, perhaps because of the shedding of its skin, it has been associated with immortality. In many traditions, the world tree is said to have a serpent residing among its roots. Because of its shape and movement, the serpent has been variously associated with the Milky Way, with lightning, and with the chaotic movement of the oceans.

Two animal types—powerful animals and sly or cagey ones—are prominent in many religions, but almost any animal has been personified as having humanlike spiritual qualities in one religion or another. Large and powerful predatory animals such as bears, eagles, and jaguars were common symbols of great spiritual power among Indians of the Americas where these animals were found. Similarly, animals that demonstrated intelligence and that tended to be seen on the fringes of human settlements, particularly the raven and the coyote (who would sometimes sneak into a human camp to steal an item of food), were often **trickster deities,** gods who acted on impulse rather than thoughtfully, who enjoyed playing jokes on others, and who often represent unconstrained or adolescent sexuality.

trickster deities
Gods who acted on impulse rather than thought-fully, who enjoyed playing jokes on others, and who often represent uncon-strained or ado-lescent sexuality.

Plants—especially psychoactive plants and medicinal herbs—are also sometimes anthropomorphized as deities or sources of mana. For instance, the psychoactive peyote cactus was called "divine" by the Aztec and is still used as a source of supernatural visions by the Huichol and Tarahumara of Mexico; its use is the central sacrament of the Native American Church in the United States.

Unusual Features of the Environment

Unusual places, such as waterfalls, caves, and mountaintops, are often treated as places of spiritual power. For instance, the Shuara of the Brazilian Amazon have traditionally made pilgrimages to waterfalls where they fasted and sought the vision that would bring them spiritual power. Caves are readily associated with ideas about the underworld, either as the land of the dead or as the place of emergence of the first ancestors. Mountaintops are sacred places of pilgrimage among both the ancient and modern Andean Indians. Such unusual places have characteristics in common that make them apt sources of supernatural symbolism. They impact the senses in ways that facilitate the entry into altered states of consciousness. The sound of falling water, much like white noise, can block out other distracting sounds during meditation. The darkness and acoustic qualities of caves give them an otherworldly quality. And the unique vistas offered by mountaintops can elicit an aesthetic thrill, or "peak experience," that can easily be thought of in spiritual terms.

Sacred places may also be erected by human effort, especially in agricultural societies that provide a sufficient economic base for the support of full-time builders. Such sacred places include shrines, churches, cathedrals and temples.

Chapter Summary

1. Religion shares many characteristics with other parts of expressive culture, such as fantasy play, art, love, and mental disorders. These institutions have fuzzy boundaries and overlap in some of their characteristics.
2. Feelings play an important role in religion, as they do in other parts of expressive culture. However, there is no distinctively religious emotion—that is, no emotion that has only a religious significance. Any human emotion may be linked to religious rituals, but different religious traditions stress different emotions.

3. Emile Durkheim emphasized the role of feelings, such as awe, respect, and reverence for things that are sacred, set apart, and forbidden as providing motivation to sustain society; the rituals that elicit these emotions are designed to influence and evoke the sacred things that are metaphors for the parts of society that must be respected and maintained.

4. Roy Rappaport pointed out that rituals arouse strong feelings in their participants, and this reinforces socially approved attitudes about whatever the rituals symbolize. Victor Turner analyzed the interplay of sensory and ideological symbols in religious rituals as a mechanism by which strong feelings are aroused in participants and then transformed to allegiance to the object of a religion's ideological symbols.

5. Rudolf Otto emphasized the importance of feelings associated with concepts of the "holy," that which elicits overpowering sense of dependence, awe, and dread. One form of the idea of the "holy" is the concept of mana, an impersonal supernatural force, or "sacredness," that is contained in sacred things and that can be manipulated by means of religious rituals. Another is the concept of mystical union with the sacred.

6. Religion also expresses feelings in the form of values. Values are higher-order feelings about what is good and bad. All religions include piety values, feelings about right and wrong behavior toward sacred things. These include taboos that forbid those behaviors believed to have negative supernatural consequences as well as positive injunctions for other behaviors. Some religions, most notably those found in societies manifesting differences in wealth, power, and social class, also support moral values with promises of supernatural consequences—rewards for following them and punishments for their violation.

7. Some social scientists have been influenced by Paul Tillich's view of religion as "ultimate concern." Defining religion in terms of the ultimate concerns of a society or social group broadens the concept of religion in a way that highlights its similarity to other institutions that are also central to defining people's commitment to a guiding system of highest-priority values. However, it also undermines the usefulness of the word *religion* to designate an institution that communicates a group's ultimate concerns within a supernaturalistic ideology. An approach that distinguishes between religion and other institutions that communicate ultimate concerns can still profit from noting the functional-equivalent effects that such nonreligious institutions have.

8. Religious symbolism is drawn from such sources as the human body and unusual features of nature. Such symbolism can carry powerful emotional significance.

Recommended Readings

1. Douglas, Mary. 1970. *Natural Symbols: Explorations in Cosmology.* New York: Random House. Douglas's original book-length discussion of the physical body as a microcosm of the social body.

2. Durkheim, Emile. 1915. *The Elementary Forms of the Religious Life.* Translated by Joseph Ward Swain. New York: Free Press. The classic analysis of Ab-

original Australian religion that lays the foundation for Durkheim's view of the role of religion in perpetuating social stability.

3. Lewis, William F. 1993. *Soul Rebels: The Rastafari.* Prospect Heights, IL: Waveland Press. A brief ethnography of the subculture and religion of the Rastafari, whose distinctive combination of ganga-smoking as a means of mystic experience, reggae music, and social struggles makes fascinating reading.

4. Millman, Lawrence. 1987. *A Kayak Full of Ghosts.* Santa Barbara, CA: Capra Press. A wonderful collection of mythic, beautiful, and often violent tales of the indigenous Inuit peoples of the Northwest Territories, Baffin Island, northern Quebec, Labrador, and both coasts of Greenland.

5. Moore, S. F., and Meyerhoff, B. G., eds. 1978. *Secular Ritual.* Atlantic Highlands, NJ: Humanities Press. Examines the role of ritual in a variety of non-religious contexts, including politics, recreation, sport, and theater.

6. Ono, Sokyo. 1962. *Shinto: The Kami Way.* Rutland, VT: Charles E. Tuttle. A brief introduction to the indigenous Shinto religion of Japan by a professor of the Shinto university, Kokugakuin Daigaku.

7. Radin, Paul. 1956. *The Trickster: A Study in American Indian Mythology.* New York: Dover. The classic anthropological discussion of Trickster deities.

8. Tedlock, Barbara. 1992. *The Beautiful and the Dangerous: Encounters with the Zuñi Indians.* New York: Penguin. Beautifully presented life-story narratives, legends, and myths based on the author's experiences among the Zuñi over more than two decades.

9. Vander, Judith. 1997. *Shoshone Ghost Dance Religion: Poetry Songs and Great Basin Context.* Urbana: University of Illinois Press. An ethnomusicological analysis of Shoshone Ghost Dance songs.

Recommended Websites

1. *http://www.religioustolerance.org/newage.htm*
   Religious Tolerance website on New Age spirituality.
2. *http://lcweb.loc.gov/folklife/*
   The Library of Congress's American Folklife site.
3. *http://www.justpunjab.com/religion/oral_literature.htm*
   A site on oral literature—including religious music and stories—in the Punjab.
4. *http://flsj.ucdavis.edu/home/sjjs/orallit/litorale1*
   Oral literature of Sephardic Judaism.
5. *http://www.csupomona.edu/~plin/folkreligion/chinesefolkrel.html*
   A site on Chinese folk religion.
6. *http://www.humnet.ucla.edu/humnet/anthropoetics/ap0501/tea.htm*
   An analysis of the Japanese tea ceremony.

Study Questions

1. How are the various institutions of expressive culture similar to one another?

2. What do we mean when we say that there are no distinctive religious emotions?
3. According to Hood, under what circumstances are experiences of mystical unity with nature most likely to occur?
4. What is one problem with defining religion as behaviors that relate to "ultimate concerns"?
5. What is similar about how the concepts of "left" and "right" are treated in many cultures?
6. Why, according to Mary Douglas, is the human body a powerful source of religious symbols?
7. What is meant by the phrase "natural symbols" and how do they differ from other kinds of symbols?
8. What characteristics do sacred places often have?
9. How do animals that frequently become symbols of the greatness of supernatural power differ from those that frequently become symbols of Trickster deities?
10. Why may symbols drawn from nature typically be characterized as "natural symbols"?

Language, Belief, and Religion

CHAPTER OBJECTIVES

When you finish this chapter, you will be able to

1. Explain the relationship between belief and interpretation of experience.
2. Compare a literalist and a figurativist approach to interpreting experiences.
3. Discuss religious diversity within nonliterate and literate societies.
4. Explain the origin and perpetuation of liturgical orders.
5. Define the difference between a restricted and an elaborated code.
6. Explain the role of linguistic taboos in defining loyalty to a religious tradition.
7. Outline the various ways in which language is used in religious rituals.
8. Define the nature of *paradoxes* and explain their function in religious ideologies.
9. Define *canon* and explain its religious function.
10. Discuss the various problems concerning the translation of sacred religious texts, including the problems of *canon, textual basis, interpretation,* and *style.*

Without language, religion could not exist. This is both because the most basic concepts of religion—ideas about gods, spirits, and other supernatural things—could not be taught were there no language with which to explain them and because language always plays a role in religious practices such as praying, chanting, or speaking charms. The sacred stories of religion may be passed on as part of an oral tradition or may be perpetuated as written texts. The case study titled "The Origin of the Hebrew Bible" illustrates how sacred written texts may evolve over centuries and how religious concepts can change even in a religion that has a tradition based on written texts.

CASE STUDY

The Origin of the Hebrew Bible

Scholarly analysis of the biblical text has yielded a great deal of insight into how the text arose. Textual analysis indicates that prior to the rise of a literate culture among the ancient Hebrews, religious stories were passed down orally in song, poetry, and sacred tales. The first written version of some of these oral traditions is now known as Genesis 2 (beginning with the second half of verse 4) through Genesis 4 and parts of ensuing chapters thereafter. This story of the creation of the world by the Hebrew deity Yahweh[1] was written down during the rise of the state-sponsored, urban temple ceremonies in Jerusalem around 950 B.C. Yahweh was portrayed in concrete and anthropomorphic terms. He formed a man (Hebrew adam*)*

---

[1] Hebrew was originally written without vowels. Thus, the name Yahweh was written with the consonants YHWH. By the time of the Roman domination of Judea, the name of Yahweh had come to be regarded as so sacred that it was no longer spoken aloud except in the Temple. Instead, devout Jews substituted the word Adonai ("Lord") or HaShem ("the Name") when referring to Yahweh or when reading aloud scriptures that contained the name Yahweh. Eventually, the Masoretic scribes developed a system for marking Hebrew vowels and began to use them when they copied the Hebrew scriptures. In respect for the custom of not pronouncing the name Yahweh, the Masoretes inserted the vowel marks for the word Adonai wherever YHWH occurred. This was intended to remind readers to substitute the word Adonai for Yahweh. Later, Christian translators mistakenly accepted these vowels as the correct ones, reading the name as YAHOWEH and chose the English spelling Jehovah as the name of the Hebrew deity.

from the soil (adamah), planted a garden for the man to live in, formed animals and let the man name them, and finally produced a companion for the man from one of the man's ribs. The stories about Yahweh's dealings with humankind recounted how the first couple ate the fruit of the forbidden Tree of Knowledge after being deceived by a serpent and how they were cast out of the garden because of this transgression. It traced their descendants down to the time of a great flood, told of the covenant that Yahweh made with Abraham, and followed his descendants until, in Exodus 19 and 34, Moses received the Law from Yahweh on Mount Sinai. This early text also included parts of Deuteronomy, which reiterates the covenant between Yahweh and the people of Israel and summarizes their obligations under that contract. The Yahwist text also included some of the psalms, particularly ones that may have been used in the Temple services.

The second major addition to the Bible arose among the northern tribes that were said to have established their independence from the Monarch around 921 when they established the separate kingdom of Israel. The religious traditions of the northern cities were more greatly influenced by the urbane cultures of the Canaanites than was that of Jerusalem, which was more isolated from the surrounding cultures in the southern highlands. The religious stories of Israel also recounted the lives of Abraham, Jacob, Joseph, and Moses, but the written version of these stories differed from that of the Yahwist tradition in several ways. In it, God was referred to by variants of the name El, the older Semitic name for the divine father of the lesser gods who ruled the various nations. The Elohist texts, as they are called, had a more intellectual style, one that spoke of God in more abstract terms than did the concrete stories of Yahweh that were written in the south. In the Elohist texts, God appears in dreams, while in the southern stories Yahweh comes in person. They emphasized the role of Israel as a Covenant people and the importance of moral and ethical rules. After the conquest of the northern kingdom by the Assyrian king Sargon II in 722 B.C., many refugees fled from Israel to the south. Jerusalem's numbers multiplied—from a town of about 5,000 people to a city of about 45,000—due to the influx of northerners who brought with them their northern religious views. In the ensuing years, the Yahwist and Elohist scriptures were combined into a single, integrated text.

The combining of the Yahwist and Elohist texts left certain fingerprints of the editorial process behind. For instance, it resulted in "doublets" of certain stories—two different versions of the same event which sometimes contradict each other in specific details, such as the number of each kind of animal that was preserved from the Flood. The two versions of the various doublets also maintain the distinctive vocabulary and style of their Yahwist or Elohist source. For instance, the Elohist writer refers to Moses's father as Jethro, while the Yahwist text calls him Reuel or Hobab; the Elohist calls the mountain on which Moses spoke to God Horeb, while the Yahwist author calls the place Sinai. Such differences simply reflect the differing versions of the traditions that evolved among the northern tribes of Israel and among those in the southern highlands.

Sometime during the reign of king Josiah (640–609 B.C.) or perhaps slightly earlier during the reign of Hezekiah (715–687 B.C.), the core of the book of Deuteronomy (chapters 5–26 and 28) was composed. As part of the religious reforms of King Josiah, who attempted to eliminate foreign influences among the religious practices of the people of Judah, it emphasized the importance of Mosaic Law by restating it to them. Its central reiteration of the Law was the "book of the Torah" that was said to have been found by Josiah in 622 B.C. and that he used in his reform efforts. The author composed the text as if it were a sermon spoken by Moses to the Israelites as they wandered in the wilderness, but its language is that of someone who was familiar with the northern tradition following the Monarchy. The Deuteronomist's style of writing reflects the northern tradition in the use of Elohist terms for God and, where they differ from those of the Yahwist author, names for geographical locations and persons. Despite his northern background, the author of Deuteronomy was likely a Levite who was associated with the royal court of Jerusalem. Some have suggested that Jeremiah might have been the author, while others have pointed to Shaphan, the scribe of the royal court and the high priest Hilkiah as possible authors.

A somewhat later author, the Deuteronomic historian, composed a prologue for Deuteronomy (chapters 1–4:40 and 29–34) and the books of Joshua through Kings, a history of the Monarchy and divided kingdom that attempts to explain why the God allowed the kingdom of Judah to fall to the Babylonians in the sixth century B.C. and to encourage the historian's contemporaries to live faithfully according to the Covenant. The historian most likely composed his work around 550 B.C. shortly after the final event in that history, the release of king Jehoiachin from prison in 561 B.C.

The final editing of the Jewish scriptures began with the addition of what is known as the Priestly text, which was made up of documents written by the priests who returned to Palestine from the Babylonian Captivity in 539 B.C. At the beginning of the Babylonian Captivity, in 587 B.C., the Jewish elite, including the priestly caste, had been deported from Palestine, but the bulk of the population of peasant farmers and artisans had remained in Palestine. Deprived of their leaders, the Jews who remained at home had been influenced by the religious practices of their neighbors, such as the Canaanites, and the worship of the gods and goddesses of these non-Jewish peoples had infiltrated Palestinian Judaism. During the same half century, Jewish priests in Babylon were influenced by the urbane intellectual tradition of Babylonia and came to view their own Judaism in broader, less parochial terms than they once had. At the same time, finding themselves surrounded and dominated by their Babylonian subjugators, they reacted very strongly against its polytheism as a means of maintaining their own, distinctive, Jewish identity. On their return to Palestine, the priests of the Captivity took as their first task, the elimination of all of the foreign gods and religious practices that they found among the peasants who had remained in Palestine. It was in this context that the Priestly text was written. The Priestly text consisted of emendations and commentaries that were added to all of the books of the Torah. They include, for instance, the creation story as told in the first chapter of Genesis, a version which—while attributing creation to the Jewish deity, Elohim, and avoiding any reference to the gods of the Babylonians—has much in common with the Babylonian creation story that had influenced its writers during their stay in Babylon. The primary purpose of these documents was to emphasize the importance of Jews remaining true to their Covenant with God, following the Law assiduously, and rejecting all pagan religious influences from Judaism. The priestly texts also emphasized the proper forms of worship, the rules that governed the behavior of the priests themselves, and the forms of the priestly ceremonies (such as the sacrificial services in the Temple). These were all things that the priestly elite saw as central to their mission of reestablishing a unified Jewish community in Palestine after their return from the Captivity. Although the priestly literature may have been added to over a period of time by various members of the priestly school of thought, some have suggested that Ezra may have been the original and primary priestly writer who organized the first five books of the Hebrew scriptures into their approximate final form.

The second major subdivision of the Hebrew scriptures was made up of the writings of the prophets. The core of the prophetic writings consisted of commentaries on the social and political events of their times and their relationships with the moral obligations of the people toward one another and their duties toward God. The prophetic tradition occurs throughout the history of the Hebrews. For instance, Abraham and Moses are portrayed as prophets by the Elohist texts, and there were prophets such as Samuel during the history of the Monarchy and the divided kingdom. Similarly, prophetic writings such as those of Isaiah, Ezekiel, and Ezra date from later times. In fact, the prophetic tradition did not die out in the culture of the Jews until at least the first century A.D., where it was still practiced among some of the Jewish sects, including Jewish Christianity. However, as we shall see, with the exception of the book of Daniel, Judaism came to accept only prophetic works written prior to about 400 B.C.

The question of what works to establish as canon (see p. 164)—that is, as authoritative, inspired scriptures—was not a pressing one in early Judaism. By the first century A.D., individual synagogues might have other texts such as psalms, proverbs, and works attributed to various prophets, in their collection of sacred texts, and these collections might differ from one synagogue to another. Nevertheless, all Jews accepted the Torah—Genesis, Exodus, Leviticus, Numbers, and Deuteronomy—as scripture, since their authorship had come by then to be attributed to the prophet Moses. Achieving a complete consensus about which books all Jews should recognize as sacred was not a pressing matter partly because the Torah was viewed as containing the full Law of God for his people; and the practice of the Law, not theology, was the defining essence of Judaism. That is, while later Christian history concerned itself intensely with issues of "orthodoxy" and "heresy" of belief, Judaism was—and remains—primarily a religion of practice rather than doctrine. Furthermore, support for the Temple and its sacred ceremonies as a defining feature of Judaism also made it less of a concern whether discussion of the Torah was supplemented by reference to other written texts. Thus, it was only after the destruction of the Temple in A.D. 68, that Judaism began to focus on refining its defining teachings and scriptures.

At the fall of Jerusalem and the Temple, Rabbi Yohanan ben Zacchai, the youngest student of Hillel the Pharisee, escaped Jerusalem by having himself smuggled out of the city in a coffin. He and other rabbis were instrumental in establishing an Academy in Jamnia (now Javnah) that created a new identity for Judaism in the post-Temple era, one in which the guiding force of Judaism was no longer the priests who controlled the sacrificial rites of the Temple, but scholars who studied the Torah in light of the oral traditions that gave it meaning. According to rabbinic tradition, it was in Jamnia in A.D. 90 that a great council of rabbis determined which books would be accepted as inspired scripture in Judaism.

Although all Jews accepted the Torah as sacred, determining what other books would be included in the Jewish canon was not without controversy. One general rule held that no books written after Ezra (about 400 B.C.) would be regarded as scripture, although after much debate an exception was made for the books of Jonah and Daniel, which had been composed after that time. Ecclesiastes was opposed by many rabbis because they felt that its pessimistic and despairing outlook was uncharacteristic of Judaism, but it was eventually accepted by the majority. The Song of Songs was strongly opposed by many of the rabbis because of its strong erotic imagery until, finally, the view prevailed that its true meaning was an allegory of God's love for Israel, not the carnal love of a man for a woman. Finally, the book of Esther was controversial for at least a century after Jamnia because the word "God" did not appear in it and because it introduced the Feast of Purim, which implied that the Torah—which does not mention Purim—was incomplete. Nevertheless, it too eventually became accepted as part of the standard list of sacred texts, and by A.D. 200 rabbinic Judaism had established the 39 books that have formed the Hebrew Bible ever since.

LANGUAGE, RELIGIOUS BELIEF, AND INTERPRETATION

Religious beliefs can be thought of as the standard way a group of people speaks about religious things; each religion (each group) has its characteristic ways of doing so. Throughout most of history religions have consisted of oral traditions passed down from one generation to the next by means of language. Since writing developed, some of these traditions took on the form of sacred written texts, but oral tradition continues to play an important role in how these texts are talked about. The standard ways in which a group does its religious talking define the unique identity of its religion.

ideology
The shared beliefs that define a social group and that are passed down from one generation to the next.

Ideology consists of the shared beliefs that define a social group and that are passed down from one generation to the next. The human capacity to use language makes it possible for human groups to develop these shared beliefs. Ideologies are important to people, in part because accepting them defines a person's membership in his or her society or group. Acceptance of a religious ideology functions as an expression of the adherent's commitment to the religious group, and loyalty is typically very important to religious groups.

When loyalty to an ideology is important, beliefs can bias our perception of what is true and what is not true so much that we cease to be objective in our interpretation of events around us. At the very least, ideologies should be understood as being like the lenses of eyeglasses. They may be clear or tinted, and how we see the world can be very different depending on which pair of glasses we happen to be wearing.

Language is central to the communication and perpetuation of religious beliefs. It is also central to the process of interpreting beliefs that goes on as part of the religious lives of believers.

Language

language
A distinctively human system of communication that governs the use of spoken symbols to communicate information.

Language is a distinctively human system of communication that governs the use of spoken symbols (see chapter 5) to communicate information. So skilled are humans at using symbols to communicate with one another that we have also developed nonspoken varieties of language such as the gestural sign language used by hearing-impaired people and **writing,** a system of symbols used to portray language in visual form. Through most of human existence, religious beliefs were communicated and perpetuated from generation to generation within the body of **oral literature,** the spoken traditions of a society. This tradition continues, but since the invention of writing, the oral religious tradition has been supplemented by the perpetuation of religious information in the form of sacred religious texts and commentaries on them.

writing
A system of symbols used to portray language in visual form.

oral literature
Tales told by word of mouth for pleasure and edification.

As do other animals, humans also communicate some important messages with signs (see chapter 5). We use signs—often quite unconsciously—in ways that naturally communicate our feelings about ourselves, those with whom we are interacting, our situation, and the topic about which we are communicating with language. The signs that express such feelings when we are using language include volume and speed of speaking; tone of voice; the emphasis given to one word or another; and even such things as eye contact, body posture, and gestures. In oral religious traditions, including **liturgies** (rituals or ceremonies practiced as forms of public worship or devotion), the sign communication that accompanies spoken symbols provides an important context that greatly influences how the audience or participants in the liturgy understand the meanings of the word symbols. Such contextual information, which normally accompanies spoken language, is not very well conveyed in written forms of the same words. Although writing includes a few conventions, such as the use of underlining for emphasizing a word or phrase or exclamation points to emphasize an entire sentence, most of the subtle information signs that accompany spoken language are lost when spoken words are translated into a written text.

liturgies
Rituals or ceremonies practiced as forms of public worship or devotion.

Language and the Interpretation of Religious Beliefs

We humans are interpreting animals. The act of interpreting what we experience comes so naturally that it commonly operates in the background without rising to the level of consciousness. The believer often overlooks the role of interpretation in formulating religious belief, confusing interpretation with fact. Of course, the religious are not alone in this. The error plagues both believer and nonbeliever alike. However, it is important for the student of religion to be aware that all belief arises through the interpretation of facts and that how symbols, such as those of a religion, are interpreted is greatly influenced by the culture of the interpreter.

Failure to recognize that belief *is* a result of interpretation is most glaringly apparent in the case of religions whose beliefs are grounded in sacred written texts when those beliefs are based on a literalist reading of the texts. When the method of scriptural interpretation is guided by a principle of literalism, it is easy for readers to perceive their reading as simply "what the Book says," as if the readers' understanding were not influenced by the rules they use to interpret the written text. But *all* understanding derived from the reading of a text are *interpretations* of that text. Trite expressions to the contrary notwithstanding, sacred texts do not "speak for themselves" or "provide their own interpretation." Believers do the interpreting. This singularly important and fundamental concept should not be forgotten by those who wish to understand religion within a social science framework.

Religious interpretation may tend more or less toward literalism or figurativism. No one is always completely literal in every reading of every text, and no one is always completely metaphorical either. We all shift mental gears, understanding some things quite literally at one time and rather figuratively at another. The same is true of religious ideologies. Some believers favor literalism over figurativism, and others have the opposite bias, but none approaches every doctrine completely literally or metaphorically. Rather, different religions may be thought of as falling along a continuum on which the differences are in the relative emphasis placed on one mode of interpretation or the other. With that in mind, let us look at the two modes themselves.

Literalism

The approach to understanding texts that assumes that they are best understood without taking the words as similes, analogies, and metaphors is called

literalism
The approach
to understanding
texts that as-
sumes they are
best understood
without taking
the words as
similes, analogies,
and metaphors.

literalism. From a literalist perspective, texts simply mean what they appear to mean "on their face." If the text says the world was created in seven "days," a truly literal interpretation would be that the creation was accomplished in seven 24-hour periods. If the text says a flood "covered the earth," then it was a universal flood, one that overran every continent worldwide. If the text says that the "sun stood still,". then its doing so was not merely an optical illusion or a psychological misapprehension of "time standing still," but a physical reality, no matter how mysterious such an occurrence would seem to be by the reader's normal understanding of physical laws.

Anthropologist Vincent Crapanzano (2000) has investigated literalist thinking in the United States and has shown that it is limited neither to religion nor to the lower social classes. For instance, numerous judges and lawyers apply literalist thinking to the law when they concern themselves with the letter of the written law. Crapanzano notes that a literal approach to interpretation tends to focus on words in their role of designating or naming things rather than in their role of (1) conveying meanings that can be recognized only if the context of the utterances is known or (2) being used to influence people rather than simply to specify information about something "out there." The literal approach assumes a simple one-to-one correlation between word and thing and ignores the ambiguity that language also has. It assumes that there is a plain and understandable meaning to every text and that this meaning can be determined with surety. Finally, according to Crapanzano, practitioners of literalism "are given to quoting or citing [the texts they accept as authoritative] on all manner of occasions" (p. 3), and they give "priority to the written—the text—over the spoken and in the case of sacred texts like the Bible, at times over experience" (p. 3).

The virtue of the literalist understanding of religious ideology is that it requires no special training, so it is a way of understanding that is available to all. It also permits the everyday understandings of grassroots believers to inform their religious views, thereby giving them a sense of empowerment as individuals who may speak their beliefs with confidence. Thus, the approach can imbue religious beliefs with a sense of immediacy and "truthfulness" that can be lacking when "doctrine" is controlled and doled out by specialists whose language is not the commonsense language of the ordinary believer.

The literalist approach is unself-conscious about its methods of interpretation, since it relies on what appears to be the face-value meaning as understood by the reader or hearer of the text. Those interpretations easily take on the aura of unquestioned "truths," since they are simply what appear to the believer to be the self-evident meanings of the texts. Indeed, the language of literalism is not likely to include the word *interpretation*. Rather, the text is viewed as if it "speaks for itself."

Since the literalist approach allows readers to draw upon their own cultural context and its presuppositions to interpret the meaning of a text, it requires no independent knowledge of the culture of the writer or interpretive sophistication on the part of readers. Meanings can be intuited just as they are in face-to-face discourse. This gives literalism an appeal and also makes the more literalist theologies both flexible and enduring. As the culture of its followers changes over generations, so do the literal understandings of its theology. The flexibility derives from the fact that as the culture of the readers changes, so too will their interpretations of what they read. Since such a theology is not grounded in historicism, the very fact of change need not be apparent to its current generation. Thus, a nineteenth-century American literalist denomination in a pro-slavery culture would readily find support for slavery in the Hebrew scriptures, while a century later members of the same denomination, no longer finding such verses salient to their current values need not be aware that their forebears did.

Nonliteralism

The approach to the text that assumes that the words may mean more than they seem to when taken at face value is called **figurativism** (or **nonliteralism**). Nonliteralist interpretations expect to find figurative language, metaphors, and similes in the texts they are applied to. Believing that the world revolves around the sun rather than the other way around, the figurativist interprets "the sun stood still" as an idiom for "the day seemed to lengthen." A "day" of creation is read as a "period" of creation, surely not just a 24-hour period.

Practitioners of figurativism recognize that texts are sometimes ambiguous and the original intent of the writer may be simply unknowable. The degree of tolerance for ambiguity that this approach requires can leave the literalist quite uncomfortable.

Nonliteralist interpretations recognize that the meaning of any text is influenced by the other parts of the text that surround it. Thus, nonliteral interpretations place a conscious emphasis on taking such contexts into account to determine the meaning of a text. For instance, a nonliteral interpretation of "covered the earth" would likely understand "earth" in the sense of a local area of land rather than as the entire world. This concern for the influence of context often extends to historical and cultural contexts as well as linguistic context, issues that will be discussed in more detail in the discussion of ethnocentrism and cultural relativism later in the chapter.

Psalm 90:4 can be used to illustrate the influence of context on an understanding of a text's meaning. It reads, "For a thousand years in your [God's] sight are like yesterday when it is past, or [literally "and"] like a watch in the night." The first half of this verse is quoted more often in religious discussions than is the last; and taken by itself, it is sometimes understood in a literal way: What God calls a "day," as in the story of the seven days of creation in the Genesis story, is a period of a thousand years. However, a nonliteralist interpretation that also includes the second half of the verse requires a different understanding: A thousand years is said to be compared both to a day and to a "watch in the night," which is much shorter than a day. What we have here cannot be intended to work like a mathematical equation, but rather is simply a way of saying that what seems a long, long time to humans is but a fleeting moment, a mere day or even less, to God, who is eternal. Indeed, the preceding context makes this the clear motif of the psalm: the opening two verses both emphasize the eternal nature of God: "you have been our dwelling place in all generations . . . from everlasting to everlasting you are God."

Figurative interpretation often requires more effort than literal interpretation because it must consider alternatives to the surface meaning of a text. As an approach, it is most fully achieved only by specialists who have extensive training in the language, culture, and history of the texts. This makes nonliteral

figurativism (or nonliteralism) An interpretation that assumes the words of the text may mean more than they seem to when taken at face value.

approaches less accessible to grassroots followers of a religious tradition and can create a status difference between the ordinary follower and the scholarly theologian whose writings may be taken as more authoritative than grassroots opinions. On the other hand, its practitioners regard a nonliteral approach as one that helps them achieve a more accurate understanding of how the text was understood by its original writer.

Balancing the Literal and the Figurative

My goal is neither to disparage the literalist nor tout the figurativist approach. Remember, no individual or shared religious ideology is simply one or the other. Religious denominations vary merely in the degree to which they use both approaches, and each has a customary consensus among its followers about how and when each approach is preferable. Even the most literal of theologies accepts some texts, such as parables and sacred poetry, as figurative, and the most nonliteral theologies take some texts literally. Religions and their diverse denominations simply differ along a continuum in how they balance the two approaches. The question to be considered now is what determines the guidelines of how literal or how figurative each group's religious ideology becomes.

A balancing of approaches exists even in a religion that relies heavily on one method or the other, especially when a literal reading of the text contradicts cultural assumptions about what "makes sense." For instance, the literalist creationist who insists that the creative "days" of the first chapter of Genesis were 24-hour periods, is nevertheless bound to interpret the same word in the second chapter that refers to "the day on which God created the heavens and the earth" to mean "a period of time," since this "day" includes several of the creative "days" in the first chapter.

Ethnocentrism and Cultural Relativism in the Interpretation of Sacred Texts

In addition to literalism versus nonliteralism, texts may be read in a way that relies on assumptions derived from the reader's own culture or that attempts to interpret the words in terms of their original cultural context. The former approach offers the benefit of flexibility in that it allows the reader to more readily apply the sacred text to his or her own life and circumstances in a way that feels fulfilling and that more easily maintains a sense of the sanctity and relevance of the text. Its drawback is the problem of *ethnocentrism* (see chapter 1), interpreting a text by the standards of meanings of one's own culture rather than by those of the writer's culture. Ethnocentrism results in misunderstanding the original meaning because it is being evaluated in the wrong cultural context. In an ethnocentric interpretation, the words of the text need not be placed in their original cultural context to understand what the author intended. Rather, it is assumed that the reader can adequately grasp their meaning, equipped with no other preconceptions than his or her own background, culture, and experience. Furthermore, one may draw on one's own internalized frame of reference quite unself-consciously, with no explicit recognition that the act of understanding is conditioned by any "frame of reference." One merely understands what one perceives the words to say on their face.

Cultural relativism (see chapter 1), the approach to interpreting meaning which holds that texts are most accurately understood in light of the cultural and historical context from which they derive, offers the opportunity for better understanding an ancient text as it would have been understood by ancient readers. But it too has drawbacks. First, its greater emphasis on the differences between the reader's own culture and that from which the text derived may leave the meaning of the text seeming less relevant to the life and times of the reader and, therefore, potentially less sacred than when viewed from a nonrelativistic viewpoint. Second, the more ancient a text is, the less information is likely to be available from which to reliably derive a relativistic understanding of its original meaning.

The way in which cultural relativism can give a more accurate understanding of a text can be illustrated by a common misunderstanding of the injunction "You shall not commit adultery" (Exodus 20:14). In contemporary, industrialized Western societies such as the United States, this text is commonly understood to forbid marital infidelity by both husbands and wives more or less equally, an ethnocentric interpretation that is compatible with secular gender norms of these societies. It is a natural reading in societies where marriage is viewed as a contract between two individuals and where children are thought of as equal descendants of both their fathers and mothers. However, a relativist approach would recognize that this would not likely have been the common interpretation in ancient Hebrew society, where descent was traced solely through men and children belonged to the father's, but not the mother's family. When family relationships are determined in this way, a wife's role in marriage involves a commitment to bear only children who are his and, therefore, legitimately entitled to claim membership in his patrilineal family—the kin who all claimed descent through the father-line back to some common male ancestor. Infidelity by a married woman was a threat to the purity of her husband's line of descent, since her infidelity could lead to the birth of children who had been fathered by some man other than her husband. Adultery (Hebrew, *na'aph*) violated a woman's obligation to bear children only by her husband, thereby adding to his family only offspring who were its legitimate members. Thus, by ancient Hebrew standards, the injunction, "You shall not commit *na'aph*" meant "Do not have sexual intercourse with a married woman." That is, the marital status of the man was irrelevant, since a man could only commit *na'aph* with a woman who was married to another man. Thus, for instance, a sexual relationship between a married man and an unmarried woman was not *na'aph*, since the woman was not married and could not, therefore, adulterate the purity of anyone's family line.

DIVERSITY WITHIN RELIGION

Diversity is not simply a matter of differences *among* cultures. No culture is homogeneous, and diversity can be found within each of the world's religions. Sometimes diversity of religious belief or practice has been treated with dramatic efforts to eradicate it, as when religious heretics were burned in 16th-century Europe. Although diversity within a religious tradition may not be welcomed, no religion exists with complete homogeneity of belief or practice. Religions differ merely in the degree to which such diversity is accepted. Were this not so, cultural change would not be possible, and religion would remain static despite the passage of time. Although part of the sanctity of most, if not all, religions is expressed as the belief that they embody ancient truths and practices in forms that have not changed, all religions do change with the passage of time, and there are differences in the specifics of belief and practice among followers of any religion.

The Intra-Group Diversity of Religious Doctrine

It is easy to speak about the ideology of a religion as if the beliefs and values of its followers were homogeneous. However, this simplifies a reality that is more complex. Individual members of any religion may differ from one another, both idiosyncratically and in terms of social differences between them, in their views about the ideology they "share." What defines the unity of a given religion is not, in fact, a true homogeneity of belief and practice, but the belief that a shared belief and practice exists. In other words, the boundaries of a particular religion are not a matter that can be defined objectively but depend on the group's own tolerance for variance among its own members.

Religious Diversity in Nonliterate Societies

In nonliterate societies, local variations in the telling of a religion's myths and in the specifics of ritual practice inevitably develop over the generations. For instance, the Shoshone Indians of the Great Basin region of the United States were a foraging people who survived in small groups. All tell many of the same religious stories that they call Coyote stories. These stories are commonly related to features of the natural environment. For instance, a character's home might be described as a particular cave, or Coyote may be said to have rested by a particular known spring. As these stories were passed down the generations among this seminomadic people, the locations did not remain fixed points within the Great Basin. Rather, each local group of Shoshone tends to associate the same stories with its own vicinity. Shoshones are tolerant of this kind of variation in the telling of their myths, and such differences do not prevent them from being accepted as proper Coyote tales.

Religious Diversity within Literate Societies

Religions with bodies of sacred written scriptures also manifest internal diversity of belief and values. As with religions that rely on oral traditions, geographically dispersed groups within the same religious tradition may show specific differences in matters of belief, values, and practice. Such diversity may be noticeable from one local congregation to another; but in multinational religions, the differences within the same religion may be especially dramatic among followers in different countries.

Diversity within Hinduism

Hinduism offers an excellent example of a religion that self-consciously accepts tremendous variation within itself. Its underlying unity exists at a higher level of abstraction than does that of religions that have a single seat of theological authority and an emphasis on "orthodoxy." Hinduism is the dominant religion of millions of people who speak a number of different languages throughout the subcontinent of India. No centralized ecclesiastical hierarchy controls the belief and practices of Hindus as a whole. As a result, great diversity has developed within this single religious tradition, whose followers still recognize one another, despite their specific differences, as belonging to the same religion.

As a religion whose ecclesiastical organization includes priests but no central seat of priestly authority for the entire religion, Hinduism has sometimes been characterized as a religion with millions of gods. Hindu theologians view Hinduism as monotheistic and hold that this diversity simply represents many different ways of portraying a single ultimate reality about god, since Hinduism is a religion with extreme tolerance for diversity in the human portrayal of god.

Throughout India, local practices and the gods who are worshiped within Hinduism vary tremendously from one region to another, even from one village to the next. Yet, despite tremendous diversity in belief and practice, the common identity of Hinduism is accepted throughout the subcontinent. This unity is seen in the acceptance of a common body of scriptures that began as oral texts but that were eventually written down from about 1500 to 500 B.C. The primary scriptures of Hinduism are the Vedas. Added to these are a set of secondary scriptures that grew up in later ages as elaborations on the Vedas. There are four Vedas—the Rigveda, the Samaveda, the Yajurveda, and the Atharvaveda. Each is divided into three parts—the Mantras (the basic hymns and verses), the Brahamas (ritualistic and interpretive explanations of the Mantras written by priests), and the Upanishads (profound mystical and philosophic extensions of the truths revealed in the Mantras).

The secondary scriptures are called the Smriti ("that which is remembered"). They are not revealed scriptures, but authoritative digests of earlier writings, manuals of philosophy, commentaries, rituals, codes of law and conduct, sacred stories, and epics.

Beyond this unity of scriptures, Hinduism is tremendously diverse, because it encompasses many local variations across the subcontinent and because Hinduism attempts to meet the needs of humanity at every level. Because of its regional diversity, Hinduism can be described as a polytheistic religion with countless gods, ritual practices, and sects. But beneath this diversity a core of doctrine defines a basic unity of thought and belief that accepts all of the diverse descriptions of the many gods as merely different manifestations of One Absolute Reality.

Three main gods form the Hindu trinity: Brahma (the Creator), Vishnu (the Preserver), and Shiva (the Destroyer). These gods embody the three basic aspects of reality as experienced by humans: creation, stability, and change. Thus, all things, including human beings (not just the gods), may be understood as manifestations of Ultimate Reality, which is the whole animate and inanimate universe. These three primary deities are worshiped under a variety of different names throughout India, the different names being thought of as different incarnations or manifestations of the same deity. In addition, the actual devotions of many people are not directed to any of the three primary gods but to one of the many other gods that have come to be recognized as belonging to the Hindu pantheon. For instance, Ganesha, the god of travelers, who is portrayed with elephantlike characteristics, is a widely venerated deity. According to the Hindu worldview, the essential self of every individual is called *Atman*. This is a transcendent, divine aspect that is one with the Ultimate Reality, or *Brahman*. Indeed, Atman may be thought of as Brahman experienced subjectively. So each person is one with all things in the universe because he or she is one manifestation of the Supreme Reality.

The multiplicity of material objects apprehended by the senses obscures and hides the true reality that pervades all things. In fact, the diverse gods, rituals, and creeds of Hinduism are thought of as merely institutions through which humans may seek to transcend the obscurity that masks Ultimate Reality. By transcending the illusions that make up the ordinary so-called reality of the senses, Hindus strive to find liberation from their particular body, which is finite, egotistical, and limited to the world of the senses. The final goal of life is *moksha*, liberation from finite human consciousness to unity with a divine consciousness of the Ultimate Reality. This unity with Brahman is thought of as a state of pure existence, pure consciousness, and pure bliss that escapes the bondage of individual experience.

Hindu life is guided by the *dharma* ("duty, law, morality, conduct"), the rules that govern life. Dharma is a guide to right conduct. It emphasizes the virtues of truth, nonviolence, sacrifice, purity, and renunciation or detachment. Hindus believe that humans are in bondage to their individual bodies in a cycle of rebirth, or transmigration of the self. The nature of each successive rebirth is determined by the law of *karma*, which operates like a moral law of cause and effect. According to the law of karma, how well or poorly one has followed the principles of dharma in one's previous life determines the characteristics of one's present condition. Similarly, morally good acts performed in one's current incarnation will have a positive influence on one's future incarnations, and morally bad acts will produce negative results.

Diversity and Hierarchy

Religions may have central ecclesiastical hierarchies that exercise authority over the body of followers. When this is the case, practice and doctrine tend to become more standardized than they are in societies without such ecclesiastical authorities or sacred written texts. In such religions, concepts such as orthodoxy and heresy may develop, and rigorous procedures such as excommunication may exist to maintain the purity of belief and practice as it is defined by the ecclesiastical elite. The Holy Inquisition of the Middle Ages, when hundreds of thousands of suspected and real religious nonconformists were put to death, illustrates how important conformity may become and how much power may be wielded in the effort to ensure the homogeneity of religion.

However, even in religions in which the right to define what constitutes religious orthodoxy is formally held by a specific, identifiable set of ecclesiastical leaders, religious diversity will still exist. Notably, even where there is a broad consensus among members of some religions that its beliefs and rituals are unquestioningly accepted by all of its followers, diversity can still be found. The diversity within such religions is not limited to marginal members who may be identified by others as only semicommitted, but can also be found among those regarded as fully participating, mainstream followers. This is especially noticeable in the contrast between the religious beliefs of ecclesiastical elites and those of the mainstream grassroots membership.

Mormonism, a Christian denomination of over 11 million members, provides an interesting example of the contrast between grassroots and elite beliefs about orthodox doctrine. To examine the diversity of belief within a religion, I (Crapo, 1987) compared grassroots beliefs of Latter-day Saints (also called LDS or Mormons) with the official positions of presidents of the same denomination. In spite of the fact that the LDS religion has authority-based concept of "revealed doctrine" in which only the presidents of the church have the authority to declare what the official position of the religion is, actual beliefs at the local level sometimes deviate from the doctrinal positions that have been expressed by LDS church presidents. In some cases the *majority* of members at the grassroots level assert as "official doctrine" views that directly oppose statements issued by more than one LDS president. For instance, 57 percent of church members in his study believed that biological evolution was contrary to the doctrines of their church, although several presidents of the church have declared the official position on evolution to be one of neutrality. Sixty-two percent regarded abortion to be a form of murder, although official church policies—though classifying most abortions as very serious sins—do not treat it as such and even classify abortions under certain circumstances as permissible. What was even more interesting than the simple fact that grassroots opinion about what constituted Mormon doctrine sometimes differed from the official views of the ecclesiastical leaders of the denomination was the fact that the grassroots consensus was sometimes firmly enough established that individuals whose personal views were the same as the official theological stance also shared the erroneous consensus of other grassroots members about what was official *and defined their own views as deviant.* For instance, 25 percent of those who personally believed in evolution thought that the official church stance was antievolutionist. It is unlikely that contrast between grassroots religious understandings and views of ecclesiastical leaders is unique to Mormonism. Religious specialists in any large religious denomination are unavoidably somewhat isolated from the grassroots membership, and such contrasts are probably inevitably found in any other large religious group.

LANGUAGE IN RELIGIOUS SETTINGS

Language is a prominent feature of religious **liturgical orders,** rituals that Rappaport (1999, p. 169) defines as "more or less invariant sequences encoded by persons other than the performers." By *encoded,* Rappaport means that the ritual symbolism was created by someone other than those who then participate in the rituals. That is, the ritual symbolism of liturgical orders is a matter of tradition that has been handed down from its original creators. Unlike those creators, who were innovators, participants in the liturgical orders view their role as one of perpetuating the ritual symbolism, which they view as sacred and therefore not to be changed. In addition to the highly predictable language of liturgical orders, less structured but still formal religious language is also an important means of establishing a sense of group identity and unity within religious congregations.

liturgical orders
More or less invariant sequences of rituals encoded by persons other than the performers.

Religious Language as Restricted Code

ritual language
The highly standardized spoken words that are predictable and spoken in a more or less invariant way.

Cultures can be thought of as ways of talking that are shared by members of the same society. The core of any culture consists of what may be called **ritual language,** the highly standardized spoken words that are predictable and spoken in a more or less invariant way. In a secular context, ritual language is used in ceremonial contexts and can be illustrated by the words spoken in ceremonies such as a military changing of the guard or the inauguration of a high official. In a religious setting, the rote language of liturgy exemplifies ritual language. Surrounding this core are the standard ways of saying things that, though still highly predictable, do have a small number of variants recognized by all speakers. In nonreligious life, such language can be illustrated by the ways people greet acquaintances with standard phrases such as "Hi, how are you!" The expected response in such rituals is also quite predictable—words like "I'm fine, how are you!" or its standard variants. Such words might be exchanged even when two people are merely passing one another. Neither learns much about the other beyond his or her mood and willingness to be civil if they do stop to chat. The formal language that is often used within religious congregations—forms of address such as "Brother" and "Sister" in some Protestant denominations or characteristic greetings such as "Shabbat shalom" in a Jewish congregation—is also at this level. Language of this standardized sort does not convey much factual information but is used primarily to establish a friendly relationship with others, acknowledge their presence, or demonstrate that one is a loyal member of the group. A less formal layer of talk with a slightly more varied repertoire of language skills, popularly known as "small talk," is used when first establishing a relationship or when friends want to interact for a while without deep conversation. The topics tend to be nonthreatening ones—like the weather, hobbies, family, and work. Again, this kind of language functions primarily to establish and perpetuate relationships rather than to communicate or analyze factual information.

Elaborated and restricted codes

restricted code
A use of language that involves relying heavily on standard idioms and relies on the hearers' ability to intuit what has not been explicitly said based on their shared background.

Ritual language, formal language, and small talk form what Basil Bernstein (1965, 1973) referred to as a **restricted code,** a way of talking that is structurally simple, that relies heavily on idioms that are shared by members of a group but may not be known to outsiders, and that functions more to establish group unity and coordinate the interaction of members of a group than to communicate and analyze information. Bernstein notes that restricted codes pack a lot of meaning into fewer words by relying heavily on standard idioms and clichés known to the members of a group. It requires members to intuit what has not been explicitly said based on their shared background.

elaborated code
A use of language in which many words are used to organize ideas and make one's thoughts explicit.

According to Mary Douglas (1970) a restricted code "draws from a . . . narrow . . . range of syntactic alternatives" that are "rigidly organized" (p. 44). A restricted code contrasts with an **elaborated code,** such as the language of academics, which is a way of communicating where many words are organized into complex syntactic structures in order to explicitly communicate fine distinctions. Such language is very effective at transferring information, but may not as quickly build rapport, establish the place of individuals within a group's hierarchy, or coordinate group interaction.

Much, perhaps most, of the everyday language used in religious settings falls under the heading of a restricted code. This is true both of the formal language of religious liturgy and of the informal language of members of a religious community when speaking among themselves, such as when members of conservative Christian denominations address one another with the kinship terms *brother* and *sister*. Knowing how to respond to the ritual use of liturgical language or to the in-group use of a restricted code in a religious setting identifies the speaker as one who shares the religious worldview of the group and marks one as a member of the group.

Restricted codes are central to the verbal interaction of priests and their congregations during rituals. For example, a Catholic priest's words and the congregation's responses in a Tridentine Mass in which Latin was the traditional liturgical language were expected to conform to the precise requirements of the ceremony.

Religious use of a restricted code includes language taboos as well as language rituals and standardized styles of talking. Like other taboos, language taboos can be thought of as "anti-rituals"—that is, as standardized *avoidances* where certain things are consistently *not said* rather than said. Like other taboos, avoiding the expression of certain ideas helps to define the boundaries of the beliefs and values of the group. Typically, group members leave unsaid, and therefore unconscious, ideas that would seem to challenge the established pattern of thinking that embodies the group's religious worldview and values. David Knowlton (1997), a Mormon anthropologist, described how the language taboos of his own religious community cause the academic discourse he and others practice to be interpreted by religious leaders as evidence of "apostasy." According to Knowlton, in the restricted code of Mormonism "good" speech is simple language. It distrusts rhetoric and other elaborate language such as that prized in academic settings. It conveys feelings that are expressive of spirituality. Speech that "communicates simply the feelings of the heart" (p. 48) is seen as evidence of loyalty to the Mormon religious community.

Sanctity as Expression of the Unspoken Order

Roy Rappaport (1999) observed that the most sacred beliefs of any religion have no empirical content and can therefore be neither verified nor falsified, yet are nevertheless treated as unquestionably true. For instance, neither the Muslim assertion that there is but one God, nor the Christian assertion that God consists of three persons, each of whom is fully God, has any ordinary-world content that can be tested through empirical observation. Furthermore, Rappaport explains that the sanctity of such beliefs is nothing more or less than their quality of being treated as unquestionable.

The Sacred as the Unsaid

Equating the sacred with the unquestionable implies that much can be learned about what is sacred in a religion by examining what goes unsaid among its adherents. In particular, if the sacred is understood as that which is "unquestionable," then the sacred is most clearly spotlighted by an examination of the **linguistic taboos** of a religion, those things that are not to be said, either because saying them will be punished by other members of the religious body

linguistic taboos
Those things in a religion that are not to be said, either because saying them will be punished by other members of the religious body or because they are believed to result in harmful spiritual consequences.

or because they are believed to result in harmful spiritual consequences. Blasphemy, speech that directly challenges the divine, illustrates the relationship between the sacred and the unspeakable. The taboo against blasphemy forbids the speaking of words that call the sacredness of deity into question. In its strongest form, blasphemy directly profanes the divine by insulting its dignity. Such direct insults were considered so unthinkable in early Hebrew times that references to cursing God were only referred to euphemistically, as "blessing God." And such acts of blasphemy were expected to result in divine punishment, even death—as where Job is told to "curse (literally, "bless") God and die" (Job 2:9). In Hellenistic times, even the simple utterance of the divine name became forbidden in Judaism except once a year by the high priest in the Holy of Holies of the Temple in Jerusalem. In milder forms, blasphemy may simply use reference to sacred things in nonsacred ways, for instance by using a term such as "God" simply as emphasis in ordinary speech.

Knowlton (1997), has discussed the "unspeakable" in Mormonism and notes that there is a strong but unspoken taboo against discussing the sacred ceremonies performed only in Mormon temples as well as a taboo against criticism and contention among members. When his own academic writing was seen as inappropriate, his religious leaders were constrained by these same taboos so that they were unable to criticize his work directly or discuss what disturbed them in his writing beyond simply saying in general terms that his published material had "concerned" the higher leaders of the church. His offense had been the violation of a language taboo, discussing in public something that should not have been spoken of, but no *specific* criticisms of his published work were raised, since the same taboos prevented his leaders from discussing the specifics of the issue. Rather, it was left to him to intuit what he should do differently to avoid offending church leaders in the future. His ability to conform without direct instruction was, in fact, a test of loyalty to the group.

One result of such linguistic taboos is that discussion of infractions relies on a restricted code in which "much social information must . . . be communicated in the form of subtle hints" (p. 49) and "the ability to decipher the restricted code becomes a sign of a person's character" (p. 49). Thus, "restriction of language embodies the morality within the community" (p. 49), since those who know the boundaries of speech will be able to intuit the nature of the infraction and realign themselves to the group's rules against directly speaking about sacred things.

Language as Part of Ritual

In addition to defining the ideology of a religion, language also plays a dynamic role in carrying out its rituals. For instance, it is central to prayer, exhortation, the singing of hymns and chants, and the performance of magical rituals where the words themselves are essential to the effectiveness of the ritual.

prayer
The use of language to influence supernatural beings and powers.

Prayer

According to Guthrie (1980), **prayer,** the use of language to influence supernatural beings and powers, is perhaps the single most universally shared example of quintessentially religious behavior. Since prayer uses language,

Figure 6.1
A Navajo Sing
One central feature of the Navajo curing
ceremony is its use of specific songs
and chants. Here a woman and her baby
are being treated by a Navajo *hataali,*
or "singer."

and language is a system of communication, it is tempting to think of prayer only as a form of communication directed toward gods, spirits, or other anthropomorphic beings who are thought of as capable of understanding language and choosing whether to respond favorably. However, spoken words can be a part of rituals that are intended to influence the behavior of mana as well as supernatural beings. For instance, the Shoshone Indians of the North American Great Basin would actualize the effectiveness of the magical ingredients for love and gambling magic by privately speaking over the materials before secreting them on the gambler's body or bringing them into contact with the object of sexual desire. But doing so was not a request for the intercession of a god or spirit. Rather, the role played by language was simply a necessary part of the ritual that activated the supernatural power of the "medicine." All ritual involves symbolic behavior, and sometimes the symbolism is embodied in the words of spoken language, even when the spoken words are not thought of as a petition to a decision-making supernatural being.

Song and Chant

Language and languagelike behavior frequently play a role in religious ritual expressed through the medium of music rather than ordinary speech. In **songs,** the speech of language is produced as a part of music, while **chants** are also sung, but use speechlike but nonmeaningful syllables rather than actual words. Both songs and chants play an important role as an aid to entering trance states in many of the world's religions.

Exhortation

Language is also used for intragroup communication within religious settings. In this context, language functions to help maintain conformity to religious values, beliefs, and ritual practice. Wallace (1966) cites *exhortation* (see chapter 2), the addressing of members of a congregation by another—often by a religious specialist such as a priest or shaman—who is acting in the role of representative of the supernatural. **Exhortation** includes giving sermons, conducting liturgies, and counseling individuals about how to put religious principles into practice in their lives. When carried out by a religious specialist, the act of exhortation also fulfills the function of communicating and reinforcing the hierarchical structure of the religious organization, since in such cases exhortation tends to be from specialists to laity or from specialists of higher authority to those lower in the hierarchy of specialists.

songs
Meaningful speech produced as a part of music.

chants
The use of speechlike nonsense syllables rather than meaningful speech produced in musical form.

exhortation
The addressing of members of a congregation by one who is acting in the role of representative of the supernatural.

recitation of
the code
Communicating
about the ideol-
ogy of the group.

Recitation of the code, communicating about the ideology of the group—for instance, in liturgical responses of a congregation to ritual exhortations by a religious specialist, in retelling the myths of the group, or in talking about the religion's beliefs and values—may be done by specialists, but it is often an important role for the laity within a congregation. As such, it has an important function in communicating both solidarity and equality within the group. Reciting the code may vary from formal recitation, in which the speakers are expected to use a precise sequence of ritual statements, to informal talking about religious ideology. However, even at the informal end of the spectrum, where language is not being used as part of an established liturgy, speakers still tend to follow implicit rules for speaking that set recitation of the code apart from the use of ordinary language in an everyday setting. For instance, special terms of address such as "Brother" and "Sister" that emphasize group unity may be adopted, religious jargon that is uncommon outside the group may be expected, syntax may become more formal or even archaic, and style of speaking—such as a particular cadence, resonance, or intonation pattern that is characteristic of the group—may be adopted. The underlying message communicated by these is "We are a unified group with common religious values and beliefs."

Glossolalia

glossolalia
The production
of sound se-
quences that have
no conventional
meanings in
speechlike acts.

Commonly called "speaking in tongues," **glossolalia** is the production of sound sequences that have no conventional meanings in speechlike acts. Glossolalia typically occurs during ecstatic trance states. In the United States, it is most commonly associated with Pentecostalism and the "Holiness" churches that are particularly common in Appalachia, where it is understood as a "gift of the Spirit" in which the speaker is believed to be praising God in an angelic language.

Glossolalia is not confined to any one religious tradition, but has been observed in diverse religions throughout the world. The sounds produced in glossolalic utterances tend to be those that are also part of the speaker's own native language.

Figure 6.2
Glossalalia
This member of an Appalachian Holiness church in West Virginia is in an ecstatic state of trance in which she is speaking in tongues while holding a venomous snake.

Paradox and the Nature of Religious Belief

The mathematician, Kurt Gödel (1962) demonstrated that no system of symbols that is complex enough to make self-referential statements—statements about itself—can be complete, since any system of communication of that complexity can be used to make paradoxical statements. **Paradoxes** are statements that are true if and only if they are false but false if and only if they are true. All religious ideologies include paradoxes, assertions of belief that can, if explicitly discussed, be thought of as theological dilemmas for which no logical solution can be found.

Paradox and Creation Stories

Creation myths are an inevitable source of paradoxes. A prime example of this fact is the Paradox of First Cause that is inherent to any attempt to explain the origin of reality: Any question about the origin of existing things must necessarily bump up against the problem that *any supernatural creator* said to have brought things into existence must, itself, have existed before those things that it created. But in that case, the creation story is incomplete unless the origin of the creator is also explained. However, any attempt to do so either produces the specter of an infinite, and therefore incomprehensible, regression of creators of creators or paradoxically defines the creator as somehow both existing (so that it can perform acts such as creating other things) and yet somehow not "existing" in a sense that needs explaining. Infinite regressions fail to explain the actual origin of things, since no First Cause, the origin of which is accounted for, is ever reached. Rather than explaining the origin of all existence, the problem is simply postponed repeatedly until the question, at some point, is no longer posed. Defining the creator as both real enough to have created the rest of reality (and therefore itself an existing thing, the existence of which needs to be accounted for) yet somehow not part of that which, by virtue of existence, needs to have its existence accounted for, is an assertion of paradox since part of the "explanation" for existence involves asserting that no explanation is necessary for some existing things.

Although paradoxes have, by definition, no *logical* solution, their existence in creation stories can be handled pragmatically in various ways that eliminate their logical threat to the viability of a religious ideology. First, they need not be spelled out explicitly within the ideology itself. For instance, a myth need not point out that the origin of the creator is unknown or unknowable. The origin story may simply assert the creator's role in bringing the world into existence in a way that simply takes for granted that no dilemma exists if the creator's origin is not discussed. This ability to not face the question can be facilitated if the creator is described in ways that contrast it strongly with mundane, existing things. This is the approach of Western creation mythologies that portray God in terms of absolute qualities such as perfection, omnipresence, omniscience, and all-powerfulness, qualities beyond mortal comprehension. When God is portrayed as incomprehensible, any question about God's nature or origin seems nonsensical. The alternative problem of the potential infinite regression of the question, "Who created the creator?" can be kept out of the spotlight if the symbolism of the creator blurs the distinction between comprehensible existing things and incomprehensible ones, by defining the creator as both humanlike, yet not human. For instance, the Yąnomamö Indians of Brazil and Venezuela (who have separate creation stories for men and women) "explain" the origin of men in a myth about "Spirit People" who predated and created men. As *spirit* entities, they

paradoxes
Statements that are true if and only if they are false but false if and only if they are true.

were not men and therefore could be used to account for the origin of men. Yet, the Spirit People were like men as well. In fact, they looked like men, lived in villages built in the same form as the circular *shabonos* of the Yąnomamö Indians, used bows and arrows, and cremated their dead just as the Yąnomamö do. Thus, although the story ultimately fails to explain the origin of all of the manlike qualities that they possess, the failure can be easily ignored because they are called "Spirit People" rather than "men."

Paradox and the Problem of Evil

The classical paradox that is built into the very structure of Western theology is the so-called Problem of Evil. In Western theology, the creator was defined as completely good, all-knowing, and all-powerful. Yet, the world the creator produced is far from perfect. How, for instance, can evil exist in a world created by a perfect and purely good creator? One would not expect a perfectly

---

 ## *"Moonblood," a Yąnomamö Origin Myth*

The Yąnomamö explain the origin of human beings by saying that they were created from the blood of Moon, one of the Yąnomamö deities. According to some Yąnomamö, this myth is specifically about the origin of men and accounts for the fierceness of males. The myth, summarized here, was been documented by anthropologists Timothy Asch and Napoleon Chagnon (1975).

According to the story of Moonblood, a group of Spirit People decided to invite some neighbors to a feast. Two brothers traveled through the forest to the village where these neighbors lived, but when they arrived, they found the shabono deserted. They decided to spend the night there before searching further. So they strung their hammocks in the shabono. During the night, the deity Moon descended from the sky and gleefully ate the cremated ashes of some of the children of the local Spirit People that were hanging from the rafters of the shabono.

The next day, the two brothers found the missing neighbors in the forest and encouraged them to take vengeance for Moon's inappropriate behavior. They returned to the shabono and found Moon still there, gloating over his deed. The younger of the two brothers, who was the more impulsive of the two, rushed to be the first to shoot at Moon; but as Moon ascended into the sky, his arrows fell short. Finally, Moon was almost out of sight when the older, more deliberate brother took careful aim. His arrow pierced Moon in his belly and blood gushed forth and fell upon the earth, where it was transformed into the first men. Where Moon's blood fell the thickest, men were so aggressive that they fought with one another until they became extinct. Where the blood fell less thickly, men were less aggressive and survived to modern times as the ancestors of the Yąnomamö and other peoples.

The Yąnomamö had high rates of warfare and killing when Chagnon (1992) studied them. He estimated that about a fourth of Yąnomamö men died violently. Under such circumstances, aggressiveness was a valued personality trait in men, and the Yąnomamö sometimes referred to themselves as the Fierce People. One function of the Moonblood myth was that it accounted for the high level of men's aggressiveness, by pointing out that their very creation was from an act of violence.

Like all creation stories, the Moonblood myth contains a paradox. Although it "explains" the origin of men, it does so by attributing their origin to supernatural beings who already embodied the characteristics that distinguish Yąnomamö men from nonhumans: their use of the Yąnomamö language when they communicate with one another in the myth, their use of Yąnomamö weapons and shabonos, their customs and values regarding the treatment of the dead, and, of course, their "fierceness" in responding to insults with violence.

good creator to create evil, and if God is all-knowing, he should have been able to think of a way to create a world that would fulfill his purposes without evil existing in it. As an all-powerful being, there should be no impediment to his actually having done so. Yet, evil exists.

Western theologians have grappled with the paradox of evil for centuries. The dilemma of the paradox seems resolvable only by acknowledging either that God is not good, not all-knowing, or not all-powerful. None of these alternatives has been palatable to most Western religions. Yet, although no logical solution exists, a variety of attempts have arisen for talking about the problem in a way that pushes the paradox off center stage. For instance, it may be said that evil is somehow beneficial to human beings in some as yet not understood way. This approach involves a new, though sometimes less noticed, paradox, since it defines "evil" as not "truly evil," yet acknowledging that why it is not cannot be comprehended. The Christian Science religion found a resolution to the problem that simply asserts that God, in fact, did not create evil, that evil actually does not exist, but that the belief in evil within God's perfect creation is merely an "illusion." Such a definition of evil as actually nonexistent despite its apparent existence is a satisfying enough approach that it has been adopted not just by one Christian denomination, but by mainstream Hinduism and Buddhism as well. Yet, though it is satisfying enough to adherents, the paradox remains on the logical level, since the approach fails to explain how the imperfection of "illusion" itself could have been created by a perfect, totally good, all-knowing, and omnipowerful creator. Now this fact of the existence of paradoxes within any religious theology should not be understood as a criticism of religion, since it is equally true of *any* complex philosophy, both religious and secular. It is simply a fact about the nature of human symbolic thought that paradoxes cannot be eliminated from any human ideology. For this reason, the existence of paradox has been embraced in some religious traditions as a statement about the beauty and wonder of the supernatural. For instance, within the Roman Catholic tradition, paradoxes are referred to in theological language as "mysteries, in the true sense of the word," meaning realities that can be known only through divine revelation, not by logic, and that are true yet ultimately incomprehensible to the human mind.

SACRED TEXTS

Sacred texts may be transmitted orally from one generation to the next when the stories that make them up are told frequently enough that they are learned by the members of each new generation who, in turn, recite them and pass them on. In societies that have a system of writing, sacred texts may be committed to writing in order to give them a life that transcends generations. In this section, we will compare the effects of these two approaches to the transmission of sacred texts.

Oral Tradition

Throughout most of human existence, religion has been perpetuated as part of an oral tradition. Since oral transmission of stories inevitably results in changes in the stories as they are told and retold over the generations, orally transmitted religious beliefs are flexible and easily adapted to new and changing circumstances. This can be seen quite well in the differences that have developed in the same myths told by different local groups of the same foraging societies. For instance, the variants in Shoshone Coyote stories described earlier in this chapter developed because when Shoshone groups migrated from place to place, storytellers made the geographical features of a story the local ones that the tellers and hearers knew instead of maintaining earlier locations that might no longer be meaningful to the audience. In contrast, written texts tie locations to fixed places.

Barre Toelken (1994) noticed how Navajo myths had evolved to accommodate the changing circumstances of Navajo life: "Several times over the past few years, I have had the opportunity to speak with *hataali* (literally, "singers") and hear their versions of the Emergence during appropriate parts of healing rituals. Many of them now include horses, cattle, sheep, and goats among those beings who came up from the lower worlds. When I asked about this apparent anachronism on one occasion, I was told by one very gifted singer, 'Of course I know that cows and sheep came here with the Spaniards. I myself never mentioned them in the ceremony until recently. But then I realized that these animals have become a part of us (as you know, we even call sheep 'the mothers of our children'), and I thought, 'how can it be a sacred story if it doesn't include all the important beings in our world?'" (p. 5).

Written Texts

Since the development of writing, a few religions have arisen whose religious beliefs are codified in written texts. Notable examples include Judaism, Christianity, Islam, Hinduism, and Buddhism. Those texts that have been formally recognized as the valid documents for establishing the doctrine and practice of a religion are referred to as the **canon** of that religion.

canon
The works that are considered religiously authoritative in a religion that has written sacred texts.

Hinduism has the oldest of written scriptures, the Vedas, including the Brahmanas and the Upanishads. The oldest of the Vedas, the Rig-Veda, was composed between 1300 and 1000 B.C. in northwest India. It consists of 1,028 hymns to the Hindu gods. The Brahmanas, composed between 1000 and 600 B.C., consist of ritual practices and philosophical discourses, and the 108 Upanishads, which were written between 600 and 300 B.C., are philosophical and metaphysical discussions of the nature of reality.

Most of the sacred texts of Judaism were written before 400 B.C. They make up the Hebrew Bible, which comprises the Torah (the Law—the first five books of the Hebrew Bible), the Nebhiim (the Prophets), the Kethubhiim (the Writings). After the destruction of the Jewish Temple in A.D. 70, Jewish sages carefully compiled and codified their understanding of the rituals and laws of Judaism and their meanings into a multivolume text known as the Talmud as a guide to a proper understanding of the Torah.

Christianity was born as a Jewish sect and regards a form of the Jewish canon as sacred texts along with a number of distinctively Christian sacred writings that were composed from about A.D. 50 through A.D. 120. These include the Gospels (which record the life of Jesus), Acts of the Apostles (which recounts some of the history of early Christianity), various Epistles (letters by

Figure 6.3
Sacred Religious Texts and Commentaries
Sacred religious texts usually include both scriptures that are regarded as having an inspired origin and later religious commentaries on those texts that are viewed as authoritative interpretations of those scriptures. These young monks in Mae Hong Son, Thailand, are reciting prayers from sacred texts.

early Christian writers) and the Revelation of John (an apocalyptic book containing prophesies about the end of the world).

The scripture of Islam, called the Qur'an, began to be written during the lifetime of Muhammad, between A.D. 610 and 632, and it was codified into its modern canonical form within two decades after his death. It consists of 114 revelations, called Suras, from God to Muhammad. They are grouped into two divisions, the Makkan, which consists of revelations given to Muhammad before his migration to Medina, and the Madinan, which came afterward. The Makkan revelations stress the unity and majesty of Allah (God), the prophetic calling of Muhammad, and the obligation of submission to the will of Allah. The Madinan revelations outline the rituals of Islam, moral and criminal laws, and guidelines for social, economic, and political life.

The scripture of Buddhism, the Tipitaka, or the Three Baskets, was written down during the first century B.C. It consists of discourses called the Sutra Pitaka, a code of monastic practices called the Vinaya Pitaka, and philosophical and doctrinal discussions called the Abhidharma Pitaka. These and other religions that base their teachings on ancient written texts have many characteristics in common because the authoritative source of their ideas and practices was fixed in writing and these writings were written in cultural milieus that differ from those of their contemporary followers and in languages that are no longer used in the native speech of those followers.

With the passage of time, sacred religious writings become less accessible to their readers because both language and culture change with time. Since language changes, contemporary readers may no longer understand the original meanings of the individual words or the idioms of the text. Since culture changes, the context in which the text was originally understood can be lost. When that happens, readers may adopt their own cultural background as the basis for interpreting the text. Both of these changes alter the way the text is understood. One adaptation to cultural and linguistic change in all of the major written religious traditions has been the development in each religion of secondary sacred writings that, although they are not regarded as canon scripture, are treated as authoritative commentaries on how the scriptures should be interpreted and on the rituals and ceremonies of the religious tradition.

Sacred Language

The language of written religious texts—the way in which the story is told as well as the ideas related—may become sanctified, especially with the passage of time, when changes in the spoken language leave the text sounding archaic. This is true even for the language of translated sacred texts. Thus, English speakers of some denominations that customarily use a centuries-old translation of scriptures may regard the style of that translation as more appropriate for a sacred text than the style of a more contemporary translation, and they may even adopt some of the older stylistic qualities of English when preaching or praying, even though English is not the original language of their scriptures and even though the earlier style that they think of as more appropriate for sacred settings did not develop until thousands of years after their scriptures were written.

Islam and the Sacredness of Original Language

There are many variants in how language may become sanctified for religious use. At one extreme, the original language of a written text may be held as sacred, so that worshipers for whom it is not a native language may be expected to learn to read the text in its original form and to use the original language in their devotions. Islam is such a case. It is Islamic belief that the revealed words of God that form the Qur'an were literally dictated to the prophet Muhammad and he merely repeated them, word for word, so that they might be written down. Since no perfect translation of those words into other languages is possible, the very thought of translating and thereby altering the words of God is frowned upon. Translations do exist, but they are not given the same stature as the Arabic text. Because of the imperfections of any translation, it is preferred that followers of Islam should learn to read the Qur'an in its original form in Arabic. Similarly, the standard prayers set forth in the Qur'an should be learned and recited in Arabic, regardless of what the native language of the worshiper may be. The universal use of Arabic as the liturgical language of Islam gives Islamic worship a degree of formal unity throughout the world that is rare in other religions.

Judaism and the Problem of Secular Uses of Sacred Language

The role of Hebrew in Judaism has parallels to that of Arabic in Islam. Thus, when it was proposed in the third century B.C. that the Hebrew scriptures be translated into Greek to make them accessible to the many Jews who lived in Greek-speaking parts of the world, the proposal was controversial even though by that time so many Jews lived outside Palestine that more spoke Greek than Hebrew. Although this translation spread rapidly throughout the world of Greek-speaking Jews, it was later rejected by the rabbis at Jamnia around A.D. 90. The consensus of the rabbis at Jamnia was that any translation would corrupt the meanings of the original text.

Hebrew is an interesting case of a sacred language, because following the destruction of Jerusalem and the dispersion of Jews throughout the rest of the world, Hebrew became extinct as a language of daily use—although it survived as a liturgical language in worship services. Thus, when the state of Israel was founded and Hebrew was established as the official language of the nation, the language was revived for ordinary use for the first time after two millennia. Returning Hebrew to nonreligious settings was naturally problematic, since the language itself had acquired a level of sanctity that was incompatible with some secular uses. Controversies arose concerning the use of Hebrew in daily life. Sacred texts are treated with reverence in Judaism and are not simply discarded when they become worn and no longer usable. Rather, they are ritually deposited in places that are specially reserved for such documents. Thus, it was understandably debated in Israel whether it would be sacrilegious for a merchant to wrap a fish he had sold in a newspaper page that was printed in Hebrew. Such issues have not all been resolved even today. For instance, in 1999 a leading Orthodox rabbi, Moshe Shaul Klein, ruled that although it would be inappropriate to erase the word "God" from a written text, it was acceptable to do so on a computer screen, since the "letters" of the word are made up of individual pixels rather than continuous strokes that form actual letters.

The Problem of Translating and Modernizing Texts

Because all languages change over generations, any written text eventually becomes increasingly difficult to read and understand. Since religions that have written sacred texts tend to also be among the larger religions and have followers who speak a variety of different languages, the original language of sacred texts is often a foreign language to many, sometimes even most, of such a religion's adherents. Thus, the question of updating and translating religious texts is one that these religions must address. Such changes can be problematic to believers, since changing the language of a sacred text may be viewed as a challenge to the authority of that text.

Problems in Translating Sacred Texts

Translation is not a simple and straightforward process, because different languages do not map one-to-one in their vocabularies and idioms, and any translator must choose from among a variety of different possible ways of modeling the original text in a new language. This means that any translation must introduce some kind of changes into the meanings of a text.

Barry Hoberman (1985) lists the four problems that are faced by translators of ancient sacred texts as the problems of canon, textual basis, interpretation, and style. The **problem of canon** is the determination of which original texts to include in a translation of scripture. This problem arises because different denominations within the same religious tradition may disagree on which original works are accepted as canon. For instance, Judaism canonized 39 books, all but two of which were written prior to about 430 B.C. Christian denominations generally accept these Jewish works as scripture and add 27 other books that make up the collection of distinctively Christian writings. However, Christian denominations disagree over a number of other works. Roman Catholicism considers as scriptural 10 other books from pre-Christian Judaism that were not adopted into the Jewish canon. These are referred to as "Deuterocanonical" books in the Catholic tradition. They are classified by most Protestant denominations as "Apocrypha," works that have historical or even inspirational value but that are not considered binding sources of doctrine: Tobit, Judith, Additions to the Book of Esther, Wisdom of Solomon, Ecclesiasticus (or the Wisdom of Jesus Son of Sirach), Baruch, The Letter of Jeremiah, Additions to the Greek Book

problem of canon The problem in determining which original texts to include in a translation of scripture.

of Daniel (The Prayer of Azariah and the Song of the Three Jews, Susanna, and Bel and the Dragon), 1 Maccabees, and 2 Maccabees. The Eastern and Slavonic Churches add four others to the Deuterocanonical collection: 1 Esdras (called 2 Esdras in the Slavonic Bible), Prayer of Manasseh, Psalm 151, and 3 Maccabees. The Slavonic Bible adds another, 3 Esdras. Thus, in a single religious tradition, there can be major disagreements about what actually constitutes the canon of scripture.

problem of textual basis
The problem of determining which particular version of the original text should be chosen as the one to be translated.

The **problem of textual basis** of a translation is the difficulty in determining which particular version of the original text should be chosen as the one to be translated. The problem of the textual basis for translating ancient sacred writings is that no original texts exist for any of the world's religions with ancient written texts. Thus translators must decide which among the various early copies is the most reliable wherever the early versions differ. This is not simply a matter of choosing one entire early document over others, since one may be closer to the original form than others in particular sentences but further from the original in others. Thus, choosing the textual basis for a translation involves choices about which early document to use for each place in which the early versions differ from one another. For instance, in the case of the Hebrew scriptures, there are two major complete texts. The older is the **Septuagint,** a translation of the Hebrew scriptures into Greek that was made in the second and third centuries B.C. The second is the **Masoretic text,** a version in Hebrew for which copies exist that date to the ninth century A.D. These two documents differ in numerous parts of the texts. The dilemma for translators is to determine which of the differences should be attributed to errors made during the translation of Hebrew into Greek and which arose within the Hebrew text itself as a result of the many generations of recopying older copies before the ninth century A.D. Which is more reliable in any given verse is not always possible to determine with certainty.

Septuagint
A translation of the Hebrew scriptures into Greek that was made in the second and third centuries B.C.

Masoretic text
A version of the Hebrew scriptures for which copies exist that date to the ninth century A.D.

problem of interpretation
The problem of how to determine the precise meaning of a word, a verse, or a passage in an ancient sacred text.

The **problem of interpretation** is the third problem in translating an ancient text—the problem of how to determine the precise meaning of a word, a verse, or a passage of an ancient sacred text. Hoberman explained this problem this way: "How do translators establish the precise meaning of a word, a verse, or a passage in the Bible? This is not the same thing as determining the best way to say it in English, although the two issues are closely intertwined and sometimes inseparable. A translator must first establish what the original text is saying before he decides how to express the meaning in the 'target' language, the language into which he is translating" (p. 50). Determining the original meaning is not always easy. After all, languages change through time both in the meanings of individual words and in grammar. To make matters worse, some words no longer have a modern counterpart. For instance, for biblical Hebrew, hundreds of words occur only once in the Hebrew Bible. This makes it impossible to compare different usages of the same word to get a better sense of its likely meaning. In such cases, it is sometimes possible to compare the various meanings that the equivalent roots have in modern or other ancient written Semitic languages to establish a likely meaning for the biblical Hebrew root. Nevertheless, as Hoberman puts it, "For hundreds of verses—in Psalms, Job, Isaiah, Hosea, and one or two other books—*any* English rendering is speculative or at best provisional" (p. 50).

The Problem of Vulgar Language
in Sacred Texts

Harvey Minkoff (1989) points out that translations of the Bible generally hide the fact that some of the original texts use a very colloquial Hebrew that was sometimes coarse, vulgar, or even obscene. The intent was clearly to emphasize a point by the use of shocking language. Yet, an accurate translation of such passages would be unacceptable to the modern reader whose sensibilities strongly contrast the sacred and the obscene, sometimes regarding even coarse or vulgar style as religiously taboo. To deal with the fact that too accurate a rendering would cause the translation to be unusable for worship, such passages are generally euphemized or sometimes even completely modified to avoid the offensive language.

Minkoff cites the Hebrew root *šgl* as a striking example. It is a very direct way of indicating sexual intercourse. It is not entirely certain how vulgar it was considered to be in ancient Hebrew society, but that it was seen that way is suggested by the fact that it occurs only four times in the Hebrew scriptures and elsewhere sexual intercourse was regularly euphemized by the use of the root *škb*, "to lie with." Minkoff explains that in each of the four places in which the root *šgl* occurs, it "appears as part of a threat or condemnation, and always with the clear intention of shocking the audience" (p. 26). The first occurrence is in Deuteronomy 28:28–30, "The Lord will strike you with madness, blindness and dismay. . . . You will be betrothed to a woman, but a stranger will *šgl* her." The second is Isaiah 13:16: "Their infants will be smashed on the ground, their houses ransacked, and their wives *šgl*[ed]." Jeremiah 3:1–2 also uses this root: "You have played the harlot with many lovers. . . . Where haven't you been *šgl*[ed]?" And so does Zechariah 14:2: "The city shall be captured, the houses ransacked, and the women *šgl*[ed]." Minkoff concludes: "Obviously, the authors of these lines deliberately chose strong language—if not actual vulgarity—in order to horrify, upset, and rattle their audience. Everything they love, the audience

is told, will be abused, debased, destroyed" (p. 26). The closest English term that has the equivalent shock value would too strongly violate contemporary religious taboos to be acceptable to English-speaking religious readers. Using Deuteronomy 28:30 as an example, Minkoff notes that only the New English Bible maintains some of the tone of the original: "The Hebrew word is gritty and down-to-earth. The original audience hearing these threats and condemnations gasped at the language and shuddered at the image" (p. 26). Yet, the New Jewish Publication Society Bible translates the relevant phrase as "another man shall enjoy her," the Jerusalem Bible gives it as "another man will have her," the King James Version renders it as "and another man shall lie with her," and the New English Bible carries the emphasis only so far as "but another man shall ravish her."

Other bodily processes are similarly euphemized in English translations. For instance, according to Minkoff,

A similar problem arises in 2 Kings 18:27 where the emissary of the Assyrians who are besieging Jerusalem calls to the Israelite soldiers on the city walls to surrender. All hope is lost, he tells them. Their allies have fallen, their gods have abandoned them, and they will soon be reduced to eating their own _____ and drinking their own _____.

"The Hebrew words in these two slots are quite explicit soldier talk: . . . [TRYHM and SYNYHS]. A footnote to this passage in the Jerusalem Bible calls our attention to the "graphic description of the straits to which the beleaguered city is reduced." Yet, JB's translation, like other modern English versions, sanitizes the horror by having the angry Assyrian soldier threaten to make his enemies "eat their own dung and drink their own urine." (p. 26)

In such cases, modern translators are faced by an unresolvable dilemma: Being true to the language of the sacred text will be offensive to the religious reader, but showing respect for the readers' religious values paradoxically requires distorting the language of the very text that they venerate.

problem of style
The problem of determining how modern or archaic, how colloquial or formal, or how literal or idiomatic a translation should be.

The **problem of style** of a translation, determining how modern or archaic, how colloquial or formal, or how literal or idiomatic the translation is, is another source of problems. Style is a particularly thorny problem in the case of religious texts, since simply reflecting the style of the original documents may result in a translation that does not match the religious sensibilities of contemporary readers. For instance, even though the archaic and formal style of the King James Version, a translation done in 1611, is no longer easily read and understood by modern readers, it has been in use for so long that readers in some Christian denominations have come to view its use of antiquated words and its formal, poetic style as indicative of the sacredness of scripture. Even though most of the New Testament was written in the common tongue of ordinary Greek speakers rather than in formal Greek style, a translation into English that uses an equivalent colloquial English can grate on the ears of some readers as sounding too unpolished to seem "sacred." Thus, translators are constantly confronted by trade-offs between faithfully reproducing the style of the original text and selecting a style that will feel comfortable to readers of the target language.

The box titled "The Problem of Vulgar Language in Sacred Texts" illustrates how differences in the values of the culture from which an ancient religious text comes and the values of a contemporary culture can create difficulties in translating the ancient text for religious use.

Another issue concerning style is the matter of the degree to which a translation should maintain the meanings of individual words or phrases versus capturing the sense of entire sentences. A translation that emphasizes the former is sometimes called a **literal** (or **formal equivalence**) **translation.** One that sacrifices the use of equivalent words for the sake of expressing the meanings conveyed by complete sentences and paragraphs is referred to as a **idiomatic** (or **dynamic equivalence**) **translation.** Both approaches have benefits as well as drawbacks.

literal (or formal equivalence) translations
Renderings of a text from one language to another that emphasize the use of the words or phrases that are most equivalent to those of the original text.

idiomatic (or dynamic equivalence) translation
A rendering of a text from one language to another that sacrifices the use of equivalent words or phrases for the sake of expressing the meanings conveyed by complete sentences and paragraphs.

A literal translation has the virtue of permitting the reader to evaluate theological implications that may turn on the original writer's choice of a single word. For instance, rendering Isaiah 7:14b as "Look, the *virgin* [Hebrew, *almah*] is with child and shall bear a son" has potentially important theological significance for Christians, but differs from the more literal rendering "a *young woman* is with child." However, as useful as a literal translation may be for clarifying specific meanings such as this, an extremely literal translation can be difficult to comprehend, since the syntax and idiom of the target language may be quite different from those of the original language. Consider for instance the following word-by-word translation of Genesis 1:20: "And saying is God, 'Roaming is the water with the roaming, living soul, and the flyer is flying over the earth on the face of the atmosphere of the heavens'" (Gen. 1:20, Concordant Version). This is hardly recognizable as the same verse of the New International Version, a dynamic-equivalent translation that focuses more on the ideas conveyed in the original than on reproducing the individual words: "And God said, 'Let the waters teem with living creatures, and let birds fly above the earth across the expanse of the sky.'"

A dynamic equivalence translation has the virtue of readability in the target language, since it conforms to the syntax and idiom the reader is used to. Its

Saint Anselm formulated a philosophical proof of the existence of God that is known as the "ontological proof." Reduced to its simplest form, Anselm began by defining God as "the most perfect conceivable being" or, in his own words, "that than which no greater can be thought." He then argued that since whatever exists in reality is more perfect than whatever does not, God must exist in reality. After all, if God did not exist in reality, then it would be possible to conceive of a more perfect being—one with all the attributes of the nonexistent God but who also exists. The merits of this argument have been debated down the centuries, and although it has been rejected by many, it has impressed enough European philosophers that one still finds it in texts on the philosophy of religion.

However, Anselm's "proof" cannot be readily made and does not sound equally impressive in every language. For instance, I noticed that it was not initially possible to translate the argument directly into the Navajo language, which originally had no word that was equivalent to the Judeo-Christian word *God* as referring to an omniscient, omnipresent, omnipotent, and totally good Creator of all things. Navajo religion was polytheistic, with many individual deities, each of whom specialized in different areas of responsibility and power. There is, for instance, a Navajo god of language, but no traditional Supreme Being.

Of course, this limitation of traditional Navajo is not an absolute impediment to translation. As is true of all languages, Navajo is perfectly capable of adapting itself to express new and innovative ideas. In fact, the English word *god* was borrowed into Navajo after contact with Christian missionaries. In contemporary Navajo, the word for the Christian Supreme Creator is spelled *gad,* which reflects the fact that it is pronounced more or less like the word sounds in spoken English. This change has made it possible to do a direct translation of St. Anselm's argument into Navajo today. Unfortunately, there is another complication. Before the English word *god* was borrowed into Navajo, there was already a Navajo word that sounded

the same. So *gad* not only means "the Christian deity," but also has its original meaning of "juniper tree." So, although it is possible to give a literal rendition of Anselm's argument in Navajo today, it is more likely to elicit a laugh than a response that it seems intuitively true. After all, even if defining a "juniper tree" as "the most perfect conceivable being" does prove that the juniper tree must really exist, to really be a juniper tree is not quite what St. Anselm had in mind!

What the Navajo story really illustrates is that there is a difference between *asserting* the existence of a thing and the necessity of its actually existing. For instance, we might substitute "unicorn" for "juniper tree" in the same argument and conclude that we must conceive of a unicorn as an existing animal if we define it as, say, "the most perfect conceivable equine." But defining a unicorn in this way would not cause a unicorn to exist. Thus, Anselm's argument merely proves that the *concept* of "God" must include belief in his existence if he is also believed to be that which is the "greatest conceivable." In other words, the idea that God does not exist is incompatible with the idea that God is "the most perfect conceivable being." Since perfection entails existence, *defining* the word "God" as perfect includes an assertion of "existence in reality" as part of the definition. But, as the Navajo speaker would readily note, *defining* a *gad* (meaning "juniper tree") as "the most perfect conceivable being" does not make it one. It is still just a tree, knotholes and all. And it is not our calling it "perfect" that makes it exist. Similarly, *defining* the word *gad* (meaning "God") as "the most perfect conceivable being" does not force such a being to exist in reality either. Our definition of the *concept* of God may not correspond to anything that really exists, even if the definition, by including "most perfect Being" as one of its elements, forces the definition to imply "existing Being" as another of its elements. The bottom line is that Anselm—and the many who have been impressed by his argument—confused language and reality.

At a time when drugs, crime, and street violence was having a devastating impact on Black youth in the United States, the African American Family Press began to publish the *Black Bible Chronicles*, a paraphrase of the Bible in Black Vernacular English. The express purpose, according to the Andrew Young (1993), former ambassador to the United Nations, congressman, and mayor of Atlanta, was the "attempt to put the most important message of life into the language of the streets" (p. v) so that the Bible would be more accessible and interesting to young people. In doing so, the African American Family Press was following the same philosophy that guided Martin Luther when he translated the Bible into the contemporary language of ordinary German speakers of his day.

The following excerpt gives a sense of how dialect differences can powerfully influence the wording of a sacred text:

Now when the Almighty was first down with his program, He made the heavens and the earth. The earth was a fashion misfit, being so uncool and dark, but the Spirit of the Almighty came down real tough, so that He simply said, "Lighten up!" And that light was right on time. And the Almighty liked what he saw and let the light hang out a while before it was dark again. He laid out a name for the light, calling it "day" time and the dark He called "night" time so that all around it made up the first day.

Compare these parallel texts and consider how much less effectively the poetic style of the 17th-century aristocratic dialect of the King James translation might communicate to speakers of late-20th-century Black Vernacular English:

King James Version: Now the serpent was more subtle than any beast of the field which the LORD God had made. And he said unto the woman, Yea, hath God said to eat of all the trees of the garden? And the woman said unto the serpent, We may eat of the fruit of the trees of the garden. But of the fruit of the tree which is in midst of the garden, God hath said, Ye shall not eat of it, neither shall ye touch it, lest ye die.

Black Vernacular English Version: Now the serpent was one bad dude, one of the baddest of all the animals the Almighty had made. And the serpent spoke to the sister and asked, "You mean the Almighty told you not to eat of all these trees in the garden?" And the sister told him, "Yeah, snake, I can eat of these trees, just not the tree of knowledge or the Almighty said I'd be knocked off."

drawback is a loss of a certain degree of specific information, material conveyed by particular words or phrases in the original that are not replicated in the target language. For the sake of readability and general comprehension, most translations of religious texts generally lean in the direction of dynamic equivalence, emphasizing the sense rather than the exact form of the original text.

The box titled "Translation and the Ontological Argument: The Navajo Example" illustrates how the characteristics of language can influence how convincing a logical argument sounds. In this example, we examine a particular problem that occurs when Saint Anselm's ontological argument for the existence of God is translated into the Navajo language.

Modernizing the Language of Sacred Texts

Since languages change over the generations, any translation of sacred texts becomes gradually less accessible to readers with the passage of time. For instance, the King James Version of the Bible was translated into English in 1611. In nearly 400 years, English has changed considerably in vocabulary and idiom, so that some verses of the King James are no longer understandable to most readers. Incense was called *confection* (Exodus 30:35) by the King James translators. An oak tree was a *champaign*. A *churl* (Isaiah 32:7) was a villain. To *prevent*

(1 Thes. 4:15) did not mean to stop something from happening but "to come before." When the kings of Israel, Judah, and Edom "fetched a compass" (2 Kings 3:9) it meant that they made a roundabout trip, and "he who now letteth will let" (2 Thes 2:7) would read "he who now restrains it is removed" in contemporary English.

Because of changes in language, translations of sacred texts must occasionally be updated if they are not to become gradually more obscure. Yet, the archaic quality of an older translation may have come to imbue it with an aura of venerableness that makes it seem more sacred than a contemporary translation, so the idea of updating the language of a sacred text may be controversial. The box titled "The Black Vernacular English Bible" illustrates how translations may differ in dialect and in stylistic qualities. Undertaken for the purpose of making the Bible more accessible to Black youth, the Black Vernacular English Bible employs the dialect they actually speak rather than the aristocratic dialect of England in the early 1600s or the dialect preferred today in university English literature classes.

LANGUAGE AND RELIGIOUS IDEOLOGY

Language may have an impact on religious ideology in three important ways. First, language is the vehicle by which a religious ideology is communicated and transmitted from one generation to the next. During this transmission, the beliefs and values of an ideology may undergo change. Second, the structure of a language may influence how intuitively true a belief may seem to its speakers and, therefore, the likelihood of a particular idea's being easily accepted. Third, since language itself changes through time, people may come to understand religious ideas that are expressed in older, traditional language in new and different ways.

Mythology as a "Disease of Language"

Friedrich Max Müller (1870) theorized that religious mythology arose as a kind of "disease of language" that developed from an inability of early humans to distinguish between the expression of concrete and abstract ideas. Descriptions of nature were phrased in "mythopoetic" language. For instance, instead of saying "It is night," speakers ancestral to the Greeks of classic times might have said, "The moon (silene) has kissed the setting sun (endymion) into sleep." With the passage of generations, such a mythopoetic description of nighttime might have come to be taken literally instead of mythopoetically, and people would misunderstand the terms *silene* and *endymion* as personal names of anthropomorphized divine beings rather than as generic terms for the moon and the setting sun, hearing the statement as part of a religious myth, "Seline has kissed Endymion into sleep." Müller's attempts to explain the rise of mythology was naive and overdrawn, since he incorrectly assumed that all mythology began with speakers who were ancestral to the Indo-European languages and that all early humans spoke only in such mythopoetic ways to talk about the world around them. Yet, the kernel idea, that descriptive terms may sometimes come to be understood anthropomorphically is certainly not without some merit. This kind of "mistake" need not be limited to changes in meaning that occur over generations, as Müller suggested, but can certainly be illustrated by the common psychology of confusing similarity with identity that is embodied in Frazer's Law of Similarity. For instance, the names of mythological characters often have ordinary meanings as generic terms: Daphne, for example, also means *laurel* in Greek, and Psyche also means *air* or *breath*. The Anglo-Saxon word for spring was oestre and the goddess of spring, Oestre, was, by the principle of similarity, the patroness of the fertility heralded by the coming of spring. The same principle easily explains why the hare, a natural symbol of fertility, was offered to her on the vernal equinox, March 21, when the longer days of spring begin to return. It is a simple step to link her name with the similar sounding word for *east*, the direction of the dawn, over which she also ruled. Such symbolic similarities can develop over a short time as well as a long one, although they can certainly also be elaborated as myths are recounted over the passage of generations, as when the rabbit became a substitute for Oestre's hare and was combined with the egg, another symbol of fertility, to form the symbolism of the modern Christian Easter, which is celebrated about the same time of year when hares were sacrificed to Oestre.

Linguistic Relativity and Religion

Müller was not the only one interested in linguistic influences on classical religious beliefs. Anthropologists Edward Sapir (1931) and Benjamin Lee Whorf (1956a,b) noticed that sometimes the ways in which we talk about reality lead us to unwarranted conclusions about it. They formulated the concept of **linguistic relativity,** the idea that the structure of a language influences its speakers' understanding of reality or, as Sapir put it, language "not only refers to experience largely acquired without its help but actually defines experience for us by reason of its formal completeness and because of our unconscious projection of its implicit expectations into the field of experience" (1931, p. 578). Alfred Korzybski (1933) expressed the idea that languages may mislead their users with the admonition to remember that "the map is not the territory." The box titled "Creation Itself Demands a Creator" in chapter 1 illustrates how the characteristics of language can be confused with facts about external reality.

linguistic relativity
The idea that the structure of a language influences its speakers' understanding of reality.

Language Change and Religious Meaning

We have seen that language change can make traditional language incomprehensible to later generations. In other cases, the change in the meanings of a religious concept can be transparent because although the denotations of the words of a common religious statement have changed, the statement remains meaningful, but with a new and different meaning than it originally had. In such a case, later generations may be unaware that their understanding of a religious text or verbal formula is quite different from that of their forebears. For instance, in the King James translation of 2 Thessalonians 5:22, "Abstain from all appearance of evil," the word *appearance* was intended to signify "to come into view." Thus, the admonition meant "Avoid evil when it first appears." To

21st-century readers, however, the English sentence still seems quite meaning-ful, but they are likely to understand the word *appearance* to mean "resem-blance" or "outward semblance of" and to mistake the meaning of the sentence as "Don't even behave in a way that might appear evil."

Another such shift in meaning is found in 2 Thessalonians 2:7, "For the mystery of iniquity doth already work: only he who now letteth will let, until he be taken out of the way," where "let" meant "to restrain or prevent" in the 1600s but now means to permit. A more contemporary rendering is found in the New Revised Standard Version: "For the mystery of lawlessness is already at work, but only until the one who now restrains it is removed." Or when the King James translators chose "peculiar" to describe the Hebrew people (in Deuteron-omy 14:2), the word meant "private property [of God]," while the modern reader would more likely think that such verses indicated that they were in some way strange. Various verses (such as Matthew 13:21; Mark 6:25; and Luke 21:9) in which the King James English used the phrase "by and by" are likely to be misunderstood today as meaning "eventually," whereas to the reader in the 1600s, the phrase had nearly the opposite meaning of "immediately."

Chapter Summary

1. Religious ideologies depend on the existence of language, through which they are expressed and communicated from one generation to the next. Those meanings are communicated with both signs and symbols. Religious beliefs may be passed on orally or, in some cases, through religious texts as well. Religious ideologies are important because they influence the way we perceive the world.
2. Religious beliefs, like those of any ideology, arise from a process of inter-preting experiences. Belief is never merely a knowledge of the facts that we experience, but also a product of how we interpret those experiences.
3. All religious ideologies include a mix of literal and figurative interpreta-tions. Literal interpretations are those that the interpreter takes to be the "face value" or nonmetaphorical meaning of an experience or religious text. A figurative interpretation is one that takes the meaning of a text to be metaphorical rather than literal.
4. Interpretations of religious texts may be either ethnocentric or culturally relativistic. Ethnocentric interpretations assume that the cultural back-ground of the interpreter is the appropriate frame of reference for under-standing the text. A culturally relativistic interpretation attempts to under-stand a text in the context of the culture in which it was created.
5. Religious diversity exists within each religious tradition as well as among different traditions. In religions with oral religious traditions, geographi-cal differences in religious beliefs, values, and traditions arise as they are passed from one generation to the next. Adaptation of religious ideologies to local settings and conditions is an important part of this process of change. In religions that rely on sacred written texts, internal religious di-versity is both geographical and hierarchical.
6. The language of liturgical orders is a special case of the more general category of the ritual language of a culture. Ritual language is a restricted linguistic

code, one that is particularly effective at building rapport, establishing the place of individuals within a group's hierarchy, and coordinating group interaction.

7. Religious language includes linguistic taboos, things that are not to be said, as well as standard ways of saying things.

8. Ritual language includes prayer, song and chant, exhortation, reciting the code, and glossolalia.

9. As a system of symbols, every religious ideology includes paradoxes, assertions about reality that are true only if they are false.

10. Religious texts may be oral or written. Written religious texts may come to be viewed as sacred and their official interpretation perceived as the standard against which orthodoxy of belief and practice is to be measured.

11. Since language changes, the original language of sacred religious texts will eventually become inaccessible to contemporary readers. Translating ancient religious texts includes problems of determining what works are to be considered *canon,* choosing which early *text* to use from the various early versions that may exist, and deciding how best to *interpret* the text and which *style* the translation should adopt.

Recommended Readings

1. Bernstein, Basil. 1973. "A Socio-Linguistic Approach to Socialization." In *Directions in Socio-Linguistics,* ed. John Gumperz and Dell Hymes. New York: Vintage Books. (Originally published in *Penguin Survey of the Social Sciences,* ed. J Gould, London: Penguin.). Bernstein's groundbreaking analysis of the use of restricted codes.

2. Carroll, J. B., ed. 1956. *Language, Thought and Reality: Selected Writings of Benjamin Lee Whorf.* Cambridge, MA: MIT Press. Though Whorf did not focus specifically on the role of language in religious settings, his arguments about the influence of language on thought provide some important insights that are applicable to religious settings as well.

3. Crapanzano, Vincent. 2000. *Serving the Word: Literalism in America from the Pulpit to the Bench.* New York: New Press. An exceptional example of ethnographic work on textual literalism and religious fundamentalism.

4. Douglas, Mary. 1973. *Natural Symbols.* New York: Random House. An important discussion of the role of natural symbols in human ideologies.

5. Finkelstein, Israel, & Neil Asher Silberman. 2001. *The Bible Unearthed: Archaeology's New Vision of Ancient Israel and the Origin of Its Sacred Texts.* New York: The Free Press. An up-to-date look at what archaeology has revealed about the Hebrew Bible.

6. Müller, Friedrich Max. 1856. "Comparative Mythology." *Oxford Essays,* Vol. 2. London: W. Parker, pp. 1–87. Müller's classic on language and religion.

7. Ong, Walter. 1982. *Orality and Literacy: The Technologizing of the Word.* London: Routledge. Discusses the characteristics of and differences between oral cultures and literate cultures.

8. Whorf, Benjamin Lee. 1956. "The Relation of Habitual Thought and Behavior to Language." In *Language, Thought and Reality: Selected Writings of Benjamin Lee Whorf,* ed. J. B. Carroll. Cambridge, MA: MIT Press, pp. 134–59.

Recommended Websites

1. *http://www.iconsoftec.com/gita/*
   The text of the Hindu scripture, the Bhagvat Gita.
2. *http://www.earlham.edu/~seidti/iam/interp_mss.html*
   A site devoted to the scholarly study of the ancient manuscripts of Christian scriptures.
3. *http://journalofbiblicalstudies.org/Links/methodology.htm*
   A site on the methodologies of exegesis and text criticism.
4. *http://www.avesta.org/avesta.html*
   This site provides access to the Zoroastrian scriptures and commentaries.
5. *http://www.wam.umd.edu/~stwright/rel/index.html*
   Links to the scriptures of a variety of religious traditions.

Study Questions

1. How did the Hebrew scriptures evolve?
2. How does figurativism differ from literalism?
3. How may one's own culture or a knowledge of the culture in which a text originated influence one's understanding of its meaning?
4. In what ways does being based on an oral tradition foster change and the development of diversity within a religious tradition?
5. Explain why the unity of a religion does not require that it be homogeneous in belief or practice.
6. What is meant when a taboo is called an "anti-ritual"?
7. How does the distinction between elaborated and restricted codes illuminate the nature of language in religious settings?
8. How does paradox function in religion?
9. Explain what is meant by the "Problem of Evil."
10. What dilemmas can be created when a religious text is translated into fully modern language?

CHAPTER 7

Religious Ritual

CHAPTER OUTLINE

CHAPTER OBJECTIVES

When you finish this chapter, you will be able to

1. Explain how rituals express meaning.
2. Explain how religious rituals help perpetuate the stability of society.

3. Recognize the multivocality in the meaningfulness of religious rituals.
4. List the various categories of ritual.
5. Explain the differences between magical and petitionary rituals.
6. Explain the psychological principles involved in magic.
7. Describe the characteristics of ritual that imbue it with a quality of sacredness.
8. Define *ultimate sacred postulates* and explain their function in religion and the role they play in liturgies.
9. Define *communitas* and explain its relationship with ritual.
10. Explain symbolism of the threefold structure that many rituals have.
11. Define *rite of passage* and explain its psychological and social functions.

Rituals are central to religious practice. They are, for instance, the primary means for attempting to mobilize supernatural power for the benefit of human beings. Rituals also communicate religious ideas in ways that cannot be done with language alone. Participation in ritual is itself an act of commitment to the ideas and values that the ritual embodies. In the case study "Shinto Belief and Ritual," we examine the importance of ritual in a Japanese religion.

CASE STUDY ————————————————————————

Shinto Belief and Ritual

Shinto is the religious system that flourished in Japan before the introduction of Buddhism. Shinto is described as kami-no-hichi, *"the way of the spirits." In the worldview of Shinto, kami inhabit the world in all its facets. Kami are found in natural features of the environment, animals, and plants. Recognizing their presence inspires awe and aesthetic wonder. Thus, Shinto places a great emphasis on an appreciation of nature, and its shrines are often associated with awe-inspiring places such as the tops of mountains.*

In Shinto mythology, three original spirits, or kami, *created other male and female kami. One pair, Izanagi and Izanami, were crossing the bridge of heaven when the male, Izanagi, thrust his spear into the ocean below. When he pulled his spear out of the water, the drops that fell from its tip were transformed into the islands of Japan. Izanagi and Izanami descended to the islands where they gave birth to other kami. Their children became the samurai, or warrior class, of Japan. Izanagi created the moon god Tsukiyomi-no-Mikoto, and the sun goddess Amaterasu. Amaterasu's grandson Ninigi became the first ruler of Japan.*

Shinto emphasizes the importance of rules of piety that are intended to insure ritual purity. Its rituals help human beings achieve oneness with the kami of nature. Spirits control the world, and they can be influenced by rituals.

Local Shinto shrines sponsor festivals, or matsuri, *that emphasize the importance of the relationship between the local human community and the kami of the local area. Seasonal matsuri are widely celebrated throughout Japan to express devotion and service to the kami and to request such things as bounty in the coming agricultural season. Matsuri have four important parts: (1) purification (*harai*), (2) offerings (*shinsen*), (3) litany (*norito*), and (4) a communal feast (*naorai*).*

*It is particularly important that priests who preside over matsuri are ritually pure and thereby fit for their duties. Ritual purity is insured by the performance of rituals that include acts such as washing. The importance of rituals for the purification of ritual uncleanness (*kegare*) is one reason Shinto is said to be a religion that centers not on moral rules but on ritual purity.*

During a festival, the kami and ancestral spirits descend from heaven to reside temporarily among the living on earth. This may be symbolized by the removal of a portable shrine, or mikoshi, from its usual sacred place, a Shinto shrine, and its transport on a palaquin into the secular community. This intrusion of the sacred into the secular space sanctifies the community during the festival. This insertion of the sacred into the community has a socially disruptive effect, the normal social order being abandoned for the duration of the festival. The realm of the kami is, in contrast to the ideally ordered nature of Japanese social life, a chaotic one. The men who carry the portable shrine into the community may be drunk on sake—appropriate for those "possessed" by the sacred—and the shrine may careen through the streets in a way that illustrates the chaos of the sacred realm.

After a shrine has arrived at its temporary place of housing in a community, offerings are made there for the kami and ancestral spirits. The offerings include prayers, special foods, and rice wine. A traditional litany is recited while the shrine is found within the community. During this period, oracles may be received that pertain to the welfare of the community, and other spiritual gifts may be manifest as evidence of the presence of the spirits. A community feast celebrates the communion of the families of the community with their ancestors and with the higher kami of the shrine. After this, a concluding ceremony sends the spirits back to their residing place in the other world and the shrine is returned to its sacred sanctuary.

An important purpose of matsuri is to renew the spiritual power (ke) of its participants, since one's spiritual energy is depleted by the natural course of participation in secular life. Ke is the energy necessary for life and growth. As one's ke is depleted, one becomes kegare, or unclean. This state of uncleanness is eliminated by participating in matsuri when communion with ancestral spirits and the greater kami, or gods, can restore one's ke.

RELIGIOUS RITUAL AND THE EXPRESSION OF MEANING

How do we know that people are "religious"? One basis for this characterization is that they espouse a set of religious beliefs. Further evidence of people's religious commitment is their participation in religious behavior. We may ask, therefore, "What do people *do* when they are being religious?" Although people may show their religious commitment in many ways, participation in rituals is part of every religion.

Rituals are not unique to religion, but they *are* the quintessential religious behavior. Rituals are the living essence of religion, religion in action. As anthropologist Anthony Wallace (1966b) has noted, rituals are central to religion in that "the goals of religion are to be achieved by performing rituals" (p. 104).

Religious Ritual

religious ritual Behavior that follows the same sequence of actions on repeated occasions, with care taken to achieve accuracy of performance; the ritual behavior is believed to mobilize supernatural powers to accomplish human ends.

Religious ritual may be defined as behavior that follows the same sequence of actions on repeated occasions, with care taken to achieve accuracy of performance. It differs from nonreligious ritual in the belief that it works to mobilize supernatural powers to accomplish human ends. Religious ritual is performed carefully with respect for its traditional form. As Wallace (1966b) put it, ritual is "ideally, a system of perfect order and any deviation from this order is a mistake" (p. 233). Typically, participants in rituals experience special feelings that are not associated with the same or similar behavior in nonreligious settings. For instance, bread and wine might be consumed at a meal without special feelings, but when eaten and drunk by Christians in the sacrament of the Lord's Supper, they may inspire strong feelings associated with the nearness of God's Spirit.

As can any human behavior, rituals typically express meanings. In fact, Raymond Firth (1973) referred to rituals as behaviors that communicate "in a formal way" ideas that are "not to be said in ordinary language or informal behavior" (p. 176). In ordinary language, speakers are generally quite aware of the meanings they intend to convey, but the meanings of rituals may be implicitly present in such a way that their participants need not be fully conscious of them. In contrast, the information content of ritual is quite low. Information, in its technical sense, is the knowledge transferred by a message. In ritual, very little knowledge is transferred, since the predictability of ritual performance makes it unlikely that participants will be able to acquire information that they did not already have access to. That is, participants are likely to already know the ideas and values that are symbolized by their ritual. As Wallace (1966b) explained this, *"a sequence of meaningful signals whose order is fixed,* so that the receiver always knows what signal will follow the preceding one, *will have no information value because there is no uncertainty to be reduced* by the outcome of each successive event" (p. 236). In this sense, Wallace declared that "Ritual may, perhaps, most succinctly be classified as communication without information" (p. 236).

However, information is not the only form of meaning. Most of the meaningfulness of ritual lies in the sense of order it creates—both in the sanctity with which it infuses the shared beliefs and values it embodies and in the order it establishes among the participants. This *sharedness* is central to ritual's meaningfulness. The meanings of ritual are not private messages between two individuals. Rather, these meanings embody important information about the ideological and social unity of the group; participation in rituals is an act that reaffirms this unity to those who already share the meanings. As Rappaport put it, "the meaning of ritual's informationlessness is certainty" (1999, p. 285).

Figure 7.1
A Monk Turning a Prayer Wheel
Ritual is the quintessential example of religious behavior. The setting sun spotlights a monk in a shaft of orange light as he turns a prayer wheel in the Labrang Monastery, China.

Ritual as Communication

Roy Rappaport (1999) has examined the role of ritual, including both ritual language and the use of nonlanguage symbols in ritual, in reducing ambiguity. He points out that participation in rituals publicly communicates acceptance of the community morality symbolized by a ritual. Even if a participant is privately not truly committed to the rules and values expressed in the ritual, the act of public acceptance obligates him or her to abide by them. The affirmation that is communicated is clear and unambiguous in a way that simple statements in words are not. Participation in ritual does more than express solidarity with the community in which it is performed; the act itself *is* a form of solidarity. Thus, simply saying "I support my religion" reveals nothing about whether the support is strong or moderate. Neither does it reveal the form that the support takes—whether it includes monetary donations, attendance at the religion's services, living its principles, or applying its values in daily life. The support referred to might be one or all of these or something else in the mind of the speaker. But actual participation in the rituals of the religion is, itself, an unambiguous act of support for the values symbolized by those rituals.

life-crisis rites
Rituals that ceremonialize the transitions of status that all members of a community pass through.

Some rituals clearly and unambiguously communicate changes in the status of participants. **Life-crisis rites,** rituals that ceremonialize the transitions in status that all members of a community normally pass through, exemplify this facet of ritual symbolism. Life-crisis rites are commonly celebrated shortly after birth, when a child is named and introduced to its community as a new member of the group; at puberty, when a child is proclaimed to be an adult; at marriage, when single persons become spouses; and at death, when the deceased are formally ushered out of the human group into a new role in the afterlife. These celebrations, especially at birth, puberty, and death, are frequently religious rituals. Indeed, the status change occurs as a result of participation in the ritual. Therefore, there is no ambiguity about whether the new status has been acquired. For instance, once a Jewish boy has celebrated a bar mitzvah in which he has spoken the traditional words, "Today, I am a man," there is no further question about his right to participate in other activities, such as being counted in a *minyan,* a Jewish prayer quorum that requires a minimum of at least 10 adults for the prayers of some liturgies.

Although rituals unambiguously communicate meanings concerning the status of participants, ritual symbols that refer to the shared beliefs and values of the group are typically *multivocalic* (see chapter 1); that is, they each communicate a variety of different, but equally appropriate religious meanings. For instance, Christian baptism performed in a denomination that requires complete immersion of the candidate in water reenacts the story of Jesus' baptism in the Jordan River. It also suggests purification or "washing away sin." The immersion might also be viewed as mimicking death, burial, and resurrection. No one of these meanings is more correct than others. Rather, they are all equally valid meanings of the ceremony. This particular kind of ambiguity in the ideological meanings of rituals is not unique to religious rituals, but is a general characteristic of the symbolism of all parts of expressive culture. The meanings of nonreligious art and literature can often be read on several different levels. For instance, on one level Herman Melville's *Moby Dick* is a yarn about an adventure

Folklorist Barre Toelken (1987) recounts his work among the Navajo and how he came to appreciate the different levels of meaning that could be found within religious stories told by the Navajo. Language is central to the Navajo religion and worldview: "The Navajos believe that language does not merely describe reality; it creates it. The telling of stories and the singing and narrating of rituals are ways of actually creating the world in which the Navajo live" (1987, p. 390). Toelken came to recognize that Navajo Coyote stories, tales about the Navajo Trickster deity who represents lack of impulse control, function on four levels.

On the first level, Coyote stories are told for entertainment. This is the level of "the surface story with all its descriptions of Coyote's selfish, humorous—and occasionally heroic—behavior" (1987; p. 390). Toelken comments on the entertainment role of Coyote stories: "On a typical evening, we would hear two or three such stories, and always the narration was accompanied by a lively discussion about the meaning and application. Under the impression that these were only 'children's stories,' I was struck by how 'adult' they sounded. The Navajo apparently brought up their children on meatier narratives than those I heard when I was young (Coyote is described as selfish, oversexed, gluttonous, foolish, self-destructive, as well as unpredictable and potentially dangerous to others). What eventually captured my intense interest, and what led to my later study of these stories, was the slowly dawning realization that they were more complex than 'mere' children's stories, that they were told to and for everyone present, and that they could only be told in the winter without serious complications. Not only were the Navajos careful to tell the stories only in the winter but they believed that the stories must be told, else their children would grow up in a meaningless world" (1996, pp. 2–3).

Coyote stories are also told as moral homilies, in which Coyote serves as the archetypical bad example of un-Navajolike behavior. The Navajo typically do not resort to corporal punishment when children's behavior violates the norms of Navajo life. Rather, stories about Coyote doing the same

kinds of things are told, and the laughter that accompanies descriptions of Coyote behaving in ways that are unacceptable in Navajo culture teaches children vicariously to recognize the shame they would feel were they laughed at for the same behavior. Toelken explains, "The Navajos, who seldom punish children physically or correct their behavior with direct criticism, often use laughter as a corrective. I noticed early on that in the Coyote stories, the very actions which brought the most laughter from the audience were those which were clearly morally reprehensible, those which—if performed by living persons—would provoke the greatest disapproval and anxiety among family and friends" (p. 3).

Coyote stories function on a third level, that of healing—"the conscious application of the story and its imagery to specific ailments and their treatments during healing rituals" (1987, p. 391). According to Toelken:

Health—either its maintenance or its reestablishment—is the main reason for performing any Navajo ritual; in fact, it can be fairly said that most rituals (or "sings") do not take place unless there is a patient with an illness (or potential illness) which can be defined so well that a particular ceremony is found to be appropriate and potentially efficacious. . . .

The healing ceremony, once chosen (or determined by a diagnostician who may use anything from stargazing to hand-trembling as methodology), can last a few hours or a few days; it may involve nighttime rituals both indoor and outdoor; in most cases it entails the creation and dismantling of sand paintings on the floor of the home in which the ceremony takes place; there might be related ritual dancing, shock rituals, body painting, burning of incense, distribution and application of medicines; throughout, there would be the singing-recitation of the myth which animates the particular ceremony, relieved now and then by pauses for normal conversation and even jokes. (pp. 7–8)

Language has a central role in Navajo curing ceremonies because the Navajo view language as a tool with which reality is created and maintained, not simply described. For the Navajo, the world was first created by being spoken into existence, and its order and balance are maintained today by the

(box continues)

(*box continued*)

recitation of sacred stories from the times of creation. Hearing ceremonies are a part of this process of maintaining the order of the universe or, when that order has been disrupted, of restoring it. Even the telling of Coyote stories for entertainment is understood as something that must be done each winter in order to perpetuate the order and balance of the Navajo world.

The role of Coyote stories as entertainment, moral education, and healing is vividly illustrated by the following example:

Coyote sees the Lizard people entertaining themselves by sliding down a steep slope on flat stones. He demands (four times) to be allowed to play and reluctantly the lizards teach Coyote how to slide. He gets overconfident, or chooses too large a stone, or a too-steep section of the slope, and the stone flips over (in some versions repeatedly, to the delight of listeners, who envision him appearing, then disappearing, under the wildly flipping stone). When the lizards find him at the bottom of the hill, he is mashed to a pulp, and there is nothing left but some fur and bones. They supply medicine and spirit power, and they dance around him until he revives and goes on his way. On the entertainment level, it is a funny story about Coyote botching up his life again; on the moral level, it dramatizes the results of inappropriate intrusion into the normal lives of others; on the medicinal level, it provides still another source of healing imagery. (p. 394)

In Navajo culture—as in that of most North American Indian societies—the number four is sacred. It is the symbol of wholeness and completion. The world has four sacred directions, the cardinal points of the compass. Elements of Navajo rituals are often repeated four times. And requests made four times are normally complied with in Navajo society. Thus, it is not surprising that Coyote stories would also function at a fourth level in the Navajo view of things. Toelken discovered this fourth level inadvertently by acting in the un-Navajo way that was encouraged by his academic subculture. In trying to dissect and analyze the elements and themes of Coyote stories, he persisted in asking questions about the specific meanings of their bits and pieces:

While I was pursuing some of these questions in the winter of 1982, an elderly singer asked that I stay on after other visitors had left his hoghan. It was late in the evening and we had enjoyed a long story-telling session. When all was quiet, he asked, "Are you ready to lose a member of your family?" When I responded negatively and with surprise, he unveiled to me a fourth level of meaning in the Coyote stories, one which I was totally unaware of, but which can readily be understood, given the nature of the information I have brought forward here. It has to do with witchcraft.

Since words and narratives have power to heal, they may also be used to injure and kill. Thus, when witches wish to damage the health of others, they use selected parts of the same Coyote stories in their rituals; the difference is that instead of integrating the story with a model of order and restoration, their idea of deployment is to use images, symbols, and allusions separately, divisively, analytically, in order to attack certain parts of the victim's body, or family, or livestock. One becomes a witch in order to gain personal fortune and power by causing weakness and death in others.

When one becomes a witch, the price of that power to destroy is paid by losing the life of a member of someone in the witch's family. Since my questions had been selective and analytical, since I was clearly trying to find out exactly what was powerful about Coyote stories, since I stood to gain by this knowledge, the old singer wanted to warn me of two possible dangers: If I became a witch, I would lose someone from my family; if others thought I was a witch, someone might try to kill someone in my family. In either case, Navajo informants would assume that my detailed knowledge indicated witchcraft, and no one would be willing to tell me stories any more. I later found out from a mutual friend that this singer was himself believed to be a powerful witch. (1987; pp. 396–97).

---

at sea. On another, it is about the human quest to tame the chaos of nature. Captain Ahab is both a man driven by obsession and a man controlled by fate, simultaneously a symbol of the ungodly man and of the godlike man. The whale may be seen as the worldly incarnation of God, the untamable chaos of nature, or the embodiment of fate with equal validity. In religious ritual this quality of multivocality is a source of the sense of transcendent meaningfulness that rituals may have for participants. The box titled "Multivocality in Navajo Rituals" illustrates how rituals may have different meanings in various contexts.

RITUAL AS SACRED UNDERWRITING
OF RELIGIOUS IDEOLOGY

Wallace pointed out that ritual is central to religion because it is the instrumental means of religion (1966b, p. 104), the means by which people seek to accomplish their religious goals. However, ritual is more than simply a means to an end, it is also the source of the sanctity of religion, both ideologically and socially.

Roy Rappaport (1999) has argued strongly that the enactment of religious beliefs in ritual itself imbues those beliefs with a sense of timelessness and sacredness. The more or less invariant form of ritual stimulates a feeling that the ideas embodied in the ritual are ancient, eternal, or timeless. The sacredness of ritual is communicated by the fact that it is carried out with care and with concern for the accuracy of its performance and attention to detail.

Ritual and Ultimate Sacred Postulates

The most sacred beliefs of a religion that define the essential basis for the rest of its ideology, what Rappaport terms a religion's **ultimate sacred postulates,** are assertions that cannot be proved or disproved because they are claims that have no empirical referents in the world of ordinary experience. Rappaport cites the Shema as a succinct statement of Judaism's ultimate sacred postulates: "Hear oh, Israel, the Lord thy God, the Lord is one." On the most overt level, it asserts the distinctive monotheism of Judaism. On a deeper level, the "oneness" of God refers to his perfection and holiness, the quality of being separate and above all other things and untainted by any quality other than perfect "goodness." The Shema also defines God's relationship to his followers. He is their "Lord" or "master," rendered in Hebrew, their *adonai,* a plural form indicating him to be supreme above all other lords or masters. And, finally, it defines God's relationship to his people. Even though they have long been dispersed through many nations, Jews are referred to by a collective name, "Israel." They are one people, a religious community, not merely a collection of individuals. God is their master, so Israel must be God's servant, a metaphor that points to the nature of Judaism as primarily a religion of practice rather than doctrine. What binds Jews together in a universal community are the rituals that demonstrate fidelity to the sacred order of God's creation, not mere belief. In Judaism, it is ritual that mediates between the individual believer and his or her God.

Ultimate sacred postulates, such as the Shema, that have been formulated as succinct and distinctive statements often play a central role in the liturgical orders of the religions that have them. For instance, Rappaport points out that the ultimate sacred postulates of Catholicism "are summarized in the Creeds, but are expressed at greater length in the canon of the Eucharist, particularly in the preface, the closing doxology and the words of institution" (1999, p. 277). In Judaism the reading of the Torah is preceded by blessings and prayers, including an abbreviated version of the Shema, and the Shema is used in prayer by observant Jews every morning and every evening.

Christianity illustrates that the ultimate sacred postulates of a religion need not be reducible to a single, succinct statement such as Judaism's Shema. For Christianity, the Creeds embody its ultimate sacred postulates. A number of

ultimate sacred postulates
The most sacred beliefs of a religion that define the essential basis for its ideology.

different creeds have been formulated in various centuries and by various Christian denominations. The most widely accepted of the Creeds is probably the Nicene Creed, written in A.D. 325. The distinctive view of divinity found in the various creeds differs from that of the Shema in its incorporation of the Trinitarian paradox into its description of the God of Christianity: God is "one God," hence Christianity maintains the monotheism of the Judaism from which it sprang. Yet God is composed of "three Persons," the Father, the Son, and the Holy Spirit, each of whom is "fully God." The Christian doctrine of the Trinity is what in Catholic theological terminology is referred to as a "mystery, in the strict sense of the word," meaning a truth not derived from logic or experience, which cannot be comprehended, but only learned by having been revealed. This paradoxical view of the godhead distinguished Christianity from the stricter monotheism of Judaism. So too did Christianity's creedal portrayal of the relationship between God and his worshipers. Although Christianity began as a Jewish sect, it soon flourished throughout the Roman Empire and ultimately gave rise to a large number of distinctive denominations. Unlike the Shema, the Christian creeds do not define Christians as "a People" or portray them as servants of God, but as individual "believers." In expanding the concept of the Godhead into three "Persons," Christianity replaced the community of "Israel" as God's servants with "the Son" as the divine mediator between God and humankind, mediation that is manifest through the pastoral service of the church and its liturgies. Although participation in the liturgies is certainly an important part of Christian life, belief itself was elevated in Christianity to play the crucial role in defining the relationship between God and the individual and in producing the salvation of the individual. Other distinctive ultimate sacred postulates in the creeds include the doctrines of the death and resurrection of Jesus and the virgin birth—the belief that the incarnation of God the Son, his birth to Mary, was a miraculous event, the pregnancy of a virgin, caused by the intervention of God the Holy Ghost.

As Christianity diverged from its Jewish roots, it modified these defining characteristics in the following ways. Although God was still viewed as "one" by the Christian community, his oneness came to be spoken of as being manifest as three divine "Persons" who were, nevertheless, held to be "one God." In this paradoxical definition of God as both "one" and "three," Christianity differs from the straightforward monotheism of Judaism. In Christianity, the Christian community does not portray the community as "a People" but as a group of individual believers. God's relationship with humankind shifted from a relationship with the community in the sense of "a People" to a relationship with individual believers, and this relationship is viewed as mediated by "the Son" on a spiritual level and by the "church" on an earthly level. While participation in the ritual life of the church is important, the belief (or "faith") of the individual moved toward center stage as the foundation of the individual's relationship with God and the salvation of the individual.

It is instructive to consider how Islam's ultimate sacred postulates differentiate it from both Judaism and Christianity. Rappaport pointed out that just as the Shema embodies the utimate sacred postulates of Judaism in abbreviated form, the Islamic declaration of faith, the Kalimat al Shahada, does the same: "I testify that there is no god but One God, and I testify that Muhummad is his Prophet." In these few words, we find important implications about the nature of God, the nature of the community of believers, and the nature of God's relationship with his followers.

Perhaps in reaction to Christianity's movement away from the simple monotheism of Judaism, the strictly monotheistic view of God is emphasized in the Islamic Kalimat al Shahada even more than in the Jewish Shema. Like Judaism, Islam has no equivalent of the Christian "church" as a mediator between the believer and God. Rather the relationship between the individual and God is a direct and personal one, as emphasized by the central role of the first-person pronoun as the repeated subject in the Islamic declaration of faith: "*I* testify that . . ." Although Islam does not lack the concept of a community of believers, it is a community of individuals whose personal relationship with God is—in the absence of a mediating church—even more central to Islam than it is in Christianity. In Islam, the ritual uttering of the declaration of faith by an individual is the act which establishes the individual's relationship with God, but the relationship is defined as that of supreme lord to individual servant. Indeed, the very term for a follower of Islam—Muslim—means "One who submits himself (to God)," and it is acts of personal obedience to the will of God rather than simple assertion of belief through which one's Islamic identity is manifest.

Religions need not formally distill their most sacred and essential doctrines into a single, succinct statement or even a somewhat more elaborate one such as the Christian creeds. Nevertheless, when this is not the case, religions can be characterized by the ultimate sacred postulates that are *implicit* in their beliefs and ritual practices. Thus, though many religions have no formal equivalent to Judaism's Shema or the Christian creeds, the symbolism of their rituals have consistencies from which ultimate sacred postulates can be inferred.

Ritual as the Ground of Sanctity for Ultimate Sacred Postulates

Ultimate sacred postulates can neither be proved nor falsified, because they make no claims with empirical content. Yet, they are regarded as unquestionably true. Why do people continue to treat some beliefs as truths that are not to be questioned even though they are not demonstrably true—indeed, even though it is clearly not possible to demonstrate their truth? Rappaport's answer is that participation in the rituals that give beliefs (including ultimate sacred postulates) their sanctity is an act of affirmation of their sanctity and truth. Even though *words* may not be able to demonstrate the truth of a religion's ultimate sacred postulates, *participation* can nevertheless reinforce acceptance of their truthfulness, since the very act of participating places one in the position of affirming that truthfulness.

Participation in ritual has the interesting characteristic of being an act of public acceptance of the beliefs and values the ritual expresses. Acceptance is different from belief. A person may participate in a religion's rituals without actually believing in the ideology that they support, but he or she cannot participate without expressing acceptance, without communicating—both to him- or herself and to others—a commitment to abide by the obligations entailed by the ritual. This distinction between acceptance and belief has important implications: "the acceptance indicated by liturgical performance being independent of belief can be more profound than conviction or sense of certainty, for it makes it possible for the participant to transcend his or her own doubt by accepting in defiance of it" (Rappaport, 1999, p. 120). As Fehean O'Doherty (1973), a Catholic priest, put it, "Faith is neither subjective conviction or certitude, but may be at its best when doubt exists" (p. 9). Rappaport concludes that since "acceptance is intrinsic to performance of the canons in which they are represented" (p. 283) yet also independent of belief, participation in a religion's rituals "makes it possible for the performer to transcend his own doubt, experience and reason by accepting in defiance of them" (p. 283). Participation in a religion's liturgical order—its rituals practiced in group settings—constitutes a declaration that the participant publicly accepts the ideology the liturgical order symbolizes. The participant is therefore obligated not to question the religious ideology that those rituals represent. In short, participation in rituals makes their message sacred.

RITUAL: INFLUENCING THE SUPERNATURAL

Human beings are not attracted to rituals simply because they are pleasing ways to express meanings. The primary motivation to participate in rituals is the belief that they are a means by which supernatural beings and supernatural power can be influenced to help human beings accomplish goals that they are unable or less likely to achieve if they rely solely on their mundane abilities. Thus people are particularly likely to turn to religious rituals when they are unable to cope with their problems through purely secular means.

The particular meanings of each ritual depend on the specific goals that it is intended to accomplish. In this section, we examine rituals meant to influence the human relationship with the natural environment and human biological and psychological states. Wallace (1966b, pp. 107–66) suggested that based on their goals, religious rituals can be classified into a number of broad categories, four of which are relevant to this section: technological rituals, therapy and anti-therapy rituals, salvation rituals, and revitalization rituals. Though other schemes for classifying rituals into different types have been suggested, Wallace's is useful and will be used here to provide an overview of the various possible uses of ritual. All of his categories except social control rituals (which will be treated in a later section) will be discussed here in their role as influencer of the supernatural.

Technological Rituals

technological rituals
Rituals used with the intent to control nature or natural processes.

divination
The use of ritual to gain access to knowledge or information unavailable by natural means.

Technological rituals, according to Wallace (1966b, p. 107), are "intended to control various aspects of nature" in ways that improve the human ability to function. In order to better make use of nature, people use rituals to seek otherwise unavailable knowledge about the world around them or to manipulate nature either to increase the availability of its resources or to prevent various unwanted conditions. The first of these goals is achieved through various forms of divination, the second through what Wallace calls "rites of intensification," and the third by means of protective rituals.

Divination

In **divination,** the use of ritual to obtain hidden knowledge, two otherwise unrelated things are believed to be spiritually connected so that one may

Figure 7.2
Shamanic Divination Ritual
This shaman is reading the palm of a client at Batu
Caves in Malaysia. Divination, like curing, is a
common part of the shamanic cult institutions of
religions throughout the world.

be used as a source of information about the other. This offers endless possibilities: Roman augurs divined propitious days for battle by interpreting the entrails of birds or the flight of birds across the sky. Water witches in the United States take the movement of a willow branch in the diviner's hands to be an indicator of the presence of water at a particular location. Answers to questions can be obtained by the movement of a handheld pendulum, by the fall of dice (or other objects) when cast, by the pattern of tea leaves in the bottom of a cup, or the shape taken by molten metal when poured into water.

Whatever the specific form of the ritual, the interpretation typically relies on the idea that the thing interpreted will be similar to what it reveals. Thus, the willow branch points to water; the Hermit card in tarot represents solitude, introspection, searching, and guidance; many leaves in tea-leaf reading represents a full life; and the flame going out in Tibetan butter-lamp divination signifies death. Many of these similarities would be recognized across cultural boundaries, though the symbolism may require knowledge of the culture from which it is derived. For instance, the similarity between death and a dying flame would need no explanation to a non-Tibetan, but that the runestone Ansuz represents speech and knowledge would likely seem more appropriate to one who knows that the name Ansuz is also the name of the first letter of the runic alphabet.

Rituals of Manipulation

Whereas rituals of divination help the human adjustment to nature by providing them with knowledge they need to make useful decisions, **rituals of manipulation** are used to act on nature directly. The first approach to manipulating nature is embodied in attempts to cause the environment to produce what humans need from it more bounteously. Wallace called such rituals for increasing the availability of important natural resources or for controlling other forces of nature in ways that improve human life **rites of intensification.** They may be performed to improve one's luck in hunting or fishing, to increase the fertility of animals or crops, to bring rain, or to otherwise improve success in obtaining an adequate subsistence.

Wallace distinguished rites of intensification from those performed for the opposite purpose of *preventing* unwanted natural circumstances such as earthquakes, storms that endanger vessels at sea, fires that can destroy homes or entire communities, or insect plagues or droughts that threaten crops. He called these **protective rituals.** They weave a beneficial spell around those things to be

rituals of manipulation
Rituals that are used to act on nature directly.
rites of intensification
Rituals for increasing the availability of important natural resources or for controlling other forces of nature in ways that improve human life.
protective rituals
Rituals used with the intent of preventing harm to human beings.

fetish
An object that
embodies the
power of a pro-
tective ritual.

protected or, sometimes, around some tangible object called a **fetish** that continues to embody the power of a protective ritual. The advantage of fetishes is that the ritual that invokes a protective benefit need not be performed repeatedly, since the fetish itself perpetuates its influence and, if small enough, can be transported by its possessor from place to place so that its effects carry over to the new locations. The Ghost Shirt of the Great Basin Ghost Dance religion is a good example of a fetish. In a time when Indians had been displaced and disenfranchised by the militarily superior forces of immigrants from the eastern United States, the Ghost Shirt offered protection against the potential dangers those immigrants represented. The wearer of a Ghost Shirt was believed to be protected from death in battle, even from gunshot wounds, a belief not fundamentally different from the contemporary use of a St. Christopher's statue or medal to make travel safer for its owner.

Taboos

Avoidance of behaviors can also be thought of as a kind of "anti-ritual," things that are *not* done rather than done. Prohibitions against performing certain behaviors are called *taboos*, (see chapter 1) a term that anthropologists borrowed from the languages of Polynesia where such rules were a very important part of people's religious life. Michael Lambek (1998) explains that taboos are an example of practices that function to create a social identity for the people who follow them. For instance, he points out that "The very name of the Tsimihety, like that of a number of other Malagasy groups, contains the negative participle, *tsy*. Tsimihety means '[those who] do not cut their hair'" (p. 118). Social identity need not be as explicitly identified as this to exist. Even when taboos do not enter into the formal definition or name of a group, their existence still functions to create a sense of in-group versus out-group identities. The practice of keeping a kosher kitchen and following its restrictions distinguishes the observant Jewish community from others. By following the taboos of the "Word of Wisdom," which forbids the use of tobacco, coffee, and alcohol as well as other substances, Mormons are repeatedly confronted with situations in which they explain their nonparticipation in common forms of American socializing, thus distinguishing their social identity from that of others.

Therapy and Anti-Therapy Rituals

therapy rituals
Rituals per-
formed by people
to improve
health and bodily
functioning.

Wallace termed those behaviors intended to influence the human body itself *therapy* and *anti-therapy rituals*. **Therapy rituals** are performed by people to improve health and bodily functioning. Every culture known to anthropologists included religious rituals for curing diseases, particularly those for which no secular cure was available. Forest Clements (1932) pointed out that in the religions of the world, beliefs about possible supernatural causes of disease fall into five categories: magic, the intrusion of supernatural "disease objects" into the victim's body, soul loss, spirit possession, and taboo violation. Therapy rituals use symbolism that is appropriate for the type of supernatural cause of a particular illness. For instance, curing illnesses caused by magic requires counter-magic. On the other hand, disease objects are usually removed by massaging the

A Shoshone Curing Ceremony

The Shoshone Indians of Utah and Nevada relied heavily on the services of native shamans for curing diseases that their herbal knowledge could not treat successfully. Such shamans were known as *puhakantən,* literally "possessors of (spiritual) power." Shamans obtained the power they used for curing illnesses from a visionary experience. The power was never theirs by right, but held by them in trust from the spirit who had appeared to them in their vision and who acted as their spirit partner, their *nəwəpuha-pəa* in curing ceremonies.

Willie Blackeye was the shaman on the Duckwater Reservation in eastern Nevada when I did my fieldwork there in the late 1960s. His reputation as a great curer was widespread throughout Nevada, and patients came to him from quite a distance from Duckwater. His power to cure came to him from his spirit partner, the Eagle, who warned him in his first vision that he must follow certain rules carefully if he wished to continue in his role as a *puhakantən.* Among these rules, he was forbidden to attempt to cure any illness that he diagnosed as "cancer," and he was not to increase his fee over the years.

A curing ceremony was preceded by a diagnosis to determine whether a cure was possible. Willie Blackeye might ask a prospective patient to take an "eagle wing" fan home and sleep under it by hanging it above the bed. That same evening,

Willie Blackeye would consult the Eagle spirit for a diagnosis. Depending on the outcome of that effort, he would accept or reject the patient on the next day.

If the patient had been accepted, he or she would bathe at sunrise on the morning of the curing ceremony and come to Willie Blackeye's home, bringing payment for the service and a gift of tobacco that would be used in the ceremony. The cure would begin at sunset. Willie Blackeye would begin the cure by smoking some of the tobacco that had been brought to him by the patient. Then he would sing a chant that he had learned from his spirit partner in his first vision. This chant was an invitation to the Eagle to come down from the mountain where he lives and give spiritual power to the shaman so that he could cure the patient's illness. Alternately smoking and chanting, Willie Blackeye would massage the patient's body to manipulate the "disease object" and eventually remove it from the patient's body. The ceremony might last for several hours, until the shaman was confident that the purification of the patient had been successful.

As a follow-up to the curing ceremony, a patient might be given several tasks that would insure a complete and permanent cure. For instance, the curing of nosebleeds was facilitated by having the patient collect some of the blood and deposit it on a red anthill.

afflicted part, manipulating the disease object, and removing it by hand or by sucking. The appropriate solution to illnesses caused by soul loss is usually a ritual in which a shaman enters a trance and sends his or her own spirit to find and retrieve the missing soul. And spirit possession is commonly treated by a ritual in which the offending spirit is overpowered and forced to leave the patient's body by the shaman. The box titled "A Shoshone Curing Ceremony" describes religious curing among the Shoshone Indians of the North American Great Basin.

Anti-therapy rituals are intended to have an effect opposite that of therapy rituals. That is, they are intended to cause discomfort, illness, and even death to the person against whom they are directed. Human beings demonstrate a powerful ability to be influenced by such rituals when they know that they have been the object of one. For instance, Herbert Basedow (1925) gave

anti-therapy rituals
Rituals intended to cause discomfort, illness, and even death to the person against whom they are directed.

191

**rituals of
salvation**
Rituals intended
to cause a tempo-
rary or perma-
nent change in
the participant's
personality.

**spirit-possession
rituals**
Rituals in which
the participant's
personality is
temporarily re-
placed by another
that is attributed
to a spirit who
has taken control
of the partici-
pant's behavior.

**ritual of becom-
ing a shaman**
A ritual in which
the participant's
personality un-
dergoes a perma-
nent change as
part of a vision-
ary experience of
leaving the body
and traveling in
the spirit world
where spirits or
deities call the
person to become
a shaman.

**rituals of mysti-
cal experience**
Rituals in which
the participant
seeks the ecstatic
experience of
oneness with the
divine.

a vivid description of the effects of a "bone-pointing" sorcery ritual among Aboriginal
Australians:

A man who discovers that he
is being boned by an enemy
is, indeed, a pitiable sight.
He stands aghast, with his
eyes staring at the treacher-
ous pointer, and with his
hands lifted as though to
ward off the lethal medium,
which he imagines is pour-
ing into his body. . . . His
cheeks blanch and his eyes
become glossy, and the expression of his face becomes
horribly distorted, like that
of one stricken with palsy.
He attempts to shriek but
usually the sound chokes in his throat, and all that one might see is froth at his
mouth. His body begins to tremble and the muscles twist involuntarily. He
sways backwards and falls to the ground, and after a short time appears to be
in a swoon but soon after he begins to writhe as if in mortal agony, and, covering his face with his hands, begins to moan. After a while he becomes more
composed and crawls to his wurley [hut]. From this time onwards he sickens
and frets, refusing to eat and keeping aloof from the daily affairs of the tribe.
Unless help is forthcoming in the shape of a counter charm administered by the
hands of the "Nangarri" or medicine-man, his death is only a matter of a com-
paratively short time. If the coming of the medicine-man is opportune, he might
be saved. (quoted in Cannon, 1942, p. 181)

Figure 7.3
Bone-Pointing in Australia
This Arunta man of central Australia is demon-
strating the use of bone-pointing to cast illness into
the body of an enemy.

Salvation Rituals

What Wallace (1996b) called **rituals of salvation** are intended to cause a
temporary or permanent change in the participant's personality. In his typol-
ogy, there are four general types of salvation rituals: spirit-possession rituals,
the ritual of becoming a shaman, mystical experience rituals, and rituals of
expiation.

In **spirit-possession rituals** the participant's personality is temporarily replaced by another that is attributed to a spirit that has taken control over the
participant's behavior. In a **ritual of becoming a shaman** the participant's personality undergoes a permanent change as part of a visionary experience in
which he or she experiences the near-deathlike experience of leaving the body
and traveling in the spirit world, where spirits or deities call the person to become a shaman. In **rituals of mystical experience,** participants seek the ecstatic
experience of oneness with the divine. In the fourth kind of ritual of salvation,
rituals of expiation, the participant engages in acts of penance or good works

Figure 7.4
Expiation Rituals
This man shows his devotion by having skewered his cheeks at the Hindu Thaipusam festival, Batu Caves, Malaysia.

to atone for sins, taboo violations, or other failings.

Revitalization Rituals

Finally, Wallace suggested that people participate in some rituals as a means of coping with widespread societal stresses such as those that are the result of natural disasters, warfare, epidemic diseases, or other problems that undermine the usual smooth functioning of a society. He calls these rituals that are typically involved in the birth of new religious movements **revitalization rituals.** In these rituals, new systems of beliefs and values are communicated and reinforced in their participants. The processes that give rise to revitalization rituals will be discussed in detail in chapter 10.

Ritual as Manipulation and Petition

The rituals of religion are intended to influence the supernatural on behalf of human beings; however, not all rituals are thought of as equally effective. We can think of rituals as falling along a continuum that measures how effective they are believed to be. Some rituals, those we call *magic* (see chapter 1), are believed to actually compel the supernatural to behave in a particular way. Their outcome is believed to be assured, as long as no mistake is made in performing them. Magical rituals are, therefore, performed in precisely the same way each time, with care and attention to detail. On the other end of the scale are **petitionary rituals,** those whose participants believe that performing them increases the likelihood of the outcome that they desire, yet without any guarantee that they will work every time.

Magical Rituals

The most precisely performed rituals are magical rituals. They are also the ones that are thought to be the most mechanical and compulsive in their effect. The underlying principles by which they are thought to work are embodied in what Sir James Frazer ([1911]1925) referred to as the laws of "sympathetic magic." He examined the use of magic in his classic work, *The Golden Bough,* and decided that all magic operates by what can be called **Law of Sympathy,** the idea that "things act on each other at a distance through a secret sympathy" (p. 12). This Law of Sympathy, he argued, is composed of two principles: "If we analyze the principles of thought on which magic is based, they will probably be found

rituals of expiation
Rituals in which the participant engages in acts of penance or good works to atone for sins, taboo violations, or other failings.

revitalization rituals
Rituals that are typically involved in the birth of new religious movements.

petitionary rituals
Rituals intended to request rather than compel the supernatural.

Law of Sympathy
The magical idea that things act on each other at a distance through a secret sympathy.

**Law of
Similarity**
The magical prin-
ciple that like
produces like or
that an effect re-
sembles its cause.

**homeopathic (or
imitative) magic**
Rituals that com-
pel the super-
natural by means
of the Law of
Similarity.

to resolve themselves into two: first, that like produces like, or that an effect re-sembles its cause; and second, that things which have once been in contact with each other continue to act on each other at a distance after physical contact has been severed" (p. 11). He referred to the first principle as the *Law of Similarity* and the second as the *Law of Contact or Contagion.*

The **Law of Similarity** is the basis of **homeopathic or imitative magic,** magic in which similar things are believed to be spiritually identical so that one can be used to influence the other. The Law of Imitation can be observed in the rituals of peoples from all parts of the world. For instance, Pueblo Indians use the idea that like begets like when they stir up frothy billows of yucca suds in cloudlike masses to induce life-giving rains in parched deserts. New Age Amer-icans follow the same principle when they engage in therapies such as "imag-ing" or "visualizing" an ovum passing through the fallopian tubes and being fertilized by a strong and vital sperm, accompanied by the sounds of lullabies, to overcome infertility problems.

Magical rituals may be used to control and manipulate supernatural beings. For instance, Kurt Seligman (1948) quotes a ritual for summoning a demon from a grimoire, or "black book," titled *Sanctum Regum:*

> Two days before the conjuration, you must cut a bough from a wild hazel tree with a new knife, that has never before been used. It must be a bough which has never carried fruit, and it must be cut at the very moment when the sun rises over the horizon.
>
> After this, take a bloodstone, as it is known by the druggists who sell it, and two blessed wax candles and select a lonely place where the conjuration may pro-ceed undisturbed. Old ruined castles are excellent, for spirits like decayed build-ings; a remote room in your house may do equally well. With your bloodstone, trace a triangle upon the floor, and set the candles at the sides of the triangle. At the bottom of the triangle, write the holy letters **I H S,** flanked by two crosses.
>
> Take your stand within the triangle with your hazel wand and the papers containing the conjuration and your demands, and summon the spirit with hope and firmness:
>
> "Emperor Lucifer, master of the rebellious spirits, I beg you to be favour-able to me, when now I call for your minister, the great Lucifuge Rofocale, as I desire to sign a contract with him. I beg also that Prince Beelzebub may protect my enterprise. O Astaroth, great count, be favourable likewise, and make it pos-sible for the great Lucifuge to appear to me in human form and force, without bad odour, and that he grant me, by the agreement which I am ready to sign with him, all the riches which I need. O great Lucifuge, I pray that you leave your dwelling wherever it may be to come here and speak to me. If you are not willing to come, I will compel you to do so by the power of the great living God, of the Son and the Spirit. Come promptly, otherwise I will torment you eternally by the power of my mighty words and by the great Key of Solomon, which he used when compelling the rebellious spirits to accept a pact. Thus appear as quickly as possible, or else I will torment you continuously by the power-ful words of the Key: Aglon Tetagram Vaycheon Stimulamathon Erohares Retragsammathon Clyoran Icion Esition Existien Eryona Onera Erasyn Moyn Meffias Soter Emmanuel Sabaoth Adomai, I call you, Amen." (1948, pp. 199–200)

The grimoire also explains how a demon, once summoned, can be forced to reveal the location of hidden treasures.

Shoshone Love Magic and the Laws of Similarity and Contagion

During my fieldwork on an eastern Nevada reservation, one 65-year-old Shoshone informant described Shoshone love magic or, as he called it, "girl medicine." His description made it clear that the concept of similarity was a rationale for the ritual actions involved:

Weasel is used for girl medicine. It is good. You take the heart out before it is dead and talk to it. You take it off someplace by yourself and talk to it. . . . You put it under your pillow for five nights, to dream about girls. The heart is mixed with *pisappih* (red face paint clay) all ground up. If you don't dream something about girls, it won't work, so you throw it away. If you do, it will work.

If you see a girl you like, but she won't pay attention to you, get a little piece of rock about half the size of your fingernail and put the medicine on the rock. Then go by her and hit her with it. When she feels it, that's a ghost. For half an hour or so, you walk around where she can see you. Then after a while she's getting worse and worse. After a while she follows you and talks to you. That's how you catch a girl, the old timers say.

Weasels are pretty little things, especially in the winter. That's why they chose it to catch a girl.

In this example we see both the Law of Similarity and the Law of Contagion at work. The former is evident in the choice of a weasels to create attraction because they "are pretty little things," and the Law of Contagion is at work when the power of the medicine is transferred by hitting the person it is intended to influence.

From Richley H. Crapo, *Cultural Anthropology: Understanding Ourselves and Others*, 2nd ed. (Guilford, CT: Dushkin Publishing Group, 1990), p. 220. Reprinted by permission of The McGraw-Hill Companies.

The **Law of Contact or Contagion,** Frazer's second principle of magic, is the idea that things which have been in contact with each other remain in contact spiritually, so that one may be used to influence the other. The Law of Contagion also implies that mana (see chapter 1) can be transferred from one object or person to another when the two come into contact with one another. The principle of contagion is used in **contagious magic,** magic in which supernatural influences are transferred through contact or things that have been in contact are used to influence one another.

The use of the Law of Similarity and the Law of Contagion in magic is illustrated in the box titled "Shoshone Love Magic and the Laws of Similarity and Contagion."

Worship Rituals

Not all ritual is done to compel supernatural powers or beings into serving human needs. Rituals may also be performed to worship or petition the supernatural. In **worship** the purpose of ritual is to express adoration, although petitionary rituals are often combined with rituals of worship to form larger ceremonies, and rituals of worship may be thought to improve the disposition of supernatural beings to grant those things requested in the petitionary parts of a ceremony. In the last instance, supernatural beings may decide to withhold the benefits that their worshipers have requested. Frazer and other Victorian anthropologists ethnocentrically contrasted magical rituals with the more worshipful style of European religious ritualism and reserved the word *religion* for the Western practice of worshiping rather than manipulating the supernatural. Of course, their contrast was overdrawn, since Western worship services often

Law of Contact (or Contagion)
The magical principle that things once in contact with each other continue to act on each other at a distance after physical contact has been severed.

contagious magic
Magic in which supernatural influences are transferred through contact or in which things that have been in contact are used to influence one another.

worship
Ritual performed to express adoration.

include not only rituals of petition but also rituals that fit the definition of magical rituals.

By contrasting the "religions" of Western society with the "magic" of "primitive cultures," Victorian anthropologists failed to recognize that compulsion and petition by means of rituals are merely alternate forms of religious rituals, forms that are best understood as contrasting ends of a continuum rather than qualitatively distinct categories. Rituals do not fall into one extreme category or the other. Rather, being compulsive or petitionary is a matter of degree. Even within the same religion, different rituals may be viewed as being more or less effective than one another. Some rituals are thought to be more reliable in their effects, while others are less so. Petitionary rituals, like magical ones, are performed because those who do them believe that they are increasing the likelihood of some human benefit. The degree of certainty of the outcome is merely lower than is true of magical rituals. And even when the rituals are thought of as compulsive, certainty is never perfect, since even magical rituals may be ineffective if they are done imperfectly or if their effectiveness is countered by someone else's magic.

Petitionary rituals, such as the various rituals of worship that are common in Western religions, are often directed toward influencing the goodwill of supernatural beings such as gods, ancestral spirits, or other benign supernatural beings. These rituals seek the favor of such beings, but since they are thought to have a mind and will of their own, petitionary rituals are thought of as requests rather than demands. Because the supernatural beings approached by these rituals may elect not to respond as participants in the rituals hope, petitionary rituals may fail to achieve their desired ends.

RITUAL AS UNDERWRITING OF SOCIAL UNITY

Rituals, particularly those enacted in group settings, are important means by which loyalty to the group is reinforced and one's position within it defined. We look at the first of these two important functions of religious rituals by revisiting ideas about the psychological significance of ritual symbolism expressed by Victor Turner and Emile Durkheim. We explore the second by an examination of rites of passage.

Social Control Rituals

rituals of social control
Those rituals aimed at maintaining the stability of society and its culture.

rituals of ideology
Rituals of social control that communicate the symbolism of the group to its participants.

Rituals that are aimed at maintaining the stability of society and its culture are called **rituals of social control.** Wallace discussed two types of these, *rituals of ideology* and *rites of passage.* **Rituals of ideology** communicate the symbolism of the group to its participants. They are, according to Wallace, "intended to control, in a conservative way, the behavior, the mood, and the sentiments and values of groups for the sake of the community as a whole" (1966b, p. 127). Examples include the preaching of sermons that exhort the audience to support the values of the religious group, congregational hymn singing, rituals that reenact the founding events of the religion itself such as Christian Passion plays at Easter time or the celebration of the Passover Seder by Jewish families.

Ritual and Social Loyalty

Victor Turner (1969) has cast a spotlight on the psychological impact of rituals on their participants. Turner argues that participating in rituals with others helps people achieve a psychological state characterized by a sense of unity and equality that he calls *communitas* (see chapter 1). Communitas involves a state of mind in which the usual hierarchical relationships between the members of a group are overcome and individuals perceive themselves as part of a community of equals. This can, according to Turner, be the source of deeply felt bonding and allegiance among the members of the group, a kind of "mystery of intimacy" that carries over into day-to-day life in a way that counteracts the antipathies that can arise due to the hierarchical relationships that society's functioning requires. Turner has observed that "Spontaneous communitas is richly charged with affects, mainly pleasurable ones" (1969, p. 139). This contrasts with the structured daily life of routine social existence, which "is filled with objective difficulties":

> Decisions have to be made, inclinations sacrificed to the wishes and needs of the group, and physical and social obstacles overcome at some personal cost. Spontaneous communitas has something "magical" about it. Subjectively there is in it the feeling of endless power. But this power untransformed cannot readily be applied to the organizational details of social existence. It is no substitute for lucid thought and sustained will. (1969, p. 138).

Yet, communitas plays an important role within the structure of society. As Turner notes, "structural action swiftly becomes arid and mechanical if those involved in it are not periodically immersed in the regenerative abyss of communitas." Though communitas may be experienced spontaneously in certain settings, its more common role is what Turner calls **normative communitas,** in which the experience of undifferentiated loyalty to others and equality of comradeship that is characteristic of communitas is incorporated into a lasting social system by its being organized into periodic ritual events. Communitas elicited in organized ritual settings evokes a generic sense of harmony and loyalty that society otherwise might lack. Thus, ritually evoked communitas functions to make the social order more enduring than it might otherwise be.

Normative communitas is organized as a structured group event. Turner notes that rituals are often described as consisting of three phases: (1) a "separation" phase in which participants are taken out of the ordinary setting in which they conduct their mundane life work and enter a sacred setting that is set apart for the ritual, (2) a "betwixt-and-between" phase that he calls the **liminal period** during which the feelings of the participants are characterized by communitas, and (3) a phase in which participants are reintegrated into their normal social life. Such a threefold sequence can function to integrate the loyalty and comradeship experienced during the liminal phase of rituals into the larger structure and hierarchy of daily nonritual life. In effect, the experience of social cohesion embodied in communitas can be carried over into the ordinary routine of life in which deference to authority is necessary for the coordination of action and the mobilization of resources that are necessary for the survival of any group.

Durkheim approached religion's role as a mechanism that functions to support or underwrite the social order from a different angle. Durkheim noted that

normative communitas Communitas in which the experience of undifferentiated loyalty to others and equality of comradeship is incorporated into a lasting social system by its being organized into periodic ritual events.

liminal period The phase of a ritual during which the feelings of the participants are characterized by communitas.

sacred things are characteristically associated with an attitude of respect of the kind that is appropriate toward moral obligations within society and toward the authority of social institutions. If people lacked such an attitude, then moral obligations would not be binding and social institutions would fail.

In Durkheim's view, religious rituals function primarily to imbue symbols of moral obligations and fundamentally important social institutions with that attitude of respect. He arrived at this view by noting the tremendous diversity among those things that are considered sacred among different peoples. He concluded that the diversity of sacred things precluded their having any common quality that would make them intrinsically sacred. In fact, things that are sacred in one religion may seem ridiculous to members of another religion. Sociologist Talcott Parsons (1949) aptly summarized Durkheim's revolutionary conclusion:

> At this point Durkheim became aware of the fundamental significance of his previous insight that the attitude of respect for sacred things was essentially identical with the attitude of respect for moral authority. If sacred things are symbols, the essential quality of that which they symbolize is that it is an entity which would command moral respect. It was by this path that Durkheim arrived at the famous proposition that society is always the real object of religious veneration. (p. 206)

To Durkheim, ritual was a means by which the collective sentiments of the social group are expressed. Exemplifying this with the ritual songs and dances among Aboriginal Australians, Durkheim wrote, "And since a collective sentiment cannot express itself collectively except on the condition of observing a certain order permitting cooperation and movements in unison, these gestures and cries [by which individuals express their feelings] naturally tend to become rhythmic and regular; hence become songs and dances" ([1895]1958, p. 247). Applied to religion in general, the functional role of religious rituals can be put this way: By evoking feelings of awe, respect, and reverence, the rituals of each religious community renew attitudes of respect for the moral order of that community as embodied in the symbolism of those rituals.

Rites of Passage

Rituals held to celebrate important changes in social status and roles at various times in the life cycle, **rites of passage,** have a stabilizing function similar to that of rituals of ideology, but they differ in easing people through changes into new roles that they are not yet accustomed to playing. Rites of passage are practiced in all human societies. Those life-cycle changes that are most widely celebrated in such rituals are the changes that occur when newborn children are named and introduced to other members of their community, when children move into adulthood, when people marry, and when people die.

Arnold Van Gennep demonstrated that religious rituals can facilitate change in the lives of individuals while reinforcing the stability of the social order in which those individuals participate. He did so by examining the rites of passage that facilitate the transition individuals from one socially recognized status to another as they progress through the stages of life that are normally experienced within their society.

The public celebration of rites of passage is a particularly common way of coping with the changes in society and in the lives of its individual members that surround (1) childbirth, (2) puberty, (3) marriage, and (4) death. The rituals

rites of passage
Rituals that define the changing statuses of individuals within their social groups as they pass through the various stages of life.

by which the social identity and roles of individuals are redefined at each of these four universal junctures in life are commonly religious. For instance, most societies have a series of rituals that organize the passage through pregnancy into the new social role of parenthood. Women may be separated from society during pregnancy, and various taboos come into play that are intended to make the pregnancy and the process of giving birth progress safely. Almost universally, there is a culminating ritual following childbirth that heralds the entry of the infant into human status and that reintroduces the woman into society as the mother of the child. Bestowing a human name on the infant is almost always part of this ceremony. Commonly, the new member of the human community is symbolically brought into contact with symbols of survival. Pygmies who survived by gathering wild foods in the Ituri Forest of Africa introduced their children to their forest provider in a religious ritual that involved tying forest vines around the children's wrists, ankles, and waists (Gibbs, 1965); the Samoans of Polynesia and the Yahgan of Tierra del Fuego bathed newborns in the sea that was their main food source (Cooper, 1946; Murdock, 1934; Service 1978); and many Christians who live in societies dominated by large cities made up mostly of strangers and who worry about crime more than food symbolically wash their children to free them from "sin." Van Gennep illustrates the naming ritual by quoting Daniel Wilson's description of practices in Gabon:

> A public crier announces the birth and claims for the child a name and a place among the living. Someone else, in a distant part of the village, acknowledges the fact and promises on the part of the people that the newborn infant shall be received into the community and have all the rights and immunities pertaining to the rest of the people. The people then assemble in the street, and the newborn infant is brought out and exhibited to public view. A basin of water is provided and the headman of the village or family sprinkles water upon it, giving it a name, and invoking a blessing that he may have health, grow up to manhood or womanhood, have numerous progeny, possess great riches, etc. (Wilson 1904, pp. 212–133, as quoted in Van Gennep, [1909]1960, p. 63).

Throughout most of human existence, individuals have been helped through the transition from childhood to adulthood with religious rites variously called *initiation rituals, puberty rituals,* or *adulthood rituals.* Though these ceremonies are generally held in and around the time of physiological puberty, Van Gennep emphasized the fact that they were really celebrating "social puberty," the transition from childhood to initiated adult status. He illustrated this with a statement by Howitt about the initiation of boys in the Maring community of the Kurnai people of Southeast Australia:

> The intention of all that is done in this ceremony is to make a momentous change in the boy's life; the past is to be cut off from him by a gulf which he can never re-pass. His connection with his mother as her child is broken off, and he becomes henceforth attached to the men. All the sports and games of his boyhood are to be abandoned with the severance of the old domestic ties between himself and his mother and sisters. He is now to be a man, instructed in and sensible of the duties which devolve upon him as a member of the Maring community. (1960, p. 532)

In adulthood rituals, children are commonly ceremoniously removed from their usual social setting. They may be taught new religious lore that was previously withheld from them. Often they undergo trials such as circumcision or scarification to demonstrate their adult capacity to endure pain. Finally, they are reintroduced to society as part of its adult social groups. The box titled "The Bar or Bat Mitzvah: A Jewish Adulthood Ritual" describes the rite of passage to adult status among Jews and explains its importance in Jewish religious culture.

Marriage is another fundamentally important transition that involves the imposition of new rules of conduct. These may involve the obligation of abandoning the somewhat more lenient rules that govern sexuality before marriage, for the expectation of sexual fidelity is commonly a part of the marriage contract. A ceremony of marriage impresses the importance of such changes on those who are moving from the unmarried state to the married one. It also dramatizes the change for the rest of the community of friends and neighbors who attend the ceremony, reminding them that they too must now respect the new obligations of the married persons. When these ceremonies are religious rather than secular, sacred authority lends its weight to the importance of the commitments to the new and different married lifestyle.

Finally, funerals mark the end of a person's human status within the community and help the survivors and the rest of the community adjust to changes that must come about in the absence of the deceased. Funeral rituals help the liv-

---

 ## The Bar or Bat Mitzvah: A Jewish Adulthood Ritual

In Aramaic, *bar* is the term for "son" and *bat* (pronounced bas in the Ashkenazic dialect) is the word for "daughter." Mitzvah means "commandment." So bar (or bat) mitzvah means "son (or daughter) of the commandment." The phrase names the public celebration of religious adulthood in the Jewish community, the time when Jews become old enough to be responsible for following the commandments.

In Judaism, children are not required to obey the Law, although they are encouraged to learn to do so as their abilities progress. At the age of 13 boys become responsible for living the commandments, while girls are understood to attain the age of responsibility at 12 years of age. This change requires no ritual, but it is commonly celebrated with a bar mitzvah for boys or a bat mitzvah for girls.

At the bar mitzvah, a boy participates in his first Aliyah, or "going up" to participate in the reading of the Torah. Minimally, this consists of his reciting a blessing over the Parshat ha-Shuvua, the weekly reading aloud from the Torah. This requires some skill, since the reading is in Hebrew. Usually, the celebrant recites at least the Haftarah

portion (the Prophetic reading) and its corresponding chant. In some congregations, the celebrant may read the entire weekly lesson. Thus, the bar mitzvah requires the celebrant to demonstrate a religiously significant adult skill—the reading of the Torah before a congregation, which is surely no mean feat for a 13-year old. Usually, the boy is also expected to give a speech that begins with the traditional phrase, "Today I am a man," since the bar mitzvah signals the beginning of his responsibility to live the commandments as an adult. The celebrant's father typically offers a prayer in which he gives thanks that he has now been relieved from the responsibility for his son's sins.

For girls, the corresponding celebration is the bat mitzvah. Since in Orthodox and Chasidic Judaism, girls are not permitted to participate in the reading of the Torah, a bat mitzvah celebration is generally carried out in a school Shabbat party similar to a birthday celebration or in a family setting at a dinner after Shabbat. In some Jewish congregations, however, the girl's bat mitzvah is identical to the bar mitzvah.

ing cope with the process of disposing of the body of the person who has moved on to a new, nonhuman status such as "spirit." They also help those closest to the deceased cope with the process of grieving by transforming it into a socially constrained process. For instance, dramatic wailing may sometimes be *mandated* rather than merely spontaneous. When this is the case, the emotion of grief is transformed into behavior that is, at least somewhat, brought under conscious control by virtue of its being ritualized. The grieving are also given reassurance of emotional support and a continued place in the community of the living by the presence and participation of acquaintances.

In general, rites of passage function to help individuals cope psychologically with the stress of change and to reassure them that they will make the transition to the habits of new roles successfully. The rituals not only give individuals a structured and traditional process for making the transition instead of casting them out on their own to find a way into their new roles, but they also provide the reassurance that what those individuals have seen others accomplish before—when they participated in the same rituals as members of the audience—they too can accomplish. Socially, rites of passage function to help the community be more conscious of the changes that its individual members go through and remember to relate to them in new ways appropriate to the new roles those individuals will play—thereby helping them to make the changes.

Pilgrimage

A **pilgrimage** is travel that is undertaken as a form of religious devotion. As acts of devotion, pilgrimages typically involve some significant elements of cost, hardship, or deprivation. Pilgrimages exist in many religious traditions, and they are found in all of the so-called "major religions" such as Buddhism, Hinduism, Islam, Christianity, and Judaism. They typically involve travel, either solitary or in groups, to locations that are regarded as sacred in either the mythology or legends of a religious tradition, and they usually involve some degree of desire on the part of participants to achieve a more spiritual psychological state or to attain spiritual insights. The act of traveling to sites that are sacred in religious myths or legends involves, at least implicitly, some sense that the pilgrims are reenacting the sacred stories associated with the pilgrimage sites. Sometimes pilgrimages include formal ritual reenactments of those stories in which the participants take the roles of supernatural beings or human characters. Thus, on one level or another, pilgrimages may be thought of as what Anthony Wallace (1966b) called rituals of salvation, rituals undertaken for the purpose of bringing about a transformation in the personalities or social statuses of the participants.

pilgrimage
Travel undertaken as a form of religious devotion.

Victor and Edith Turner (1978) examined Christian pilgrimages and developed a model in which pilgrimage is a transitional state, one that is a reversal of the pilgrim's previous state. As such pilgrimage challenges or subverts the existing social order: In complex societies, pilgrimages are undertaken as voluntary acts by individuals rather than as religiously organized, mandatory processes that everyone in a particular social group participates in together. In this respect, the pilgrimages of the religions of socially complex societies contrast with those in small-scale society that are mandatory, that occur at set times, that are undertaken under the guidance of others, and that function to reinforce the existing social order.

Victor Turner (1971) emphasized pilgrimage as a *liminal* state, a state of transition in which normal social boundaries and hierarchies are dissolved and participants experience a relationship of communitas with one another. He cited C. K. Yang (1961) to illustrate the special sense of community that can arise among fellow pilgrims:

> For three days and nights, the emotional tension and the religious atmosphere, together with the relaxation of certain moral restrictions, performed the psychosocial function of temporarily removing the participants from their preoccupation with small-group, convention-ridden, routinized daily life and placing them into another context of existence—the activities and feelings of the larger community. In this new orientation local inhabitants were impressed with a distinct sense of community consciousness. (p. 89)

The concept is illustrated dramatically in Malcolm X's description of his own experience in a hajj to Mecca, a statement also cited by Turner:

> You may be shocked by these words coming from me. But on this pilgrimage, what I have seen and experienced has forced me to *rearrange* much of my thought-patterns previously held and to *toss aside* some of my previous conclusions. . . . During the past eleven days here in the Muslim world, I have eaten from the same plate, drunk from the same glass, and slept in the same bed (or on the same rug)—while praying to *the same God*—with fellow Muslims, whose eyes were the bluest of blue, whose hair was the blondest of blond, and whose skin was the whitest of white. And in the *words* and in the *actions* and in the *deeds* of the "white" Muslims, I felt the same sincerity that I had felt among the black African Muslims of Nigeria, Sudan, and Ghana. We were *truly* all the same (brothers)—because their belief in one God had removed the "white" from their *minds*, the "white" from their behavior, and the "white" from their attitude. I could see from this, that perhaps if white Americans could accept the Oneness of God, then, perhaps, too, they could accept in reality the Oneness of Man—and cease to measure, and hinder, and harm others in terms of their "differences" in color. (pp. 340–41)

Other researchers have argued that this is not necessarily the case and that pilgrims may bring with them diverse agendas so that pilgrimage itself involves relationships of dialogue, contest, and diversity of viewpoints that participants may negotiate among themselves. As Glenn Bowman (1991) put this:

> Pilgrimage is above all an arena for competing religious and secular discourses [that] deconstruct the very category of "pilgrimage" into historically and culturally specific behaviors and meanings. For, if one can no longer take for granted the meaning of a pilgrimage for its participants, one can no longer take for granted a definition of the phenomenon of "pilgrimage" either. (pp. 2–3)

Places of pilgrimage may be defined by special natural features of the environment, such as mountains, forests, waterfalls, or caves. They may be architectural or artifactual objects of veneration such as temples, cathedrals, shrines, or icons. And they may even be defined by the presence of sanctified humans—for instance, living holy persons or the remains of deceased saints may attract pilgrims.

The box titled "The Hajj: Pilgrimage in Islam" exemplifies religious pilgrimage by describing the most important Islamic pilgrimage.

Islam has five essential acts of worship that are known as the Five Pillars of Islam. One of these is the obligation—for those whose circumstances make it possible—to make the Hajj, or pilgrimage, to Mecca (Makkah) in Saudi Arabia. The purpose of the Hajj is to worship Allah (God) at the Kabah, the sacred house at Mecca that, according to the Qur'an, was built by Abraham and his son Ishmael. The Kabah, a cubical building housing a black stone, is constructed of gray stone and marble, with three pillars supporting the roof and suspended lamps. The entire Kabah is covered with an enormous cloth of black brocade, but this covering is removed for the rituals of the Hajj.

The hajj is a scheduled event. It occurs during the 12th month of the Islamic lunar calendar. To participate in the hajj, each pilgrim must travel to Mecca. Before arriving in Mecca, pilgrims change their ordinary clothing for the simple clothing of the hajj: two seamless white sheets for men and simple white dresses and scarves for women. On arriving in Mecca, the first act of the pilgrimage is a ritual called the *tawaf*. In this ritual, pilgrims walk around God's house, the Kabah, seven times in a counterclockwise direction. At the beginning of each circuit they pray, "(I begin) in the Name of Allah who is Most Great. O Allah! (I perform) believing in thee, confirming Thy Book, fulfilling Thy Pledge, and following the Way of Thy Prophet, Muhammad—Blessing and peace upon him!" As they walk around the Kabah, they repeat another standard prayer: "Labbayka Allahumma Labbayk," which means "Here I am at your service, O God, Here I am!" and other prayers that declare their monotheistic belief in but one God. The intent of this ritual is to awaken in each pilgrim's mind the centrality of God in all things, the recognition that God is the center of their lives and the source of all meaning. During the circling of the Kabah, pilgrims who manage to reach the innermost part of the circling crowd—which numbers in the thousands—may attempt to kiss or at least touch the Black Stone which is set in the main corner of the building. Although this is not a requirement for a valid hajj, it is considered to be a special blessing to those who accomplish it, since the Black Stone is believed to be the only remaining stone of the original building erected by Abraham and Ishmael. The stone itself, which is thought to be a meteorite, is believed to have been brought to earth by the angel Jibral (Gabriel) to be set as the cornerstone of God's House. Those who touch or kiss the stone feel a special connection with the sacred history involved.

Next comes the *sa'i*, a brisk walk in which pilgrims hurry back and forth seven times between two small hills named Safa and Marwah. In so doing they reenact the Biblical and Qur'anic story of Hajar's (Hagar's) desperate search for life-giving water and food for her son Ishmael and herself after they were sent into the desert by Abraham. The sa'i also symbolizes pilgrims' dedication to spend all of their energy pursuing the path of God. Pilgrims may then drink from a spring called Zamzam that is believed to have miraculously appeared by the will of God to provide for Hajar and Ishmael's needs.

After the run between Safa and Marwah, pilgrims travel several miles to the plain of Mina, where they camp for the night. The next morning they travel to the plain of Arafat, where they spend the day in prayer and supplication. Here once again pilgrims pray, "Lord, I am present, Lord, I am present." In so doing, they remind themselves that they will be present before God on the Last Day of Reckoning when all will be judged by God. That night they move to a new campsite at Muzdalifa between the plains of Mina and Arafat. The following morning the pilgrims return to Mina, where, at a place called Jamrae-Uqba, they throw seven pebbles at a stone pillar that represents the devil. This symbolizes their rejection of Satan and the polytheism that he fostered. By casting stones at the pillar, pilgrims remind themselves that their relationship with Satan is one of enmity and renew their dedication to drive Satan from their lives. After this, the pilgrims sacrifice an animal such as a sheep and distribute the meat to family, friends, and poor and needy people in the community. The sacrifice itself symbolizes the sacrifice of one's self, a declaration of faith that one is willing even to die

(box continues)

(*box continued*)
in the service of God. This is very expressive of the very name, Islam, which means "submission." True believers in the One God should completely submit themselves to God; and nothing, neither Satan, nor pride, nor even their own lives, should stand between them and Allah.

The final rituals of the Hajj require pilgrims to return to Mecca, where they once again perform a *tawaf* and a *sa'i*. The close of the Hajj is marked by a festival, the Eid al-Adha, which is celebrated with prayers and the exchange of gifts in Muslim communities everywhere.

SOCIAL INEQUALITY AND RITUALS OF RESISTANCE

Social unity need not imply social equality. Rituals play a role in maintaining all parts of a social order, including class distinctions and other social inequalities. They may also play a role in resisting these inequalities in support of a different social order than the prevailing one.

Religion and Social Inequality

The role of religion in perpetuating the stability of social inequality is illustrated by the case of the Barakumin of Japan. Ohnuki-Tierney (1987) estimates that there are about three million Barakumin in Japan. They form an underclass thought to be descended from those who performed polluting tasks such as working with hides or handling corpses. Today, Barakumin have other menial occupations, but their social pollution continues. For instance, they are sometimes referred to as *eta-hinin,* which means "very polluted/unclean nonpersons," or even as *yotsu,* a term for four-legged animals.

The pariah status of the Barakumin included their segregation into their own communities, and this segregation was reflected in religious practice as well. For instance, Buddhist temples in Barakumin communities were referred to as *eta-dera,* or "impure temples." The Buddhist doctrine of *karma,* the belief that people's behavior in their past lives is the cause of their current circumstances, provided a ready justification for Japanese society's treatment of the Barukamin as a polluted class. When Buddhist priests recorded the names of Barakumin who had been given a Buddhist funeral service in the temple's records and even on the burial tombs, it was common for a derogatory epithet such as "beast," "humble," "ignoble," "servant" to be associated with the name to indicate that the deceased was of Baraku origin. Thus, religion reinforced the social stigma carried by the Barakumin.

In contrast, rituals of resistance undermine the power of a social order. This was an important role for religion among Black slaves in America. In resistance to the imposition of inequality, Blacks sometimes met secretly to discuss their spiritual concerns and sometimes did so more openly. For instance, the Black preacher John Jasper achieved great popularity among Whites as well as Blacks in many parts of the South during the American Civil War. Although his preaching was patterned after the popular evangelical Christian style of the day and his topics did not offend a White audience, he sometimes conveyed hidden messages of hope to his Black audience at the same time. His most popular sermon was overtly a fundamentalist tirade against the scientific idea that the earth revolves around the sun, in which he used biblical verses to demonstrate that it is the sun that revolves around the earth. By overtly refuting this example of scientific "natural law," he could use examples such as God's stopping the movement of the sun at the behest of Joshua to suggest that slavery—which was widely justified as another part of the "natural order of things"—was something God could also bring to a stop.

Revitalization Movements as Resistance

Anthony Wallace suggested that some rituals help participants cope with widespread societal stresses such as those that result from natural disasters, warfare, epidemic diseases, or other problems that undermine the usual smooth functioning of a society. He calls these rituals, typically involved in the birth of new religious movements, *revitalization rituals;* they can arise as part of a social group's efforts to cope with and resist change that has been imposed from outside. In these rituals, new systems of beliefs and values are communicated and reinforced in their participants. The processes that give rise to revitalization rituals will be discussed in detail in Chapter 10.

Chapter Summary

1. Rituals are the quintessential religious behavior. They embody important information about the ideological and social unity of a group, and participation in rituals reaffirms this unity to those who already share in it.
2. Participation in rituals publicly and unambiguously communicates acceptance of the community morality symbolized by a ritual.
3. Religious symbols are characteristically multivocal in having many equally valid meanings.
4. Religious rituals do not have just one correct meaning. Rather, they express many different meanings simultaneously.
5. The enactment of religious beliefs in ritual imbues those beliefs with a sense of timelessness and sacredness.
6. The most sacred beliefs of a religion that define the essential basis for the rest of its ideology, a religion's ultimate sacred postulates, are assertions that cannot be proved or disproved because the claims they make have no empirical referents in the world of ordinary experience. A religion's ultimate sacred postulates often play a central role in its liturgical orders.
7. The purpose of religious rituals is to influence the supernatural. Technological rituals are performed to control various aspects of nature. Therapy and anti-therapy rituals function to influence the human body. Social control rituals are intended to maintain the stability of society. The purpose of rituals of salvation is to cause a temporary or permanent change in the participant's personality. Revitalization rituals are conducted to help people cope with large-scale societal stresses.
8. Religious rituals differ in the degree of anticipated effectiveness. Magical rituals are performed mechanistically, with great attention to detail and pre-

cision in their performance. They are thought of as compulsive in their effect, when they are performed correctly. Petitionary rituals are performed with the intent of influencing supernatural beings. Although their performance is believed to increase the likelihood of a desired outcome, it is understood that the supernatural beings they are intended to influence may choose not to grant that outcome.

9. Magical rituals use two symbolic principles: the idea that like produces like or that an effect resembles its cause and the idea that things which have once been in contact with each other continue to act on each other at a distance after physical contact has been severed.

10. Participating in rituals with others helps people achieve a sense of unity called *communitas*, in which the usual hierarchical relationships between the members of a group are overcome and individuals perceive themselves as part of a community of equals.

11. Rituals are often described as consisting of three phases: (1) a "separation" phase in which participants are taken out of the ordinary setting in which they conduct their mundane life work and enter a sacred setting that is set apart for the ritual, (2) a "betwixt-and-between" phase called the "liminal period" in which the feelings of the participants are characterized by communitas, and (3) a phase in which participants are reintegrated into their normal social life.

12. Religious rituals called rites of passage can facilitate change in the lives of individuals while reinforcing the stability of the social order in which those individuals participate. They are typically performed when individuals pass from one socially recognized status to another, especially when they progress through the stages of life that are normally experienced within their society: birth, puberty, marriage, and death.

13. Religion may be a source of motivation for social change and conflict as well as for stability.

Recommended Readings

1. Durkheim, Emile. 1958. *The Rules of the Sociological Method.* Translated by Sarah A. Solovay and John H. Mueller. Glencoe, IL: Free Press. First published in French, 1895.

2. Middleton, John. 1960. *Lugbara Religion: Ritual and Authority among an East African People.* Oxford: Oxford University Press. A classic anthropological analysis of religion in its social context.

3. Morinis, A., ed. 1992. *Sacred Journeys: The Anthropology of Pilgrimage.* Westport, CT: Greenwood Press. A key work for understanding pilgrimage.

4. Morinis, A. 1984. *Pilgrimage in the Hindu Tradition: A Case Study of West Bengal.* Delhi: Oxford University Press.

5. Ohnuki-Tierney, Emiko. 1987. *The Monkey as Mirror: Symbolic Transformations in Japanese History and Culture.* Princeton: Princeton University Press. An examination of Japanese culture that emphasizes the interplay of culture and ritual.

6. Ortner, Sherry. 1978. *Sherpas through Their Rituals.* Cambridge: Cambridge University Press. Ortner demonstrates how the fundamental assumptions of a people are portrayed in their ritual performances.

7. Swanson, Guy. 1974. *The Birth of the Gods: The Origin of Primitive Beliefs.* Ann Arbor: University of Michigan Press. Tests a number of hypotheses concerning the Durhkheimian view that religion is a symbolic portrayal of important parts of a society's social organization.
8. Turner, Victor. 1969. *The Ritual Process: Structure and Anti-Structure.* Chicago: Aldine.

Recommended Websites

1. *http://www.accesstoinsight.org/lib/bps/wheels/wheel402.html#ch1*
   A summary of the rituals and ceremonies of Sri Lankan Buddhism.
2. *http://www.siu.edu/~anthro/mccall/children.html*
   A site about rites of passage and cultural identity.
3. *http://www.artsednet.getty.edu/ArtsEdNet/Resources/Maps/wed.html*
   Weddings as a rite of passage.
4. *http://dushkin.com/webquester/anthrosites/funeral.html*
   Funerals as a rite of passage.
5. *http://www.nd.edu/~jneyrey1/miracles.html*
   Provides social science perspectives on religious healing.

Study Questions

1. What did Wallace mean when he said that rituals have "no information value"?
2. What social functions do rites of passage play?
3. According to folklorist Barre Toelken, what are the four levels of meaning in Navajo Coyote stories?
4. How do magical rituals differ from petitionary rituals?
5. In what sense did Wallace contend that rituals are the central core of religion?
6. What is the social function of the Jewish bar mitzvah?
7. How is it possible that anti-therapy rituals appear actually to be able to cause death?
8. Why does the fact that the weasel is considered pretty by the Shoshone make it an appropriate animal to use in love magic?
9. What is the main social function of participation in ritual?
10. How does the state of communitas contrast with the structured daily life of routine social existence?
11. What are the common characteristics of pilgrimage?
12. Illustrate the role that religion may play in stimulating social change.

CHAPTER 8

Religious Social Organization

CHAPTER OUTLINE

Case Study: The Vision Quest among the Plains Indians
Religious Practices
    Cult Institutions
Religious Practitioners
    Shamans
    Box: Wicca, Contemporary European-American Shamans
    Sorcerers
    Box: Navajo Skinwalkers
    Priests
    Prophets
Religious Social Organization
    Types of Religious Organizations and the Evolution of Religion
    Denominational Size and Support for Societal Values

CHAPTER OBJECTIVES
When you finish this chapter, you will be able to

1. Analyze the structure of religions in terms of cult institutions.
2. Discuss the status of shamans and the roles that they play.
3. Compare and contrast the concepts of sorcerer and shaman.
4. Compare and contrast the roles of shamans, priests, and prophets.
5. Explain how cult institutions are organized into various types of religion.
6. Discuss the social characteristics that are associated with the practice of spirit-possession rituals and spirit-travel rituals.

All religions bring people together in settings where they cooperate in performing rituals. Even in the least complex societies, these group activities include a division of labor that differentiates religious specialists from others. The simplest form of religious specialization need only involve two persons, the specialist and a client, while religious specialists in more complex societies may be organized into hierarchies of cooperating religious specialists. In the case study, "The Vision Quest among the Plains Indians," we first examine the role of personal rituals that are meaningful in a larger religious system.

CASE STUDY

The Vision Quest among the Plains Indians

Individualistic cult institutions played a prominent role in the religions of most of the Plains Indians. The best-known example was the famous "vision quest" that was practiced throughout the Plains cultural area. In the vision quest, young men attempted to establish a personal relationship with a supernatural patron or helper through a period of social isolation and fasting. Normally, they fasted and did without drink for four days, asking for pity from the spirits. In some tribes, the supplicant would also engage in other forms of self-punishment to gain the pity of the spirits. For instance, Robert Lowie (1954) pointed out that Crow Indians "usually cut off a finger joint" (p. 158) as part of the vision quest.

In his lonely and uncomfortable isolation, the vision-quest supplicant might be rewarded with a vision of a spirit or might feel the spirits communicated with him through sounds such as a rustling of leaves or the call of a bird. Lowie gives the example of Crow Indians who "tell how on their lonely vigil they saw a spirit or several spirits riding along, how the rocks and trees in the neighborhood turned into enemies who attacked the horsemen, but were unable to inflict any harm." For the supplicant, "the symbolical meaning of these apparitions is that the spirits are making the visionary invulnerable" (p. 159).

According to Lowie, "The supernatural beings who befriend man vary enormously in character. Animals were very frequent visitants of Plains Indians; buffalo, elk, bears, eagles (sometimes conceived as birds producing thunder by flapping their wings), and sparrow hawks constantly figure in the narratives, but also quite lowly beasts such as dogs or rabbits. . . . Celestial patrons are also frequent, stars figuring prominently among the Pawnee. Fanciful creatures of more or less human shape likewise appear in visions, e.g., a dwarf with a very powerful musculature. Sometimes the patron comes in human guise but in disappearing assumes his true shape or otherwise gives a clue to his identity" (pp. 159–160).

According to Lowie, "the spirit normally taught the Crow a sacred song, instructed him just how he must dress in battle or if a man was to become a doctor what medicines or curing devices he must use, and frequently imposed certain taboos as to diet or behavior" (p. 160). Once the relationship was established, a spirit patron would continue to help its human partner throughout his life, making him more successful in acquiring horses, in war, and in other pursuits. The vision quest was not a once-in-a-lifetime event. Rather, individuals might participate in vision quests repeatedly throughout their lives, each time acquiring new instructions that would strengthen their spiritual power. Lowie explains that "Often the visionary not only wore some token of his vision or painted it on, say, his shield cover, but also on the strength of successive visions assembled the ingredients to build up a 'medicine bundle,' i.e., a wrapper containing a set of sacred objects indicated by the spirit. A Pawnee bundle contained as a minimum one pipe, tobacco, paints, certain birds, and corn—all assembled in a container of buffalo hide that was hung from the wall of the lodge" (p. 160).

In those societies that cannot afford the services of *full-time* religious specialists, religious statuses are not organized into a neat series of totally separate roles. For instance, the same individual might make use of both sorcery and shamanism. So, before defining the various possible specialists that might be found, we must first consider the different kinds of religious activities that religious practitioners participate in.

Cult Institutions

cult institution
A set of rituals all having the same general goal, all explicitly rationalized by a set of similar or related beliefs, and all supported by the same social group.

individualistic cult institution
The rituals of a religion that involve only one individual.

Anthony Wallace (1966b, pp. 75–96) coined the phrase **cult institution** to refer to "a set of rituals all having the same general goal, all explicitly rationalized by a set of similar or related beliefs, and all supported by the same social group." All cult institutions can be described in terms of the social relationships involved in carrying out their rituals. The simplest cult institutions involve only one person. A group of rituals carried out by one person is what Wallace called an **individualistic cult institution.** These institutions include rituals such as personal prayer in which practitioners perform religious rituals for their own benefit.

All religions have individualistic rituals that anyone may perform on occasions; performance is not limited to a class of specialists. Individualistic rituals include all those rituals that individuals perform on their own initiative to make their own lives less stressful than they otherwise would be. They include prayer and other rituals for maintaining or improving health, finding food and shelter, protecting oneself from any form of danger, finding lost objects, or fulfilling any of the thousands of other needs that individuals may have.

shamanic cult institution
The rituals of a religion that involve at least two persons, the ritual practitioner and a client who is intended to benefit from the performance of the practitioner.

The **shamanic cult institution** involves at least two persons, the ritual practitioner and a client who intends to benefit from the performance of the practitioner. Again, the practitioner need not necessarily be a specialist in performing shamanic rituals, although she or he may specialize in such rituals on a part-time basis. Shamanic rituals may be performed for all the same purposes as individualistic rituals are. The shamanic cult institution exists simply because sometimes individuals may not be willing or able

Figure 8.1
A Shamanic Curing Ceremony
This Kalahari San shaman, while in a trance, lays his hands on the patient in order to cure him.

to rely on their own ability to influence supernatural beings or forces sufficiently well enough to be satisfied with their own performance of individualistic rituals. When that is the case, they may turn to someone else whom they believe to be more skilled or successful at performing effective religious rituals. A woman in labor might perform her own rituals to facilitate the process of childbirth, but she might also ask a relative, the midwife, or someone else to give her the added support of her or his ritual intervention as well. An ill person might not be satisfied with personal prayer as a means of recovery and might ask for shamanistic rituals to be performed by someone else, hoping that these might better insure recovery. In other words, shamanic rituals are like individualistic rituals, but they are performed for the benefit of someone else.

The **communal cult institution** consists of all the rituals that members of the same religion participate in as group activities for the benefit of all involved in the ritual or even of the entire community of which they are a part. Since the performance of communal rituals requires organizing a number of people, religions that have communal cult institutions often have at least some communal rituals that are scheduled by the calendar or in situations that normally bring people together, such as communal hunts or meetings between neighboring groups for political or economic purposes. Nevertheless, communal rituals can sometimes also be organized by an individual who calls together a group for that purpose, as, for instance, when a family head asks all members of the household to participate in a communal fast and prayer for some need that has arisen that will affect the entire household or community.

communal cult institution
The rituals that members of the same religion participate in as group activities for the benefit of all involved in the ritual or even the entire community of which they are a part.

The last of Wallace's cult institutions is the **ecclesiastical cult institution,** in which a religious specialist is charged with performing rituals for the benefit of an entire congregation. Such rituals are often scheduled by the calendar or convened on the authority of the regular practitioner. Ecclesiastical rituals are more specialized than are those of the other cult institutions, which may more easily be performed on the spur of the moment or with little preparation. Since they are performed by specialists who may have devoted much time and energy perfecting their ritual skills, they may have a degree of elaborateness and intricacy that individualistic, shamanic, or even communal rituals may not have. They include exhorting the group

ecclesiastical cult institution
The rituals of a religion in which a religious specialist is charged with performing rituals for the benefit of an entire congregation.

Figure 8.2
A Communal Ritual
As part of the communal cult institution of their religion, members of the Church of Lord Jesus in Jolo, West Virginia, handle dangerous rattlesnakes and drink strychnine during a worship service.

through sermons, blessing crops, insuring the success of military expeditions, and other traditional rituals that are performed by a specialist to benefit a community or some part of it.

RELIGIOUS PRACTITIONERS

Since religious rituals are sometimes practiced in group settings, the description of any religion requires consideration of the kinds of religious specialists who are involved in conducting rituals and ceremonies for others and the ways these specialists are sometimes organized in respect to one another. We will now examine four types of religious specialists: shamans, sorcerers, priests, and prophets.

Shamans

Shamanism is thought by some to be the most ancient of religious practices because it has been found in all of the technologically simplest societies that anthropologists have studied. Cave paintings in France that are about 25,000 years old appear to document the existence of practitioners of shamanic rituals. In the religions of the least technologically developed of human societies, the foraging peoples, shamans have remained the principal religious practitioners into contemporary times; and shamans can be found within industrialized societies as well, plying their trade as spirit mediums, diviners, fortune-tellers, and astrologers.

Where shamanism is the sole system of religious rituals, all individuals are able to perform rituals on their own behalf and are believed to have access to the same supernatural powers as anyone else. There are no religious leaders to monopolize the right to perform certain rituals or to assert religious authority over the lives of others. The only religious specialist is the **shaman,** a part-time, charismatic religious specialist who conducts rituals for individual clients. Shamans differ from other persons only in their reputation for skill and effectiveness in performing rituals, so they are often sought out by others to do rituals on their behalf.

shaman
A part-time practitioner of religious rituals who serves individual clients.

Shamans may be men or women. They are charismatic individuals who are believed to have been called to their role by visionary experiences. Eliade (1974, p. 43) describes the vision a shaman experiences as a symbolic death and resurrection. He cites the case of a Yurok-Samoyed shaman named Ganykka who said, "Once when he was beating his drum the spirits came down and cut him in pieces, also chopping off his hands. For seven days and nights he remained unconscious, stretched on the ground. During this time his soul was in the sky, journeying with the Spirit of Thunder and visiting the god Mikkulai" (p. 38). He also recounts the story of an Avam Samoyed shaman in these words: "Sick with smallpox, the future shaman remained unconscious for three days and so nearly dead that on the third day he was almost buried. His initiation took place during this time. He remembered having been carried into the middle of a sea. There he heard his Sickness (that is, smallpox) speak, saying to him: 'From the Lords of the Water you will receive the gift of shamanizing. Your name as a shaman will be *Huottarie* (Diver)'" (p. 39), after which the shaman's spirit visited the Lady of the Water and her husband, the Lord of Madness and various Lords of nervous disorders, and other deities who gave him the power of curing illnesses.

Shamanic rituals are used for many reasons—for instance, to find lost objects, to bless tools and weapons so they will be more effective, to provide amulets that protect people from various harm, to cure diseases, or to perform any other task that requires the control of religious powers with more skill than a potential client personally possesses. In performing these services, the most basic skill of the shaman is the ability to enter trance states and communicate with and control spirits. William Howells (1986) put it this way: "A shaman is a medium and a diviner, but his powers do not stop there. He differs from other men in general, . . . because he can shift gears and move in the plane of the supernatural. He can go at will to the other world, and he can see and treat with souls or spirits, meeting them on their own ground" (p. 125). The shaman may call spirits to his or her presence, be possessed by them so that they may speak through the shaman, control them with magic for the benefit of clients, or practice **soul flight,** sending the soul out of the body to travel to the spiritual plane, visit spirits, and obtain information for clients. Jarich Oosten (1986) summarizes characteristics of Inuit shamans, called *angakkut* (singular, *angakok*), this way: "The angakkut controlled techniques of trance which enabled their souls to leave their bodies, and to travel in the worlds of souls and spirits. But even if they were not in trance they could perceive souls and spirits, which could not be seen by other Inuit. Illumination and sharp vision were marked characteristics of the angukkut among the Inuit in Canada. 'When a person becomes an angakok, a light covers his body. He can see supernatural things. The stronger the light is within him, the deeper and farther away he can see, and the greater is his supernatural power' (Boas 1907:133). Rasmussen refers to the *qaumaniq* or *angakua* [variant spelling of *angakok*], lighting or enlightenment, which enabled the angakkuq to see through the darkness and to perceive hidden things (cf. Rasmussen 1929:112–3)" (p. 120).

Knud Rasmussen (1926a) gives a vivid account of the soul flight of an Iglulik Eskimo shaman on behalf of a sick client:

> The shaman sits for a while in silence [in a darkened house], breathing deeply, and then, after some time has elapsed, he begins to call upon his helping spirits, repeating over and over again: "The way is made ready for me; the way opens before me!"
>
> Whereat all present must answer in chorus: "Let it be so!" . . .
>
> And now one hears, at first under the sleeping place: "Halala—he—he—he, halala—he—he—he!" and afterwards under the passage, below the ground, the same cry: "Halala—he!" And the sound can be distinctly heard to recede farther and farther until it is lost altogether. Then all know that he is on his way to the ruler of the sea beasts. (p. 461)

The ground has opened up and the shaman's spirit travels down to the bottom of the sea where he eventually reaches the goddess Takánakapsâluk, the patroness of animals, who sends illness and withholds game from hunters when she has been neglected. There he curries the favor of the goddess by stroking her hair and combing out its tangles. Upon returning to his body, the shaman then

soul flight
Sending the soul out of the body to travel the spiritual plane, visit spirits, and obtain information for clients.

leads the members of the client's community in confessing a series of taboo violations, since the sins of people have gathered about the body of the sea goddess and must be removed by confession. Once she has been propitiated properly, Takánakapsâluk will remit the illness that has come about because of these sins and will reward the household with an abundance of game.

Joan Townsend (1997) explains that "The induction of a shamanic state of consciousness can be accomplished in a variety of ways including drumming, dancing, chanting, fasting, and meditation. In some societies, notably in Middle and South America and Siberia, hallucinogens may be used to induce the state." (p. 442). Richard Noll (1985) contends that shamans make use of an innate human capacity, the ability to experience mental imagery to produce their visions. The neophyte shaman undergoes a two-phase process, first learning "to increase the *vividness* of his visual imagery through various psychological and physiological techniques" that allow the shaman to "block out the noise produced by the external stimuli of perception and to attend to internal imagery processes, thus bringing them more clearly into focus. . . . Once the novice shaman can report more vivid imagery experiences, a second phase of shamanic mental imagery training is aimed at increasing the *controlledness* of the experienced visual imagery contents, actively engaging and manipulating the visionary phenomena" (pp. 445–46). The full-fledged shaman is, in other words, able to induce vivid visual imagery and to control the contents of the visionary experience.

Shamans may have learned the rituals that they use, but they also have the skill to creatively alter them to better meet the needs of individual clients. One of the more common problems of life for which people seek out the services of a shaman is illness, so the shaman has sometimes been referred to as a "magico-religious curer." But this is an oversimplification, since shamans provide many other kinds of services as well. For instance, an Apache friend of mine had a shotgun blessed by a shaman so that it would be more effective when he used it to hunt deer. Nevertheless, in all societies in which shamans are the principal religious practitioner, they cure illnesses; and they are probably asked to perform cures more than any other task.

Shamanic Curing

Although all cultures recognize that some illnesses can be treated by non-religious techniques such as the use of herbs, religious cures are based on the belief that some illnesses are caused by supernatural forces. These fall into five major categories: soul loss, spirit possession, object intrusion, witchcraft or sorcery, and taboo violation.

Soul Loss

soul loss
The belief that one's spirit has left one's body, causing the body to languish, sicken, and, perhaps, to die.

The belief that one's spirit has left one's body, causing the body to languish, sicken, and, perhaps, die is called **soul loss.** Soul loss may be thought of as the result of sorcery or witchcraft or may be thought to have happened because the spirit of the victim was dislodged from the body by a "magical fright." The belief in soul loss is particularly common in societies where children are strongly socialized to be independent and self-reliant—that is, where people are concerned about the importance of succeeding through personal effort and where being dependent on the help of others is looked down on as evidence of personal weakness. This is exemplified by a story that a Bolivian friend shared with me. He and a half dozen men once took a horseback trip that was planned to last for over a week. One of the riders, a colonel in the military, was passing a large tree when one of its branches snapped and fell, startling both the rider and his horse. He began to worry that the incident had dislodged his spirit from his body, that it was wandering aimlessly and he would die if it were not recovered. The men decided to end the trip and return to La Paz so that the colonel could be treated by a shaman for soul loss.

Spirit Possession

The belief in **spirit possession** as a cause of illness holds that an unfriendly spirit has entered a person's body and caused suffering. Spirit-possession beliefs are most common in societies in which child-rearing emphasizes the importance of being helpful and supportive of others rather than independent and assertive. Being possessed may symbolize the patient's stress about being dominated by powerful others. In spirit-possession illnesses, the task of curing involves removing the offending spirit from the body of the patient. Like soul loss, spirit possession may be thought of as caused intentionally by a witch or sorcerer, or it may simply be the act of a spirit who decides to invade a human's body.

spirit possession
The belief that a
spirit has entered
one's body and
now controls its
actions.

In socially complex societies in which hierarchies of authority are common, the religious solution might be for a priest to exercise divine authority and "command" the evil spirit to depart. However, in socially simple societies without the basis for a metaphor of religious "authority" of this kind, the symbolism of the cure is likely to be phrased in terms of a personal conflict rather than a conflict of authority. The invading spirit must be overcome and dominated or cast out by someone personally strong enough to do so. Four approaches are common. First, the shaman might use magic that is powerful enough to force the spirit to leave. A variant of this approach would be to make the patient's body uncomfortable for the spirit to inhabit so that it will choose to leave. For instance, the shaman might torture the patient, as was sometimes done in medieval Europe when persons were believed to have been possessed. A second approach would be for the shaman to wrestle with the evil spirit until it is forced to submit to the greater strength of the shaman, who may then remove it. Such a contest might be acted out bodily by the shaman, or the shaman might enter a spirit travel trance and send his or her own spirit into the body of the victim to carry out the fight. A third approach would be for the shaman to send another spirit, one greater than the one in the patient's body, to fight with the offending spirit. Finally, in some societies patients are taught the shamanistic skill of controlling spirits so that they can learn to control the spirit which vexes them.

object intrusion
The belief that
explains illness
by attributing it
to the presence
of a foreign body,
a "disease ob-
ject," in the pa-
tient's body.

Object Intrusion

The theory of **object intrusion** explains illness by attributing it to the presence of a supernatural foreign body, a **disease object,** in the patient's body. Again, this form of illness can be caused by sorcery or witchcraft, but it may also occur spontaneously. The cure for object intrusion involves removing the disease object by a ritual of sucking it from the body, massaging the body to manipulate the object until it can be removed, or symbolically brushing away

disease object
A supernaturally
powerful object
that causes illness
when it enters or
is magically pro-
jected into a vic-
tim's body.

Wicca is a neopagan religion that was formed in the 1950s and popularized by a retired British civil servant, Gerald Gardner, and his initiate and High Priestess Doreen Valiente. According to the U.S. Armed Forces handbook for chaplains, "After the repeal of the anti-Witchcraft laws in Britain in 1951, Gerald Gardner publicly declared himself a witch and began to gather a group of students and worshipers. In 1962, two of his students, Raymond and Rosemary Buckland (religious names: Lady Rowan and Robat), emigrated to the United States and began teaching witchcraft here. At the same time, other groups of people became interested in witchcraft by reading books by Gardner and others. Many covens were spontaneously formed from a combination of research and individual inspiration. These self-created covens are today regarded as just as valid as those who can trace a 'lineage' of teaching back to England" (U.S. Chaplains Service Institute, 1990, p. 231).

Wicca is polytheistic, accepting the existence of many gods and goddesses from a variety of different religious traditions, but most Wiccans believe that there is a creative force in the universe known as the One or the All. Although little can be known about the One itself, it is manifest in nature and throughout the natural processes and cycles of nature. Most Wiccans believe that the divine creativity is manifest in some form of two coequal divinities, the Great Mother goddess, who embodies the symbols of the earth and the moon, and her male consort, the God, who is manifest as the sun, the sky, the forest, the hunt, and the grain of the fields. Wiccans may also accept the existence of many other gods and goddesses, including ones found in a variety of other religious traditions.

All Wiccans recognize eight Sabbats or "Days of Power" during the year. Four occur on the solstices, and four are based on folk festivals. In *Yule*, the shortest day of the year (between December 21 and 23), the Goddess gives birth to the God, her son. This is a time of darkness when the God is not yet strong. The second day of February marks *Imbolg*, when the Goddess recovers from giving birth, and the God grows stronger as the days

lengthen until its warmth fertilizes the earth, and seeds begin to germinate. *Ostara* (March 21–23, when the night and day are of equal length) marks the first day of spring, when the God reaches maturity as the fertility of the Goddess is seen on the earth. On *Beltane* (April 30), which begins the time of vitality, God enters manhood and the Goddess becomes his lover. The summer solstice, or *Litha* (June 21–23), begins the season when the powers of nature become strongest. *Lughnasadh,* or *Lammas* (August 1), is the celebration of the first harvest. The God begins to lose his strength, and the Goddess watches in sorrow for his impending death. *Mabon,* the autumnal equinox (September 21–23), marks the completion of the harvest, and the God prepares to die. *Samhain* (October 31) is the Wiccan New Year's celebration, when the God dies and Wiccans hold the feast of the dead to remember departed kin and friends.

Wicca is a good illustration of the fact that religious ideology is tremendously diverse and a particular religion may not fit perfectly into the neat categories that have arisen in the social sciences to talk about religion. Is the practitioner of Wicca a "witch"? The answer is not altogether clear. At its core, becoming a practicing Wiccan can be thought of as becoming aware of one's innate spiritual ability to relate to and use the creative force that permeates all reality. As Raymond Buckland (1986) put it, "We practice rites to attune ourselves to the natural rhythms of life forces" (p. 9). Many Wiccans therefore emphasize the importance of meditation and visualization techniques by which one's inner powers can be realized. Wiccans sometimes describe themselves as having always had an intuitive empathy for animals or as being "sensualists" by nature, traits that suggest a perception of Wicca as involving innate characteristics. Yet Wiccans may also practice rituals to channel the creative forces of nature. Thus, there are characteristics in Wicca that crosscut the anthropological categories of witch versus shaman/sorcerer, reminding us that these distinctions sometimes have fuzzy boundaries.

(box continues)

(*box continued*)

Wicca has no "commandments," but is guided by two general principles, the Threefold Law and the Wiccan Rede. The Threefold Law states, "All good that a person does to another returns threefold in this life; harm is also returned threefold." This principle is frequently cited by Wiccans as the reason why they use their powers only in ways that do not harm others. The Wiccan Rede is best known in its short form: "These eight words the wiccan rede fulfill; An' harm ye none, do what ye will." The Rede is understood to be an equivalent to the Golden Rule, recommending an ethic of behavior that does not harm others, but it is also taken to be a descriptive truth: The creative powers of the universe respond to the human will.

One interesting aspect of Wicca is its grassroots organization. Wicca has no ecclesiastical hierarchy, no central authority, and no unified doctrine to which all must subscribe. Rather, like Hinduism, it can be defined by broad similarities of belief and practice yet accepts much diversity when it comes to both the specific theological symbols its followers use and the autonomy of local congregations. Indeed, Wiccans generally recognize that practitioners of the "Craft," as it is commonly called, include both lone, self-taught practitioners called "solitaries" and followers who are "initiated" into Wiccan traditions as members of congregations called "covens." The lack of a centralized ecclesiastical hierarchy has allowed numerous diverse styles of Wicca to flourish, as individual covens have developed their own distinctive approaches. Thus, Wicca includes not only those who follow the pattern laid down by Gerald Gardner, who first popularized Wicca, but also those who follow "Alexandrian" Wicca, founded by Alexander Sanders, a student of Gardner; Dianic Wicca (named for the goddess of wisdom, Diana), which was founded by Zsuzsanne Bedepest and which is popular in some feminist circles; the Covenant of the Goddess, which was incorporated in 1975 as a church under U.S. law but unites covens that represent a variety of different traditions; Fairie Wicca, which draws from British fairy lore; and Celtic Wicca, which emphasizes the Celtic deities. These are but a few of the diverse strands of Wicca that form the pattern of its fabric.

Who is attracted to Wicca? The answer to this question is central to understanding that religion is a means by which human beings find fulfillment. No religion has equal appeal to all individuals. Rather, the personal characteristics that our life circumstances have fostered in us predispose us each toward different religious orientations. Wicca embodies values of gender equality, the beauty of "feminine" symbolism as a guide to life, and the ability of individuals to find strength and dignity within themselves as individuals. As such, it is unsurprising that it has attracted a significant following among feminists who object to gender inequality and to hierarchies of authority that rely heavily on "masculine" symbols of power and subordination. The inner spiritual power that Wicca portrays as available to all individuals who cultivate it has much in common with the secular value of nonaggressive personal assertiveness that nonreligious feminists also advocate as an ideal for liberating individuals from the "disempowering" effects of "patriarchy." And because Wicca's positive ethics is centered in the Threefold Law and offers the hope of success through a nonhostile form of personal spirituality, it also holds an understandable attraction to individuals who perceive themselves as not having achieved personal success or validation as individuals in the mainstream social system.

---

spiritual contaminants from the patient's body. A variant of this idea is the Shoshone belief that each individual has a *mukua*, a spirit shaped like a ball of feathers that resides in the forehead and that can become contaminated, causing illness. The cure involves removing the *mukua*, cleaning it, and replacing it.

Sorcery and Witchcraft

As was explained in chapter 4, the use of magic to harm others is known to anthropologists as *sorcery*, while *witchcraft* is the use of an inborn power to work

Though they are commonly called "witches" in American English, Navajo "skinwalkers" are a good illustration of the anthropological concept of sorcerers. In Navajo, the skinwalker is called *yenaldlooshi*, "he who trots along here and there on all fours with it." Their name comes from the fact that they are believed to have the ability to don an animal skin and take on the shape of that animal. Skinwalkers symbolize the opposite of desirable Navajo behavior. They reverse the usual Navajo curing ceremonies, commit incest, prefer the night, visit cemeteries, kill their own relatives, and even participate in cannibalism and necrophilia.

Margaret Brady (1984) explains that "According to traditional Navajo belief, skinwalkers climb on top of a hogan when a family is asleep and drop pollen, specially made from the ground bones of human infants, down the smoke hole (Downs 1972, 110). Contact with this substance brings the sleeping person ill health, social problems, and sometimes death" (p. 1). According to Brady, skinwalker lore permeates Navajo life from childhood: "Downs says that it is common for older children to dress up in coyote skins, painting their faces with charcoal and other paints, and to appear suddenly to terrorize infants and very young children (1972, 111). . . . Besides this 'playing skinwalker,' almost every evening, the older children, from eight through twelve years old, tell stories about skinwalkers and witches to the younger toddlers and soon have them in a state of utter fear (Downs 1972, 111)" (pp. 60, 61). Brady gives the following example of a skinwalker story told by one 11-year-old child in her study:

One time there was a boy and a girl. They stayed home by theirselves. And their mother and father went somewhere. And then that little girl got scared and that little boy said, he said, "What are you scared of?" She said, "I'm scared of something." She heard something running around the house—a lot of things like horses. Then she said, "If something gets me, you run outside, jump on the horse, tell the horse to run real fast and don't stop, 'til whatever chases you loses you." And then that night that boy slept on top of the hogan. That little girl um that little girl um went in one of the corners of the room. Then those things, those werewolves came in. Then it said, "Check all

the corners, look around, then if you can't find anything check again and find that little girl, and cut off her head." Then that little boy saw the dancer and jumped on the horse and started running. The horse really started running. Then those other guys started running after them. Those other guys started running, came close; then almost one was holding the horse's tail so they could catch up. And then it uh missed his tail. Then it let go and then it fell down. The others kept running, that other kept running. Then that boy he came to his grandma, grandmother and grandfather's house. And then he told them what happened. He said he saw his little sister dead in the house and then they went over there with some guns. The next morning those wolves tracked into the mountains, where rocks, where a cave, a hole is.

Then he went in there and he saw a lot of heads of people in there. Then his grandfather, grandfather and father of the people he shot them all and then . . . that's all. (pp. 73–74)

Skinwalker stories contain themes that express the fears of their tellers. The fear of skinwalkers in children's stories is often associated with being alone at night. For adults, skinwalker tales are reminders that safety resides among relatives and that strangers are potentially dangerous. Who is most likely to be suspected of being a skinwalker? Brady points out that the wealthy and powerful are more likely to be suspected than others. Skinwalkers, she notes, have much in common with the rich, with politicians, and even with the aged and with Navajo curers—all of whom have more power or success than does the ordinary Navajo. "Singers and witches are very closely identified; the same linguistic term is sometimes applied to both medicine men and witches (Kluckhohn 1944, 7). All singers are expected to be familiar with some aspects of witchcraft (Kluckhohn 1944, 27). Sometimes it is believed that a singer will be in partnership with a witch: the witch will make the victim ill and then the singer will cure him. Afterwards, witch and singer split the fee. . . . It is this same sense of power that makes both rich men and politicians suspect. Men who suddenly become wealthy are often accused of being grave-robbers and hence witches or skinwalkers (Reichard [1950]1963, 2)" (p. 53).

(box continues)

Navajo cultural values emphasize the importance of maintaining good family relationships, of cooperating with others, and of personally striving to maintain a dynamic harmony—what Navajos call *hozho*, or a state of "beauty"—with the natural environment. Yet, Navajo life also fosters the need for autonomy and independent action by individuals who often find themselves without the social support network of kin and community that their culture values. Many Navajo, for instance, survive through employment in the non-Navajo urban market economy away from their family ties. In earlier times, rugged individualism was also fostered within Navajo culture. Marriage customs, for instance, typically took men away from their own kin and local community. Survival by gardening and sheepherding in a vast desert environment was difficult, and there were personal conflicts within communities because of limited resources. There were also political conflicts between Navajos and their non-Navajo neighbors. And today, more and more Navajos find themselves isolated from family because they have migrated to cities for employment in predominantly non-Navajo communities. So the values of cooperativeness and harmony were not always the day-to-day realities of life. Whatever else they might be, skinwalkers are apt symbols of deviation from the Navajo ideals of *hozho*, cooperativeness, and respect for family ties; and Navajo witchcraft beliefs and stories about skinwalkers symbolize the tensions between these two contrasting aspects of Navajo life.

ill. Both are also common explanations for illness. Sometimes the sorcerer or witch is believed to have caused illness by having stolen the victim's spirit, by having sent a spirit to possess the body of the victim, or by having "shot" a disease object into the victim's body. Other times the explanation may be that the sorcerer or witch has caused the illness more directly—the sorcerer by magically inducing the illness or the witch by simply consciously or unconsciously desiring the patient to sicken.

Taboo Violations

Finally, it may be believed that illness results from a **taboo violation,** the breaking of a spiritual rule for which illness is the consequence. This belief is particularly common in societies where a child must learn many rules before it is equipped to survive as an adult. For instance, it was a common explanation for illness among the Inuit who lived in the Arctic. Rasmussen (1926b) gives an account of a shaman guiding a patient through a cure by confession. Drawing on his knowledge of the patient, the shaman asks leading questions to elicit a series of confessions, each of which proves insufficient to achieve the cure. With each new revelation of a taboo violation, the audience calls out a plea that she be forgiven by the offended spirit. Through much soul-searching and community expression of support, the patient is finally reassured that she will be released from the effects of her transgressions and that she will therefore recover from her illness.

taboo violation
The belief that illness may result from the breaking of a spiritual rule.

A contemporary shamanistic religion is described in the box titled "Wicca, Contemporary European-American Shamans." This box also illustrates how native terminology may differ from that used by anthropologists—while most Americans, and some Wiccans, associate the term *witch* with practitioners of Wicca, most anthropologists would describe them as *shamans*.

Sorcerers

sorcerer
One who uses
magical rituals
for socially unap-
proved purposes.

Like shamanism, sorcery is the use of magical rituals to cause supernatural pow-ers or beings to fulfill human ends; but, unlike shamanism, sorcery uses these rituals to harm other people. A **sorcerer** is simply one who uses magical rituals for socially unapproved purposes. What differentiates the sorcerer from the shaman, then, is not the rituals that each uses, but the ends to which they are put. Indeed, the same individual might be both a sorcerer and a shaman, us-ing rituals sometimes to harm and sometimes to help others. Diamond Jenness (1935) described six techniques that were used by Ojibwa sorcerers to cause harm to their victims. They could induce magical harm through the Law of Contagion by sketching a victim's image on the ground and placing super-natural "medicine" made from plants over the part of the image where they wanted the pain to be felt in the victim's body. Or a wooden image of the victim could be carved and tied to a poplar tree to cause the death of the victim when the thread broke and the image fell. The Law of Contact could be utilized by scratching the victim with a poisonous spine called a *bagamuyak* that was ob-tained through trade because it came from a plant that did not grow locally. Supernatural "medicine" could be also sprinkled on a victim's food so that its effects would be taken into the victim's body. The "medicine" of sorcery could be mixed with a victim's fingernail or hair clippings, shreds of fur from his or her clothing, or even charcoal from the victim's campfire to bring the super-natural power into indirect contact with the victim. Finally, the "contact" could be highly symbolic when it occurred in the form of "shooting" into the victim's body a disease object made by chewing the leaf of a plant called *zobiginigan* to-gether with a small stick or bone. The box titled "Navajo Skinwalkers" discusses the symbolism and the social functions of the Navajo belief in a distinctive kind of sorcerer.

Priests

priests
Religious special-
ists who mediate
between the su-
pernatural realm
and humans by
performing tradi-
tional rituals for
congregations at
scheduled times.

While shamans work with individual clients, **priests** mediate between the su-pernatural realm and humans by performing traditional rituals for congrega-tions at scheduled times. While the success of shamans depends on their per-sonal charisma and their personal visionary ability, priests have authority within an ecclesiastical organization. According to Joachim Wach ([1931]1944), "The authority of the priest depends upon the charisma of his office. The call-ing, not the call, characterizes the priest" (p. 360).

Also unlike shamans, priests tend to be *full-time* religious specialists. Al-though this is not a defining characteristic, it is typically the case: The status of priest originates when societies are economically productive enough to pro-duce sedentary communities large enough to support full-time religious practi-tioners, who serve the entire community, or even a subset of the community, rather than simply performing for individual clients who seek them out. The rit-uals performed by priests are also typically conducted according to an estab-lished calendar, so that members of the congregation can anticipate when each ceremony will be held.

Wach ([1931]1944) notes that the priest's "primary function is the conduct of worship" (p. 362) and that central to this purpose is "the role which preparation and education play in the priesthood" (p. 362). The rituals performed by priests are not based on their personal inspiration, but represent established ceremonies that are handed down over the generations. As such, they must be learned by candidates for priestly offices, whose role is best understood as that of conservators of tradition. Again, this contrasts with the ritual life of shamans, who may creatively innovate and alter the specifics of a ritual to fit the needs of individual clients. As conservators of an established tradition of rituals, priest-candidates are typically trained and eventually certified as competent to hold the office of priest by an organized body of established priests. The more economically productive and socially complex a society tends to be, the more likely it is that its priests will be organized into complex ecclesiastical hierarchies, within which individual officeholders will be assigned different religious responsibilities. Within such organizations, order and tradition tend to be the watchword. As Wach puts it, "A greater emphasis is placed on the exactness of the cultic performances as a prerequisite of their efficacy" ([1931]1944, p. 363).

Given the contrasting roles of shamans and priests, it is hardly surprising that the two kinds of practitioners tend to regard one another as competitors rather than allies. With the rise of an organized priesthood, shamans tend to become marginalized, and followers of the priestly religion may be formally forbidden to seek out their services. But given the needs that shamans fulfill, priests themselves may take on some of the roles for their own followers that shamans normally perform. Thus, in addition to their defining role as performers of rituals for entire congregations, Wach explains ([1931]1944, p. 366) that priests may also become guides, advisers, comforters, "pastors," and "confessors." As conservators of tradition, they also tend to become sources of information about correct doctrine and proper social standards of conduct. In the latter role, they may be expected to be role models of piety within their communities.

Finally, according to Wach, "The priest is the guardian of traditions and the keeper of the sacred knowledge and of the technique of meditation and prayer. He is the custodian of the holy law, which corresponds to the cosmic moral and ritual order, upon which the world, the community, and the individual depend. As an interpreter of this law, the priest may function as judge, administrator, teacher, and scholar, formulate standards and rules of conduct, and enforce their observance" ([1931]1944, p. 365). All of these roles flow out of the priest's function as a *conservator* rather than innovator of tradition. His primary mandate is the maintenance of the religious status quo and, by extension, the social status quo in the community of which his congregation is a part.

Prophets

Victor Turner (1972, pp. 81–82) explained that **prophets** are the charismatic founders of new religions who base their teachings on the claim of personal revelation from the supernatural rather than from the study and interpretation of a preexisting theology. Like shamans, prophets are charismatic religious

prophets
The charismatic founders of new religions who base their teachings on the claim of personal revelation from the supernatural rather than from the study and interpretation of a preexisting theology.

innovators, but they do more than simply modify existing rituals to meet the needs of specific clients. They create entire systems of rituals and beliefs that may differ in important ways from those already practiced among the same people. Prophets may draw upon already existing religious symbolism, but the entire religious "package" they create is something new and innovative *as a complete system of religious thought, values, and practices.* They are, in short, the founders of new religious traditions.

According to Max Weber ([1922] 1963), the charisma of a prophet includes "the capacity to achieve the ecstatic states which are viewed, in accordance with primitive experience, as the preconditions for producing certain effects in meteorology, healing, divination and telepathy" (p. 47). That is, prophets are viewed as individuals who are imbued with divine power, including the power to affect natural

Figure 8.3.
A Prophet
Wovoka, the Northern Paiute prophet who founded the Ghost Dance religion.

conditions such as the weather, to cure illness, and to divine hidden knowledge, including the thoughts of others. Unlike priests, who are simply conservators of doctrine and practice, they—like shamans—are able to enter trance states and access and use divine power directly instead of merely channeling it in ways that the traditional rituals already permit.

RELIGIOUS SOCIAL ORGANIZATION

Anthony Wallace's (1966b) concept of *cult institutions,* sets of rituals that are defined by the relationships between their practitioners and their beneficiaries, can be used to describe the social organization of each religion. Since each religion is a system composed of various cult institutions, the social organization of a religion consists of the various social relationships between ritual practitioners and their audiences within all of the cult institutions that make up that religion.

Types of Religious Organizations and the Evolution of Religion

It turns out that when we categorize religions based on the ways in which cult institutions are grouped together, only three organizational types are found:

shamanic religions, communal religions, and *ecclesiastical religions.* Wallace noted that "In societies containing an ecclesiastical cult institution, there will also be communal, shamanic, and individualistic institutions. Where there is no ecclesiastical institution, but a communal one, there will also be shamanic and individualistic varieties. And where there is neither ecclesiastical nor communal, there will be shamanic and individualistic" (1966b, p. 88). In other words, shamanic religions have the structurally simplest organization of cult institutions. Communal religions add communal cult institutions to those found in shamanic religions, and ecclesiastical religions make use of all the cult institutions found in communal religions and combine them with ecclesiastical cult institutions.

Shamanic Religions

The religions with the simplest social organizations are those that Anthony Wallace (1966b) called **shamanic religions,** in which rituals may be performed by individuals in their own behalf or by shamans in behalf of clients who seek them out. According to anthropologists William Lessa and Evon Vogt ([1958] 1965), shamanic religions tend to be common in societies that have foraging subsistence economies. However, they are not limited to societies with purely foraging economies. For instance, shamanic religions were found among Asian and Siberian pastoralists. According to Wallace, they were the typical religious type in the circumpolar regions: "*Circumpolar shamanism* is found among Eskimos, northern Athapascan and Algonkian hunters, the Paleo-Siberians, central Asiatic steppe and forest tribes, and the Lapps" (p. 97). Shamanic religions are also found in isolated pockets in the tropical forests of the Andaman Islands, Malaya, and central Africa that, like the circumpolar area, were not readily invaded by horticultural peoples.

Wallace typified the shamanic religions as having individualistic cults that dealt with matters of death and day-to-day taboos. The shamanic cult institutions dealt with curing illness and divination. The ideologies of the shamanic religions generally had few major deities, and these did not typically interact with human beings except in unusual circumstances. Circumpolar shamanic religions tended to share the symbolism of supernatural Keepers of the Game, who could withhold hunting success when angered by human beings, and a world-tree motif.

Communal Religions

Religions that include a communal cult institution working in consort with a shamanic and an individualistic cult institution are called **communal religions.** They tend to be found in more socially complex societies than the simpler foraging societies could support. Societies with communal religions bring people together in larger, often semi-permanent communities. Thus, most often they are found in horticultural societies, although they are also found in some of the more affluent foraging societies. Geographically, they are particularly prominent in native North America, central Africa, Oceania, Melanesia, and Australia. Wallace characterized the communal religions as usually having

shamanic religions Religions in which only personal and shamanic rituals or ceremonies are performed.

communal religions Religions in which the rituals of individuals and shamans may be supplemented by others that are performed by groups of individuals in their own behalf or for the welfare of the entire community.

polytheistic pantheons in which major deities each controlled specific aspects of nature. "Rituals are performed in which many lay persons participate actively; a ritual calendar is related to seasonal, life crisis, and other cyclical events. The mythology is rich and variegated, although the gods are not for the most part heroic figures" (Wallace, 1966b, p. 97).

Ecclesiastical Religions

ecclesiastical religions
Religions that have ecclesiastical, communal, shamanic, and individualistic cult institutions.

The **ecclesiastical religions**, those which have ecclesiastical, communal, shamanic, and individualistic cult institutions, are typical of agricultural societies or horticultural societies that are economically productive enough to support large communities, markets, and many economic specialists. According to Turner (1972) these are societies "where the more common ceremonial is a public rite performed for the benefit of a whole village or community. Such rites are often calendrical, or performed at critical points in the ecological cycle" (p. 438). The pantheons of ecclesiastical religions have high gods—or in some cases, a single supreme deity—who are thought to be involved in upholding the political institution of their respective societies as well as control-

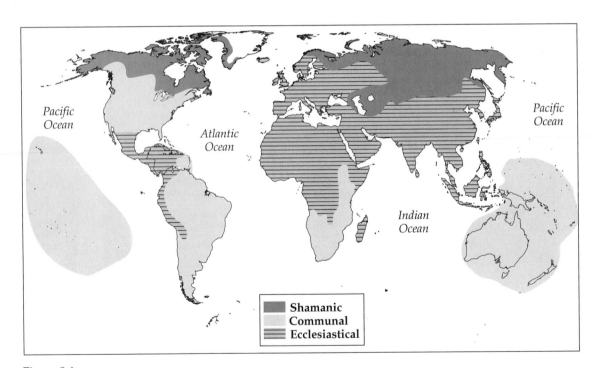

Figure 8.4
World Map of Religious Types
The most complex religious social organizations are found among the economically and politically most powerful societies and have spread at the expense of the socially less complex religious systems that tend to be most prominent in marginal areas such as the far north and far south, in tropical forest regions, and in other isolated areas.

ling aspects of nature. Their worship involves a priesthood that is often a full-time occupation. It also involves the building of temples and other permanent places of worship.

Nation-states are societies in which social classes exist and in which power is unequally distributed throughout most institutions, including the religious system. Since the status of the shaman is defined by his or her personal charisma rather than any authority of office, shamanism is at a disadvantage when it competes with ecclesiastical religions whose practitioners lay claim to authority and whose authority is legitimized by a hierarchy of fellow practitioners. Generally then, shamanism becomes a marginalized form of religion within nation-states. As Jane Atkinson (1992) noted, "Shamanic traditions have long been the target of institutionalized religion and state powers. Echoing Weber, Lewis (146:34 [1981, p. 34]) writes, 'If certain exotic religions thus allow ecstasy to rule most aspects of their adherents' lives, all the evidence indicates that the more strongly-based and entrenched religious authority becomes, the more hostile it is toward haphazard inspiration.' Such hostility is not limited to religious authority" (p. 315).

Denominational Size and Support for Societal Values

In large-scale societies, religions have followings that may number from millions to just a few. One form of religious change is the birth of new religious movements. The smaller of these ecclesiastical religions are known as *sects* and *cults.*

Sects and Cults

Religious denominations in large-scale societies vary in their degree of support for mainstream social values. The larger ecclesiastical religions tend to be accepting of mainstream social values. The smallest religious groups, called sects and cults, often espouse values that may diverge from more mainstream members of the societies in which they are found. **Sects** are denominations that work within an established religious tradition but regard their distinctive doctrines and practices as uniquely true and valid in contrast with those of other denominations whom they judge to have departed from correct belief and practice. Their approach to scriptural interpretation tends to be literalist. The membership of sects is largely based on adult conversion, and members are viewed as an exclusive or "elect" group of faithful who have been saved from the world through their commitment to the denomination, its standards of moral purity, and its doctrines. Commonly, sects lack an emphasis on a highly trained clergy and rely instead on high participation by ordinary lay members to carry out the work and rituals of the organization. Sects are often—though not necessarily—led by a single charismatic leader who has more-or-less direct contact with the grassroots members and who exercises authoritarian control over the organization. They are often hostile or at best indifferent to the larger society, which is seen as embodying values that contrast markedly with their own.

sects
Small ecclesiastical religions that are composed primarily of first-generation converted members and that espouse religious ideologies that they view as representing pristine truths lost by other denominations within the same religious tradition.

Sects may remain small and benign, offering their members a sense of special identity that they do not find in the larger society. They may also grow in numbers and may, in the process, become increasingly less critical of mainstream society if their membership becomes more representative of society at large. In some cases, a sect's alienation from or hostility toward society at large can escalate into outright conflict between government and the sect. One such case was the conflict between the Bureau of Alcohol, Tobacco, and Firearms and the Branch Davidians that led to the deaths of nearly a hundred members of the sect at their Waco, Texas, facility in 1993. Another case was the People's Temple, in which the founder, Jim Jones, exercised powerful control over his followers, whom he eventually required to die in an act of mass murder/suicide in response to Jones's fear that the sect was about to be destroyed by the U.S. government.

**cults
(new religious movements)**
Small ecclesiastical religions that are composed primarily of first-generation convert members and whose religious ideologies are not derived from the major religious or cultural traditions of the society in which they develop.

Cults (or **new religious movements**) are quite similar to sects, but while sects view themselves as reintroducing something thought of as an original truth that they believe has been lost by others, cults typically espouse an ideology that is new and different from the mainstream traditions of the society in which they arise. The contrast between their own ideology and those of their society's mainstream religions is the primary distinction between a cult and a sect. Although cults can develop their distinctive ideologies locally, their beliefs are often derived from foreign cultural traditions. Cults also tend to be even smaller than sects and typically have an even stronger tendency to be led by a single charismatic leader. They are also more likely to adopt a separatist approach to society at large, expecting their members to hold themselves more strictly apart from interaction with outside society than do sects.

"Rajneeshism," as it is sometimes called in the United States, illustrates how an imported religious tradition can gain a devoted following yet experience social conflicts with the mainstream society in which it has taken root. Rajneeshism is named after its founder, Bhagwan Shree Rajneesh, who was born in Kuchwada, Madhya Pradesh, India, in 1931 and was also known as the Bhagwan Shree Rajneesh. He taught a spiritual path that derived from Hinduism, Jainism, Zen Buddhism, Taoism, Christianity, ancient Greek philosophy, and other religions. In 1981, he came to the United States, where his teachings found fertile ground among college-aged people. In 1984, his American converts founded a commune of 4,000 inhabitants called Rajneeshpuram in eastern Oregon, where they sought spiritual enlightenment and freedom from the anxieties of modern American life through meditation and other Eastern techniques. In addition to its resident population, Rajneeshpuram also sponsored occasional festivals that brought together as many as 15,000 other followers or investigators of Rajneeshism. The movement taught a brand of ecstatic meditation and regarded sexuality as a means of experiencing the divine as well. Such practices were alien to the mainstream American population of the nearby community of Antelope, Oregon, which held legal jurisdiction over the land on which the commune had been founded. The antagonism led to conflicts such as the Antelope city council's refusing to grant building permits to the commune. When the city council repeatedly refused to grant business licenses to followers of Rajneesh, members of the commune were able to elect their own candidates to the city council. One of their first acts was to rename the city of Antelope as City of Rajneesh. Eventually, conflicts with state and federal government authorities led to Rajneesh's return to India, where he adopted the name Osho. A number of top aides were accused and convicted of various crimes, and Rajneeshpuram was abandoned, although Osho still has numerous followers within the United States.

Despite the marginality or elitist nature of their beliefs and values, new religious movements and sects do not recruit their followers primarily from among the more socially dispossessed and deprived members of society. Rather, their converts tend to be young, well-educated, and from middle-class family backgrounds. Much of the attraction of new religious movements may derive from their small, face-to-face nature, which allows them to provide a greater sense of close personal relationships among their members.

Churches

If sects or cults continue to attract more and more followers, they may remain doctrinally distinct from other denominations and continue to assert their special claim to having truths that other religious groups lack. However, sometimes growth in membership leads them toward an increasingly mainstream set of religious values. If, as they grow, they begin to emphasize their common ground with other denominations, they may become simply one of a number of different but equally mainstream denominations. Such larger religious groups that conform to the mainstream social values of their society have commonly been referred to as churches. **Churches** are the largest and ideologically most mainstream ecclesiastical religions. Because of their size, they tend to have bureaucratically organized and highly trained religious specialists. Their mainstream status is reflected in a more compromising approach to doctrine that supports the existing values and social structures of society at large and that emphasizes the application of doctrine for living *within* the larger society. Its theology tends toward harmonizing religion and secular philosophy, such as mainstream science. Instead of viewing salvation as a matter of individual worth, purity, and commitment, it is more likely to emphasize the role of grace and church sacraments.

churches
The largest and ideologically most mainstream of the ecclesiastical religions.

Chapter Summary

1. All religions are a system of cult institutions, sets of rituals all having the same general goal, all explicitly rationalized by a set of similar or related beliefs, and all supported by the same social group. The four kinds of cult institutions are individual, shamanic, communal, and ecclesiastical.
2. Shamans are part-time religious practitioners who perform shamanic rituals in behalf of individual clients when called on to do so. Shamans are accepted as religious specialists because of their personal charisma and established reputation as successful practitioners. They typically enter trance

states during their ritual performances and may alter established rituals as they feel inspired to fit the particular needs of specific clients.

3. Shamanic curing relies on the belief in one or more of five religious ideas about supernatural causes of illness: soul loss, spirit possession, object intrusion, taboo violation, and witchcraft and sorcery.

4. Priests are religious specialists who perform ecclesiastical rituals, rituals in behalf of entire congregations, often at scheduled times. Unlike shamans, priests are conservators of established religious traditions rather than religious innovators. Their role is based on the authority of their office rather than personal charisma.

5. Prophets are the charismatic founders of new religions who base their teachings on the claim of personal revelation from the supernatural rather than from the study and interpretation of a preexisting theology. Like shamans, prophets are charismatic religious innovators, but they do more than simply modify existing rituals to meet the needs of specific clients. They create entire systems of rituals and beliefs that may differ radically from those practiced among the same people previously.

6. Religions are a system of two or more cult institutions. The oldest and simplest of religions are shamanic religions that consist of individual and shamanic cult institutions. Communal religions add a communal cult institution to the individualistic and shamanic ones. Ecclesiastical religions include individualistic, shamanic, communal, and ecclesiastical cult institutions.

7. Ecclesiastical religions include sects, cults, and churches. Both sects and cults tend to be small groups that rely heavily on recruiting new members for perpetuating themselves. Both tend to be at least somewhat at odds with the values and beliefs of the larger society of which they are a part. They differ primarily in that the religious beliefs of sects belong to the same general religious tradition as do the mainstream religions of their own society, while cults perpetuate a religious tradition that differs from that of the mainstream of their own society. Churches tend to have a larger membership than cults and sects and tend to be supportive of the mainstream secular values of the societies in which they are found.

Recommended Readings

1. Baer, Hans A. 1988. *Recreating Utopia in the Desert: A Sectarian Challenge to Modern Mormonism.* Albany, NY: State University of New York Press. A study of the Aaronic Order (also called the Levites), a communitarian millenarian sect that developed out of the Mormon tradition.

2. Brown, K. M. 1991. *Mama Lola: A Vodou Priestess in Brooklyn.* Berkeley: University of California Press. A descriptive study of a vodou community in the United States.

3. Eliade, Mircea. 1974. *Shamanism: Archaic Techniques of Ecstasy.* Translated by Willard R. Trask. Princeton: Princeton University Press. The classic analysis of shamanism by an articulate author.

4. Hogbin, Ian. 1970. *The Island of Menstruating Men: Religion in Wogeo, New Guinea.* Prospect Heights, IL: Waveland Press. An excellent examination of Wogeo religion and its gender symbolism.

5. Hostetler, John, & Gertrude Enders Huntington. 1997. *The Hutterites in North America.* New York: Harcourt Brace. An ethnographic study of a communal religious group with settlements in the Great Plains of the United States and Canada.

6. Lame Deer, John (Fire), & Richard Erdoes. 1972. *Lame Deer, Seeker of Visions: The Life of a Sioux Medicine Man.* New York: Simon & Schuster. The biography of a Lakota Sioux shaman from the Rosebud Reservation in South Dakota.

7. Noel, Daniel C. 1997. *The Soul of Shamanism: Western Fantasies, Imaginal Realities.* New York: Continuum. Discusses the various ways shamanism has been viewed in Western cultures and examines the psychology of shamanistic practice.

8. Sharon, Douglas. 1978. *Wizard of the Four Winds: A Shaman's Story.* New York: Free Press. A fascinating account of a Peruvian shaman who perpetuates pre-Columbian techniques for curing.

Recommended Websites

1. *http://www.circlesanctuary.org/aboutpagan/Intro2Wicca.html*
   A good firsthand source about Wicca.
2. *http://www.whisperingstone.com/information-shaman-pub-siberia.htm*
   Excerpts on shamanism from *Aboriginal Siberia* by Czaplicka.
3. *http://www.nando.net/prof/caribe/origins.html*
   An excellent resource on Vodoun.
4. *http://www.geocities.com/Athens/Agora/6654/*
   Homesite of the Church of Jah Rastifari.
5. *http://www.ne.jp/asahi/moriyuki/abukuma/*
   A site on Max Weber's sociology of religion.

Study Questions

1. What was the purpose of the Plains Indian vision quest, and what were its common characteristics?
2. What are Wallace's "cult institutions," and how can religions be understood as being organized around them?
3. What are the four common beliefs about supernatural causes of illness?
4. What social characteristics tend to be common where soul loss is an important explanation for illness?
5. What child-rearing practices may create a predisposition for spirit-possession beliefs and why?
6. Even though they sometimes refer to themselves as "witches," why are followers of Wicca better understood, in anthropological terminology, as shamans?

7. How do priests differ from shamans?
8. According to Wach, what are the common characteristics of the ways priests carry out their roles?
9. How does a prophet differ from a shaman or a priest?
10. What are the ways in which sects commonly differ from churches?

CHAPTER 9

Religion and Society

CHAPTER OUTLINE

Case Study: Religion and Society in Ancient Sumer

Religion and the Social Order

Religion and Gender

CHAPTER OBJECTIVES
After you have read this chapter, you will be able to

1. Explain the influences of religion on the political organization of society.
2. Describe several examples of theocratic government.
3. Discuss the religiosity of political leaders.
4. Describe the concept of a civil religion and explain how it develops.
5. Discuss relationships between governmental support for religion and secularization.
6. Explain how subsistence economies influence the role of gender in religion in foraging societies.
7. Discuss gender symbolism in religion.
8. Explain how gender stratification influences gender roles in religion.
9. Describe a number of examples of women's spirit-possession cults.

As Karl Marx (1867) wrote, "The religious world is but the reflex of the real world." In this chapter we examine that idea by analyzing some of the relationships between religion and its social environment. Religion does not exist in a vacuum. It is a part of a social order. As such, it influences and is influenced by the other institutions of the society or societies in which it is found. In previous chapters we noted that various parts of religion are influenced by such things as a society's child-rearing practices, the presence or absence of a class system, and the nature of its judicial system. In this chapter, we look in more detail at the interplay between religion and the political system and between religion and its society's gender system. In the case study, "Religion and Government in Ancient Sumer," we examine the relationships between religion and government in the world's first theocratic society.

CASE STUDY

Religion and Government in Ancient Sumer

The oldest known human civilization was the southern Mesopotamian society known as Sumer. The people of ancient Sumer built towns and temples for 500 years before they finally produced a full civilization with true cities. The origin of their civilization is usually dated at 3500 B.C., when the city of Ur came into existence on the shore of the Tigris River. The urban population of Ur and the other cities of Sumer—Adab, Ashak, Bad-tibira, Erech, Kish, Lagash, Larak, Larsa, Nippur, Sippar, Umma, Eridu, Isin, and Kullab—that followed soon after Ur were supported by plow agriculture, which was very productive in a region of rich delta soils.

The people of Sumer followed a polytheistic religion. There were hundreds of gods in the pantheon of Sumer, but the greatest were "those who decree fate." These seven great gods were An, Ninhursag, Enki, Enlil, Nanna, Utu, and Inanna. The highest god was An, king of the Igigi, or sky gods, and benevolent father of the Anunaki, the second generation of gods who mostly dwell on earth. An had several consorts. By his consort Nammu, the primeval sea, An fathered Enki, the god of wisdom, and Ninhursag, who represented the great primal mountain that arose from the sea. As an embodiment of the Great Mother goddess, Ninhursag was known by many names. In her role as the earth goddess, she was known as Ki, which was perhaps the oldest of her names. She was sometimes referred to as Ninmah, or "Exalted Lady," or as Aruru, the womb goddess and midwife of the gods. Since it was she who fashioned human beings out of clay and gave them life, she was also called Nintu, the "Lady Who Gave Birth." Ninhursag and Enki produced the goddess Ninsar, who gave birth to the goddess Ninkur, who was the mother of Uttu, the goddess of weaving and clothing. Ninhursag was also a consort of her father, An, and under the name of Antu or Ki, which are earlier names of the primeval earth goddess, she gave birth to various other gods and demons. Among their many children, the most prominent was Enlil, the god of storms, who became the king of the Anunaki, the gods who dwelt on earth.

Enki, the god of wisdom, fashioned the earth that floats in the midst of the primeval ocean. For some time, the gods resided on the earth, where they labored to cultivate their food and to establish order. At first, they lived together in a primeval paradise called Dilmun where there was no illness, where no one aged, and where there were no predatory animals that preyed on the flocks. Disharmony did arise once, in a story that may be echoed in the much later Hebrew myths about the divine paradise of Eden, which include the eating of a forbidden fruit as the cause of human mortality and the creation of Eve from Adam's rib. In the Sumerian tale, while the gods still lived in Dilmun, Enki ate some plants that had been created by Ninhursag, and she cursed his body with eight great afflictions. The other gods, not wishing to lose the wisest among them, pleaded with Ninhursag to relent, and she finally gave in. To cure his illnesses, Ninhursag brought forth eight goddesses, each of whom pro-

nounced a blessing that cured one of his illnesses. One of these goddesses was Ninti, whose name means both "Lady of the Rib" and "Lady of Life." She cured the affliction that Ninhursag had pronounced against Enki's rib.

Nanna, the son of Enlil and Enlil's consort Ninlil, was the Sumerian moon god. He too had great influence over the lives of humankind, as did his son Utu, the sun god and god of justice, and Nanna's daughter Inanna, goddess of fertility, love, and war.

Sumerian religion taught that humankind was created for one purpose: to be servants of the gods, toiling to relieve the gods from the drudgery of life. Thus in ancient Sumer, the relationship of worshipers to gods was like that of serfs to their lords. Their labor in the fields released the gods from the work of producing their own food. Of course, a few humans rose to positions of power and luxury as priests who served each city's god or goddess or as a king whose power was based on his role as head of the military. But the lot of the ordinary human was to serve the gods and their earthly lords; and even priests and lords knew that they were subordinate to the gods, since, like other humans, they were mortal and doomed to die and since they too were plagued by the demons that brought illness and suffering to mortal humans.

The mythology of Sumer also included the oldest known story of a great Flood. The Flood was sent by Enlil, who became angered when his sleep was disturbed by the raucous partying of human beings on earth. Enki, being the wisest of the gods, realized that to slay humankind would be a great mistake, since the work of human beings allowed the gods to live in luxury instead of having to toil themselves. So, secretly, Enki spoke to the king of the trade city Shurupak and warned him of the coming deluge. This Sumerian Noah, who was named Ziusudra, was therefore able to escape the seven-day downpour on a barge that housed his family and their animals. After the Flood, Enlil realized that he had made a rash mistake in trying to destroy the humans who toil for the gods, and he decreed that Ziusudra should be made immortal and dwell forever in Dilmun.

Each of the cities of Sumer was regarded as the property of one of the gods or of a divine couple. For instance, the god Enlil claimed the city of Nippur as his own, while Enki ruled over the city of Shurupak. Inanna called Uruk (biblical Erech) her own, and Nanna was the god of Sumer's first city, Ur. The center of each city was a temple, built for the city's god or gods to live in. The temple was built atop a large raised platform or ziggurat and surrounded by a walled ceremonial precinct. Within the grounds of the ceremonial precinct were dormitories for the priests who served the gods and who acted, in behalf of the city's ruling god, as city managers. The precinct also housed warehouses within which were stored the tithes that the people paid as tribute to their god. The fields worked by farmers were not considered their own property, but were owned by the god of the city, who allotted each farmer the land that he was permitted to work. As cities grew, shrines of other gods might also be built in them, but they were always secondary to that of the god who claimed the city as his or her own.

Sumer was a socially stratified society, one that distinguished between members of the ruling class and commoners, between the wealthy and the poor. Gender was also stratified, and women generally played roles that were subordinate to those of men, but the women of early Sumer did have more equality with men than did women of later Mesopotamian societies. For instance, they were able to own property and transact business. Nevertheless, we know less about the lives of women than of men. There is one reference to a woman who was a tavern owner and well-off enough to have paid for the restoration of a temple; she even rose to the position of ruler of her city. However, the most frequent reference to a woman's occupation in writings from Sumer is that of prostitute. Prostitutes included both ordinary prostitutes and sacred prostitutes. The latter were priestesses who served in temples dedicated to goddesses, such as the Mother goddess in one of her embodiments or Inanna, the goddess of love and human fertility. Sex with a sacred prostitute was believed to be a means by which men could commune with and worship the goddess.

The oldest priestess cult was probably that of Inanna, goddess of both the passion of love and of war. In Uruk, at the celebration of the Sumerian New Year, the king spent the night with the chief priestess of Inanna in her sacred bedchamber. Their union was believed to renew the fertility of the earth and ensure abundance for the kingdom in the coming year. In this yearly ceremony, the king and the priestess reenacted the Sumerian myth of the demise and resurrection of Inanna's consort Damuzi (biblical Tammuz), the shepherd god who also had power over the fertility of plants. In this myth, Inanna descended to the Underworld to visit her sister Ereshkigal, who ruled there. As Inanna had anticipated, Ereshkigal attempted to imprison her there as one of her own subjects. Having expected this, Inanna had asked Enki to insure her safe return to the surface world. Enki does so by creating two creatures who win Ereshkigal's favor and obtain Inanna's corpse from her. Enki restores Inanna's body to life with the Bread of Life and the Water of Life but Inanna's rescue can only be bought at the expense of providing a scapegoat to replace her in the Underworld. When Inanna returns to Uruk, she discovers that in her absence her husband Damuzi has not been mourning her but has been enjoying his life as sole ruler of Uruk. In anger, Inanna chooses him as her scapegoat and banishes him to the underworld. However, his absence has dire consequences, since he is the patron of plant fertility, and the crops wither under the devastating heat of the summer sun. To avoid disaster, Inanna arranges for him to return to earth for six months of the year, while his sister Geshtinnana, the patroness of vineyards, takes his place. Damuzi's return to earth brings the autumn rains and ensures a plentiful harvest in the spring. His sister's return heralds the harvest of the vineyards in the fall. Thus, their alternation in the Underworld and their semi-annual return to earth symbolize the changing of the seasons.

Prostitutes play an important role in several Sumerian myths and legends, perhaps because of the high status of sacred prostitutes who served as priestesses in some of the Sumerian temples. In one of these legends, a prostitute plays a key role as a civilizing influence in the lives of the subjects of Gilgamesh, the tyrant king of Uruk. Gilgamesh was a demigod, the son of a mortal father and the goddess Ninsun. Being half divine, Gilgamesh is unaware of how tiring work is for his subjects, whom he overtaxes in the building of the city's defensive walls. He also exercises the right to sleep with every virgin bride on her wedding night. When his subjects complain to the gods about their mistreatment, Enlil creates Enkidu, a savage whose strength matches that of Gilgamesh, to fight with Gilgamesh. Enkidu is a wild man who lives among the wild animals outside the city. When word of him comes to the city, Gilgamesh calls upon a prostitute to entice Enkidu and to introduce him to life in the city. She is successful in introducing Enkidu not just to sex but also to the civilized life of Uruk. There, Gilgamesh and Enkidu meet and engage in combat to determine who is more powerful. After seven days of fighting, the two opponents declare a truce and become lifelong companions and friends who have many adventures together.

RELIGION AND THE SOCIAL ORDER

Durkheim's contention that religious symbolism is based on the organization of society itself has been investigated by a number of anthropologists. The most ambitious single study of the relationship between religious beliefs and social organization was conducted by anthropologist Guy Swanson (1974). Swanson formulated a series of specific hypotheses that he derived logically from Durkheim's model and tested these with a cross-cultural sample made up of one society from each of 50 world culture areas. Swanson argued that what he called **sovereign groups** would be the most likely sources of religious beliefs in a society. These sovereign groups have "original and independent jurisdiction over some sphere of life" (p. 20). As the parts of society that actively control how society functions, they would, Swanson contended, have the power to inspire respect and compliance in their members. In examining monotheism, polytheism, ancestral spirits, reincarnation, the human soul, supernatural sanctions for the violation of moral rules, and sorcery, Swanson established that relationships existed between various kinds of sovereign groups and religious beliefs (see chapter 5).

sovereign groups
The parts of a social organization that have original and independent jurisdiction over some sphere of life.

Religion and the Political System

The relationships between religion and society are not simply a matter of religious beliefs being influenced by the nature of the social order. It is also true that religion influences believers' social behavior, and therefore religion influences the social order as well as being influenced by it. Religion has an effect on all of society's institutions, because religious people participate in them all. Here we examine religion's influence on the political life of society.

In societies that have no specialized political institutions, religion can serve as an important mechanism of social control—but not just as a source of values to guide people's social behavior. Religion can also impose sanctions for the violation of social norms. For instance, Beatrice Whiting (1950) examined sorcery cross-culturally and found that its practice is most common in societies where accusations of criminal conduct are not judged by a legal official but where, instead, aggrieved parties turn to retribution when their rights have been violated. In the absence of an effective judicial system, sorcery functions as a kind of religious system of justice in which practitioners are sought out by aggrieved parties and hired to perform rituals designed to harm the wrongdoer. Thus, although sorcerers are thought of as antisocial persons who magically harm others, often for their own benefit, they nevertheless may be tolerated because their skills can be put to use for socially beneficial purposes.

In societies in which full-time governmental specialists exist, the influence of religion on a society's politics is particularly interesting. Both religion and politics have authority to influence how people live. The political institution obtains its authority when people yield power over their lives to political leaders for a variety of practical reasons. Whether it arises from a community's desire for better military defense or coordination of public economic projects that benefit the common welfare or from its fear of challenging those who have imposed their rule upon them, authority arises from the people who are governed, either by their willing consent or by default. In contrast, religious authority is believed to arise from supernatural sources.

Since religion has authority among its followers, its authority can be a source of added support for the legitimacy of a political system. In fact, all of the world's early, pristine civilizations—Sumer, Egypt, the Indus Valley civilization,

The Latter-day Saint migration to the North American Great Basin was organized and directed by the leaders of the church. The Church of Jesus Christ of Latter-day Saints (LDS) had a hierarchical ecclesiastical organization in which the local heads of "wards" (congregations) were called bishops. The bishops of a given area were presided over by a stake president, and stake presidents reported directly to church leaders in Salt Lake City. The highest ecclesiastical leader was the president of the church, who was spoken of as a "Prophet, Seer, and Revelator" and was believed to receive his direction from God through revelation.

The hierarchical structure of the LDS church and the belief that the decisions of one's ecclesiastical leaders were inspired by God made it very easy for the church to organize the process of colonizing the Great Basin and surrounding areas. New converts to the LDS religion throughout the world were encouraged to participate in what Latter-day Saints called "the Gathering" by emigrating from their homelands and traveling to Utah. The church even organized the process of migration by chartering ships and organizing wagon trains from the eastern states to Utah Territory. The church itself set up a "Perpetual Immigration Fund" to pay the way for Saints who could not afford the cost of travel to the United States, with the understanding that persons so aided would pay back the cost of their travel when they could afford to do so.

On arriving in Utah Territory, LDS immigrants found that the church even provided suggestions about where they should settle within the territory. Thus, the church might request groups of members to colonize new settlements in areas within the territory where the leaders knew that arable land was available to be homesteaded. Salt Lake City was settled first, but soon waves of settlements began to spread north and south as smaller towns were settled along the Wasatch Mountain range and eventually into areas that would later become parts of Idaho, British Columbia, Arizona, Nevada, and southern California.

Since the church organization played such an influential role in organizing the economic as well as religious lives of Mormon settlers, it is unsurprising that it was drawn upon to fulfill the same role in the political life of Mormon communities as well. For instance, LDS bishops, who functioned as the judges of religious matters, were called upon to serve as justices of the peace when secular courts were needed; and when Mormons chose their first territorial governor, Brigham Young, the president of the church, organizer of the settlement of the territory, and a man who was regarded by Mormons as an inspired prophet of God, was viewed by Mormons as the natural choice for that job. The territorial legislature was also dominated by those men whom Mormon settlers looked up to as leaders in their communities—that is by men who were already leaders in their religious communities. Thus, the creation of the territorial government of the Great Basin pioneers serves as an excellent example of at least one way in which a theocratic political system can quite naturally arise out of the preexisting system of religious authority and how a shared system of religious beliefs can function to support the establishment of a political organization.

theocracies
Societies whose governments are based on the religious authority of their leaders.

the Chinese civilization of the Huang Ho River Valley, the Olmec civilization of the Gulf of Mexico, and the earliest Andean civilizations—appear to have had **theocracies,** societies whose governments were based on the religious authority of their leaders. Most of these were governed by priests in the name of a god, and in Egypt the king himself was considered a god. The box titled "Religion and Government in Territorial Utah" describes the role of religion in the founding and governing of the frontier territory that became the state of Utah.

The west African kingdom of Ashanti is a good example of a society in which the legitimacy of the political institution can be supported by religion.

The Ashanti kingdom arose early in the 18th century and lasted until 1874, when the British deposed the then currently ruling king. The kingdom was established by Osai Tutu, who unified the previous independent chiefdoms of the Ashanti. Very soon, the right of the Ashanti kings who followed this unification to rule began to be supported by the belief that Osai Tutu's chief adviser and head priest, Komfo Anokye, had brought down from the sky the Golden Stool on which Osai Tutu and the ensuing Ashanti kings sat. Thus, the miraculous origin of the Golden Stool, which represented the ancestors of the Ashanti people, made it a powerful sacred symbol of the legitimacy of the authority of the Ashanti kings. Ashanti kings governed in the name of the ancestors, and each took an oath to the Earth Goddess and his ancestors to rule according to their expectations. The theocratic nature of the Ashanti government is further illustrated by the fact that all crimes were considered to be sins and offenses against the ancestors. As sins, all crimes were believed to endanger the welfare of the Ashanti people, since the ancestors' goodwill was necessary for the continued well-being of Ashanti society. To avoid the anger of the ancestors, all crimes were—in theory—punishable by death, and execution would be carried out unless the penalty was waived by the king himself, who could do so, since his authority was from the ancestors and he ruled in their behalf. In practice, the death sentence was commuted by the king in most instances, but the sacredness of Ashanti law is illustrated by the handling of suicides. Suicide was classified as a form of murder, which was viewed as the most heinous of sins. It was also an affront to the sacred authority of the king, who alone had the right to have anyone put to death. It is therefore understandable that anyone who was convicted of having attempted suicide was sentenced to death, which was carried out by beheading. In fact, the symbolic importance of murder as a sin against the ancestors and an abrogation of the king's divine authority was so great that the bodies of successful suicides were also brought to court, tried, and—if convicted—beheaded. Sorcery and witchcraft were also regarded as sins and were punishable by strangling or other means of execution that did not involve the shedding of blood. Persons accused of crimes could request that their guilt or innocence be determined by a religious ordeal. In most cases, the accused person would drink poison. His or her survival was understood as unquestionable supernatural proof of innocence.

Religion and Political Loyalty

Bernard Spilka, Ralph Hood, and Richard Gorsuch (1985) pointed out that "Spiritual systems are based on certain core doctrines that may be identical to, or spring from, the same sources as political tenets. Political institutions often legitimize, or culturally rationalize, their existence by utilizing religious themes. . . . The force of political ideology and action is strengthened when it becomes religious" (p. 116). This fact is commonly used by politicians to increase their support among citizens. Spilka and his colleagues note, for instance, that Franklin Roosevelt called such religious references in political speeches "God stuff," and Ronald Reagan referred to God repeatedly in his speeches. The call to religion in support of politics is not necessarily calculated, although it certainly can be. It can also be a simple reflection of the harmony between religious and political values in the minds of the politicians themselves. Peter Benson and

Dorothy Williams (1982) documented that, at least in the United States, political leaders tend to score higher than average in various measures of religiosity.

The Concept of Civil Religion

civil religion
The shared religious beliefs and values that cross-cut denominational boundaries in complex societies.

Governments need not be theocratic in order for religion to function in ways that enhance their legitimacy in the eyes of believers. In 1967, Robert Bellah introduced the concept of **civil religion**—the shared religious beliefs and values that cross-cut denominational boundaries in complex societies—to the study of religion and its relationship to society. Looking specifically at the United States, he conceptualized the "civil religion" of America as the religious dimension of American public life that cross-cut denominational boundaries and consisted of sacred symbols and rituals that portrayed the fundamental values of American social life in religious terms. Americans, he pointed out, often paint themselves as a modern "Israel" whose God is actively interested in the country's welfare and history. The sacred texts of American civil religion include the Declaration of Independence, the "divinely inspired" U.S. Constitution, and the Gettysburg Address. The figures of its mythology include George Washington, the American Moses who could not "tell a lie" even in childhood and who led his people out of bondage to the English "pharaoh," and Abraham Lincoln, who gave his life for the rebirth of his nation and whose Gettysburg Address preaches a Gospel of love and reconciliation. Its sacred holidays include Memorial Day, Thanksgiving Day, Veterans Day, and—at the time of his writing—the birthdays of Washington and Lincoln. American civil religion draws heavily on biblical archetypes such as Exodus, the Chosen People, the Promised Land, and sacrificial death and rebirth. In short, civil religion does for the United States, a country whose citizens belong to many different specific religious denominations, what Durkheim believed the shared religion of smaller-scale societies did for them: It provides a public system of religious symbols and rituals that transcends the denominational differences of Americans and imbues the important institutions of their society with a sense of sacredness that inspires loyalty to society as a whole. As P. L. Benson (1981) put it, "Civil religion provides a kind of divine stamp of approval of the social order as it now exists" (p. 50). The civil religion of the United States includes a number of holidays. Some of these, such as the celebratory period of Christmas and Hanukkah, were derived from religious holidays. Others, such as Thanksgiving Day and Memorial Day, have become quasi-religious holidays in the civil religion. For instance, Memorial Day began as a day of remembrance of those who died in war but has evolved into a day when many families visit cemeteries and place flowers on the graves of other deceased relatives as well.

Politics and Civil Religion

state churches
Religions that are sponsored and economically supported by the governments of nation-states.

A number of western European countries have legally recognized **state churches**, religions that are sponsored and economically supported by the governments of their respective nation-states. Wilson (1982) points out that "In Sweden, where the church is virtually a department of state, and where it is supported by taxation, the church remains financially strong, even though attendance at services is phenomenally low. In Britain, where the association with

Until 1999, Sweden was a country with an official state church. When children were born to any member, they were automatically "joined" to the church as members, whether they were later baptized or not. Before 1860 it was impossible to resign from the church. Before 1950, one could only resign one's membership by joining another Christian denomination.

In the Swedish state-sponsored church, clergy were both pastors and civil servants. That is, their salaries were paid by the government. The money for the support of the church came from a church tax that was levied on all Swedish inhabitants. Nonmembers were not exempt, but paid a "dissenter tax" at a lower rate than that paid by members. This public money was allocated by the government for various religious purposes that benefit the state church.

One might expect that such political support for a religion would be a bulwark against secularization, but an interesting legal case arose in the early 1990s that illustrates how such a system can also blur the lines between religion and politics. Rudolf Ernström was enrolled as a member of the state church at birth, but by the time he became an adult he had also become an atheist. As a nonbeliever, he left the state church and began to pay a lower church tax. Then, some years later, he decided to run in a public election for a seat in his local church-council, which plays an important role in local politics.

Under Swedish law, membership in the state church is a requirement for anyone who runs for public office. So Rudolph Ernström went to his vicar and requested that he be readmitted to the church. The vicar, knowing that he was a confirmed atheist, felt that this was religiously unacceptable and so refused his request. Now, the vicar was not just a pastor, but—since his salary was paid by the government—also a civil servant. Mr. Ernström was not just a would-be politician but also a lawyer. And as a citizen of Sweden who had been enrolled as a member of the country's state church at birth, he felt that his civil rights had been violated by the refusal to readmit him as a member. So he brought a suit against the vicar and the vicar's superiors in Stockholm who had supported the vicar's decision and argued that he had a legal right to be a member of the state church. The case was heard by the Administrative Court of Stockholm, which ruled in his favor, a decision that essentially meant that even an atheist had a right to be a member of the church.

Since the parish did not appeal the decision, Rudolph Ernström's membership in the state church was reinstated, making him eligible to run for office in the 1991 election as a member of the Atheist/Agnostic Party.

the state persists in a somewhat more attenuated form, and where the church receives no public funding, attendances are not so low, but voluntary donations are very small" (p. 151). Thus, *secularization* (see chapter 10), a decreased role for religion in social life, as measured by individual participation and voluntary financial support for the religious organization, may still be prominent despite government efforts to promote religion. The box titled "An Atheist Joins a State Church" illustrates how state sponsorship introduces secular qualities into a religious organization by examining an interesting legal case that involved the Swedish state church.

In the United States, a somewhat different pattern of secularization has occurred. In this case, the constitutional principle of separation of church and state has prevented the development of a state-recognized religion. As a result, a large number of denominations coexist with more or less equal influence and public acceptance. Wilson (1982) points out that "in the United States, with its high immigrant and highly mobile population, churches have functioned as much more basic foci of community identity than has been their role in settled societies" (p. 152). Religious participation and voluntary financial support for religious organizations is high in U.S. denominations, but Wilson points out that "few observers doubt that the actual content of what goes on in the major churches in Britain is very much more 'religious' than what occurs in American churches; in America secularizing processes appear to have occurred *within* the church, so that although religious institutions persist, their specifically religious character has become steadily attenuated" (p. 152).

Religion and the Economic System

Karl Marx viewed religion as part of a larger system of social institutions in which the primary function of religion is to stabilize society, keeping it the way it is. Religion itself was, in his view, ultimately conditioned by the economic order of the society it functioned to stabilize. Where the economic system creates stress for members of society—for instance, where the economic system produces class differences in which the working class is deprived of the benefits of its own labor by the upper classes that own and control what the working classes produce—religion offers the poor an alternative source of fulfillment, albeit an illusory one. In his words (1844), "Religious distress is at the same time the expression of real distress and the protest against real distress. Religion is the sigh of the oppressed creature, the heart of a heartless world, just as it is the spirit of a spiritless situation. It is the opium of the people. The abolition of religion as the illusory happiness of the people is required for their real happiness. The demand to give up the illusion about its condition is the demand to give up a condition which needs illusions" (p. i).

The function of religion in reinforcing economic differences can be illustrated with the Hindu caste system. The castes are a religion-based system of social classes, each of which has its own ritual obligations and appropriate occupations. Traditionally, the system was described as having four main castes and a pariah category of "outcastes" that was legally abolished in 1949. Each caste was further subdivided into jatis, which were occupational categories. Membership in a jati was by birth, and sets of rules governed acceptable occupations, foods, marriage, and association with other jatis. In the caste system, priests and educators belonged to the highest caste. Rulers belonged to the second-highest caste, while merchants, artisans, and farmers belonged to the one below. The lowest caste consisted of unskilled laborers and servants of the higher castes. Outcastes performed the most menial and symbolically polluting work, such as removing dead animals from a village, working with leather, and disposing of garbage. They were not permitted to visit a village temple or use the village well. Even letting their shadow fall on a person of an upper caste was considered polluting. Religiously, birth into one caste or another or into the pariah class was understood as a natural result of one's behavior during past lives. Thus, religious belief functioned to perpetuate the status quo, including the economic differences that were based on jati membership.

Max Weber (1904) reversed Marx's relationship between religion and economics and argued that religious ideology is a powerful force in determining the characteristics of an economic system. For instance, Weber contended that the development of the Protestant ethic, which arose during the Reformation, laid the foundations for the later rise of capitalism as an economic system. Protestantism, according to Weber, had a more "this worldly" orientation than did pre-Reformation religion. It therefore had implications for people's economic life. The Protestant ethic replaced the previous religious emphasis on piety—often through withdrawal from the world into monasticism—with an emphasis on "good works" as a duty toward God and as a sign that one had been saved by God. Good works required performing one's earthly duties and obligations and prioritizing work over pleasure, a philosophy that did much to aid the rise of business and, eventually, industrialization.

Anthropologists today differ in their treatment of religion as primarily a cause or an effect, but most recognize that there are important relationships between religion and economics. Swanson's (1974) correlations between social forms and religion included several economic traits that are useful predictors of religious characteristics. For instance, Swanson found that societies with occupational specializations such as blacksmiths, fishers, and carpenters were more likely to have a polytheistic belief in superior gods than were societies that lacked such specializations. He determined that the presence of debts was a predictor of the belief in personal souls and that the presence of interpersonal differences in wealth was most often associated with the religious belief that the supernatural realm rewards conformity to moral principles.

RELIGION AND GENDER

The ways that gender is manifest in religion, which is a conservative institution reinforcing the stability of society, are generally based on how gender is organized in society at large. In societies where men and women are social equals, women may be as likely as men to hold positions of religious responsibility. Where gender is stratified, so too is gender in the religious system.

The oldest and socially least complex of human societies are those in which people survived by foraging for wild foods. In these societies, called bands in anthropological literature, religious specialization was limited to the presence of shamans, who might be either male or female practitioners. However, women do not have social equality with men in all band societies. Whether they do is largely a function of how the available food resources influence the economic division of labor. According to Ernestine Friedl (1975), the division of labor by gender in foraging societies depends on the subsistence adaptation of the foraging group to its specific environment. Friedl grouped foraging into four basic types: individual foraging, communal foraging, plant-focused foraging, and animal-focused foraging.

Individual foraging is common in environments like forests where meat is a relatively unimportant resource. Because meat is not a major resource, both men and women gather their own plant foods, with men providing primarily for themselves and women foraging for themselves and their children. In this subsistence pattern, men and women are typically equal in social power and prestige, and both men and women may become shamans. For instance, among the Indians of northern California, where the staple food was flour ground from forest nuts such as the acorn, women were the social equals of men, and shamans were always women.

Communal foraging is most common in environments such as the North American Great Basin, where the major meat resource is fish or small game, and plant foods are most easily collected by cooperative labor. For instance, hunting typically involves women and children driving animals toward nets where they are killed by the men of the group. The game is normally divided at the site among all who participate, and men gain no particular prestige from their role in hunting. Although men may be thought of as the "hunters" of the group and may devote some of their time to hunting while women are gathering wild plants, the animals hunted by individual men are small game. With small game, individual male hunters do not bring enough surplus meat home for customs to develop in which men gain high status by making gifts of their extra meat to other men. As a result, women and men tend to be thought of as equals, and both men and women may become shamans if they are so inclined.

In environments where plant resources easily supply most of the food from areas near camp, people engage primarily in plant-focused foraging. In these societies, women spend a great deal of time collecting wild plant foods near camp, and men tend to range farther from camp in order to supplement these plant foods with meat. Although 60 to 70 percent of the group's staple foods may be supplied by women, men's social prestige and power are often higher than women's because whenever men bring more meat to camp than their own families need, they share the surplus with the less successful hunters of other families and are given high status by their neighbors as a result. Among plant-focused foragers, such as the Plains Indians of North America, women might sometimes become shamans, but this religious specialization was more often practiced by men.

Finally, in environments that offer little in the way of plant foods but have enough fish and animal life to support foraging bands, animal-focused foraging was the basis of subsistence. Here the basic foods were fish and large game hunted by men. In animal-focused foraging, women are economically dependent on men because women do not contribute directly to the food supply. Their responsibilities become primarily domestic ones such as the processing of the meat and skins brought in by the men. Often in those societies, men even make the tools that women use, a practice that also perpetuates women's dependence on men. Here, men's sharing of their surplus catch with other men becomes an even more important mechanism that raises men's social rank. Especially where the meat resources are large game animals, the pursuit of status by sharing meat that requires high levels of skill and aggressiveness in the hunt may result in high levels of competitiveness and aggression among hunters. The economic dependence of women on men in societies that depend largely on meat for their food supply is often associated with low social status for women. In these societies, shamanism tends to be a largely male occupation.

gender symbolism
Symbols and metaphors that reflect the social roles of men and women.

That a culture's symbolism includes **gender symbolism,** symbols and metaphors that reflect the social roles of men and women, has been documented repeatedly and for quite some time now (see, for instance, Ortner, 1974, and Strathern, 1980). Sanday (1981) has demonstrated that the gender differences of society often show up even in how people describe the world around them. In societies where women play subordinate roles, untamed nature is often symbolized as "female," while culture is viewed as a symbolically "masculine" realm. For instance, among the ancient Hebrews of the Mosaic era, Yahweh, the deity who leads the Hebrews in their conquest of Canaan, has the decidedly masculine characteristics of a war god. Sanday also noted that masculine deities tend to dominate the mythologies of the more patriarchal societies, while egalitarian societies emphasize feminine symbolism. Thus, where women are highly subordinate to men, creation stories typically emphasize male gods who come from the sky and themes of warfare, aggression, and sexuality. In these very patriarchal societies, humans tend to be created either out of the god's body, by acts of sexual intercourse, or through self-fertilization by the god. In such societies, whatever is identified with women is often regarded as supernaturally dangerous to men. For instance, according to M. Meggitt (1964), among the Enga of the western New Guinea highlands, men obtained their wives from competing neighbors and marriage was thought of as being with "the people we fight" (p. 218). Enga men believed that women's menstrual blood was a dangerous substance that could destroy men's ability to achieve wealth, pigs, or success in war.

In male-dominant societies, the negative symbolism associated with women may also take a more active form, even portraying women as the originators of various forms of evil, such as sin, illness, and death. For instance, in the Judeo-Christian creation story, Eve first commits sin by being disobedient to God, thereby bringing death into the world along with the curse of pain in childbirth. Similarly, in Greek mythology Pandora failed to control her impulsiveness and curiosity and so brought illness, greed, and death into the world.

On the other hand, female deities and female symbolism predominate in the creation stories of egalitarian societies. Birth, creativity, and progress usually originate from *within* something such as water or earth. In egalitarian societies, female creators either work alone or are aided by male deities in bringing forth humans from the earth, molding them from clay, transforming them from plants or animals, or carving them from wood. For instance, among the Iroquois of the Great Lakes region of North America, women were regarded as equals of men, and the supreme creator was a female deity, the Ancient Bodied One; her daughter was the deity who gave birth to humans. Similarly, among the egalitarian Yuchi Indians of North Carolina, humans originated from the union of the earth with a drop of menstrual blood that had fallen from the Sun, a female deity (Speck, 1909, pp. 205–7).

Gender in the Religious Institution

Gender stratification—unequal access to social power based on gender—is often associated with religious practices such as segregating males and females during rituals, excluding women from religious roles, or—where the most prestigious religious rituals are controlled by male priests—by restricting women's religious lives to participation in lower-status shamanistic rituals. For instance, the male-only ceremonial houses of South America and the New Guinea highlands and, according to some ethnographers, male ceremonial groups among aboriginal Australians supported male dominance because they had political, economic, and religious functions as well as religious ones. Typically, women were not permitted to participate in or even observe the religious rituals practiced by men in these settings.

gender stratification Unequal access to social power based on gender.

women's cults
Religious groups in which female shamans enter trances and become possessed by spirits to serve as mediums, diviners, and curers for their clients.

In gender-stratified societies, males may attempt to monopolize knowledge of the myths of human origin and of the orthodox rituals of religion. According to E. Bourguignon and L. Greenberg (1973), where men are socially and religiously dominant, spirit-possession symbolism may figure prominently in women's religious ritualism. For instance, in many Islamic countries, where men monopolize the roles of priests and where the mosque is considered a men's place of prayer, women may participate in a variety of **women's cults** in which female shamans enter trances and become possessed by spirits to serve as mediums, diviners, and curers for their clients. Similarly, Korean shamanism is predominantly a women's religious specialization that contrasts with the ecclesiastical role of male priests. According to I. M. Lewis (1971), Korean shamanism provides women with a psychological outlet for the stresses of their subordinated roles in Korean secular life.

Men's and women's roles as shamans and priests, as well as the role they are thought to play as sorcerers and witches, are intimately tied to the social organization and culture of their society. In many societies where the religious social organization was solely organized around the practice of shamanism, both men and women

Figure 9.1
A New Guinea Men's House
In parts of New Guinea, male dominance was supported by the religious ideology, and women and children were excluded from men's initiation rites; men maintained separate residences from their wives. This is the interior of a men's house in New Guinea.

might become shamans. The charismatic nature of shamanism allowed the individual characteristics of would-be practitioners to play a major role in whether they gathered a following of clients who would seek out their services; and charismatic individuals of either sex had a better chance of doing so than they would in a religious system where practitioners had to be accepted into an established bureaucratic hierarchy of priests who controlled admission into their own ranks. So religious practitioners of both sexes were most common in the shamanic religions of foraging societies and societies in which simple horticulture was practiced. This was particularly so where men and women contributed about equally to their family's income and where family organizations larger than the nuclear family were absent or, in their presence, when lineages or clans were not based on descent solely through the male line.

The shamanic specialty becomes gender-linked when the social system predisposes it to. For instance, although both women and men can be shamans, female practitioners of shamanism are more likely to make use of spirit-possession rituals while male practitioners are more likely to emphasize soul-travel trances. Since these two practices are not equally distributed throughout the world's societies, there are noticeable gender differences by social types. For instance, Bourguignon (1973, pp. 3–35; 1976) has noted that societies where spirit-possession rituals are prominent and, thus, where women are most likely to be the predominant shamanic practitioners, tend to be more socially complex and have a greater emphasis on communalistic social life and stronger social hierarchies than those in which spirit-possession rituals are uncommon. Spirit travel as the primary shamanic activity tends to be practiced more often by males and under the opposite social circumstances. Spirit-possession trances are not the exclusive province of female shamans, and spirit flight is not practiced only by men. And there are many shamanic societies in which men and women *both* practice as shamans, performing the same ritual services of either type.

One reason for the greater likelihood of female predominance in the spirit-possession rituals of more complex social systems is that in many of these societies both shamanism and women have been marginalized and disempowered. In these very patriarchal societies, women and socially marginal men as well may be drawn toward shamanism as a psychological outlet for their desire for higher social status or greater power. Spirit-possession symbolism allows them to behave in dominant and powerful ways that are not available to them outside this religious sphere.

In state-level societies, hierarchy is fundamental to how society is organized, and the status of shaman tends to become marginal with respect to that of the higher-status priestly office. Within the religious organization, legitimate shamanic roles tend to be taken over by priests themselves, who may sometimes perform shamanic rituals for individual members of the same congregations they otherwise serve as priests. The shaman, as an independent religious specialization, tends to become stigmatized by the priesthood itself but may continue to exist as a marginal occupation.

The priestly offices of state-level societies tend also to be stratified by gender, with men being the dominant actors as priests, especially at the highest ecclesiastical levels of the priestly bureaucracies. Particularly in those societies in which women's roles are restricted in their access to power within the public arena, women may be the predominant players in the arena of shamanism. Lewis (1971) suggested that women's prominence in the marginal shamanic cults of very patriarchal societies serves as a psychological "safety valve" that allows women who could otherwise not legitimately play powerful roles in a public setting to do so. When serving as a shaman, the usual gender hierarchy can be reversed, and the female shaman may behave very strongly as she exercises control over spirits and even gods in behalf of her client, who may be male or female. Thus, a woman who is not permitted to exercise secular power as, say, a politician, may exercise its spiritual equivalent when she gives guidance and direction to her clients of either sex. The box titled "Women as Shamans in Islamic Saint Cults" illustrates the role of women in marginal shamanic cults in Islam in Sudan and on the island of Mayotte.

Women as Shamans in Islamic Saint Cults

I. M. Lewis (1971) argues that women tend to be particularly involved in spirit-possession cults in societies where women are particularly subordinate to men. Possession cults permit women to find a religiously validated identity that ameliorates their subordination in the mainstream culture of their societies. He (1986) suggests that the differences between the roles of men in mainstream Islamic worship and those of women in spirit-possession cults such as the zar cult of Sudan help define mainstream Islam. Janice Boddy (1989), who has also studied the zar cult, makes the similar observation that "the dialectic between the zar and Islam on a religious level corresponds to that between women and men in an everyday world pervaded and informed by sexual complementarity. It is important to realize that if women are constrained by their gender from full participation in Islam, men are constrained by theirs from full participation in the zar" (p. 6).

According to Boddy, Sudanese villagers view possession by zar spirits as an illness that can be helped by ritual observance. Women, especially married women, are thought to be particularly vulnerable to attacks by zayran (plural of zar) because the spirits are attracted to things such as henna, perfumes, jewelry, and beautiful clothing used by women. Men's involvement in the public rituals of Islam are also thought to protect them from zar attacks.

When possessed of a spirit, the woman enters a state of trance. The zayran also cause suffering, illness, and disorder within the lives of those they possess. Possession by a zar is treated by participation in the zar cult, which can alleviate the problem but not cure it. Symptoms are relieved by propitiating the spirit in a ceremony conducted by women. Drumming and the singing of chants invite the afflicting spirit to enter the body of the person it has troubled. When the afflicted person enters a trance, the spirit can be identified and asked what offerings it wishes or what other demands it wants to make in return for no longer plaguing the woman. Though her symptoms are ameliorated by this, no permanent cure can be said to have been accomplished, since the woman and the zar remain in a perpetual partnership in which the spirit may possess her again in future ceremonies. Thus, the woman must continue to participate in the zar cult throughout her life to avoid a relapse of her spirit-caused illness or other afflictions.

Although men denounce the propitiation of the zayran, such spirits are mentioned in the Qur'an, so the belief in their influence is not seen as contrary to Islam. When, occasionally, a man is diagnosed as suffering from the attack of a zar, he does not participate in the propitiation ceremonies of women, because the sexual segregation of men and women is a barrier to that, and because men condemn the ceremony as counter to their Islamic beliefs. Instead, men resort to exorcism by means of Islamic medicine and rituals. Nevertheless, though they publicly argue that the possession trances and ritual propitiation of the spirits is heretical, men commonly support the participation of their female kin in the women's rituals. This is partly out of concern that an exorcized spirit might retaliate against women, who are regarded as more vulnerable than men. Boddy and Lewis also suggest that men's tolerance of the women's cult gives them the opportunity to participate "in what they ostensibly condemn as superstition and heresy" (Lewis 1986, p. 196), not just by providing money for the offerings given to the spirits but also by listening to and watching the rituals from afar.

Michael Lambek (1993) found a similar symbiosis between Islam and women's spirit-possession rituals on the island of Mayotte, which lies between Madagascar and the coast of Tanzania. As in Sudan, the relationship between Islam and spirit possession is gendered. Lambek explains that "Islam is embodied and reproduced largely and most saliently by men, possession by women" (pp. 62–63). Possession offers women an opportunity to express their identity as powerful individuals that Islam does not. Hence, women are more likely to become possessed than are men. As in Sudan, women's participation in possession rituals can be a source of power. For instance, Lambek explains that "Mediumship provides an avenue . . . through which capable women can exercise their authority and play

(box continues)

(box continued)

a significant role in the *mraba* [their family] and the community. This can protect or further their own interests, for example, enabling sisters to continue to lay immoral claims upon their brothers after the parents' death" (p. 334). Men, in contrast, are "expected and enabled to display their moral concerns in the universalistic arena provided by Islam" (p. 335). Lambek estimates that about 25 percent of the population is possessed.

In Mayotte the spirits that possess are of two kinds, called *trumba* and *patros*. The first are more like humans in their relationships with other trumba and more involved in human affairs. For instance, the senior trumba may be spirits from the royal lineages of the island. The patros spirits are more powerful; they prefer blood as food, and their power is more associated with nature and the wild. Like the zar, both the trumba and patros cause illness and problems between people. In fact, the initial possession is typically manifest as a lingering illness that can be cured only by the successful removal of the spirit. Once removed, however, a spirit may decide to enter into a permanent mediumship relationship with the person who was possessed. In the process the spirit is "tamed," and its speaking through the person it possesses becomes part of the moral discourse of the community. Lambek explains that in the early stages of mediumship, women are often possessed by glutinous and libidinous spirits, but gradually they are replaced by more sedate and dignified senior spirits. Each spirit has an individual identity, and the same spirit may successively possess members of different generations of the same family. Thus, spirit possession can symbolize the kinship connections of a particular medium, and the spirit may speak in behalf of the moral concerns of the medium's family.

In Mayotte, the "first signs of possession often . . . follow a crisis or loss" (p. 335)—that is, a situation where the afflicted person has experienced weakness or lack of control. The possession itself permits the individual to assert control once again, but in an indirect way, since his or her dominant behavior is thought to be under the control of the possessing spirit. When people are made ill by spirits, they consult a religious specialist called a *fundi*, who manages the possession ceremony. Like the client, the fundi is someone, male or female, who has been possessed by a spirit, but the fundi has the ability to consult his spirit and act as a medium to provide clients with advice concerning their problems. As in the zar cult, the afflicting spirit may be placated with offerings and by following various taboos. The ceremonies are worked out cooperatively by the fundis and their clients. Interestingly, in Mayotte, where women are not as socially subordinate as are women in Sudan, the possession cult is not exclusively controlled by women to the exclusion of men; but possession still afflicts women primarily, and women are prominent in the fundi role.

Chapter Summary

1. Religion influences and is influenced by its broader social and cultural contexts.

2. Religious symbolism is influenced by the organization of society itself, including such organizational facts as the kind of sovereign groups in that organization.

3. In societies that have no specialized political institution, religion can serve as an important mechanism of social control.

4. In societies that have full-time governments, religion may provide support for the authority of government.

5. In religiously heterogeneous societies, a shared system of religious beliefs and values, called a *civil religion,* may develop.

6. Political efforts to support religion can make it more socially prominent without necessarily increasing individual participation or voluntary financial support for religion.

7. In the simplest of societies, men and women typically have equal access to religious roles, but as societies grow socially more complex, particularly societies with gender stratification, the religious roles of women may be subordinated to those of men.

8. In gender-stratified societies where men monopolize religious ideology and rituals of the public religious organization, women sometimes play major roles in marginalized spirit-possession cults as an alternative source of religious prestige and power.

9. Gender relations in society are often a source of symbols and metaphors that are prominent in religious ideology and mythology.

10. Religious practitioners of both sexes were most common in the shamanic religions of foraging societies and societies where simple horticulture was practiced. In contrast, the role of priest in ecclesiastical religions tends very often to be dominated by male practitioners.

Recommended Readings

1. Boddy, Janice Patricia. 1989. *Wombs and Alien Spirits: Women, Men, and the Zar Cult in Northern Sudan.* Madison: University of Wisconsin Press. A fascinating discussion of the social functions of the zar cult in Sudan, emphasizing its relationship with gender.

2. Frankfort, Henri. 1948. *Kingship and the Gods: A Study of Ancient Near Eastern Religion as the Integration of Society and Nature.* Chicago: University of Chicago Press. Describes the religions of the major civilizations of the ancient Near East and their political functions.

3. Gellner, David N. 2001. *The Anthropology of Buddhism and Hinduism: Weberian Themes.* Delhi: Oxford University Press. An anthropological examination of Buddhism and Hinduism from a Weberian perspective.

4. Kingsborough, Susan Farrell. 1996. *The Power of Gender in Religion.* New York: McGraw-Hill. Eleven essays examine the interplay between gender and religion.

5. Layman, Geoffrey C. 2001. *The Great Divide: Religious and Cultural Conflict in American Party Politics.* New York: Columbia University Press. Documents the changing role of religion in American politics from the early 1960s through the late 1990s.

6. Middleton, John. 1960. *Lugbara Religion: Ritual and Authority among an East African People.* Oxford: Oxford University Press.

7. Van Gennep, Arnold. 1960. *The Rites of Passage.* 1908. Translated by Monika B. Solon and Gabrielle L. Caffee. Chicago: University of Chicago Press. The classic work on rites of passage.

8. Weber, Max. 1904. *The Protestant Ethic and the Spirit of Capitalism.* London: Allen & Unwin. Weber's classic work on the influence of religion on economic development.

Recommended Websites

1. *http://theothervoices.org.za/religionsa.htm*
   Sources on women and religion in South Africa.

2. *http://matrix.bc.edu/*
   A site that documents the medieval women's religious communities of Europe.
3. *http://pubpages.unh.edu/~cbsiren/sumer-faq.html#A1.2*
   An excellent source on the religion of ancient Sumer.
4. *http://members.tripod.com/~Lhamo/*
   A site about women in Buddhism.
5. *http://www.academicinfo.net/religindex.html*
   Provides information on church-state relationships from the time of ancient civilizations to the present.

Study Questions

1. What does Guy Swanson mean by *sovereign groups?*
2. Why may the early civilizations of the world have been so consistently theocratic societies?
3. How has the process of secularization differed in Europe and the United States?
4. Explain how subsistence customs influence the role of women in religious practices in foraging societies.
5. What was the origin of the Ashanti Golden Stool and what did it symbolize?
6. Briefly describe the characteristics of the United States' *civil religion.*
7. What specific kinds of religious roles do women play in many Islamic countries, where men monopolize the roles of priests and where the mosque is considered a men's place of prayer?
8. How does gender symbolism differ in the creation myths of patriarchal and egalitarian societies?
9. What are the common characteristics of societies in which spirit-possession rituals are prominent?
10. Explain why women's participation in spirit-possession cults has sometimes been described as a psychological "safety valve."

CHAPTER 10

Religious Adaptation
and Change

CHAPTER OUTLINE

CHAPTER OBJECTIVES

After you have read this chapter, you will be able to

1. Explain how the sacred symbols and rituals of religion contribute to the stability of the society of which it is a part.
2. Define syncretism and explain why some religions are more willing to borrow beliefs and practices from other religious traditions.
3. Discuss religion as part of a society's adaptation to its environment.

4. Discuss the process of secularization and its causes.
5. Discuss the circumstances under which new religious movements arise and outline the stages of a revitalization movement.
6. Define the characteristics of religious fundamentalism and explain the circumstances that make fundamentalism attractive to some people.
7. Discuss why religion is likely to continue to play a role in society in the future.

Religion is often a conservative force in society. Its beliefs have an aura of timelessness or antiquity because they are thought of as having derived from the times of mythology, and the values it espouses support the social order of the religious community. Nevertheless, religion does change and may even be a force for change in broader society. In this chapter, we explore some of the principles that govern the ways in which religion adjusts and changes as its circumstances change. We begin with a case study "The Birth of a New Religious Movement: The Ghost Dance Religion," that examines the most dramatic form of religious change, the origin of a new religious movement.

CASE STUDY

The Birth of a New Religious Movement: The Ghost Dance Religion

James Mooney (1896) described a new religious movement called the Ghost Dance Religion that arose among the Great Basin Paiute Indians of the late 1800s and then became particularly popular among the neighboring Plains Indians. The Ghost Dance was first preached by a Northern Paiute prophet named Wodziwob at a time of widespread deprivation among western Indians. He had learned in a vision that the Great Spirit was going to bring the spirits of the dead back to earth, remove the White foreigners who dominated the Indians, and transform the earth into a paradise for believers. To facilitate the coming of this millennial age, Wodziwob taught two basic practices—ritual bathing for purification and a simple dance in which dancers, decorated in black-, white-, and red-painted designs, lined up in a circle that was broken at one point to allow their ancestors to enter. The Ghost Dance spread rapidly from the Great Basin to the Indians of northern California, where impoverishment was particularly acute. After about five years, disillusionment set in because the promised millennium had not materialized, and the movement fell into abeyance until it was revived in 1886 by a new Northern Paiute prophet, Wovoka, who was also known by the name of Jack Wilson (see Figure 8.3). This time it spread among the Indians of the plains, where the traditional culture based on bison hunting had been devastated by the near extinction of the great herds that had once migrated yearly through the plains. Wovoka's vision, like that of Wodziwob, promised a coming millennium in which Whites who did not become one with the Indians would be blown away by terrible winds. In preparation, Indians were to give up fighting, lying, stealing, and drinking whiskey. They were also to revive Wodziwob's dance and wear white cotton. In 1890, the Ghost Dance spread to the Sioux and other Plains Indians. The Sioux had lost 9 million acres of their traditional hunting lands, and the Ghost Dance offered them hope of a return to better days. Despite its rejection of belligerence, when the Ghost Dance became popular among the Sioux in 1890, the U.S. government feared that it would lead to a revival of hostility and attempted to arrest Sitting Bull, who was killed in the resulting fight. The conflict escalated and ended in the massacre of over 300 Sioux at Wounded Knee Creek.

THE CONSERVATIVE FUNCTION OF RELIGION

The primary social function of religion is the maintenance of social stability. Like the flywheel in an engine, it is normally a conservative force that inhibits social change by lending its support to tradition and the status quo. This is why, in times of gradual social change in society at large, religions tend to teach values that may be perceived by many as more adapted to the previous generation's needs than to their own under current circumstances. With time, though, most religions will adjust to the new status quo and give their support to the current ways of doing things rather than continuing to support the older value system. Thus, for instance, in Victorian times one might have heard sermons against women wearing dresses that revealed the ankle at church, but revealing the ankle is no longer an issue a century later in the same denominations. Even in a "conservative" denomination where dress standards might still be addressed, the sermon is not likely to recommend ankle-length hemlines today. Like flywheels, religion resists change, but does adjust to it when it happens and comes to support the new mainstream way of life with the same vigor that it supported the one before.

The role that this "flywheel" function of religion plays in the stability of a society should not be underestimated. Examples of how religion supports society's mainstream values are legion. Perhaps the most interesting are examples of religions whose traditional doctrine is based on ancient scriptures whose teachings nevertheless manage to incorporate the current civil values of their own society even when those bear no relationship to the culture embodied in their scriptures. For instance, many North American Christian denominations find scriptural support for the current taboos against language deemed obscene in "polite company" by expanding the originally narrow commandment "Do not take the name of God in vain" as if it were an injunction against all socially unacceptable speech. Biblical Hebrew followed no such injunction. In fact, numerous verses would be rather obscene by contemporary standards, a fact hidden by translators for the sake of contemporary social and religious sensibilities. Minkoff (1989) points out that the Talmudic commentary *Megillah* explicitly supports the practice of substituting euphemisms for impolite words when reading aloud the original Hebrew text: "The rabbis taught: Wherever an indelicate expression is written in the text, we substitute a more polite one in reading. For *yišgalenah* [the root of which is the vulgar Hebrew term for intercourse] read *ijiškabenah* [from the root for "to lie down with"]." Thus, contemporary social values prevail over loyalty to the original text, making it possible to view the text as supporting those contemporary values.

The adaptation of religious values to fit current societal values can happen over even shorter time spans than the previous illustration suggests. For instance, the Latter-day Saint (Mormon) religion, which supported the practice of polygamous marriage by its members in the late 1800s, is now mainstream in its members' preference for monogamous marriage. Such change in what may be perceived as "religious values" occurs in all religions. It happens because people tend to harmonize their religious and social values so that the two are not in conflict.

Figure 10.1
Religious Change.
These priests perform an elaborate purification rite for the safety of a prototype of
Japan's FSX fighter. Religion often emphasizes tradition and the ancientness of its ritu-
als, but it does change incrementally to adapt its practices to new circumstances.

Durkheim's Insight

Emile Durkheim was the first social scientist to emphasize the harmony between religious and societal values. He was interested in uncovering the "origins" of religion by looking at religion in what he and many at the time thought
of as the simplest of human societies, that of the Aboriginal Australians. Although he did not contribute lasting insights into the evolution of religion, his
study of Aboriginal Australian society and religion led to a fundamentally important insight: Religious symbols are intimately connected to the social order
and help to perpetuate it by instilling loyalty to it in a process whereby symbols
that are metaphors for society's basic institutions are imbued with feelings of
sacredness.

According to Durkheim, Aboriginal Australian societies illustrated the unity
between religion and respect for important social institutions quite dramatically. Australia was populated by foraging peoples who lived in seminomadic
groups. A central tenet of Australian religion was the concept of **totemism,** the
belief that humans are divided into different social groups based on their different spiritual affinities to various plant or animal species. The concept of
totemism played an important role in identifying and differentiating the different clans to which people belonged in two ways: (1) each clan was symbolized
by a particular totemic plant or animal, and (2) clan members were believed to

totemism
The belief that
humans are di-
vided into differ-
ent social groups
based on their
different spiritual
affinities to vari-
ous plant or ani-
mal species.

have personal souls of the same type as the clan's totem. Thus, although the symbolism of totemism embodied religious meanings, it simultaneously denoted membership in the very groups out of which Australian society was built. As Durkheim ([1895]1958) put it, "The god of the clan, the totemic principle, can therefore be nothing else than the clan itself, personified and represented to the imagination under the visible form of the animal or vegetable which serves as totem" (p. 236).

Totemic distinctions played an important role in maintaining social cohesiveness both within clans and between clans. For instance, although the economics of foraging forced clan members to live in different wandering communities, totemic ceremonies periodically brought members of the same totemic clan together for the purpose of renewing the fertility of their clan animal or plant. This was believed to be important, since totems were generally important food resources. Participation in these ceremonies reinforced clan solidarity that otherwise might have been undermined by the dispersion of the clan into different local groups. Since membership in a totemic clan entailed the belief that one's spirit was the same kind of spirit that also resided in the plant or animal of the clan's totem, eating that particular food would be spiritually akin to cannibalism. So, the fertility ceremonies of each clan and the abstinence of each clan's members from the food that their rituals were believed to increase were seen as benefiting members of other clans—those who would harvest that food resource. Thus, totemic beliefs and practices improved goodwill between different clans.

Durkheim believed that what was true of Aboriginal Australian religion was true of religion in general. His view, which is still very influential, held that religion everywhere embodies the same moral authority as does society at large, and religion cloaks important parts of its society's social system with an aura of sanctity that engenders respect for and obedience to that society's institutions and customs. By doing this, religion motivates people to follow customs that benefit society at large even if they do not recognize why following those customs is beneficial.

Durkheim's insight about Australian totemism was found to be applicable to other societies in which the religious concept of totemism was also found. Alexander Goldenweiser (1931) found that, despite specific differences, societies with totemic ideologies had two things consistently in common: social groups that perform different functions and the practical need for them to distinguish themselves from one another. Totemism is simply a religious ideology that imposes itself on such groups because creating symbols that distinguish them from one another fulfills a preexisting social need. In his words,

> In a community subdivided into social units, such as clans, the first demand is for some kind of classifiers, preferably names, which would identify the separate units and yet signify their equivalence by belonging to one category. Again, hereditary kinship groups, such as clans, with a strong feeling of common interest and solidarity tend, so sociopsychological experience shows, to project their community spirit into some concrete thing which henceforth stands for the unity of the group and readily acquires a certain halo of sanctity. It often happens with such objects that certain rules of behavior develop with reference

to them, both positive and negative rules, prescriptions, and restrictions. Such objects thus become symbols of the social values of the group. (p. 381)

The close alliance between social institutions and religious beliefs can be illustrated by considering how the subordinated status of women in late-15th-century Europe was reflected in religious literature. The box titled "Gender in Late Medieval Religious Writing: Excerpt from *Malleus Maleficarum, 1486*" gives a vivid portrayal of religious and social attitudes toward women in that era.

Gender in Late Medieval Religious Writing: Excerpt from Malleus Maleficarum, 1486

Religion reinforces the values of the society of which it is a part by elevating those values to sacred ones. The reflection of the social order in religious symbolism is illustrated dramatically in the portrayal of women in medieval writing. The following excerpt from a tract on witchcraft written in 1486 clearly shows the low status of women during that period:

Since women are feebler both in mind and body, it is not surprising that they should come under the spell of witchcraft. For as regards intellect, or the understanding of spiritual things, they seem to be of a different nature from men; a fact which is vouched for by the logic of the authorities, backed by various examples from the Scriptures. Terence says: Women are intellectually like children. . . .

But the natural reason is that she is more carnal than a man, as is clear from her many carnal abominations. And it should be noted that there was a defect in the formation of the first woman, since she was formed from a bent rib, that is, a rib of the breast, which is bent as it were in a contrary direction to a man. And since through this defect she is an imperfect animal, she always deceives. . . . And it is clear in the case of the first woman that she had little faith. . . . And all this is indicated by the etymology of the word; for Femina comes from Fe and Minus, since she is ever weaker to hold and preserve the faith. And this as regards faith is of her very nature.

Therefore a wicked woman is by her nature quicker to waver in her faith, and consequently quicker to adjure the faith, which is the root of witchcraft. . . .

If we inquire, we find that nearly all the kingdoms of the world have been overthrown by women. . . . Therefore it is no wonder if the world now suffers through the malice of women.

And now let us examine the carnal desires of the body itself, whence has arisen unconscionable harm to human life. Justly may we say with Cato of Utica: If the world could be rid of women, we should not be without God in our intercourse. For truly, without the wickedness of women, to say nothing of witchcraft, the world would still remain proof against innumerable dangers. . . .

Let us consider another property of hers, the voice. For as she is a liar by nature, so in her speech she stings while she delights us. Wherefore her voice is like the song of the Sirens, who with their sweet melody entice the passers-by and kill them. For they kill them by emptying their purses, consuming their strength, and causing them to forsake God. . . .

To conclude. All witchcraft comes from carnal lust, which is in woman insatiable. See Proverb 30: There are three things that are never satisfied, yea, a fourth thing which says not, It is enough: that is, the mouth of the womb. Wherefore for the sake of fulfilling their lusts they consort even with devils. More such reasons could be brought forward, but to the understanding it is sufficiently clear that it is no matter for wonder that there are more women than men found infected with the heresy of witchcraft. And in consequence of this, it is better called the heresy of witches than of wizards, since the name is taken from the more powerful party. And blessed by the Highest Who has so far preserved the male sex from so great a crime: for since He was willing to be born and to suffer for us, therefore He has granted to men this privilege.

Such a view of women is not likely to be penned by any contemporary European religious writer, now that women have entered nondomestic life on an equal legal footing with men. Nevertheless, under the system of gender inequality that prevailed in the 15th century, Sprenger and Kramer's arguments for the role of women in witchcraft would have seemed eminently "logical" because religion represents and validates the underlying structure of a society.

From Jacob Sprenger and Henry Kramer, *Malleus Maleficarum*, ed. and trans. by Montague Sommers (New York: Benjamin Blom, 1970), pp. 44–47.

RELIGIOUS CHANGE: ADAPTATION

adaptation
Change toward
becoming more
adjusted to the
environmental
circumstances
with which
a people must
cope.

Despite religion's stability function, religion can and does change. The symbols that make up its ideology may be reinterpreted in ways that reflect the perceived needs of the current body of believers. For instance, U.S. denominations that once vigorously defended slavery as a divinely authorized institution are not likely to do so today, even though they rely on the same book of scripture that they did before. One form of change may be defined as becoming more adjusted to the environmental circumstances with which one must cope. This kind of change, called **adaptation,** may ultimately lead to a long-lasting stability.

The Cultural Ecology of Religion

Cultural ecology and related approaches, such as cultural materialism, study the ways in which cultures adapt to their specific habitats. They assume that culture is an adaptive mechanism, a means by which humans adjust to their environment and cope with their survival needs. The great diversity of religious beliefs and practices makes it easy—especially by focusing on examples of beliefs and practices that differ greatly from one's own—to portray religion as irrational or even bizarre. However, religion is part of the system of culture and, as such, can be seen as playing a role in the human adaptation to the circumstances of survival. Doing so helps make religion seem more understandable and less irrational because it illuminates religion's roles in the broader system of survival strategies that human beings practice in different environments. The box titled "Hindu Veneration of the Zebu Cow in India" demonstrates how a religious practice that might seem irrational from the ethnocentric perspective of an American student is actually an economically functional adaptation.

The Hebrew Pig Taboo

In contrast with Douglas's symbolic analysis of the Hebrew food taboos (see chapter 4), Harris (1972, 1974) has examined the taboo against eating pigs among the Hebrews and argues that this taboo is also economically adaptive: "During periods of maximum nomadism, it was impossible for Israelites to raise pigs, while during the semi-sedentary and even fully village farming phases, pigs were more of a threat than an asset" (1972, p. 35).

The Hebrew pastoralists of the ancient Near East occupied arid, unforested plains and hills that could not be easily irrigated. As ruminants, cattle, sheep, and goats—the "clean" foods of the Hebrews—were well adapted to this environment. They are cost-effective to raise because they can live on foods—like grasses—that humans do not eat. In contrast, pigs eat the same foods as humans and therefore compete with those who raise them for such things as grains, tubers, nuts, and fruits. Furthermore, pigs are native to forests where abundant shade is available to prevent them from overheating. Since pigs cannot cool their bodies by sweating, they are poorly suited to the hot, arid environment in which the Hebrews lived. In such an environment, they require water, not just to drink but also to wallow in to keep cool. Providing pigs with water for such a purpose would divert a scarce resource in the arid environment of the Hebrews from much more productive uses such as farming and cattle-raising.

Marvin Harris (1974) argues that religion often plays a role in perpetuating the stable adaptation of a society to its environment. In his view, the material conditions of life have a great influence on religious ideology, since material conditions must be coped with successfully if a culture is to survive. His approach to explaining the adaptive benefit of cow veneration in India illustrates this adaptive role of religion quite well.

In English, the idiom "sacred cow" refers to something that people are irrational about and treat as exempt from criticism or question. It originated in the ethnocentric appraisal of British colonial administrators who regarded the Hindu veneration of the *zebu* cow as irrational in the face of widespread hunger in India. Here, they thought, was meat on the hoof, unused and, therefore, wasted, side by side with starving people. Yet, anthropologists who are interested in how religion functions within the ecology of a human society have suggested that this appraisal of the situation was superficial and misplaced. According to Marvin Harris, "Contrary to expectations, studies of energy costs and energy yields show that India makes more efficient use of its cattle than the United States" (1974, p. 31).

According to Harris, the current role of the zebu cow in Hindu life is the result of changing conditions. He points out that until about 600 B.C. Indians did eat beef. Then cattle became less common on the subcontinent but continued to be eaten by the elite of society, the priestly-caste Brahmins and members of other high castes—the very people who today are religiously expected to follow the strictest vegetarian diets. This declining

(box continues)

Figure 10.2
The Sacred Cow of India.
The zebu cow is sacred to Hindus of India and shares the road with automobiles and the sidewalk with people. In addition to its status as a sacred symbol as the "mother of India," the zebu plays an important role in farming that makes it economically and ecologically more sound to preserve than slaughter it.

(*box continued*)

role cattle play as a food source resulted from a decline in the cost-effectiveness of raising herds of cattle as food and a rise in importance of other economic roles for cattle.

The living zebu cow is economically important in India. Its dung serves as fertilizer in the fields and as fuel for cooking in the home. Oxen are yoked together to pull plows. The veneration of the zebu means that the cows can wander and forage weeds along the roadsides by day without being molested by others until they return home to be milked and penned up for the night. Valuable acreage can be used to grow food for peasant families instead of fodder for cows. In fact, venerating the zebu instead of developing a beef industry yields even greater savings for Indian farmers who need animal labor to produce their food. Cattle raised as food must be fed many more calories of food that could be eaten by humans than their flesh provides. Thus, many more calories of food are available if the same acreage is devoted to producing grain for human consumption. In the United States, three fourths of all farm acreage is devoted to raising fodder for animals instead of food for people. This system is quite feasible using an industrialized system of farming and petrochemical fertilizers, but establishing a beef industry in India would remove millions of acres of land from producing food for human beings, and millions of Indians would suffer greater hunger, not less. In short, the veneration of the zebu cow in India is far from irrational; instead, the religious system helps maintain an economic pattern that is quite adaptive.

Harris (1977) summarizes the changes that led to the current sacred status of the zebu cow in India this way:

The tabooing of beef was the cumulative result of the individual decisions of millions and millions of farmers, some of whom were better able than others to resist the temptation of slaughtering their livestock because they strongly believed that the life of a cow or an ox was a holy thing. Those who held such beliefs were much more likely to hold onto their farms, and to pass them on to their children, than those who believed differently. . . . Under the periodic duress of droughts caused by failures of the monsoon rains, the individual farmer's love of cattle translated directly into love of human life, not by symbol but by practice. Cattle had to be treated like human beings because human beings who ate their cattle were one step away from eating each other. To this day, monsoon farmers who yield to temptation and slaughter their cattle seal their doom. They can never plow again even when the rains fall. They must sell their farms and migrate to the cities. Only those who would starve rather than eat an ox or cow can survive a season of scanty rains. (p. 147)

Aztec Ritual Cannibalism

Following a similar viewpoint, Michael Harner (1977) examined possible nutritional implications of human sacrifice in the Aztec civilization. Human sacrifice was practiced in a number of early human civilizations in various parts of the world, but Aztec society was unique among them in not tabooing cannibalism. Aztec aristocrats, including soldiers who captured living enemies for sacrifice, were permitted to eat the flesh of those sacrificial victims—but peasant farmers were not. Harner accounts for this by pointing out that the Aztecs' protein needs were primarily met through vegetable crops from which the body can synthesize protein; they had insufficient meat resources to meet protein needs. Thus, protein deficiency was a problem during times of drought when crops of beans and corn were insufficient to meet the population's protein needs. The tactics of Aztec warfare emphasized capturing live victims for sacrifice, and warriors who captured sacrificial victims were permitted, along with their families, to eat parts of the meat from the bodies of the captives they offered as sacrifices.

Harner estimated that the number of human sacrifices performed by the Aztecs was equivalent to 1 percent of their population. Although this would not have been sufficient to fill the protein needs of the entire population during times of drought, it did provide incentive for peasant farmers to join the military and support the government during times of stress. By supporting the state instead of rebelling against it, their families were fed by the government until the drought ended; and if they were successful in capturing enemy warriors for sacrifice, their families also had the luxury of eating meat.

The Maring Ritual Regulation of Warfare

Roy Rappaport (1966, 1967, 1984) examined the role of rituals in the regulation of warfare and the use of resources among the Tsembaga Maring people of New Guinea. The Tsembaga, like other subgroups of the Maring people, were horticulturalists whose staple crops were root crops—taro, sweet potatoes, yams, and manioc—and a large variety of greens. The Tsembaga also raised herds of pigs, but they killed and ate pigs only in times of stress, such as sickness or warfare, as parts of religious rituals.

When the pig herds were small, they were easily cared for and fed on substandard tubers, so there was little competition between them and their human owners. In fact, they contributed to the sanitation and livelihood of the community by eating garbage and by eliminating weeds in the gardens where they were penned toward the end of the first harvest. Their rooting also softened the ground in the gardens.

Pigs played a central role in the cycle of warfare among the Tsembaga. When hostilities were formally declared between neighboring groups, ritual prohibitions were put into place on sexual intercourse, on men's eating of foods prepared by women, and on drinking liquids while on the battleground. Pigs were killed ritually at this time, and men ate heavily salted pig fat just before fighting. Fighting occurred only on clear, sunny days, and the combination of heat, salt, and lack of water reduced the length of each day's fighting. After each engagement, warriors ate lean pork, helping them recover some of the nitrogen lost during stressful fighting.

A war might last for weeks. When it ended, the victors performed a ritual planting of *rumbim* plants along the new border to mark their claim to any captured territory. The ritual planting of the rumbim ended the taboos on sexual intercourse and the foods prepared by women from lowland animal species. During the planting ritual, the Tsembaga also promised their ancestral spirits to show their gratitude for the aid they had given them during the warfare by holding a *kaiko*, a pig festival in which pigs would be ritually sacrificed to feed the ancestral spirits. This required many pigs, since the meat was also used to feast the human allies who had helped the victors win the war. In fact, it typically took at least five years to a decade or even more to raise enough pigs to hold a kaiko. During this period, peace prevailed between the former enemies, and a taboo was in force against eating highland animal species associated with the ancestral spirits.

As the herds grew in preparation for a kaiko, they became increasingly expensive to the Tsembaga, since they could no longer be fed solely on garbage and substandard tubers. Thus, more and more work was required in gardening as the size of the herds increased. Immediately before a kaiko, the Tsembaga might have to be growing food on over a third more fields than were needed when the herds were small. Large herds were also the source of more social problems within a village as well. For instance, as pigs became more numerous, so did the likelihood that a neighbor's garden might be invaded by someone's pigs, resulting in disputes over the damage caused or the pig killed by the irate gardener. Thus, the growing costs of raising pigs eventually led to the decision that there were enough pigs in the village to hold a kaiko for the ancestors, who ate the spiritual substance of the ritually slaughtered pigs, and for the village's allies, who came to eat the meat.

The beginning of a kaiko was signaled by planting formal boundary stakes along the boundary established by the previous war and by uprooting of the rumbim plants that had marked them until then. Then pigs were slaughtered, the taboo on eating highland animals was ended, and a year of feasting, trading, and dancing began. During the kaiko, all of the adult pigs were killed, so the size of the herds were radically reduced again. Allies who attended the kaiko and danced on a village's dance ground during the festival were formally committed to fight alongside the village's warriors in its next war. The kaiko ended with a major pig slaughter. After this, participants were free to formally declare war again.

Rappaport summarized the role of religious ritual in the Tsembaga adaptation to their ecosystem this way:

> Ritual among the Tsembaga and other Maring, in short, operates as both transducer, "translating" changes in the state of one subsystem, and a homeostat, maintaining a number of variables which in sum comprise the total system within ranges of viability. To repeat an earlier assertion, the operation of ritual among the Tsembaga and other Maring helps to maintain an undegraded environment, limits fighting to frequencies which do not endanger the existence of the regional population, adjusts the man-land ratios, facilitates trade, distributes local surpluses of pig throughout the regional population in the form of pork, and assures people of high quality protein when they are most in need of it" (1967, p. 30).

Montagnais-Naskapi Divination

Omar Kayam Moore (1957) analyzed the Montagnais-Naskapi technique of divining where to find game and argued that using this religious method to decide where to hunt could help maintain the long-term viability of hunting in the barren lands of the Labradorian Peninsula's interior plateau. According to Moore,

> Animal bones and various other objects are used in divination. The shoulder blade of the caribou is held by them to be especially "truthful." When it is to be employed for this purpose the meat is pared away, and it is hung up to dry, and finally a small piece of wood is split and attached to the bone to form a handle. In the divinatory ritual the shoulder blade, thus prepared, is held over hot coals for a short time. The heat causes cracks and burnt spots to form, and these are then "read." The Naskapi have a system for interpreting the cracks and spots, and in this way they find answers to important questions. One class of questions for which shoulder blade augury provides answers is: What direction should hunters take in locating game? . . .
>
> When a shoulder blade is used to locate game, it is held in a predetermined position with reference to the local topography, i.e., it is directionally oriented. It may be regarded as "a blank chart of the hunting territory . . ." (Speck, p. 151). Speck states (p. 151) ". . . as the burnt spots and cracks appear these indicate

the directions to be followed and sought." If there is a shortage of food, the shoulder-blade oracle may be consulted as often as every three or four days and, of course, the directions that the hunts take are determined thereby. (p. 70)

Moore argues that since this method of determining where to go to hunt involves so many uncontrollable variables—such as the structure of the individual bone, the temperature of the fire, and how long and how close the bone is held to the fire—the effect of this ritual is to randomize the locations where hunters try to find game. This is likely to be a less successful way of actually finding game than would be relying on the opinions of skilled hunters who have known the territory for a lifetime. However, the very fact that this method lowers the success rate increases the probability that the already scarce game will not be overhunted. In other words, the very fact that divination fails more often than expert opinion insures the long-term survival of a needed commodity and, therefore, the long-term survival of this hunting society.

Syncretism

Contact between different cultures often results in one culture's borrowing traits from another. This process of mixing cultural traits often affects religion as well as other parts of culture, and numerous examples of religious **syncretism,** the mixing or blending of religious beliefs and practices, result from contact between different religious traditions. This kind of change can be viewed as a kind of adaptation to the broader social environment in which a religion exists. Haitian Voodoo illustrates the role of syncretism, in producing new religions. The deities of Voodoo derive largely from the Yoruba Fon, Ibo, and Dahomean cultures of West Africa. The name *Voodoo* itself is from the Dahomean and Togoan term for a "god," "spirit," or "sacred object." The box titled "Haitian Voodoo" illustrates the process of syncretism that brought together African and Roman Catholic religious symbolism in Haiti.

> **syncretism, (religious)** The mixing or blending of religious beliefs and practices that results from contact between different religious traditions.

Syncretism has been common among most religions. The common religious attitude about the beliefs and practices of other religions is "If it works, we'll use it too." The attitude that rejects the beliefs and practices of other religions is common among Western religions such as Christianity and Islam, but is not the norm among human religions. Rather, such an exclusivist approach seems to develop in the religions of state societies where the secular government claims to be the sole legitimate legal authority. The religions of expansionist states tend toward such a view as well as a proselytizing approach to religion that attempts to spread their ideology among other peoples, just as secular government attempts to dominate them politically. But it can arise from a protectionist attitude, one that seeks to preserve the threatened purity of its religious symbols, among religions of societies that are dominated by more powerful neighbors.

RELIGIOUS CHANGE: SECULARIZATION

Especially in societies where members live in small, face-to-face communities and share a single religious ideology, religion is highly integrated into the daily operation of other institutions such as politics. However, in societies with large

According to Karen Brown (1987), Voodoo is the religion practiced by 80 to 90 percent of Haitians. She explains that "Voodoo is an African-based, Catholic-influenced religion that serves three (not always clearly distinguished) categories of spiritual beings: *lemò, lemistè,* and *lemarasa* (respectively, "the dead," "the mysteries," and "the sacred twins"). According to Jacob Pandian (1991), "Voodoo mythology and ritual derive from the Dahomean and other West African cultural archetypes of spirituality and power; the model of ritual specialists is also derived from the West African traditions. The priest (*hungan*) and priestess (*mambo*) have their followers 'who voluntarily place themselves' under their authority" (p. 126).

Voodoo congregations typically have elaborate initiation rituals. Their rituals usually include food offerings to the gods and spirits, and spirit-possession trances play a central role in the ceremonies. Spirit possession permits human communication with gods and other spirits, including spirits of the dead. It is also common for twins to be venerated as supernatural. Both sorcery and healing rituals are also practiced. Each congregation is led by a religious specialist—a hungan or mambo—who is trained to interact with the gods, to guide the rituals of the congregation, to interpret the beliefs of Voodoo, and to give sound spiritual advice by such techniques as palm reading, reading cards, or dream interpretation.

Melville Herskovitz (1937) noted that because the African religious practices of Haitian slaves was "handicapped by social scorn and official disapprobation, the followers are almost inevitably split into local groups, each of which is dominated by the personality of the priest whose individual powers furnish the principal drive toward any outer organization the cult-group under his charge may achieve" (p. 536–37). The fragmented social organization of Voodoo also resulted in much diversity in which traditional African gods were equated with particular Catholic saints. However,

Herskovitz listed a number of the more common correspondences:

Legba, the god who in Dahomey guards crossroads and entrances to temples, compounds, and villages, is widely worshiped in Haiti where, as in Dahomey, he must "open the path" for all other supernatural powers and hence is given the first offering in any Haitian *vodoun* ceremony. Legba is believed by most persons to be the same as St. Anthony, for the reason that St. Anthony is represented on the *images* as an old man, poorly dressed, carrying a wand which supports him as he walks. Some hold that Legba is St. Peter, on the basis of the eminently logical reason that St. Peter, like Legba, is the keeper of keys and opens the door. By most persons, however, St. Peter is usually believed to be a *loa,* or *vodoun* deity, without any African designation, being called the *loa* St. Pierre, though this again is disputed. . . . Damballa, the Dahomean rainbow-spirit deity, is one of the most widely worshiped and most important Haitian *vodoun* gods. . . . The saint identified with Damballa is St. Patrick, on whose *image* serpents are depicted. (p. 538)

According to David Levinson (1996), "the African God Bodye, the "Good God," is linked with the Christian God" (p. 237).

Another important concept of Voodoo is that the human soul is composed of five parts: the *corps cadavre,* or mortal body; the *n'âme* or spirit; the *z'e'toile,* or star of destiny; and the two major parts of the soul, *ti-bon-ange,* or personality, and the *gros-bon-ange,* or cosmic life force that animates each individual.

In Haiti, Voodoo has developed somewhat different forms in rural and urban areas. Rural Voodoo tends to be organized as a family-based system of rituals carried out to placate spirits that might influence the welfare of the extended family. In cities, the priests and priestesses of congregations play a more central role in organizing and conducting rituals, and ceremonies tend to follow a regular calendar that can be anticipated by nonrelated participants.

Figure 10.3
Change in Religion.
Drawing upon symbolism from other religions is one means by which religions change and adapt to new circumstances. In Our Lady of Guadalupe Church on the Zuñi Reservation in New Mexico hang portraits of the Virgin Mary. Above the pictures of the Stations of the Cross, depicting scenes of the Crucifixion, are murals of more than two dozen life-sized kachinas, the spirit-beings of Pueblo culture. The artist, Alex Seowtowa, a Roman Catholic Indian, has combined the traditions of his Pueblo culture with those of Christianity.

populations, religion may become less involved in the day-to-day business and running of other institutions, a process called *secularization.*

The Secularization Process

Peter Berger (1967) defined **secularization** as "the process by which sectors of society and culture are removed from the domination of religious institutions and symbols" (p. 107), and Bryan Wilson (1982) described it as "the diminution of the social significance of religion" (p. 149). Secularization is a natural result of changes in a society as its population grows and its institutions, including religion, become more specialized. It consists of three main interdependent elements. The first is *institutional specialization and differentiation.* As population grows, a society's economic, political, educational, familial, and religious institutions become more specialized and more separated and distinct from one

secularization
The process by which sectors of society and culture are removed from the domination of religious institutions and symbols.

another in the roles they play. This is easily seen when we contrast the simplest of social systems, that of foraging peoples, with that of the industrialized nations. In the former, the local community of 50 or 60 people consists of two groups, family and friends, and this face-to-face community can function without being divided into distinct institutions. Instead, the institutions of life blur into one another: Family rears children, conducts religious rites, produces income, and plays a role in the governance of the community. In industrialized societies, each institution is more or less specialized in the services it performs and is staffed by specialists who are not likely to be kin to one another, share the same politics, or even be from the same communities. They may adhere to different religious traditions; and the policies they institute may not be based on, backed, or supported by the various religions of their constituents.

In the earliest of the world's civilizations, governments were theocratic and combined religious and political authority in the hands of the same societal leaders. By the time the United States was founded, religion still had great influence on government. Indeed, many other nations had "state religions" that were fostered by the government, but government officials in most of these nations nevertheless were no longer religious officials as well, and their authority was primarily secular. The authors of the U.S. Constitution took a further step of formally forbidding an entanglement of religion and government by constitutionally prohibiting the establishment of a state religion. Yet, religion as an institution still influenced matters that informed the views of political leaders. Today, in the same country, the public educational system generally does not overtly foster religious belief, government is expected to be religiously neutral in its policies, and worship within religious congregation is a weekly scheduled event led by religious specialists with whom members of the congregation may have little if any interaction the rest of the week.

The second major element of secularization is a shift in the *ideology of day-to-day decision making* from one that is heavily influenced by a worldview filled with supernatural beings and forces to one that emphasizes a rational, utilitarian, and empirical (or scientific) way of seeking solutions to problems. Such a change is a natural outgrowth of institutional specialization, particularly outside the religious institution itself, since the decision-makers come to see the problems they must deal with more and more in terms of the specialized concerns of their own work the more their own institution becomes differentiated from the religious institution.

Third, secularization includes a decline in the role of supernatural beliefs and practices in the day-to-day activities of individuals. They may still value a supernaturalistic worldview in their personal lives; but as secularization progresses, that worldview comes into play less and less as they interact with others. The decline of religion in interpersonal interaction occurs when life shifts from small communities, where personal relationships and a shared moral order are bases for daily life, to large-scale communities, where impersonal interaction with strangers is the norm.

Technological Change and Secularization

Leslie White (1947) contended that technological development is the driving force behind other cultural change in general and secularization in particular. According to White, the expansion of technology brings with it secular ways of thinking. As more and more things are controlled by means of technology, those things tend to be thought about in utilitarian rather than religious ways. Thus, as human technological control over the world grows, the realm of things understood primarily in religious terms contracts.

The influence of technological development on ideology is particularly noticeable if one compares the ideologies of the world's technologically simplest societies, those that have survived by foraging for wild foods since before the rise of food domestication, with the ideologies of the world's industrialized societies. In the former, many more things are understood in religious terms. The renewal of game is often the subject of religious rituals, and the success of the hunt, though it does involve the skilled use of hunting equipment, is commonly augmented by rituals as well. In contrast, food production in industrialized societies is almost entirely in the hands of specialists who rely on industrialized farm equipment, irrigation, petrochemical fertilizers, and insecticides that give producers tremendous control over their work. Religious rituals are generally not a part of the routine; and for the vast majority of people, obtaining food is a purely secular matter of a trip to the supermarket.

Secularization may result in more efficiency and effectiveness in accomplishing the nonreligious goals of nonreligious institutions such as the economic system, but it is not an unmixed blessing. For the nonreligious individual, a completely secular approach to politics, economics, or family life may seem completely "logical" and comfortable, but the declining presence of religion as a dominant factor in the functioning of society's institutions can be a source of stress for religious individuals. Religion is not an isolated, compartmentalized part of the religious individual's psyche. Rather, it is integrated into his or her daily life and plays an important role regardless of what institution—politics, family, education, economics, or recreation—one is involved in at the moment. For the religious, the social expectation of a secularized society that religion is not relevant to the goals and activities of other institutions is contrary to their own worldview and practice. Thus, dealing with secularized institutions can be stressful.

This dissonance between the social process of secularization and the psychology of religious individuals has resulted in repeated societal conflicts about secular trends throughout U.S. history. For instance, the legal battles concerning "separation of church and state" are waged anew in each generation without permanent resolution. A case in point is the 1980 Supreme Court decision in the *Stone v. Graham case*, which arose in Kentucky. In that decision, the Supreme Court declared it a violation of the First Amendment for the Ten Commandments to be posted in public schools. According to that decision, "The preeminent purpose for posting the Ten Commandments on schoolroom walls is plainly religious" and "The Ten Commandments are undeniably a sacred text in the Jewish and Christian faiths." As such, the practice was not constitutionally permissible.

Yet, although the increased secularization of public education that the *Stone v. Graham* decision supported came from the highest judicial authority in the country, this did not result in an easy or complete change in the attitudes of everyone it affected. And the desire for a less secularized society has emerged repeatedly since then, sometimes with the same symbol, the Ten Command-ments, as the central focus of attention. Officials in Kentucky, Indiana, and South Carolina have tested the limits of the 1980 decision by posting the Ten Commandments in other public buildings, such as county offices. Judges in Ala-bama and Texas have posted Bible verses in their courtrooms. In 1996 by a vote of 27 to 1 the Tennessee Senate passed a resolution that urged families, busi-nesses, places of worship, and public schools to post the Ten Commandments. In 1997 and 1998, the U.S. House of Representatives and the Indiana legislature considered nonbinding resolutions that supported the Ten Commandments, and 200 public officials in Congress have posted the Ten Commandments in their public offices. And in 1999 the Ten Commandments were removed from a Campbell County, Kentucky, public school where they had been placed despite the 1980 Supreme Court decision. What all this illustrates is that the principles governing a social system and leading to increased secularization of its institu-tions can be at odds with the intuitive preferences that many have for infusing religion throughout all aspects of life.

According to sociologist Bryan Wilson (1982), "Secularization occurs in association with the process in which social organization itself changes from one that is communally-based to a societally-based system" (p. 153). By "communally-based," he means based on personal, face-to-face relationships with other well-known individuals, the way society is organized in small com-munities. By "societally-based" he means organized around the impersonal as-sociations that are common in large-scale state societies. As societies evolved from the smaller, community-based system of organizing what goes on based on personal relationships between acquaintances to the larger, impersonal states of today whose institutions are run by bureaucracies, religion tended to play an increasingly smaller role in the day-to-day interaction of individuals with one another in all institutions except the institution of religion itself.

Secularization was a natural by-product of population growth and the dis-appearance of the integrated "community" as a comprehensive guide for living. According to Wilson, "The large-scale societal system does not rely, or seeks not to rely, on a moral order, but rather, relies wherever possible on technical order. In this sort of social arrangement, much less importance is attached to personal dispositions, to conformity with a code of custom, to the education of emotions, to the processes of socializing the young into responsible humane personal atti-tudes. After all, if, by time-and-motion studies, data-retrieval systems, credit ratings, conveyor belts, and electronic eyes, we can regulate human activities and, in particular, their vital economic functions, then why burden ourselves with the harrowing, arduous, time-consuming weariness of eliciting moral be-havior?" (Wilson, 1982, p. 161). While religious values shared by the community played a prominent role in guiding people's behavior in all aspects of commu-nity life, in a system built around "technical order," the religious institution be-came much less important as a shared basis for most human dealings with one another. Although religion cannot reverse the process of secularization in soci-ety at large, membership in a religious community can offer those for whom the loss of an integrated community is a source of personal stress a community-like religious environment in which they can participate. Membership in a religious denomination has served this role throughout U.S. history and is one of the reasons for the high rate of religious participation in the United States compared with European countries.

267

CHAPTER 10
Religious Change:
Secularization

A society organized around "technical order" is, according to Wilson, "an inhospitable context for the religious *Weltanschauung*":

> Religious institutions compete on increasingly unfavorable terms with other agencies which seek to mobilize and manipulate men's resources of time, energy, and wealth. These agencies can employ, much more effectively than traditional religion, all the techniques of modern science and organization; they are unhindered by the types of impediment to the adoption of rational systematization that are found even in the new religions. Religious perceptions and goals, religiously-induced sensitivities, religiously-inspired morality, and religious socialization appear to be of no immediate relevance to the operation of the modern social system. For every social problem, whether of economy, polity, law, education, family-relations, or recreation, the solutions proposed are not only non-religious, but solutions that depend on technical expertise and bureaucratic organization. Planning, not revelation; rational order, not inspiration; systematic routine, not charismatic or traditional action, are the imperatives in ever-widening arenas of public life. (pp. 176–77)

Wilson suggests a number of examples of specific stresses that can arise from secularization:

> The discontents of modern man have much to do with the sense of alienation that a rational order induces. . . . Men learn to cope with the world in terms of personal trust, parental love, personal intimacies, and local involvements; their early years are spent in a small, stable community of intimate relationships and enduring affections. Traditionally, the world into which the child was socialized had strong continuities with the world in which the adult would live out the dispositions implanted in childhood—sometimes with the selfsame people. In the modern world, however, there are profound discontinuities between the situation of socialization and the impersonal contexts in which the individual will live out most of his life. . . . The unrest is of many kinds. It includes concern about demoralization and the breakdown of civic order in urban contexts more extensive and more intricately organized than any that ever before existed. It recognizes, and is alarmed by, new techniques of social control, public surveillance, and the invasion of privacy. It is fed by growing awareness of the exploitation and pollution of the natural environment, towards which man has lost his old sense of reverence. It responds to the knowledge that violence can be systematically organized on a scale hitherto unparalleled by governments and even by terrorists. It embraces widespread uncertainty caused by recurrent betrayals of democratic principles by subterfuge and corruption. Our modern discontents include all these matters that belong to the public domain. They also include our awareness of the changing quality of personal relations; the sense of loss of community life; the disenchantment that men feel when they recognize just how invasive of personal life have become the precepts that govern the market-place and the factory, and how much has been lost in human sensitivity. (pp. 177–78)

Routinization of Charisma

As groups become larger, they tend to develop a hierarchy of managers and decision-makers whose control is based on the authority of their office rather than personal charisma but whose authority becomes increasingly restricted to

**routinization
of charisma**
The process by
which, as groups
become larger,
they tend to de-
velop a hierarchy
of managers and
decision makers
whose control
is based on the
authority of
their office rather
than personal
charisma and
whose authority
becomes increas-
ingly restricted to
their own area of
specialization.

their own area of specialization. Max Weber referred to this process as the **routinization of charisma.** The religious institution can be affected by secularization as it too becomes more bureaucratized and its practitioners become more and more specialized. In complex religious organizations, religious specialists are often organized into a hierarchy so complex that individual specialists are not involved in the full religious life of congregations.

RELIGIOUS CHANGE: ACCOMMODATION, CONFRONTATION, AND RESISTANCE

Although religion can be a powerful conservative force, it is also capable of adjusting to social change, and it is sometimes even a powerful motivator for resistance and change in a social order.

The very belief that it is based on unchanging truths can allow religion to provide strong legitimation for any social change that it supports. Some religions have demonstrated a striking willingness to accommodate social change. For instance, Shinto has a long history of incorporating changes in Japanese society into its own beliefs and practices. When Buddhism was introduced into Japan in A.D. 538, the Buddha was accepted as a kami. Buddhist shrines were often built near Shinto shrines, and in A.D. 743 the goddess Amaterasu revealed at one of Shinto's most venerable shrines that she and the Buddha were simply two manifestations of the same divine reality. Shinto and Buddhist priests developed a division of labor in which Shinto priests performed marriage ceremonies and Buddhist priests performed funerals. In embracing syncretism, Shinto supported rather than opposed the social changes brought about by Chinese influence in Japan. Today, it is common for many people in Japan to practice both Shinto and Buddhism. In recent times, Shinto has adapted quite readily to the introduction of Western technology into Japanese life.

Religion has often played a role in cultural resistance movements. Mohandas Gandhi's use of his role as a spiritual leader to preach nonviolent resistance to the British in India and the Reverend Martin Luther King's advocacy of nonviolent resistance to obtain civil rights for Black Americans illustrate how religion may play an active role in the advocacy of social and cultural change. Another dramatic example of religion as resistance was the clandestine practice of Voodoo and various similar practices that preserved African religious forms in the Caribbean. Practices that drew upon African religious symbolism were a source of strength that helped African slaves resist slavery. In Jamaica, Ashanti religious practices were drawn on by slaves to form what came to be known as Obeah. Practitioners called Obeah men were believed to have the power to cure or kill with the use of herbs and magic. They became highly respected leaders among Blacks and sometimes had a following of thousands. They always played a central role in slave rebellions and other forms of cultural resistance to the dominance of White plantation owners.

In her analysis of the transformation of religious fundamentalism into an active force in American politics, anthropologist Susan Harding (2000) described how religion has continued to play a role in the advocacy of social change in America during the past two decades. By offering an alternative vision of the direction of social change, religious fundamentalists such as Jerry Falwell and his "Moral Majority" movement have reacted against contemporary circumstances and pressed for a different kind of change that conforms to the values they espouse.

In state societies, religion has sometimes been a powerful engine of social and cultural change, as Max Weber showed in his analysis of the role of the Protestant ethic in paving the way for industrialization and capitalism (see chapter 9).

RELIGIOUS CHANGE: REVITALIZATION MOVEMENTS

Typically, religious change is slow and incremental. However, under certain circumstances religious innovation can bring new religious ideologies and rituals into existence in relatively short amounts of time. New religions are typically born in response to social stresses.

Religious Innovation and Nativistic Movements

Although religion normally emphasizes stability and functions to inhibit social change, under special circumstances religion may play a prominent role in revolutionary social change. Such religious change often occurs in times of social upheaval—for instance, as part of what Ralph Linton (1943) called **nativistic movements,** attempts of native peoples to reassert parts of their traditional cultures as a reaction against domination by foreign powers. Many new religions were born in the nativistic movements that arose following European colonization of Africa, Australia, Oceania, Asia, and the Americas. They included "cargo cults" in Melanesia, *terra sans mal* movements in South America, the Handsome Lake religion and the Ghost Dance religion among North American Indians, millenarian movements in frontier America, Black separatist churches, Jewish messianic movements, and various Islamic Mahdic movements.

nativistic movement
The attempt of native peoples to reassert parts of their traditional culture as a reaction against domination by foreign powers.

Melanesian Cargo Cults

Peter Worsley (1957, 1959) explored Melanesian examples of new religious movements. He described how the coming of Europeans to some parts of Melanesia was seen as the beginning of access to the material goods or "cargo" that the Europeans seemed to have in abundance. He explained (1959) that

> The initial enthusiasm for European rule, however, was speedily dispelled. The rapid growth of the plantation economy removed the bulk of the able-bodied men from the villages, leaving women, children and old men to carry on as best they could. The splendid vision of the equality of all Christians began to seem a pious deception in face of the realities of the color bar, the multiplicity of rival Christian missions and the open irreligion of many Whites.
>
> For a long time the natives accepted the European mission as the means by which the "cargo" would eventually be made available to them. But they found that acceptance of Christianity did not bring the cargo any nearer. They grew disillusioned. The story now began to be put about that it was not the Whites

who made the cargo, but the dead ancestors. To people completely ignorant of factory production, this made good sense. White men did not work; they merely wrote secret signs on scraps of paper, for which they were given shiploads of goods. On the other hand, the Melanesians labored week after week for pitiful wages. Plainly the goods must be made for Melanesians somewhere, perhaps in the Land of the Dead. The Whites, who possessed the secret of the cargo, were intercepting it and keeping it from the hands of the islanders, to whom it was really consigned. In the Madang district of New Guinea, after some 40 years' experience of the missions, the natives went in a body one day with a petition demanding that the cargo secret should now be revealed to them, for they had been very patient. (pp. 122–23)

In this environment of perceived deprivation, a series of **cargo cults** arose that claimed to have the secret of the cargo and offered rituals that would bring the cargo to their followers. In some places, Worsley explained, "In the New Testament they find the Apocalypse, with its prophecies of destruction and resurrection, particularly attractive" (p. 123). Worsley reported that in 1946, many Melanesians in the central highlands of New Guinea were expecting the end of the world and the dawning of a new day in which, following three days of darkness, "Great Pigs" would descend from the sky, bringing the long-awaited cargo from the ancestors in the heavens. In preparation for the end, they built landing strips on the mountains, put up bamboo antennas in imitation of the radio antennas that Europeans had at their airfields, and butchered all of their pigs to celebrate the impending end of the old order.

American Millenarian Movements

America gave rise to a number of millenarian religious movements in both the 19th and 20th centuries. **Millenarianism** is the religious belief in a future "Golden Age" in which the evils of today's world no longer exist; it is often thought that the new age will be ushered in by the action of powerful supernatural forces. Typically, the transformation from an old, evil world to an ideal millennium is conceived of as the result of divine intervention, not a natural evolution toward a better society. Often, though not necessarily, the divine intervention is expected to involve an **apocalypse,** a cataclysmic end of the world, often in the near future, that will be brought about by divine intervention; it is often expected to be accompanied by major economic and political disasters and warfare between the righteous and the evil. Throughout world history, apocalyptic millenarian movements have been particularly common as dates, depending on the calendar in use, approached the end of full thousand-year periods—for instance, in Europe in A.D. 1000.

The Revitalization Process

More recently, Anthony F. C. Wallace (1956) analyzed the process by which new religious movements arise in response to major cultural stress and found regularities that make up what he referred to as the **revitalization process.** According to Wallace, the revitalization process unfolds as a four-part sequence. Normally, religion operates as a force for stability in a culture in which change is a slow, step-by-step and recurring process that can be understood as a kind of dy-

---

cargo cults
Melanesian religious movements that claimed to have the secret of the cargo (material goods) and offered rituals that would bring the cargo to their followers.

millenarianism
The religious belief in a future "Golden Age" in which the evils of today's world no longer exist; often expected to be ushered in by the action of powerful supernatural forces.

apocalypse
A cataclysmic end of the world, often viewed as being in the near future, that will be brought about by divine intervention and that is often expected to be accompanied by major economic and political disasters and warfare between the righteous and the evil.

revitalization process
The process by which new religious movements arise in response to major cultural stress.

namic equilibrium. Wallace refers to this normal state as a **period of cultural stability.** But sometimes various forces, such as prolonged warfare, epidemic disease, ecological disaster, or cultural contact with an alien society that is much more powerful, can push a culture out of its usual state of stability into a **period of increased individual stress.** This is a time when members of society respond to the larger-than-usual problems of life with various forms of individual deviance, including crime, illness, and various kinds of individual deviance. The third state, the **period of cultural distortion,** begins when some members of society begin to band together into special-interest groups to try to overcome the stresses in their lives. This period is characterized by organized as well as individual deviance, including alcoholism, venality in public officials, sexual deviance, black market economies, and widespread distrust of the established bureaucracy. The activities of the special-interest groups and their conflicts with the established bureaucracies add to the stresses of life for other individuals and can lead to the fourth stage, the **period of revitalization.** In this period an individual or group of individuals create a plan for building a new way of life, a utopia in which the problems around them will be done away with.

Revitalization Prophets

Often the vision of a new culture is created by an individual, the **revitalization prophet,** who experiences something akin to a temporary psychotic break with reality, which he or she perceives to be a supernatural revelation. During the revelatory state, the prophet undergoes *mazeway resynthesis* (see chapter 3) and develops new, seemingly more insightful ways of thinking about the problems of his or her society and formulates a plan for overcoming those problems and establishing a new, "millennial" way of life. Since many people are having trouble dealing with the cultural distortion their society is undergoing, this message may make more sense to them than does the ideology of the old, establishment culture. As converts flock to the prophet, the old bureaucracy is likely to respond to the rapid growth of the movement as a threat to its own existence. The ensuing conflicts with the "establishment" can lead to the suppression of the revitalization movement, the expulsion of its followers from society, or a successful rise to power by the leadership of the revitalization movement. In the latter case, a way of life with new values, religious beliefs, and rituals is established as the society's new steady-state culture.

The Social Milieu of Revitalization Movements

Wallace saw an analogy between the revelatory experience of the revitalization prophet and temporary psychotic episodes such as those of reactive schizophrenia, which psychiatrist R. D. Laing (1961) viewed as a kind of self-curing psychological disorder. This analogy may have some merit when one looks solely at the visionary experience of someone like the revitalization prophet who is responding psychologically to major societal stresses. However, sociologist Rodney Stark points out that the **revelatory experience,** the subjective experience of feeling that one has received an answer to one's prayers, is actually a quite common experience among ordinary people in normal times. Seen in this broader context, the revelatory experience is not an abnormal psychological process at all: "Revelations are merely the most intense and intimate

period of revitalization
A time when an individual or group of individuals create a plan for building a new way of life, a utopia in which the problems around them will be done away with.

revitalization prophet
An individual who creates a vision of a new culture during something akin to a temporary psychotic break with reality.

revelatory experience
The subjective experience of feeling that one has received an answer to one's prayers.

fundamentalism
A religious movement that (1) emphasizes beliefs based on scripture as absolute truth, (2) has a worldview that portrays its followers as being opposed by powerful or dangerous enemies, and (3) engages in political activism aimed at recruiting others to the "fundamentals" and creating a society guided by these religious beliefs and values.

form of religious or mystical experiences—those episodes involving perceptions and sensations which are interpreted as communication or contact, however slight with the divine" (Stark, 1999, p. 291). He argues that "Although religious experiences do occur among the mentally ill and sometimes are caused by fasting or drugs, overwhelmingly they occur among normal, sane, sober people (Stark and Bainbridge 1997: 129–55). Indeed, there is an immense body of evidence suggesting that quite ordinary mental phenomena can be experienced as some sort of mystical or religious episode involving contact with the supernatural being (Hood 1985) and that many (perhaps even most) people in most societies have such experiences (Gallup International 1984; Greeley 1975; Yamane and Polzer 1994)" (p. 292). The reason that this has been noticed less than has the revelatory experience of the revitalization prophet is that, in normal times, the revelatory experiences simply "provide[s] an experiential validation of faith" (p. 292), what Stark elsewhere calls a "confirming experience" (1965). In other words, although many ordinary people experience some degree of what they interpret as a divine answer to their prayers, the revelatory experience normally renews their faith in their current religious system and its symbolism. Stark concludes that it is not the psychological process in the revitalization experience that differentiates the revitalization prophet from everyone else, but the situation of social stress in which a revitalization revelation occurs. In normal circumstances, the small day-to-day stresses of life that motivate personal prayer tend to result in revelatory experiences, when they occur, that renew one's faith in one's existing religion. In times that Wallace calls periods of cultural distortion, people's dissatisfaction with the old status quo is so great that the perceived message of the revelatory experience is more likely to be one that challenges the mainstream religious system supporting the established order. Like the revelatory experiences of persons in less stressful settings, the revitalization prophet receives a message that the problems of life can be assuaged by the support of religion; but in this case, the religious symbolism simply differs from that of the old religions whose worldview and values no longer seem adequate to account for the widespread social inequities of a period of cultural distortion.

Revitalization movements have occurred in various parts of the world among Melanesians, Aboriginal Australians, the tropical forest peoples of South America, and North American Indians. They have also occurred in the form of separatist churches and millenarian, messianic, and Mahdic movements among Christians, Jews, and Moslems.

Modern Fundamentalist Revivals: Responses to Secularization

Religious **fundamentalism** is found in various religious traditions, including Christianity, Judaism, Islam, Hinduism, and Buddhism. In all of these different religious traditions, fundamentalist movements share three characteristics: (1) an emphasis on religious "fundamentals," beliefs that Martin Marty (1993) described as "the rock-solid, hard-binding, time-tested, text based verities that give believers total assurance and total missions" (p. 5), (2) a worldview that portrays its followers as being opposed by powerful or dangerous enemies, both supernatural and human, and (3) political activism aimed at recruiting others to their "fundamentals," fighting back against the enemies they perceive as being opposed to their beliefs and values, and creating a society that is guided by their religious beliefs and values. According to Marty, the enemies that fundamentalists perceive as threatening to overwhelm them include "Satan, the devil, the West, pluralism, relativism, skepticism, immorality, modernity, violating signals of mass media, uncongenial educational institutions, unfriendly governments, or the tribes next door" (1993, p. 3).

Authoritarianism and Dogmatism in Beliefs and Values

In their beliefs, fundamentalists emphasize literal interpretations of sacred written texts, which may be either scriptures or earlier sacred legal and lifestyle traditions that arose from the application of scriptures. Their approach to these sacred sources is one of **authoritarianism,** advocating the importance of obedience to authority. In principle, the scriptures or sacred traditions are viewed as the authority to which followers must submit themselves. However, in practice, this value of respecting the authority of the sacred sources functions to motivate followers to defer to the authority of those religious specialists who interpret the sacred sources to other followers.

In their practice, fundamentalists stress the importance of the rules of ritual piety outlined in their sacred texts. Adherence to these beliefs and practices defines the "fundamentals" of each of the different fundamentalist religions. The fundamentalist approach to beliefs and values is one of **dogmatism,** stating opinions about and interpretations of the authoritative texts as if they were established fact rather than judgments that might be subject to error.

Adversarial Worldview

The **adversarial worldview** of fundamentalist religions perceives history as guided by a conflict between the forces of good and evil. Fundamentalist beliefs may embody this conflict in supernatural symbols such as God versus Satan, but may also divide the human world in ways that set themselves, as followers of God, up against various human groups that are seen as enemies of the fundamentalist cause. These human enemies include other religious groups that fall outside the fundamentalist camp. These groups "should know better," since their members are religious, but they betray the fundamentalist vision of religion. They also include a variety of secular groups whose values seem to fundamentalists to clash with their own values and goals. Marty (1993) notes that the fundamentalist vision is "in every case we have come across, patriarchal, and much concerned with issues of gender, sexuality, intimacy, familiality, the life cycle" (p. 6). Feminists and groups that follow an "alternative lifestyle" are natural enemies to the conservative gender and sexual values of fundamentalists. But government and public education are also frequently singled out for the support they are perceived to give to nonfundamentalist minority groups and to tolerance for diversity. Avoiding such enemies may involve adopting a separatist posture in which members withdraw from contact with outside groups. Within the group, the concern for avoiding the "evils of the world" may show up as an emphasis on orthodoxy of belief and culling out "false beliefs" among the group's own members.

The adversarial worldview of fundamentalist sects can sometimes escalate into outright conflict, sometimes with tragic consequences. For instance, an

authoritarianism
Worldview that advocates the importance of obedience to authority.

dogmatism
The statement of opinions and interpretations from authoritative texts as if they were established fact rather than judgements that might be subject to error.

adversarial worldview
A viewpoint in which history is perceived as guided by a conflict between the forces of good and evil.

ideology that viewed the U.S. government as a threat to its survival led the Branch Davidian followers of David Koresh to arm themselves heavily against potential attack. Government agencies responsible for the control of regulated firearms responded to this arming with a siege of the Branch Davidian's Mount Carmel Center at Waco, Texas, in 1993, a conflict that ended in a classic self-fulfilling prophecy, the death of 135 members of the cult in a conflagration.

Fundamentalists typically also reject the secularization of society and the economic, political, and gender-role changes that have occurred in social life during the past half century throughout the world. Fundamentalists particularly reject the separation of religion from other spheres of life, such as politics and social custom, holding that all behavior should be governed by the religious beliefs and values that they hold sacred.

Political Activism

fundamentalist political activism
A tendency to be involved in secular politics in order to challenge the evils perceived in society rather than withdrawing from the larger society to avoid those evils.

Fundamentalist religions are characterized by **fundamentalist political activism,** a tendency to be involved in secular politics in order to challenge the evils perceived in society rather than withdrawing from the larger society to avoid those evils. The activism of fundamentalist movements includes heavy involvement in efforts to recruit new followers. Fundamentalist missionaries can be seen handing out pamphlets at airports and train stations. Fundamentalists actively work in the political arena to turn government away from promoting secularization and toward establishing policy that supports their system of religious values. Government, in their view, should be subordinate to and a conservator of fundamentalist religious values.

Fundamentalism as a Reaction against Secularization

Bryan Wilson (1982) suggested that the process of secularization was a source of stress for some people and that this could be a motivation for increased religiosity, particularly for the attachment to religious models that call for a return to a less secularized way of life. This proposal contributes to our understanding of why religious fundamentalism, with its strong opposition to the changes of "modernization," might appeal especially to persons who perceive themselves as victims of the social changes of this century.

According to Wilson (1982), "The discontents of modern man have much to do with the sense of alienation that a rational order induces" (p. 177). Traditional society was organized around stable communities grounded in a consensus about the moral order of life. Religion was ideally suited to life in the traditional community and could provide a supernatural rationale for its moral order, but according to Wilson (1982), "The large-scale societal system does not rely, or seeks not to rely, on a moral order, but rather, wherever possible, on technical order. In this sort of social arrangement, much less importance is attached to personal dispositions, to conformity with a code of custom, to the education of the emotions, to the processes of socializing the young into responsible humane personal attitudes" (p. 161). The depersonalized system of large scale can, itself, be a source of discontent that can become the basis for new religious forms. Thus, strangely, secularization can be a cause of the rise of new religious commitments.

Numerous studies have pointed out that industrialization is associated with increasing economic inequality both among individuals and groups. Efforts of policymakers to deal with inequalities between mainstream society and economically disadvantaged minorities have had some success, but they have also been a source of stress for middle-class members of society who find themselves gradually falling behind. When individuals experience **relative deprivation** (or **status discrepancy**), the perception of a discrepancy between their expectations of success and their actual achievements, a great deal of dissatisfaction can result. Also feeling resentment toward various minorities whom they perceive as having been "favored" by government policies while they find themselves slipping behind, those experiencing status discrepancy feel anger toward secularized society and its policies. Relative deprivation has been suggested by sociologists as a major force in the rise of religious fundamentalism's popularity, since the fundamentalist sects of every religious tradition reject secularization and hold out the promise of a return to the ideals of the traditional community and its religion-based moral order.

relative deprivation (status discrepancy) The perception of a discrepancy between one's expectations of success and one's actual achievements.

American Christian Fundamentalism

The fundamental beliefs of Protestant fundamentalists in North America are based on their interpretation of the Judeo-Christian scriptures. Social scientists borrowed the term "fundamentalist" from "the Five Fundamentals" often cited as accepted by all Protestant fundamentalists: (1) the inerrancy of the Bible as the literal word of God, (2) the virgin birth of Christ, (3) the bodily resurrection of Christ, (4) the belief that Christ, through his death by crucifixion, atoned for human sins, and (5) the expectation that Christ will literally return one day to establish his kingdom on earth. Protestant fundamentalism has a strong element of political activism aimed at returning U.S. society to a 1950s style of family with "traditional" gender roles, a symbol of the time before women and other minorities had moved into competition with White men in the private-sector economy and of a day in which neighborhoods still had a sense of community built on a religion-based moral order.

For Catholic fundamentalists, papal doctrine from the decrees of the Council of Trent in the 16th century up to but not including the Second Vatican Council in the 20th century are sources of fundamental beliefs and values. Fundamentalist Catholics object to some of the changes that have occurred within Catholicism beginning with the Second Vatican Council. They would prefer, for instance, a return to the Latin mass, the mass celebrated with the priest facing away from the congregation toward the altar at the front of the church, the host (or wafer) of communion given to communicants only by the priest and not by eucharistic lay ministers, and all readings during the mass read by the priest alone without the use of lay readers, a continued observance of meatless Fridays, and the avoidance of meat through all of Lent. Fundamentalist Catholics would most particularly oppose the use of women as eucharistic ministers and would lament the fact that many orders of nuns no longer require the wearing of habits. Again, one perceives in Catholic fundamentalism an idealization of times past, particularly of the era preceding Vatican II, and a strong focus on the values of religious and social traditionalism.

Creationism: A Contemporary American Religion

Fundamentalist religious leaders in the United States have opposed scientific views about human evolution since Darwin first proposed them. In the 19th century, Darwin outlined the natural mechanisms that could guide evolutionary change in living things. Such mechanisms were a potential threat to religious ideas, since the process did not require a role for God, and incorporating them into a religious model would have required a major change in the fundamentalists' literal approach to interpreting scripture. Instead, they chose to oppose the introduction of evolutionary ideas into the United States school system. They successfully supported efforts to pass laws that forbade the teaching of evolution in states where their followers had sufficient numbers to command the respect of legislators. In 1925, John Scopes, a Tennessee high school teacher, was convicted and fined $100 for teaching his biology students that humans had evolved from simpler animals.

In the past decades, a new form of religious fundamentalism has developed in the United States, taking for itself the name **Creation Science.** The major creationist organizations are the Institute for Creation Research, which makes its home at Christian Heritage College, and the Creation Science Research Center. Creationist organizations do not carry out original scientific research in the traditional sense. Instead, they gather material published by scientists in any field that they judge relevant to their interests in opposing evolution and use these within their argument for a creationist view of the universe. They also participate actively in lobbying to bring about legislation that forbids the teaching of evolution within the public schools without giving equal time to creationist ideas.

What do creation "scientists" believe? This is not an easy question to answer, since their views are not systematically defined as is usually the case within the sciences. Generally, creationists are outspoken anti-evolutionists, refusing to believe that either life or the universe itself has evolved through time, even under divine direction. They believe that the universe came into existence suddenly by the act of a creator. Contrary to the dominant opinions of astronomers, physicists, geologists, biologists, and anthropologists, they believe that the universe, the earth, and all living things came into existence at about the same time, probably between 6,000 and 13,000 years ago. Individual creationists are divided on whether the process took six days or 6,000 years. They agree that the basic "kinds" of living things were created with essentially the same traits that they have today. There seems to be no accepted definition of what constitutes a "kind," but creationists are in agreement that whatever it is, the only change that can occur in living things is within a "kind" and that one "kind" cannot evolve into another. Fossils of extinct living forms, creationists believe, were creatures that died suddenly as a result of a major, catastrophic, worldwide flood.

If creationist beliefs sound as if they were based on a fundamentalist religious interpretation of Genesis, it is probably no coincidence. To join the Creation Research Society, one must sign a statement that reads in part, "The Bible is the written Word of God, and because we believe it to be inspired throughout, all its assertions are historically and scientifically true."* The logo of the Creation Science Research Center surrounds the phrase, "In the beginning God. . . ." The religious basis for their beliefs seems clear, but their work of lobbying for the teaching of creationism within the public schools requires that they portray their views as "scientific" to sidestep the constitutional prohibitions that prevent state-supported schools from teaching or promoting sectarian religious doctrines.

From Richley H. Crapo, *Cultural Anthropology: Understanding Ourselves and Others*, 2nd ed. (Guilford, CT: Dushkin Publishing Group, 1990), pp. 235–36. Reprinted by permission of The McGraw-Hill Companies.

Conference on Evolution and Public Education: Resources and References, edited by P. Zetterberg (St. Paul, MN: University of Minnesota Center for Educational Development, 1981), p. 80.

The box titled "Creationism: A Contemporary American Religion" briefly describes a religious movement that attempts to find scientific support for fundamentalist Christian scriptural interpretation.

Islamic Fundamentalism

Just as its Christian counterpart does, Islamic fundamentalism values a return to life guided by holy text. Islamic fundamentalists draw their nonnegotiable beliefs and values from the *sharia*, Islamic laws that arose from the application of the Qur'an to the governing of Islamic societies. Politically, Islamic fundamentalists also value a drawing together of other institutions, especially law and the state, under the authority of religion. Since secularization in Islamic countries was largely coupled with Westernization, Islamic fundamentalist rejection of secularized institutions has a strong element of opposition, particularly to Western influences that are perceived as a source of the decline of a central role for religion in public life. This was illustrated most dramatically by the attack of September 11, 2001, on the World Trade Center in New York by members of al-Qaeda, a terrorist organization that espouses an extremely politicized version of Islamic fundamentalism.

According to Fatima Mernissi, Islamic fundamentalism "is the product of two extremely modern phenomena: rapid urbanization and state-funded (therefore democratic) mass education" (1987, p. xviii). Fundamentalists tend to be educated, high achievers—college students, engineers, professionals, and office workers—whose expectations for upward mobility have not been met. Mass education of both sexes has undermined traditional gender-role values. It has created a generation of young men who are "faced with job insecurity or failure of the diploma to guarantee access to the desired job" (xxiv) and who must postpone marriage, and of women, "faced with the pragmatic necessity to count on themselves instead of relying on the dream of a rich husband [and] themselves forced to concentrate on getting an education" (xxv). Under these conditions, a turn to religious fundamentalism is attractive. According to Mernissi, "The conservative wave against women in the Muslim world, far from being a regressive trend, is on the contrary a defense mechanism against profound changes in both sex roles and the touchy subject of sexual identity" (p. xxviii).

Creation Science A new form of religious fundamentalism that espouses an anti-evolutionary view of human origins that is grounded in a literalist view of the biblical creation myth.

The Future of Religion

Nineteenth-century scholars, seeing the steady advance of science from the Enlightenment through the Victorian era, predicted the eventual demise of religion. They envisioned a society guided by a fully rational, scientific philosophy. We can now see that such views were naive at best. Even processes such as secularization can, as we have seen, give rise to new religious movements. What, then, does the future hold for religion?

The arena within which the scope of science has expanded at the expense of religion is the quest for fulfilling the most basic human needs—the needs of food, shelter, and biological survival. Scientific thinking and the secularization of life that proceeds from the application of utilitarian thinking has a natural tendency to supplant religious belief and practice in these areas because they demonstrably help people meet those important needs more successfully

**existential
questions**
Questions about
why humans ex-
ist, the meaning
and purpose of
life and death,
and the role of
values in human
life.

than does religion. However, human life is more than the mere meeting of material needs. Religion is likely to have a greater continuing appeal than does the utilitarian philosophy of science within the arenas of ideology and social organization.

In the realm of ideology, religion has a stronghold unchallenged by science in terms of **existential questions,** questions about why humans exist, the meaning and purpose of life and death, and the role of values in human life. Technological sophistication is unlikely to undermine the desire for answers to questions such as "Why do I exist?," "How should I live?" or "Will I cease to exist at death?" Religions are likely to continue to offer answers to these and similar existential questions.

Socially, religion has always played an important role in creating a sense of community, a feeling that individuals have a place within a body of like-minded others who value one another's welfare and believe in a shared moral order that guides the life of the community. As we have seen, the very processes of secularization that can undermine these things can stimulate the rise of new religious communities that provide these values.

Anthropomorphism and the Endurance of Religion

As you read in chapter 1, Stewart Guthrie (1980) suggested that religion is best defined as the systematic application of anthropomorphic thinking to understanding nonhuman things. This definition has important implications for any question about the future of religion.

Victorian scholars who viewed religion as belief in supernatural or super-empirical things and who considered the beliefs of science, being based on careful observation of empirical reality, to be more "rational" sometimes wondered why people should have even developed irrational religious ideologies. Occasionally, they opined that religion might eventually be completely supplanted by science-based rationality. Guthrie's approach highlights the fact that by focusing on the substance of religious beliefs—ideas about gods, spirits, and other "supernatural" things—these earlier scholars were led to ask the wrong question. Anthropomorphic thinking, the central feature of his definition, is a cognitive process rather than a list of specific beliefs. This shift of emphasis from the substance of things believed in to the cognitive processes by which beliefs are created puts a spotlight on the *similarities* between religious and scientific thinking and thereby makes it clear that religious ideologies are not as "irrational" as their highly diverse cosmologies can make them appear.

As Guthrie puts this change in emphasis on how to address the persistence of religion,

> Once we see religion as anthropomorphism, the question—Why does religion persist?—changes to, Why do humanlike models persist? This question is easier to answer. Humanlike models persist because they identify and account for the crucial components of our world: humans and their activities and effects. Because such models are vital, employing them is our first, our automatic, and our most powerful approach to the world. In sum, religion arises and persists because the strategy from which it stems often succeeds in identifying phenomena—real humans and their actions—that are uniquely important. (1993, p. 201)

Guthrie points out that *all* thinking—scientific and nonscientific—makes use of analogies. Humans often seek to understand the unknown by comparing it with the known. Some of these analogies, or models, are mechanical, drawing on the world of nonliving things as comparisons: Atoms can be compared to solar systems to make them more comprehensible to students. Living beings such as humans can also be used, as when constellations of stars are said to be arranged in the form of a hunter, a bull, or a crab. Although scientists prefer to avoid anthropomorphism, humans make useful and intuitively rather appealing models for a wide range of phenomena.

According to Guthrie, anthropomorphism, the tendency to see humanlike qualities in nonhuman things, is so natural and understandable that the persistence of religion is therefore quite understandable. The essence of religion, anthropomorphism, is an approach to understanding the world around us that is often very useful, since humans often are involved in the things we wish to understand. It is also an approach that is very flexible—humans make good models for a wide range of phenomena. And the use of human models has an appeal precisely because we are humans. Put a slightly different way, scholars should not have been asking why most people are religious, but rather why a few are not. Religious thinking is, in other words, a very natural process, and so scholars should not expect it to be abandoned by most human beings, who, after all, do not make their living by puzzling out how things work using nonhuman models the way scientists do. Rather, scholars should expect religion to persist, as long as life confronts people with questions they feel a need to answer in ways that seem intuitively meaningful.

Chapter Summary

1. Religion often functions as a conservative force within society. Its sacred symbols are derived from those characteristics of a society's social organization that need to inspire respect and deference for society to function. By transforming these traits into sacred symbols, religion inspires people to support those customs that insure the stability and continuity of society even if they otherwise would not recognize the importance of doing so.
2. Despite its conservative nature, religion does change. One source of change is syncretism, the borrowing of religious traits from other religions.
3. Religion is part of the system of culture and, as such, can be seen as playing a role in the human adaptation to the circumstances of survival.
4. Especially in societies where members live in small, face-to-face communities and share a single religious ideology, religion is highly integrated into the daily operation of other institutions such as politics. However, in societies with large populations, religion may become less involved in the day-to-day business and running of other institutions, a process called *secularization*. Causes of secularization include population growth, which makes it increasingly likely that important transactions will occur among strangers, and increasing technological control of parts of nature that were previously understood only in religious terms.
5. Although religion normally emphasizes stability and functions to inhibit social change, religion may play a prominent role in revolutionary social

changes under special circumstances. Such religious change often occurs in times of social upheaval, producing new religions that offer a new system of religious beliefs and values and the promise of societal reform.

6. Religious fundamentalism is (1) an emphasis on religious "fundamentals," the "rock-solid, hard-binding, time-tested, text based verities that give believers total assurance and total missions," (2) a worldview that portrays its followers as being opposed by powerful or dangerous enemies, both supernatural and human, and (3) political activism aimed at recruiting others to the "fundamentals," fighting back against the enemies fundamentalists perceive as being opposed to their beliefs and values, and creating a society that is guided by their religious beliefs and values. One circumstance that can make religious fundamentalism more attractive is the personal dissatisfaction that arises from status discrepancy, a perceived discrepancy between a person's expectations of success and his or her actual achievements.

7. Religion can also play an important role in social change and cultural resistance.

8. Conditions of societal stress sometimes gives birth to new religious traditions or the transformation of previous traditions.

9. Nineteenth-century scholars, seeing the steady advance of science from the Enlightenment through the Victorian era, predicted the eventual demise of religion. They envisioned a society guided by a fully rational, scientific philosophy. This anticipation that religion would disappear as society became increasingly secularized now seems naive in having ignored the psychological and social functions that religion can continue to play even in a highly secularized society.

Recommended Readings

1. Carpenter, Joel A. 1997. *Revive Us Again: The Reawakening of American Fundamentalism.* New York: Oxford University Press. Traces the fall and rise of religious fundamentalism in the American 20th century.

2. Harding, Susan Friend. 2000. *The Book of Jerry Falwell: Fundamentalist Language and Politics.* Princeton: Princeton University Press. A perceptive examination of the transformation of American fundamentalist Christianity into a powerful political force.

3. Hargrove, E. C. 1986. *Religion and Environmental Crisis.* Athens: University of Georgia Press. Examines religion in the context of ecological issues.

4. Harris, Marvin. 1974. *Cows, Pigs, Wars, Witches: The Riddles of Culture.* New York: Random House. A very readable book that argues for an adaptive basis for many religious practices.

5. Rappaport, Roy. 1979. *Ecology, Meaning, and Religion.* Richmond, CA: North Atlantic Books. A collection of essays on religion from an ecological perspective.

6. Rashid, Ahmed. 2000. *Taliban: Militant Islam, Oil, and Fundamentalism in Central Asia.* New Haven: Yale University Press. An informed analysis of the complex religious, political, and economic influences on the rise of the Taliban to political power and its imposition of a highly politicized form of Sunni fundamentalist Islam on Afghanistan.

7. Saliba, John. 1995. *Perspectives on New Religious Movements.* London: Geoffrey Chapman.
8. Scheffel, David. 1990. *In the Shadow of the Antichrist: The Old Believers of Alberta.* Lewiston, Petersborough, Ontario: Broadview Press. An accessible description of the most conservative branch of Eastern Christianity and the members' life of separateness from the mainstream culture of Canada.

Recommended Websites

1. *http://www.unc.edu/courses/reli099a/links/links.html*
   Links to websites about a variety of new religious movements.
2. *http://wwww.dushkin.com/webquester/antrosites/santaria.html*
   A good source of information about religious syncretism in Santaria.
3. *http://www.tibet.com/*
   The Dalai Lama homepage, with much information about both Tibetan Buddhism and religion and politics in Tibet.
4. *http://www.cesnur.org/*
   Center for the Study of New Religions website.
5. *http://www.unification.net/*
   Homepage of the Reverend Sun Myung Moon's Unification Church.
6. *http://www.multiplex.com/1/Heavensgate/index.html*
   A mirror site of the original Heaven's Gate webpages.
7. *http://www.branchdavidian.com/*
   The official website of the Branch Davidian survivors.

Study Questions

1. Explain how, according to Marvin Harris, the sacredness of the zebu cow to Hindus provides a validation for adaptive strategies.
2. What ecological circumstances does Michael Harner believe to have been at the root of Aztec cannibalism?
3. According to Roy Rappaport, how did religious ritual regulate warfare among the Tsembaga Maring of New Guinea?
4. What are the four stages of a revitalization movement?
5. What are the characteristics of religious fundamentalism wherever it is found?
6. Illustrate from your own knowledge how rituals that randomize choices might reduce social conflict or prove adaptive in the long run.
7. What effect did Leslie White believe increasing technological complexity has on religion?
8. According to Bryan Wilson, what social functions can membership in a religious community have that may mitigate the stressful effects of secularization for some members of society?
9. Outline the characteristics of fundamentalist religions.
10. Why should religious fundamentalism not be thought of as a religious orientation of the less well-educated?

Glossary

activism See *political activism, fundamentalist.*

adaptation Change toward becoming more adjusted to the environmental circumstances with which a people must cope.

adversarial worldview A viewpoint for understanding the world in which history is perceived as guided by a conflict between the forces of good and evil.

aesthetic distance The state of mind in which a distressful emotion is experienced in a balanced, real-but-safe way; it is felt strongly enough to be involving yet not so intensely as to overwhelm.

affectlessness The response to extreme stress that manifests itself as no emotion at all.

altered states of consciousness See *trance states.*

ancestor worship The practice of placating souls of deceased ancestors who can be influenced to give aid to their descendants.

ancestral spirits The souls of deceased persons who continue their helpful involvement in the day-to-day earthly affairs of their descendants.

anger An emotion felt when one is distressed about the outcome of interaction with others and perceives the problem as being the fault of the other person.

animatism The belief in an impersonal spiritual force.

animism The belief in spiritual beings.

anthropology A field in the social sciences that bases its conclusions on the study of a broad range of different ways of life.

anthropomorphism Thinking that perceives human qualities in the nonhuman world.

anti-therapy rituals Rituals intended to cause discomfort, illness, and even death to the person against whom they are directed (see also *therapy rituals*).

anxiety A generalized unpleasant physiological state similar to fear but without consciousness of a known danger.

apocalypse A cataclysmic end of the world, often viewed as being in the near future, that will be brought about by divine intervention and that is often expected to be accompanied by major economic and political disasters and warfare between the righteous and the evil.

authoritarianism Worldview that advocates the importance of obedience to authority.

canon The works that are considered religiously authoritative in a religion that has written sacred texts (see also *canon, problem of*).

canon, problem of The problem of determining which original texts to include in a translation of scriptures.

cargo cults Melanesian religious movements that claimed to have the secret of the cargo and offered rituals that would bring the cargo to their followers.

catharsis The sudden, spontaneous discharge of emotional tension when a distressful emotion occurs at aesthetic distance.

ceremony A complex sequence of rituals.

chants The use of speechlike nonsense syllables rather than meaningful speech produced in musical form.

churches Large religious denominations whose religious idealogies tend to support the customs and values of the societies in which they are found; they rely on highly trained, professional religious leaders to carry out their rituals.

civil religion The shared religious beliefs and values that cross-cut denominational boundaries in complex societies.

communal cult institution The rituals that members of the same religion participate in as a group for the benefit of all involved in the ritual or even the entire community of which they are a part.

communal religions Religions in which the rituals of individuals and shamans may be supplemented by others that are performed by groups of individuals in their own behalf or for the welfare of the entire community.

communal rituals Rituals performed by groups of individuals in their own behalf or for the welfare of the entire community.

communitas Feelings of unity achieved by a religious community during the performance of sacred rituals (see also *normative communitas*).

contagious magic Magic in which supernatural influences are transferred through contact or in which things that have been in contact are used to influence one another.

cosmogony The part of a religious ideology that consists of stories describing the origin of the gods, nature and the universe, and human beings.

cosmology Beliefs about the nature of and principles by which the universe is believed to operate.

Creation Science A new form of religious fundamentalism that espouses an anti-evolutionary view of human origins grounded in a literalist view of the biblical creation myth.

cross-cultural comparison The use of information about a large number of diverse cultures to create statistically valid statements about the relationships between religion and other parts of culture.

cult institution A set of rituals all having the same general goal, all explicitly rationalized by a set of similar or related beliefs, and all supported by the same social group (see also *communal cult institution, ecclesiastical cult institution, individualistic cult institution,* and *shamanic cult institution*).

cults   See *new religious movements.*

cultural anthropology   The subdivision of the field that specializes in the study of human ways of life.

Cultural Diversity Data Set   A sample of 200 cultures chosen to represent the various regions of the world within which neighboring societies share many cultural features.

cultural relativism   The approach to interpreting meaning that holds that the meanings of any custom are most accurately understood in light of the cultural context from which they derive.

culture   A learned system of beliefs, feelings, and rules for living that is shared by a group of people and that is outwardly manifested in behavior and artifacts.

culture myths   Religious stories that recount the exploits of heroes, demigods, and other supernatural beings in a time past when the human way of life was being implanted.

deities   See *gods.*

disease object   A supernaturally powerful object that causes illness when it enters or is magically projected into a victim's body.

distress   Unpleasant psychological response to feeling stress.

divination   The use of ritual to obtain knowledge or information unavailable by natural means.

dogmatism   Opinions and interpretations that view authoritative texts as if they were established fact rather than judgments that might be subject to error.

dynamic equivalence   See *idiomatic translation.*

ecclesiastical cult institution   The rituals of a religion in which a religious specialist is charged with performing rituals for the benefit of an entire congregation.

ecclesiastical religions   Those religions that include priests and ecclesiastical rituals.

ecclesiastical rituals   Rituals performed by priests for the benefit of the entire congregation.

elaborated code   A use of language in which many words are used to organize ideas and make thoughts explicit.

elaborating metaphors   Key symbols that provide more detailed information about a complex system to make it more comprehensible.

emotion   A combination of the feelings involved in a particular pattern of stress and thoughts about the nature of the situation in which the feelings occur.

empirical observation   Data collecting that is carried out in a definable context that can be repeated and confirmed by more than one observer.

ethnocentrism   The attitude that one's own culture is superior to other cultures and that its concepts can therefore be used as the natural standard for interpreting and evaluating what goes on in other societies.

ethnographies   Descriptions of ways of life that are written by anthropological fieldworkers.

etiological myths   Tales that recount the origins of religious rites and social customs.

eustress Stress that is subjectively experienced as a vitalizing, positive experience.

evil eye The belief that some individuals have the power, intentionally or unintentionally, to harm others whom they envy.

exhortation The addressing of members of a congregation by one who is acting in the role of representative of the supernatural.

existential questions Questions about why humans exist, the meaning and purpose of life and death, and the role of values in human life.

expressive culture The customs and institutions of a culture that are most involved with organizing and expressing feelings, often by means of meaningful individual rituals or group ceremonies, games, and festivals.

faith The unskeptical acceptance of ideas that does not demand that those ideas be based on observations through the normal senses or supported by the evidence of testing.

fear The distressful emotion associated with the perception that one has insufficient power to avoid danger.

fetish An object that embodies the power of a protective ritual.

fieldwork The anthropological method of collecting accurate information about customs by living among the people being studied and participating in their way of life.

figurativism (or nonliteralism) An interpretation that assumes the words of the text may mean more than they seem to when taken at face value.

formal equivalence translations See *literal translations*.

functional equivalents Institutions or customs that have a similar effect on the stability of a society.

functions The effects that part of a culture have on the stability of a society and on how its customs are carried out.

fundamentalism An orientation toward religion that is characterized by (1) an emphasis on text-based beliefs as absolute truth, (2) a worldview that portrays its followers as being opposed by powerful or dangerous enemies, both supernatural and human, and (3) political activism aimed at recruiting others to one's beliefs, fighting back against the enemies one perceives as being opposed to one's beliefs and values, and creating a society that is guided by one's religious beliefs and values.

fundamentalist political activism See *political activism, fundamentalist*.

gender stratification Unequal access to social power based on gender.

gender symbolism Symbols and metaphors that reflect the social roles of men and women.

ghosts Disembodied human souls that linger and do harm to living humans.

glossolalia The production of sound sequences that have no conventional meanings in speechlike acts.

gods (deities) Supernatural beings who control major forces within the universe, such as storms, plant or animal fertility, or warfare.

grief The distressful emotion experienced when a person plays his roles in a way that brings less honor than he believes those in the same kind of relationships normally receive.

guilt The distressful emotion experienced when a person believes he has harmed another by using more power than he was entitled to.

high gods Supernatural entities who are not regarded as supreme themselves, but who each exercise great power over some major force within the universe.

homeopathic magic See *imitative magic.*

ideological symbols Those conventional signs used in rituals to express allegiance to society and its social values and morality, conformity to its customs and laws, and acceptance of the established relationships between the individuals and groups that make up society.

ideology The shared beliefs that define a social group and that are passed down from one generation to the next.

idiomatic (or dynamic equivalence) translation A rendering of a text from one language to another that sacrifices the use of equivalent words or phrases for the sake of expressing the meanings conveyed by complete sentences and paragraphs.

imitative magic (homeopathic magic) Magic in which similar things are believed to be spiritually identical so that one can be used to influence the other.

individualistic cult institution The rituals of a religion that involve only one individual.

individualistic rituals Religious behavior, such as private prayer or an adherence to the taboos of a religion, that an individual performs for his or her own benefit.

internal environment Experienceable physiological and psychological processes that occur within the human organism.

interpretation, problem of The problem of how to determine the precise meaning of a word, a verse, or a passage in an ancient sacred text.

key scenarios Symbolic portrayals of means–ends relationships that order action by symbolizing ways to appropriately act out those relationships

key symbols Symbols that inspire strong positive or negative feelings; they are regarded as very important by those in whose culture they are found, are surrounded by rules such as taboos, are found in many different contexts, and are surrounded by cultural elaboration such as having many words to refer to them.

language A distinctively human system of communication that governs the use of spoken symbols to communicate information.

Law of Contact (or Contagion) The magical principle that things once in contact with each other continue to act on each other at a distance after physical contact has been severed.

Law of Similarity The magical principle that things that are similar to each other are spiritually identical so that ritual treatment of one will have an effect on the other.

Law of Sympathy The idea that things act on each other supernaturally at a distance (see also *imitative magic, Law of Contact,* and *Law of Similarity*).

legends Stories about the early times in human existence that follow the times of mythology and whose characters, though heroic, are more like modern humans.

life-crisis rites Rituals that ceremonialize the transitions of status that all members of a community pass through.

liminal period The phase of a ritual during which the feelings of the participants are characterized by communitas.

linguistic relativity The idea that the structure of a language influence affects its speakers' understanding of reality.

linguistic taboos   Those things associated with a religion that are not to be said, either because saying them will be punished by other members of the religious body or because they are believed to result in harmful spiritual consequences.

literalism   The approach to understanding texts that assumes that they are best understood without taking the words as similes, analogies, and metaphors.

literal translations (formal equivalence translations)   Renderings of a text from one language to another that emphasize the use of the words or phrases that are most equivalent to those of the original text.

liturgical orders   More or less invariant sequences of rituals encoded by persons other than the performers.

liturgies   Rituals or ceremonies practiced as forms of public worship or devotion.

magic   Religious rituals that are believed to actually compel the supernatural to behave in a particular way as long as they are done without error (see also *petitionary rituals*).

mana   Supernatural force or power.

Masoretic text   A version of the Hebrew scripture for which copies exist that date to the ninth century A.D.

matrifamilies   Families in which mothers and their relatives have authority over the husband and his children.

mazeway resynthesis   A psychological process in which a person reorganizes his system of values and the way he understands his own identity, the nature of human society, and the nature of the natural environment.

millenarianism   The religious belief in a future "Golden Age" in which the evils of today's world no longer exist; it is often thought that this age will be ushered in by the action of powerful supernatural forces.

monotheism   The belief in a high deity who maintains order within the universe as a whole and who is supreme over all other supernatural beings.

moral values   Rules about good and bad behavior toward other human beings, as religious obligations.

multivocalic   Having the quality of being appropriately interpreted in a number of different ways.

mystical experience   An ecstatic psychological state of feeling oneself merged with the divine.

mysticism   A sense of timeless and spaceless union, or oneness, with the divine that is accompanied by profoundly positive feelings.

mythemes   The basic relationships that are predicated in myths, that constitute a myth's smallest units of meaning, and that are the building blocks of the myth's underlying structure.

mythic story line   The sequence of events in a myth that compose the tale which accounts for the orderliness of the universe and which validates the customs and values of the society to which it belongs.

mythic symbols   Objects or events in a myth or legend that each stand for or represent some important element of the supernatural realm, the order of nature, the human role within creation, or relationships between these.

mythology   The collective body of a religion's myths.

myths   A religion's sacred stories about supernatural beings and powers and their roles in creating the universe and living things.

nativistic movements   Religious movements that result from the attempts of native peoples to reassert parts of their traditional culture as a reaction against domination by foreign powers.

naturalistic thinking   Thinking that distinguishes carefully between the human experience of internal objects and events and the experience of external phenomena and that explains internal phenomena in terms of biological processes and external phenomena in terms of other external phenomena.

natural symbols   Symbols that have the same meanings across cultural boundaries; objects or acts at least some of whose possible meanings are derived from their perceived attributes or normal human uses.

nature myths   Tales that account for the origin of the phenomena of nature.

new religious movements (cults)   Small religious groups that espouse an ideology that is new and different from the mainstream traditions of the society in which it is found.

nonliteralism   See *figurativism.*

normative communitas   Situation in which communitas, the experience of undifferentiated loyalty to others and equality of comradeship, is incorporated into a lasting social system by its being organized into periodic ritual events.

numinous   Pertaining to a feeling of the dependence of one's own existence; the emotion of a creature; the feeling of being submerged and overwhelmed by one's own nothingness in contrast to that which is supreme above all creatures.

object intrusion   The belief that an illness has been caused by the presence of a foreign body, a "disease object," in the patient's body.

oral literature   Tales told by word of mouth for pleasure and edification.

overdistanced   Adjective describing an experience that fails to evoke any emotions at all.

pantheon   The supernatural powers and beings of any cosmogony.

paradoxes   Statements that are true if and only if they are false but false if and only if they are true.

participant observation   A process of participating with and observing subjects in their natural setting.

period of cultural distortion   Part of a revitalization process that begins when some members of society begin to band together into special interest groups to try to overcome the stresses in their lives.

period of cultural stability   The normal state of a culture that is characterized by dynamic equilibrium in which change is a slow, step-by-step and recurring process.

period of increased individual stress   The part of a revitalization process in which a culture is pushed out of its normal state of stability by forces such as prolonged warfare, epidemic disease, ecological disaster, or cultural contact with an alien society that is much more powerful.

period of revitalization   Part of a revitalization process in which an individual or group of individuals create a plan for building a new way of life, a utopia in which the problems around them will be done away with.

petitionary rituals Rituals intended to request rather than compel the supernatural (see also *magic*).

piety values Rules that govern the behavior of people toward the supernatural itself.

pilgrimage Travel undertaken as a form of religious devotion.

political activism, fundamentalist A tendency to be involved in secular politics in order to challenge the evils perceived in society rather than withdrawing from the larger society to avoid those evils.

polytheism A belief in many gods, none of whom is supreme over the others.

prayer The use of language to influence supernatural beings and powers.

priests Religious specialists who mediate between the supernatural realm and humans by performing traditional rituals for congregations at scheduled times.

primogeniture The inheritance of property by the eldest child.

profane The realm of ordinary, everyday, work-a-day world experience.

projection The treatment of internal images and ideas as if they were externally real.

prophets The charismatic founders of new religions who base their teachings on the claim of personal revelation from the supernatural rather than from the study and interpretation of a preexisting theology.

protective rituals Rituals performed for the sake of preventing unwanted natural circumstances such as earthquakes, storms that endanger vessels at sea, fires that can destroy homes or entire communities, or insect plagues or droughts that threaten agriculture.

psychological equilibrium A subjective state of well-being.

psychological functions The effects of following a custom or of participation in an institution on the psychological states of the individual participants.

recitation of the code Communicating about the ideology of the group.

reincarnation The idea that spirits may be reborn, usually into one's own group, after a period of existence in the spirit world.

relative deprivation (status discrepancy) The perception of a discrepancy between one's expectations of success and one's actual achievements.

religious ritual Behavior that follows the same sequence of actions on repeated occasions with care taken for accuracy of performance; the ritual behavior is believed to mobilize supernatural powers to accomplish human ends.

religious technology Objects that function as religious symbols rather than as objects of utilitarian use.

restricted code A use of language that involves relying heavily on standard idioms and relies on the hearers' ability to intuit what has not been explicitly said based on their shared background.

revelatory experience The subjective experience of feeling that one has received an answer to one's prayers.

revitalization process The process by which new religious movements arise in response to major cultural stress (see also *period of cultural stability, period of increased individual stress, period of cultural distortion,* and *period of revitalization*).

revitalization prophet The founder of a new religion who formulates its new worldview, values, and rituals as a result of the experience of *mazeway resynthesis*.

revitalization rituals Rituals that are typically involved in the birth of new religious movements.

rites of intensification Rituals for increasing the availability of important natural resources or for controlling other forces of nature in ways that improve human life.

rites of passage Rituals held to celebrate important changes in social status and roles at various times in the life cycle.

ritual language The highly standardized spoken words that are predictable and spoken in a more or less invariant way.

ritual of becoming a shaman A ritual in which the participant's personality undergoes a permanent change as part of a visionary experience in which he or she experiences a near-deathlike experience of leaving the body and traveling in the spirit world where spirits or deities call the person to become a shaman.

rituals Stereotyped sequences of behaviors that associated with particular emotions and that are rationalized—that is, made meaningful—by the supernatural beliefs of the performers (see also *anti-therapy rituals, magic, petitionary rituals, protective rituals, religious ritual, revitalization rituals, rites of intensification, rites of passage, ritual language, ritual of becoming a shaman, rituals of expiation, rituals of ideology, rituals of manipulation, rituals of mystical experience, rituals of salvation, rituals of social control, spirit possession rituals,* and *therapy rituals*).

rituals of expiation Rituals in which the participant engages in acts of penance or good works to atone for sins, taboo violations, or other failings.

rituals of ideology Rituals that communicate the symbolism of the group to its participants.

rituals of manipulation Rituals that are used to act on nature directly.

rituals of mystical experience Rituals in which the participant seeks the ecstatic experience of oneness with the divine.

rituals of salvation Rituals that are intended to cause a temporary or permanent change in the participant's personality.

rituals of social control Those rituals aimed at maintaining the stability of society and its culture.

root metaphors Symbols that order conceptual experience by serving as points of reference for conceptual experience.

routinization of charisma The process by which, as groups become larger, they tend to develop a hierarchy of managers and decision-makers whose control is based on the authority of their office rather than personal charisma and whose authority becomes increasingly restricted to their own area of specialization.

sacred The quality of things that differ from the profane, or ordinary, everyday, work-a-day world, and are set apart and forbidden because of the special feelings they inspire.

sects Denominations that work within an established religious tradition but regard their distinctive doctrines and practices as uniquely true and valid in contrast with those of other denominations whom they judge to have departed from correct belief and practice.

secularization The process by which sectors of society and culture are removed from the domination of religious institutions and symbols; the diminution of the social significance of religion.

sensory symbols   Those conventional signs whose meanings relate to physiological facts and processes such as mother's milk, blood, menstruation, birth, semen, genitalia, sexual intercourse, excreta, and death and that produce strong feelings in participants in ritual that use them.

Septuagint   A translation of the Hebrew scriptures into Greek that was made in the second and third centuries B.C.

shaman   A part-time, charismatic religious specialist who conducts rituals for individual clients.

shamanic cult institution   The rituals of a religion that involve at least two persons, the ritual practitioner and a client who is intended to benefit from the performance of the practitioner.

shamanic religions   Religions in which only personal and shamanic rituals or ceremonies are performed.

shamanic rituals   Rituals performed by a religious specialist for the benefit of an individual or a group of clients when called upon to do so.

shame   The distressful emotion experienced when one believes that one is receiving more respect from others than is deserved.

signs   Objects or actions that have a natural meaning, based on the similarity between them and what they stand for, their consistent co-occurrence in nature with the things they stand for, or a connection between the two that is determined by biology.

songs   Meaningful speech produced as a part of music.

sorcerer   One who uses magical rituals for socially unapproved purposes.

sorcery   The use of learned magical rituals to harm other human beings.

soul   A spirit that is believed to animate the human body.

soul flight   Sending the soul out of the body to travel the spiritual plane, visit spirits, and obtain information for clients.

soul loss   The belief that one's spirit has left one's body, causing the body to languish, sicken, and, perhaps, to die.

sovereign groups   The parts of a social organization that have original and independent jurisdiction over some sphere of life.

spirit possession   The belief that a spirit has entered a person's body and taken control of his or her behavior, sometimes—particularly if the experience was not achieved intentionally through ritual—causing distress and/or illness.

spirit-possession rituals   Rituals in which the participant's personality is temporarily replaced by another that is attributed to a spirit who has taken control of the participant's behavior.

spirit-possession trance   A trance state that is subjectively experienced as giving up or losing personal control over one's actions while control is assumed by a spirit that has entered one's body.

spirit-travel trances   See *visionary trances.*

spirits   Supernatural beings whose power and influence is tied to a particular location or human group and whose power and influence is less than that of gods.

state churches   Religions that are sponsored and economically supported by the governments of nation-states.

status discrepancy   See *relative deprivation.*

stress The physiological changes by which the body begins to mobilize its energies to ward off disease or bodily tension from other causes.

structural meaning Meaning that is encoded into the way a story is organized; the relationships among the mythic symbols of myths and legends that form the underlying structure of the story and that convey a message concerning the tensions or conflicts in a society's ideology.

style, problem of The problem of determining how modern or archaic, how colloquial or formal, or how literal or idiomatic a translation should be.

summarizing symbols Key symbols that represent what a system means to the participants generically.

supernatural Pertaining to beings and powers that are believed to lie beyond the realm of natural things.

supernatural sanctions for violation of moral rules Supernatural punishments for violating moral rules or rewards for obeying them.

supernaturalistic philosophies Systems of thought that help us feel that we are a part of the world around us, rather than apart from it.

supernaturalistic thinking Thinking that confuses the locus of an experience by treating internal phenomena as extensions or results of external ones or external objects and events as extensions of the human ego.

Supreme Being A supernatural entity who is believed to have greater power than all other supernatural beings combined.

symbolism The expression of meaning through the use of symbols.

symbols Objects or events that stand for something else only because humans have established a consensus about what they mean (see also *ideological symbols, key symbols, sensory symbols, summarizing symbols,* and *symbolism*).

syncretism The process of mixing cultural traits often affects religion as well as other parts of culture.

system A group of interrelated parts.

taboo violation In the diagnosis of illness the belief that illness may result from the breaking of a spiritual rule.

taboos Rules against doing things that are believed to offend supernatural beings or trigger negative supernatural effects of mana.

technological rituals Rituals intended to control various aspects of nature in ways that improve the human ability to function.

textual basis, problem of The problem of determining which particular version of the original text should be chosen as the one to be translated.

theocracies Societies whose governments are based on the religious authority of their leaders.

theogonic myths Religious stories that recount the origins of the gods or supernatural beings.

therapy rituals Rituals performed by people to improve health and bodily functioning (see also *anti-therapy rituals*).

totem A symbolic representation of the kind of spirit believed to be shared by members of the same totemic clan.

totemism The belief that humans are divided into different social groups based on their different spiritual affinities to various plant or animal species.

trance states (altered states of consciousness) Psychological states in which a person loses his or her usual sense of separateness from the world and engages in supernaturalistic thinking.

trances Altered states of consciousness characterized by supernaturalistic thinking.

trickster deities Gods who act on impulse rather than thoughtfully, who enjoy playing jokes on others, and who often represent unconstrained or adolescent sexuality.

ultimate concerns An individual's or group's highest-priority values that are used as the ultimate reasons for things; whatever people take seriously without any reservation and what therefore is the source of the meaning of life for them; a set of symbolic forms and acts that relate humans to the ultimate condition of their existence.

ultimate sacred postulates The most sacred beliefs of a religion that define the essential basis for the rest of its ideology.

underdistanced Adjective describing an experience in which an emotion is felt so strongly that it is overwhelming.

value system A set of judgments about the goodness or desirability of things.

values Combinations of rules and corresponding feelings about what ought to be or not be, what is good or evil, desirable or undesirable.

visionary trances (or spirit-travel trances) A trance state that involves hallucinatory experiences which—though not necessarily—may even seem like an "out of the body" experience, one in which the ego seems to leave the body and is able to move about the environment or even enter a usually unseen spiritual realm while the body remains behind.

witch A supernatural being with the outward appearance of a human who has the innate power to do supernatural harm to human victims.

witchcraft The use of an innate, spiritual power to harm others.

women's cults Religious groups in which female shamans enter trances and become possessed by spirits to serve as mediums, diviners, and curers for their clients.

worldview Beliefs about the nature of reality, what kinds of rules it follows, how it came to be the way it is, and what supernatural beings and powers were involved in its origins.

worship Ritual performed to express adoration.

writing A system of symbols used to portray language in visual form.

zar cult A Sudanese women's spirit-possession cult.

Bibliography

Aberle, David. 1965. "A Note on Relative Deprivation Theory as Applied to Millenarian and Other Cult Movements." In *Reader in Comparative Religion*, 3rd ed., ed. William A. Lessa and Evon Z. Vogt, pp. 528–31. New York: Harper & Row.

Aberle, David. 1966. *The Peyote Religion among the Navaho*. London: Aldine.

Alland, Alexander. 1977. *The Artistic Animal: An Inquiry into the Biological Roots of Art*. Garden City, NY: Anchor Books.

Apffel-Marglin, Frédèrique. 1995. *Wives of the God-King: The Rituals of the Devadasis of Puri*. Delhi: Oxford University Press.

Asch, Timothy, and Napoleon A. Chagnon. 1975. *The Ax Fight*. Video. Watertown, MA: Documentary Educational Resources.

Atkinson, Jane Monnig. 1992. "Shamanism Today." *Annual Review of Anthropology* 21, pp. 307–30.

Basedow, H. 1925. *The Australian Aboriginal*. Adelaide, Australia: F. W. Preece.

Bellah, Robert. 1964. "Religious Evolution." *American Sociological Review* 29, pp. 358–74.

Bellah, Robert. 1964. "America's Civil Religion." *Daedalus* 1 (Winter), pp. 1–21.

Benson, Peter L. 1981. "God Is Alive in the U.S. Congress, but Not Always Voting Against Civil Liberties and for Military Spending." *Psychology Today* 15, no. 12, pp. 47–57.

Benson, Peter L., and Dorothy L. Williams. 1982. *Religion on Capitol Hill: Myths and Realities*. San Francisco: Harper & Row.

Berger, Peter. 1967. *The Sacred Canopy*. Garden City, NY: Doubleday.

Bergman, Robert. 1973. "A School for Medicine Men." *American Journal of Psychiatry* 130, no. 6, pp. 663–66.

Bernstein, Basil. 1965. "A Socio-Linguistic Approach to Social Learning." In *Penguin Survey of the Social Sciences*, ed. J. Gould, pp. 144–68. Harmondsworth: Penguin.

Bernstein, Basil. 1973. "A Socio-Linguistic Approach to Socialization." 1965. In *Directions in Socio-Linguistics*, ed. John Gumperz and Dell Hymes. New York: Vintage Books.

Boas, Franz. 1907. *The Eskimo of Baffin Land and Hudson Bay*. New York: American Museum of Natural History, *Bulletin of the American Museum of Natural History* 15.

Boddy, Janice Patricia. 1989. *Wombs and Alien Spirits: Women, Men, and the Zar Cult in Northern Sudan*. Madison: University of Wisconsin Press.

Borgoras, Waldemar. 1907. *The Chuckchee—Religion.* New York: American Museum of Natural History, *Memoirs of the American Museum of Natural History* 11, part 2.

Bourguignon, E., and L. Greenberg. 1973. *Homogeneity and Diversity in World Societies.* New Haven, CT: Human Relations Area Files.

Bourguignon, Erika. 1973. "Introduction: A Framework for the Comparative Study of Altered States of Consciousness." *In Religion, Altered States of Consciousness, and Social Change.* Columbus: Ohio State University Press.

Bourguignon, Erika. 1976. *Possession.* San Francisco: Chandler & Sharp.

Bourguignon, Erika. 1979. *Psychological Anthropology: An Introduction to Human Nature and Cultural Differences.* New York: Holt, Rinehart & Winston.

Bowman, Glenn. 1999. "Christian Ideology and the Image of a Holy Land: The Place of Jerusalem Pilgrimage in the Various Christianities." In *Contesting the Sacred,* ed. John Eade and Michael J. Sallow, pp. 98–121. London: Routledge.

Brady, Margaret K. 1984. *Some Kind of Power: Navajo Children's Skinwalker Narratives.* Salt Lake City: University of Utah Press.

Brown, Karen McCarthy. 1987. "Voodoo." In *The Encyclopedia of Religion,* Vol. 15, ed. Mircea Eliade, pp. 296–301. New York: Macmillan.

Buckland, Raymond. 1986. *Complete Book of Witchcraft.* St. Paul: Llewellen.

Cannon, Walter B. 1942. "The 'Voodoo' Death." *American Anthropologist* 44, pp. 169–81.

Chagnon, Napoleon A. 1992. *Yąnomamö.* 4th ed. Orlando, FL: Harcourt Brace Jovanovich.

Clements, Forest E. 1932. *Primitive Concepts of Disease.* Berkeley: University of California Press, *Publications in American Archaeology and Ethnology* 32, no. 2.

Coe, Michael. 1975. "Death and the Ancient Maya." In *Death and the Afterlife in Pre-Columbian America,* ed. E. P. Benson, pp. 87–104. Washington, DC: Dumbarton Oaks Research and Library Collections, Conference at Dumbarton Oaks, 17 October 1973.

Cohn, Werner. 1967. "'Religion' in Non-Western Culture?" *American Anthropologist* 69, pp. 73–76.

Cooper, J. M. 1946. "The Yahgan." In *Handbook of South American Indians,* ed. J. H. Stewart. *Bureau of American Ethnology Bulletin* 143, no. 1, pp. 97–98.

Cowdery, Warren A. 1835. Unpublished manuscript. Salt Lake City: LDS church archives.

Crapanzano, Vincent. 2000. *Serving the Word: Literalism in American from the Pulpit to the Bench.* New York: Free Press.

Crapo, Richley H. 1987. "Grass-roots Deviance from Official Doctrine: A Study of Latter-Day Saint (Mormon) Folk-Beliefs." *Journal for the Scientific Study of Religion* 26, no. 4, pp. 465–85.

Crapo, Richley H. 1995. *Cultural Anthropology: Understanding Ourselves and Others.* 4th ed. Guilford, CT: Brown & Benchmark.

D'Andrade, Roy G. 1961. "Anthropological Studies of Dreams." *In Psychological Anthropology,* ed. F. L. K. Hsu, pp. 296–332. Homewood, IL: Dorsey.

d'Aquili, Eugene, and Andrew Newberg. 1999. *The Mystical Mind: Probing the Biology of Religious Experience.* Minneapolis: Fortress Press.

Deardorff, Merle. 1951. "The Religion of Handsome Lake." In *Symposium on Local Diversity in Iroquois Culture.* Washington: Bureau of American Ethnology, Bulletin 149.

Debrunner, Hans W. 1961. *Witchcraft in Ghana: A Study on the Belief in Destructive Witches and Its Effects on the Akan Tribes.* Accra: Presbyterian Book Depot.

Douglas, Mary. 1966. *Purity and Danger: An Analysis of Concepts of Pollution and Taboo.* London: Routledge & Kegan Paul.

Douglas, Mary. 1970. *Natural Symbols.* New York: Random House.

Downs, James F. 1972. *The Navajo.* New York: Holt, Rinehart & Winston.

Durkheim, Emile. 1958. *The Rules of the Sociological Method.* 1895. Translated by Sarah A. Solovay and John H. Mueller. Glencoe, IL: Free Press.

Durkheim, Emile. 1961. *The Elementary Forms of the Religious Life.* 1912. Translated by Joseph Ward Swain. New York: Collier Books.

Eliade, Mircea. 1959. *The Sacred and the Profane: The Nature of Religion.* San Diego: Harcourt Brace Jovanovich.

Eliade, Mircea. 1974. *Shamanism: Archaic Techniques of Ecstasy.* 1951. Translated by Willard R. Trask. Princeton: Princeton University Press.

Evans-Pritchard, E. E. 1974. *Nuer Religion.* New York: Oxford University Press.

Fernandez, James. 1974. "The Mission of Metaphor in Expressive Culture." *Current Anthropology* 15, pp. 19–146.

Firth, Raymond. 1973. *Symbols: Public and Private.* Ithaca: Cornell University Press.

Frazer, Sir James George. 1925. *The Golden Bough: A Study in Magic and Religion.* 1911. New York: Macmillan.

Freed, Stanley A., and Ruth S. Freed. 1964. "Spirit Possession as Illness in a North Indian Village." *Ethnology* 3, no. 2, pp. 152–71.

Freud, Sigmund. 1907. "Obsessive Acts and Religious Practices." *Zeitschrift fur Religionpsychologie* 1, pp. 4–12. In *The Collected Papers of Sigmund Freud,* vol. 9. Translated by J. Riviere. Edited by J. Strachey. London: Hogarth Press.

Freud, Sigmund. 1928. *The Future of an Illusion.* Translated by W. D. Robson-Scott. Edinburgh: Horace Liveright and the Institute of Psycho-analysis.

Freud, Sigmund. 1930. *Civilization and Its Discontents.* New York: Jonathan Cape and Harrison Smith.

Freud, Sigmund. 1949. *Outline of Psycho-analysis.* 1940. Translated by J. Strachey. London: Hogarth.

Freud, Sigmund. 1950. *The Interpretation of Dreams.* 1900. Translated by Abraham A. Brill. London: Allen & Unwin.

Freud, Sigmund. 1964. *The Future of an Illusion.* 1927. Garden City, NY: Anchor Books.

Fried, M. N., and M. H. Fried. 1980. *Transitions: Four Rituals in Eight Cultures.* New York: Norton.

Friedl, Ernestine. 1975. *Women and Men: An Anthropologist's View.* New York: Holt, Rinehart & Winston.

Geertz, Clifford. 1966. "Religion as a Cultural System." In *Anthropological Approaches to the Study of Religion,* ed. Michael Banton, pp. 1–46. London: Tavistock.

Geertz, Clifford. 1973. *The Interpretation of Cultures.* New York: Basic Books.

Gibbs, J. L., ed. 1965. *Peoples of Africa.* New York: Holt, Rinehart & Winston.

Gluckman, Max G. 1959. *Customs and Conflicts in Africa.* Oxford: Blackwell.

Gmelch, George. 1978. "Baseball Magic." In Annual Editions: Anthropology 00/01, ed. Elvio Angeloni, pp. 177–81. Revised version of "Supersition and Ritual in American Baseball" *Elysisan Fields Quarterly* 11, no. 3 (1992), pp. 25–36.

Gödel, Kurt. 1962. *On Formally Undecidable Propositions.* New York: Basic Books.

Goldenweiser. Alexander. 1931. "Totemism." In *The Making of Man,* ed. V. F. Calverton, pp. 363–92. New York: Random House.

Greeley, Andrew M. 1975. *Sociology of the Paranormal: A Reconnaissance.* Beverly Hills: Sage.

Guthrie, Stewart Elliott. 1980. "A Cognitive Theory of Religion." *Current Anthropology* 21, no. 2, pp. 181–203.

Guthrie, Stewart Elliott. 1993. *Faces in the Clouds: A New Theory of Religion.* New York: Oxford University Press.

Hallowell, A. Irving. 1960. "Ojibwa Ontology, Behavior, and World View." In *Culture in History: Essays in Honor of Paul Radin,* ed. Stanley Diamond. New York: Columbia University Press.

Harding, Susan Friend. 2000. *The Book of Jerry Falwell: Fundamentalist Language and Politics.* Princeton: Princeton University Press.

Harner, Michael. 1977. "The Ecological Basis for Aztec Sacrifice." *American Ethnologist* 4, no. 1, pp. 117–35.

Harris, Marvin. 1972. "Riddle of the Pig." *Natural History* 81, no. 8, pp. 32–36.

Harris, Marvin. 1974. *Cows, Pigs, Wars, Witches: The Riddles of Culture.* New York: Random House.

Harris, Marvin. 1977. *Cannibals and Kings: The Origins of Culture.* New York: Random House.

Haught, James A. 1996. *2000 Years of Disbelief: Famous People with the Courage to Doubt.* Amherst, NY: Prometheus Books.

Herskovitz, Melville J. 1937. "African Gods and Catholic Saints in New World Religious Belief." *American Anthropologist* 39, pp. 635–43.

Hertz, Robert. 1973. "The pre-eminence of the Right Hand: A Study of Religious Polarity." 1909. Translated by Rodney Needham. In *Right and Left: Essays on Dual Symbolic Classification,* ed. Rodney Needham, pp. 3–31. Chciago: University of Chicago Press.

Hoberman, Barry. 1985. "Translating the Bible." *The Atlantic,* February, pp. 43–58.

Hood, R. W. J., Jr. 1977. "Eliciting Mystical States of Consciousness with Semistructured Nature Experiences." *Journal for the Scientific Study of Religion* 16, pp. 264–70.

Hood, R. W. J., Jr. 1978. "Anticipatory Set and Setting: Stress Incongruities as Elicitors of Mystical Experience in Solitary Nature Situations." *Journal for the Scientific Study of Religion* 17, pp. 279–87.

Horton, Robin. 1960. "A Definition of Religion, and Its Uses." *Journal of the Royal Anthropological Institute* 90, pp. 201–26.

Horton, Robin. 1967. "African Traditional Thought and Western Science." *Africa* 37, pp. 50–71, 155–87.

Horton, Robin. 1982. "Tradition and Modernity Revisited." In *Rationality and Relativism,* ed. Martin Holis and Steven Lukes, pp. 201–60. Cambridge, MA: MIT Press.

Howells, William. 1986. *The Heathens: Primitive Man and His Religions.* 1948. Salem, WI: Sheffield.

Howitt, A. W. 1904. *The Native Tribes of South-east Australia.* London: Macmillan.

Huntingon, W. R. 1973. "Death and the Social Order: Bara Funeral Customs (Madagascar)." *African Studies* 32, pp. 65–84.

Huxley, Julian. 1957. *Religion without Revelation.* New York: NAL.

Inglehart, Ronald, Miguel Basañez, and Alejandro Moreno. 1998. *Human Values and Beliefs: A Cross-Cultural Sourcebook: Political, Religious, Sexual, and Economic Norms in 43 Societies: Findings from the 1990–1993 World Value Survey.* Ann Arbor: University of Michigan Press.

Jansen, Karl L. R. 1997. "The Ketamine Model of the Near-Death Experience: A Central Role for the NMDA Receptor." *Journal of Near-Death Studies* 16, pp. 5–26.

Jenness, Diamond. 1935. *The Ojibwa Indians of Perry Island: Their Social and Religious Life.* Ottawa: J. O. Patenaude.

Judd, Daniel K. 1999. "Religiosity, Mental Health, and Latter-Day Saints." In *Latter-Day Saint Social Life: Social Research on the LDS Church and Its Members.* Provo, UT: Religious Studies Center, Brigham Young University, Specialized Mongraphs, no. 12.

Jung, Karl. 1938. *Psychology and Religion.* New Haven: Yale University Press.

Jung, Karl. 1958. *Psyche and Symbol.* New York: Doubleday.

Kardiner, Abram, and Ralph Linton. 1939. *The Individual and His Society.* New York: Columbia University Press.

Kardiner, Abram, and Ralph Linton. 1945. *The Psychological Frontiers of Society.* New York: Columbia University Press.

Kemper, T. D. 1978. *A Social Interactional Theory of Emotions.* New York: Wiley.

Kenton, E., ed. 1927. *The Indians of North America.* 2 vols. New York.

Kluckhohn, Clyde. 1944. *Navajo Witchcraft.* Boston: Beacon Press.

Kluckhohn, Clyde. 1959. "Recurrent Themes in Myths and Mythmaking" *Daedalus* 88, pp. 268–79.

Knowlton, David. 1997. "Intellectual Politics and the Unspeakable in Mormonism" *Sunstone* (April), pp. 46–51.

Korzybski, Alfred. 1933. *Science and Sanity: An Introduction to Non-Aristotelian Systems and General Semantics.* 5th ed. Englewood, NJ: Institute of General Semantics.

Kramer, Samuel Noah. 1981. *History Begins at Sumer.* 1956. Philadelphia: University of Philadelphia Press.

Kroeber, Alfred. 1900. *The Eskimo of Smith Sound.* Bulletin of the American Museum of Natural History, vol. XII, 1899, Article XII, pp. 265–327. New York: American Museum of Natural History.

Laing, R. D. 1961. *The Politics of Experience.* London: Penguin Books.

Lambek, Michael. 1998. "Taboo as Cultural Practice among Malgasy Speakers." In *Religion in Culture and Society,* ed. John R. Bowen. Boston: Allyn & Bacon.

Lambert, William, Leigh Triandis, and Margery Wolf. 1959. "Some Correlates of Beliefs in the Malevolence and Benevolence of Supernatural Beings: A Cross-Societal Study." *Journal of Abnormal and Social Psychology* 58, pp. 162–69.

Lansing, J. Stephen. *Priests and Programmers: Technology of Power in the Engineered Landscape of Bali.* Princeton: Princeton University Press.

Larson, D. B., K. A. Sherrill, J. S. Lyons, F. C. Craigie Jr., S. B. Thielman, M. A. Greenwold, and S. S. Larson. 1992. "Associations between Dimensions of Religious Commitment and Mental Health Reported in the *American Journal of Psychiatry* and *Archives of General Psychiatry:* 1978–1989." *American Journal of Psychiatry* 149, pp. 557–59.

Leach, Edmund. 1969. *Genesis as Myth and Other Essays.* London: Jonathan Cape.

Leighton, Alexander H., and Dorothy C. Leighton. 1949. *Gregorio, the Hand-Trembler: A Psychobiological Study of a Navaho Indian.* Harvard University, *Papers of the Peabody Museum of American Archaeology and Ethnology* 40, no. 1.

Lessa, William A., and Evon Z. Vogt, eds. 1965. *Reader in Comparative Religion: An Anthropological Approach.* New York: Harper & Row.

Levinson, David. 1996. *Religion: A Cross-Cultural Dictionary.* New York: Oxford University Press.

Lévi-Strauss, Claude. 1955. "The Structural Study of Myth." *Journal of American Folklore* 67, pp. 428–44.

Lévi-Strauss, Claude. 1969. *The Raw and the Cooked.* Vol. 1 of *Introduction to a Science of Mythology.* New York: Harper & Row.

Lévi-Strauss, Claude. 1973. *From Honey to Ashes.* Vol. 2 of *Introduction to a Science of Mythology.* New York: Harper & Row.

Lévi-Strauss, Claude. 1978. *Myth and Meaning.* London: Routledge & Kegan Paul.

Lewis, Ioan M. 1971. *Ecstatic Religion: An Anthropological Study of Spirit Possession and Shamanism.* Baltimore: Routledge & Kegan Paul.

Lewis, Ioan M. 1981. "What Is a Shaman?" *Folk* 23, pp. 25–35.

Lewis, Ioan M. 1986. *Religion in Context: Cults and Charisma.* Cambridge: Cambridge University Press.

Linton, Ralph. 1943. "Revitalization Movements." *American Anthropologist* 58, pp. 264–81.

Lowie, Robert. 1927. *Primitive Religion.* New York: Liveright.

Lowie, Robert H. 1954. "The Vision Quest among the North American Indians." In *Indians of the Plains,* by Robert H. Lowie. New York: McGraw-Hill.

Lucas, D. W. 1968. "Pity, Fear and Katharsis," Appendix 2 in Aristotle's *Poetics.* Oxford: Clarendon Press.

Malinowski, Bronislaw. 1935. *Coral Gardens and Their Magic.* 2 vols. London: Allen & Unwin.

Malinowski, Bronislaw. 1954. *Magic, Science, and Religion and Other Essays.* 1925. Garden City, NY: Doubleday.

Marett, Robert R. 1909. *The Threshold of Religion.* London: Methuen.

Marty, Martin E. 1993. "Fundamentalism and the Scholars." *The Key Reporter* 58, no. 3, pp. 1, 3–6.

Marx, Karl. 1844. "Introduction." In *Contributions to the Critique of Hegel's Philosophy of Law.* DeutschFranzösische Jahrbücher.

Marx, Karl. 1867. *Das Kapital.* Hamburg: Verlag von Otto Meissner.

Meggitt, M. 1964. "Male-Female Relationships in the Highlands of Australian New Guinea." In *New Guinea: The Central Highlands,* ed. J. B. Watson. Washington, DC: American Anthropological Association, Special Publication 6, no. 4, pt. 2.

Mernissi, Fatima. 1987. *Beyond the Veil: Male–Female Dynamics in Modern Muslim Society.* Bloomington: Indiana University Press.

Messing, Simon D. 1958. "Group Therapy and Social Status in the Zar Cult of Ethiopia." *American Anthropologist* 60, no. 6, pp. 1120–26.

Metcalf, P. 1991. *Celebrations of Death: The Anthropology of Mortuary Ritual.* New York: Cambridge University Press.

Minkoff, Harvey. 1989. "Coarse Language in the Bible? It's Culture Shocking!" *Bible Review* (April), pp. 22–27, 44.

Mooney, James. 1896. "The Ghost Dance Religion and the Sioux Outbreak of 1890." *14th Annual Report of the Bureau of American Ethnology, 1892–93,* Part 2. Washington, DC: Bureau of American Ethnology.

Moore, Omar Kayam. 1957. "Divination—A New Perspective." *American Anthropologist* 59, no. 1, pp. 69–74.

Müller, Friedrich Max. 1856. "Comparative Mythology." *Oxford Essays.* Vol. 2, pp. 1–87. London: W. Parker and Son.

Müller, Friedrich Max. 1870. *Lectures on the Science of Language.* New York: Scribner.

Murdock, Georg Peter. 1934. *Our Primitive Contemporaries.* New York: Macmillan.

Nadel, S. F. 1952. "Witchcraft in Four African Societies: An Essay in Comparison." *American Anthropologist* 54, no. 1, pp. 18–29.

Needham, Rodney. 1972. *Belief, Language, and Experience.* Oxford: Blackwell.

Noll, Richard. 1985. "Mental Imagery Cultivation as a Cultural Phenomenon: The Role of Visions in Shamanism." *Current Anthropology* 26, no. 4, pp. 443–61.

Obeyesekere, Gananath. 1984. *Medusa's Hair: An Essay on Personal Symbols and Religious Experience.* Chicago: University of Chicago Press.

Ohnuki-Tierney, Emiko. 1987. *The Monkey as Mirror: Symobolic Transformations in Japanese History and Culture.* Princeton: Princeton University Press.

Oosten, Jaarich G. 1986. "Male and Female in Inuit Shamanism." *Études/Inuit/Studies* 10, nos. 1–2, pp. 115–131.

Ortner, Sherry B. 1973. "On Key Symbols." *American Anthropologist* 15, no. 5, pp. 1338–46.

Ortner, Sherry B. 1974. "Is Female to Male as Nature Is to Culture?" In *Women, Culture, and Society,* ed. M. Z. Rosaldo and L. Lamphere, pp. 67–87. Stanford, CA: Human Relations Area Files.

Otto, Rudolph. 1923. *The Idea of the Holy: An Inquiry into the Non-Rational Factor in the Idea of the Divine and Its Relation to the Rational.* Translated by John. W. Harvey. London: Oxford University Press.

Pandian, Jacob. 1991. *Culture, Religion, and the Sacred Self: A Critical Introduction to the Anthropological Study of Religion.* Englewood Cliffs, NJ: Prentice-Hall.

Parker, Arthur C. 1913. *The Code of Handsome Lake, the Seneca Prophet.* Albany, NY: State Museum Bulletin, no. 163.

Parker, Seymour. 1962. "Eskimo Psychopathology in the Context of Eskimo Personality and Culture." *American Anthropologist* 64, pp. 76–96.

Parsons, Talcott. 1949. "The Theoretical Development of the Sociology of Religion." In *Essays in Sociological Theory Pure and Applied,* by Talcott Parsons, pp. 52–66. Glencoe, IL: Free Press.

Paul, Robert A. 1975. "The Sherpa Temle as a Model of the Psyche." *American Ethnologist* 3, pp. 131–46.

Pritchard, James B., ed. 1958. *The Ancient Near East: An Anthology of Texts and Pictures.* London: Oxford University Press.

Radin, Paul. 1937. *Primitive Religion.* New York: Dover.

Ramesh, Asha, & H. R. Philomena. 1984. "The Devadesi Problem." In *International Feminism: Networking against Female Sexual Slavery,* ed. Kathleen Barry, Charlotte Bunch, and Shirley Castley, pp. 82–87. New York: International Women's Tribune Centre.

Rappaport, Roy. 1966. Ritual in the Ecology of a New Guinea People: An Anthropological Study of the Tsemba Maring. Ph.D. diss., Columbia University.

Rappaport, Roy. 1967. "Ritual Regulation of Environmental Relations among a New Guinea People." *Ethnology* 6, pp. 17–30.

Rappaport, Roy. 1984. *Pigs for the Ancestors: Ritual in the Ecology of a New Guinea People.* 2nd ed. New Haven: Yale University Press.

Rappaport, Roy. 1999. *Ritual and Religion in the Making of Humanity.* London: Cambridge University Press.

Rasmussen, Knud. 1926a. "An Eskimo Shaman Purifies a Sick Person." In *Report of the Fifth Thule Expedition, 1921–24,* vol. 7, no. 1. *Intellectual Culture of the Iglulik Eskimos.* Copenhagen: Gyldendalske Boghandel, Nordisk Forlag, pp. 133–41. Reprinted in abridged form in *Reader in Comparative Religion: An Anthropological Approach,* ed. William Lessa and Evon Vogt, pp. 410–14. New York: Harper & Row, 1965.

Rasmussen, Knud. 1926b. "A Shaman's Journey to the Sea Spirit." In *Report of the Fifth Thule Expedition, 1921–24,* vol. 7, no. 1. *Intellectual Culture of the Iglulik Eskimos.* Copenhagen: Gyldendalske Boghandel, Nordisk Forlag, pp. 133–41. Reprinted in abridged form in *Reader in Comparative Religion: An Anthropological Approach,* ed. William Lessa and Evon Vogt, pp. 460–64. New York: Harper & Row, 1965.

Rasmussen, Knud. 1929. *The Intellectual Culture of the Iglulik Eskimos, Report of the Fifth Thule Expedition, 1921–24.* Vol. 8 (2–3). Copenhagen.

Reichard, Gladys. 1963. *Navaho Religion.* 1950. Princeton: Princeton University Press.

Root-Bernstein, Robert, & Donald L. McEachron. 1982. "Teaching Theories: The Evolution-Creation Controversy." *The American Biology Teacher* 44, October, pp. 413–20.

Rooth, Anna Brigita. 1957. "The Creation Myths of the North American Indians." *Anthropos* 52, pp. 497–508.

Saler, Benson. 1977. "Supernatural as a Western Category." *Ethos* 5, pp. 31–53.

Saler, Benson. 1993. *Conceptualizing Religion: Immanent Anthropologists, Transcendent Natives, and Unbounded Categories.* New York: E. J. Brill.

Sanday, Peggy. 1981. *Female Power and Male Dominance: On the Origins of Sexual Inequality.* New York: Cambridge University Press.

Sandner, Donald. 1979. *Navaho Symbols of Healing.* New York: Harcourt Brace Jovanovich.

Sapir, Edward. 1931. "Conceptual Categories in Primitive Languages." *Science* 74, p. 578.

Scheff, Thomas. 1977. "The Distancing of Emotion in Ritual." *Current Anthropology* 18, no. 3, pp. 483–505.

Schoek, Helmut. 1955. "The Evil Eye: Forms and Dynamics of a Universal Superstition." *Emory University Quarterly* 11, pp. 153–61.

Seligman, Kurt. 1948. *Magic, Supernaturalism, and Religion.* New York: Pantheon Books.

Selye, Hans. 1976. *The Stress of Life.* New York: McGraw-Hill.

Service, Elman R. 1978. *Profiles in Ethnology.* New York: Harper & Row.

Silverman, Julian. 1967. "Shamans and Acute Schizophrenia." *American Anthropologist* 69, pp. 21–31.

Simmons, Leo W. 1942. *Sun Chief: The Autobiography of a Hopi Indian.* New Haven: Yale University Press.

Smith, Anne M. *Shoshone Tales.* Salt Lake City: University of Utah Press.

Speck, F. 1909. *Ethnology of the Yuchi Indians.* Philadelphia: University of Pennsylvania Press. Anthropological Publications of the University Museum, Special Issue, no. 1, pt. 1.

Spilka, Bernard, Ralph Hood, and Richard Gorsuch. 1985. *The Psychology of Religion: An Empirical Approach.* Englewood Cliffs, NJ: Prentice-Hall.

Spiro, Melford. 1966. "Religion: Problems of Definition and Meaning." In *Anthropological Approaches to the Study of Religion,* ed. Michael Banton, pp. 85–126. London: Tavistock.

Spiro, Melford E., and Roy G. Andrade. 1958. "A Cross-Cultural Study of Some Supernatural Beliefs." *American Anthropologist* 60, pp. 456–66.

Starhawk. 1989. *The Spiral Dance: A Rebirth of the Ancient Religion of the Goddess.* San Francisco: Harper.

Stark, Rodney. 1965. "A Taxonomy of Religious Experience." *Journal for the Scientific Study of Religion* 5, pp. 97–116.

Stark, Rodney. 1999. "A Theory of Revelations." *Journal for the Scientific Study of Religion* 38, no. 2, pp. 287–307.

Stark, Rodney, and William Sims Bainbridge. 1997. *Religion, Deviance, and Social Control.* New York: Routledge.

Strathern, M. 1980. "No Nature, No Culture: The Hagen Case." In *Nature, Culture, and Gender,* ed. C. P. MacCormack & M. Strathern, pp. 174–222. Cambridge: Cambridge University Press.

Swanson, Guy E. 1974. *The Birth of the Gods: The Origin of Primitive Beliefs.* Ann Arbor: University of Michigan Press.

Swift Arrow, Bernadine. 1974. "Funeral Rites of the Quechan Tribe." *Indian Historian* 7, pp. 22–24.

Tambiah, Stanley J. 1973. "Form and Meaning of Magical Acts: A Point of View." In *Modes of Thought: Essays on Thinking in Western and Non-Western Societies.* London: Faber & Faber.

Tedlock, Barbara. 1992. *The Beautiful and the Dangerous: Encounters with the Zuni Indians.* New York: Viking Penguin.

Thompson, Lady Gwen. 1975. "Wiccan-Pagan Potpourri." *Green Egg* 8, no. 69.

Tillich, Paul. 1948. *The Shaking of the Foundation.* New York: Scribner's.

Tillich, Paul. 1963. *Christianity and the Encounter with the World Religions.* New York: Columbia University Press.

Toelken, Barre. 1987. "Life and Death in the Navajo Coyote Tales." In *Recovering the Word: Essays on Native American Literature,* ed. Brian Swann and Arnold Krupat, pp. 388–401. Berkeley: University of California Press.

Toelken, Barre. 1994. Native American Reassessment and Reinterpretation of Myths. Unpublished paper presented at Symposium on Myth, University of Illinois, Bloomington, Illinois.

Toelken, Barre. 1996. "From Entertainment to Realization in Navajo Fieldwork." In *The World Observed: Reflections on the Fieldwork Process,* ed. Bruce Jackson and Edward D. Ives, pp. 1–17. Urbana: University of Illinois Press.

Toffelmeier, G., and K. Luomala. 1936. "Dreams and Dream Interpretation of the Diegueino Indians of Southern California." *Psychoanalytic Quarterly* 2, pp. 195–225.

Torrey, E. Fuller. 1986. *Witch Doctors and Psychiatrists.* New York: Harper & Row.

Townsend, Joan B. "Shamanism." In *Anthropology of Religion,* ed. Stephen D. Glazier, pp. 429–69. Westport, CT.: Greenwood Press.

Tozzer, Alfred. 1907. *A Comparative Study of the May and the Lacandones.* New York: Macmillan.

Turnbull, Colin M. 1961. *The Forest People: A Study of the Pygmies of the Congo.* New York: Simon and Schuster.

Turner, Victor W. 1967. *The Forest of Symbols: Aspects of Ndembu Ritual.* Ithaca: Cornell University Press.

Turner, Victor W. 1969. *The Ritual Process: Structure and Anti-Structure.* Chicago: Aldine.

Turner, Victor W. 1971. Pilgrimages as Social Processes. Paper presented at the Department of Anthropology, Washington University, St. Louis, in February 1971. Reprinted in Victor Turner. *Dramas, Fields, and Metaphors: Symbolic Actions in Human Society,* by Victor Turner. New York: Cornell University Press, 1974, pp. 166–230.

Turner, Victor W. 1972. "Religious Specialists." In *International Encyclopedia of the Social Sciences,* ed. David L. Silts, vol. 13, pp. 437–44. New York: Crowell Collier and Macmillan.

Turner, Victor W., and Edith Turner. 1978. *Image and Pilgrimage in Christian Culture.* New York: Columbia University Press, Lectures on the History of Religions Series.

Tylor, Edward Burnett. 1873. *Primitive Culture: Researches into the Development of Mythology, Philosophy, Religion, Language, Art and Custom.* 2nd ed. 2 vols. London: John Murray.

Tylor, Edward Burnett. 1958. *Primitive Culture: Researches into the Development of Mythology, Philosophy, Religion, Language, Art and Custom.* 1871. London: John Murray.

Tylor, Edward Burnett. 1960. *Anthropology.* 1881. Ann Arbor: University of Michigan Press.

Underhill, Ruth. 1955. *Mysticism: A Study in the Nature and Development of Man's Spiritual Consciousness.* New York: Noonday Press.

U.S. Chaplains' Service Institute. 1990. *Religious Requirements and Practices of Certain Selected Groups: A Handbook for Chaplains.* Montgomery, AL: U.S. Chaplains' Service Institute.

Van Gennep, Arnold. 1960. *The Rites of Passage.* 1909. Translated by Monika B. Vizedom and Gabrielle L. Caffee. Chicago: University of Chicago Press.

Wach, Joachim. 1944. *Sociology of Religion.* Chicago: University of Chicago Press.

Wallace, Anthony F. C. 1956. "Nativistic Movements." *American Anthropologist* 45, pp. 230–40.

Wallace, Anthony F. C. 1958. "Dreams and Wishes of the Soul: A Type of Psychoanalytic Theory among the Seventeenth Century Iroquois." *American Anthropologist* 60, no. 2, pp. 234–48.

Wallace, Anthony F. C. 1966a. *Culture and Personality.* New York: Random House

Wallace, Anthony F. C. 1966b. *Religion: An Anthropological View.* New York: Random House.

Wallace, Anthony F. C. 1967. "Dreams and the Wishes of the Soul: A Type of Psychoanalytic Theory among the Seventeenth Century Iroquois." In *Magic, Witchcraft, and Curing,* ed. John Middleton, pp. 171–90. Garden City, NY: Natural History Press.

Warner, W. Lloyd. 1958. *A Black Civilization: A Study of an Australian Tribe.* 1937. New York: Harper & Row.

Weber, Max. 1904. *The Protestant Ethic and the Spirit of Capitalism.* London: Allen & Unwin.

Weber, Max. 1963. *The Sociology of Religion.* 1922. Translated by Ephraim Fischoff. Boston: Beacon Press.

White, Andrew Dixon. 1896. *A History of the Warfare of Science with Theology in Christendom.* 2 vols. New York: Appleton.

White, Leslie A. 1947. "The Expansion of the Scope of Science." *Journal of the Washington Academy of Sciences* 37, 181–210.

White, Leslie A. 1959. *The Evolution of Culture: The Development of Civilization to the Fall of Rome.* New York: McGraw-Hill.

White, Leslie A. 1969. *The Science of Culture: A Study of Man and Civilization.* 1949. New York: Farrar, Straus and Giroux.

Whiting, Beatrice. 1950. "A Cross-Cultural Study of Sorcery and Social Control." In *Paiute Sorcery,* ed. Beatrice Blyth Whiting, pp. 82–91. New York: *Viking Fund Publications in Anthropology,* no. 15.

Whiting, J. W. M., and I. L. Childe. 1953. *Child Training and Personality: A Cross-Cultural Study.* New Haven: Yale University Press.

Whorf, Benjamin Lee. 1956a. "Languages and Logic." In *Language, Thought, and Reality: Selected Writings of Benjamin Lee Whorf,* ed. J. B. Carroll, pp. 233–45. Cambridge, MA: MIT Press.

Whorf, Benjamin Lee. 1956b. "The Relation of Habitual Thought and Behavior to Language." In *Language, Thought, and Reality: Selected Writings of Benjamin Lee Whorf,* ed. J. B. Carroll, pp. 134–59. Cambridge, MA: MIT Press.

Williams, Frederick G. 1832. Unpublished manuscript. Salt Lake City: LDS Church Archives.

Wilson, Brian. 1980. Kut: Catharsis, Ritual Healing, or Redressive Strategy? Paper presented at the Conference on Korean Religion and Society, Mackinac Island, Michigan.

Wilson, Bryan. 1982. *Religion in Sociological Perspective.* New York: Oxford University Press.

Wilson, Daniel. 1904. *Western Africa.* Quoted in R. H. Nassau. *Fetichism in West Africa: Forty-One Years' Observations and Superstition.* London: Duckworth.

Wixen, Joan. 1976. "Author of Roots Recalls Emotion of Discovery." *Detroit News,* June 15, p. B 12.

Worsley, Peter. 1957. *The Trumpet Shall Sound: A Study of "Cargo" Cults in Melanesia.* London: MacGibbon & Kee.

Worsley, Peter. 1959. "Cargo Cults." *Scientific American* 200 (May), pp. 117–28.

X, Malcolm. 1966. *Autobiography of Malcolm X.* New York: Grove.

Yamane, David, and Megan Polzer. 1994. "Ways of Seeing Ecstasy in Modern Society: Experiential-Expressive and Cultural-Linguistic Views." *Sociology of Religion* 55, pp. 1–25.

Yang, C. K. 1961. *Religion in Chinese Society.* Berkeley: University of California Press.

Young, Andrew. 1993. "Foreword." In *Black Bible Chronicles.* Book 1: *From Genesis to the Promised Land.* New York: African American Family Press.

Credits

Text

Excerpts from "The Creation Epic," trans. F. A. Speiser. In James B. Pritchard, ed., *The Ancient Near East: An Anthology of Texts and Pictures.* Copyright © 1958 by Princeton University Press. Reprinted by permission of Princeton University Press.

Alexander Alland Jr.: From *When the Spider Danced* (Garden City, NY: Anchor Books, 1975), pp. 125–26. Reprinted by permission of Alexander Alland Jr.

Kurt Seligmann: From *Magic, Supernaturalism and Religion* by Kurt Seligmann, copyright 1948 by Pantheon Books Inc. Used by permission of Pantheon Books, a division of Random House, Inc.

Barre Toelken: From "Life and Death in the Navajo Coyote Tales." In Brian Swann and Arnold Krupat, eds., *Recovering the Word: Essays on Native American Literature* (Berkeley: University of California Press, 1987). Reprinted by permission of Barre Toelken.

Barre Toelken: From "Native American reassessment and reinterpretation of myths." Unpublished paper presented at Symposium on Myth, University of Indiana, Bloomington, Indiana, 1994, p. 5. Reprinted by permission of Barre Toelken.

Anthony F. C. Wallace: From *Religion: An Anthropological View* by Anthony F. C. Wallace, copyright © 1966 by Random House, Inc. Used by permission of Random House, Inc.

Brian Wilson: From "Kut: Catharsis, ritual healing or redressive strategy?" Paper presented at the Conference on Korean Religion and Society, Mackinac Island, Michigan, 1980. © 1980 by Brian Wilson.

Bryan Wilson: From *Religion in Sociological Perspective* (Oxford: Oxford University Press, 1981). Reprinted by permission of Oxford University Press.

Photos

Author Photo, provided by Richley H. Crapo

© Lindsay Hebberd/CORBIS, Figure 1.1

Bonnie Glass-Coffin, Figure 1.2

© Bruno Barbey/Magnum Photos, Figure 2.1

Courtesy Dept. of Library Services, American Museum of Natural History, Negative #319671/Photo. Rota, Figure 3.1

Index

bold page numbers indicate definitions
f indicates a figure
n indicates a footnote. For example, "142n1" means the information appears on page 142 in footnote 1
t indicates a table

Grossini, Dennis, 51–52
Guilt, **65**
Guthrie, Stewart Elliott, 20–21, 24, 158, 278–279

Habits, contrast with rituals, 36
Hair, as source of natural symbols, 78, 132–133
Haitian Voodoo, 263
Haley, Alex, 118
Hallowell, A. Irving, 11
Handedness, as source of natural symbols, 133
Handsome Lake, 55
Harding, Susan Friend, 268–269, 280
Hargrove, E. C., 280
Harner, Michael, 258
Harris, Marvin, 21, 96, 256, 257, 258, 280
Haught, James A., 95
Heaven's Gate community, 117
Hebrew language and secular used of sacred language, 166–167
Hebrew religion; *See* Judaism
Hebrews of Mosaic era
    Yahweh given masculine characteristics of war god, 243
Herskovitz, Melville J., 263
Hertz, Robert, 133
High gods, **32**
Highway hypnosis, 71
Hillel, 145
Hinduism
    caste system, 240
    diversity within religion, 152–154
    moral values, 35
    pilgrimages, 201
    primary and secondary scriptures, 153
    Problem of Evil, 163
    renunciation of worldly life as expressive culture, 127, 127*f*
    sacred texts, 164
    Sri Lankan female aesthetics and hair symbolism, 133
    zebu cows, veneration of, 257–258, 257*f*
Hoberman, Barry, 167, 168
Hogbin, Ian, 229
Holiness churches and social standing of members in United States, 69
Holy, experience of, 123–126
Homeopathic (or imitative) magic, **194**
Hood, R. W. J., 78
Hood, R. W. J., Jr., 126
Hood, Ralph, 237
Hopi Indians
    kachina masks, 107
    sacred clowns and religious rituals, 120
    witches and witchcraft, 103
Horticultural societies, 86, 223, 224
Horton, Robin, 49, 50, 67
Hostetler, John, 229
Howells, William, 58, 213
Howitt, A. W., 199
Huichol, and use of peyote cactus, 137
Human artifacts as religious symbols, 105–108
Human body
    as material metaphor in preformance of ritual, 130
    natural symbols, source of, 129–133
    rituals influencing, 190–192
Human psyche; *see* Psyche
Humanistic approaches to defining religion, 5
Humans as models for complex phenomena, 20
Hunsberger, B., 78
Huntington, Gertrude Enders, 229

Huntington, W. R., 66
Hutterites, 229
Huxley, Julian, 7
Hypnotic and trance states, parallels between, 59–60

Ideological symbols, **122**
Ideology; *See also* Religious ideology
    day-to-day decision making, and secularization, 264
    defined, **146**
    religion and existential questions, 278
    rituals of ideology, 196
    variation in, 155
Idiomatic (or dynamic equivalence) translation, **169**, 171
Iglulik Eskimo shaman, 213
Illnesses, beliefs concerning supernatural causes, 214–216
Imitative magic (homeopathic magic), **194**
India
    Devadasi priestesses, 41, 41*f*
    Hinduism, diversity within religion, 153
    reincarnation beliefs, 100
    sacred cows, 257–258, 257*f*
    sexual religious beliefs and practices, 40
    Shanti Nagar, spirit possession in, 61–62
    spirit possession as anxiety disorders, 61
    Toda people of Deccan Plateau, religious beliefs and practices, 40
Individualistic cult institution, **210**, 223
Indus Valley civilization, as theocracy, 235–236
Industrial societies, 212, 264, 265
Initial rituals, 199
Inquisition (Middle Ages), 154
Inspiration, as religious behavior, 39
Institutional specialization and differentiation, and secularization, 262
Intellectual functions of religion, 49–50
Interpretation, problem of, **168**
Inuit people
    food taboos and social responsibility, 9
    shamans (angakkut), 213
    taboo violations and shamanic curing, 216
Iroquois Indians
    ceremonial curing rituals, 67*f*
    dream therapy, 76
    dreams and ceremonies, 38
    egalitarian society and role of women in religion, 243
    Handsome Lake, religion of, 55
Isaiah 7:14b, 169
Isaiah 13:16, 170
Isaiah 32:7, 171
Islam
    Hajj (pilgrimage), 202, 203–204
    Islamic fundamentalism, 276
    Kalimat al Shahada, as summary of ultimate sacred postulates, 186–187
    moral values, 35
    pilgrimages, 201
    sacred texts, 165
    sacredness of original language, 166
    sharia (Islamic laws), 276
    women as shamans in Islamic saint cults, 246–247
    women's cults in Islamic countries, 244
Italy
    evil eye, belief in, 104
Iwasaka, Michiko, 109

Jansen, Karl L. R., 75
Japan
    Barakumin, as example of religion perpetuating social inequality, 204

purification ceremony, 253*f*
Shinto, incorporating Buddhist beliefs and practices, 268
Shinto beliefs and rituals, 179–180
Jasper, John, 204–205
Jenness, Diamond, 216
Jeremiah 3:1–2, 170
Job 2:9, 158
Jones, Jim, 117, 226
Judaism
    Abraham's offer of hospitality as key scenario, 84
    adultry, cultural relativism in interpretation of sacred texts, 151
    bar mitzvah, 182, 200
    bat mitzvah, 200
    blasphemy, and religious linguistic taboos, 158
    food taboos of Leviticus, study of, 93–94, 127
    forms of address as restricted code, 156
    Hebrew bible, origin, 142–145, 164
    kosher kitchens, as taboos, 35, 126–127, 190
    life-crisis rites, 182
    Masoretic text, 168
    menorah, as ideological symbol, 122
    mikvah ceremony, 136
    minyan, 182
    moral values, 35
    Passover Seder, 34, 39, 112–114, 196
    pig taboo, 94, 256
    pilgrimages, 201
    religious ritual implements, 107
    sacred texts, 142–145, 164, 167, 168, 170
    secular used of sacred language, problem of, 166–167
    Septuagint, 168
    Shema, as statement of ultimate sacred postulates, 183, 184, 185
    social standing of members in United States, 69
    trees, symbolism of, 135
Judd, Daniel K., 58
Judeo-Christian religion; *see* Christianity

Kachina masks, 107
Kalweit, Holger, 78
Kardiner, Abram, 18–19
Karma, 154, 204
Kemper, T. D., 63, 64*t*
Kenton, E., 76
Ketamine model of the Near-Death Experience, 75
Key scenarios, **84**
Key symbols, **84**, 109
King, Martin Luther, 268
King James bible, 169, 171, 173, 174, 175
2 Kings 3:9, 170
2 Kings 18:27, 170
Kingsborough, Susan Farrell, 248
Klein, Moshe Shaul, 167
Kluckhohn, Clyde, 86, 93, 220
Knowlton, David, 157, 158
Korean shaminism, 244
Korzybski, Alfred, 174
Kosher rules, 127–128
Kramer, Henry, 255
Kramer, Samuel Noah, 132
Kroeber, Alfred, 37
!Kung San foragers, gods of east and west, 134
Kut healing ritual (Korea), 73
Kwakiutl Indians, human sacrifice rituals, 40

Symbols and symbolism; *see* Religious symbols and symbolism
Syncretism (religious), **261**, 263

Taboos; *See also* Food taboos; Supernatural
  common characteristic of religion, 101, 126
  defined, **9**, 190
  malagasy, 190
  mana, 9
  negative piety values, 35
  religious anti-rituals, 157, 190
  as religious behavior, 38
  religious language and linguistic taboos, 157–158
  religious taboos and social responsibility, 9–10
  violations, 190, **216**
Talayesva, Don, 120
Taliban, 280
Tambiah, Stanley J., 130
Tapirapé vision trance, 74*f*
Tarahumara, use of peyote cactus, 137
"Taxonomy of Religious Experience, A" (Stark), 272
Technical order and secularization, 266–267, 274
Technological change and secularization, 264–267
Technological rituals, **188**, 188–190, 189*f*; *See also* Rituals
Tedlock, Barbara, 124–125, 139
Ten Commandments, legal controversies in United States, 266
Textual basis, problem of, **168**
Theocracies, 235–237, **236**, 264
Theogonic myths, **31**
"Theory of Revelations, A" (Stark), 272
Therapy rituals, **190**, 190–191
1 Thessalonians 4:15, 171
2 Thessalonians 2:7, 171, 175
2 Thessalonians 5:22, 174
Thielman, S. B., 58
Tillich, Paul, 16, 128
Toelken, Barre, 104, 109, 164, 184–185
Toffelmeier, G., 74
Torah (Jewish scriptures), 145
Torrey, E. Fuller, 59
Totem, **15**
Totemism
  in Aboriginal Australian societies, 15, 121, 253–254
  defined, **253**
Touch, to obtain or transfer supernatural power, 38
Townsend, Joan B., 214
Tozzer, Alfred, 134
Trance states (altered states of consciousness)
  common elements, 71
  defined, **70**
  in expressive culture, 116
  Navajo hand trembler, 118–119, 119*f*
  and religion, 71–74, 72*f*
Trances; *see* Spirit-possession trances; Trance states (altered states of consciousness); Visionary trances (or spirit-travel trances)
  daydreaming, 71
  dreams as religious experiences, 74–75
  expressive culture, characteristic of, 115
  highway hypnosis, 71
  mystical religious experiences, brain processes during, 75, 77

overview, 70–71
  religious trance, 72*f*
Translation of sacred texts, 167, 168–172
Trees, as source of natural symbols, 134–135
Triandis, Leigh, 19
Trickster deities, **137**
Trobriand Islanders, and magic, 16, 50–51
Turnbull, Colin M., 2
Turner, Edith, 201
Turner, Victor W., 17, 25, 35, 110, 122, 123, 197, 201, 202, 207, 221, 224–225
Tylor, Edward Burnett, 8–9, 49

Ultimate concerns, religion as, **16**, 128–129
Ultimate sacred postulates, **183**, 185–187
Underdistanced, **66**
Underhill, Ruth, 57
United States
  American Christian fundamentalism, 275–276
  Black slaves, religion and rituals of resistance, 204–205
  civil religion in, 238
  literalist thinking, 148
  millenarian movements, 270
  secularization in, 239–240
  separation of church and state, 239–240, 264
  social standing and membership in particular religious denominations, 69
Urination, as source of natural symbols, 131–132
U.S. Chaplains' Service Institute, 217
Utah, religion and government in territorial times, 236

Valiente, Doreen, 217
Values
  defined, **35**
  as guides for behavior, 35, 126–129
  religion as, 16
Van Gennep, Arnold, 36, 129, 198–199, 248
Vander, Judith, 139
Vecsey, C., 43
Violation of moral rules, supernatural sanctions, 101–102
Violation of social norms, religious sanctions, 235
Visionary trances (or spirit-travel trances)
  and anxiety disorders, 58
  characteristics of, 74
  defined, **72**
  dreams, similarities to, 74–75
  near-death experiences, 75, 77
  as practice of male shamans, 245
  Siberian, 216
  Tapirapé vision trance, 74*f*
  vision quest, 209
Vogt, Evon Z., 16, 43, 128, 223
"Voodoo" (Brown, Karen McCarthy), 263
Voodoo religion, 261, 263, 268

Wach, Joachim, 219, 221
Wallace, Anthony F. C., 16–17, 38, 53, 55, 57, 76, 124, 159, 180, 181, 183, 188, 190, 192, 193, 196, 201, 205, 210, 222, 223, 224, 270–271, 271
Warner, W. Lloyd, 51
Washington, George, 238
Water, as source of natural symbols, 136
Water of Life, in Sumerian religion, 234
Waterfalls, as source of natural symbols, 137
Weber, Max, 14, 222, 240, 241, 248, 268, 269

Western Europe
  state churches in, 238–239
Western theology and Problem of Evil, 162–163
White, Leslie A., 19–20, 71, 75, 95, 264–265
Whiting, Beatrice, 235
Whiting, J. W. M., 102
Whorf, Benjamin Lee, 174, 176
Wicca, 107, 136, 217–218
Williams, Dorothy L., 237–238
Williams, Frederick G., 56
Wilson, Brian, 73
Wilson, Bryan, 238, 240, 262, 266, 267, 274
Wilson, Daniel, 199
Wilson, Jack; *see* Wovoka
Witches and witchcraft
  accusations of, as threat to end suspicious behavior, 103
  evil eye, 103–105
  Hopi Indians, 103
  law enforcement, witchcraft as functional equivalent of, 102
  Malleus Maleficarum, 255
  men's and women's roles tied to society's social organization and culture, 244
  Navajo Indians, 29, 104, 105, 132, 185, 220–221
  Salem witchcraft trials, 70
  shamanic curing, 216
  sorcery, contrasts between, 102–105
  testing accused persons by dunking in river, 136
  viewed as sin in Ashanti kingdom, 237
  Wicca, 107, 136, 217–218
  witchcraft, defined, **102**, 216
  witchcraft myths, themes of, 93
Wixen, Joan, 118
Wolf, Margery, 19
Women's cults, 73, **244**
Worldview, **85**; *See also* Religious worldview
Worship, **195**
Worship rituals, 195–196
Worsley, Peter, 269–270
Wovoka, 222*f*, 251
Writing, **146**

Yąnomamö Indians
  origin myth, 87–88, 161–162
Yahgan (Tierra del Fuego)
  birth, rites of passage, 199
Yahweh, written versions of name, 142n1
Yamane, David, 272
Yang, C. K., 202
Yenaldlooshi. *See* Navajo skinwalkers, 220
Yokuts Indians, 107*f*
Young, Andrew, 173
Young, Brigham, 236
Yuchi Indians
  egalitarian society and role of women in religion, 243
Yurok-Samoyed shaman, 212

Zar cult
  Ethiopia, 60–61
  Sudan, 246–247, 248
  zar, defined, 60
Zechariah 14:2, 170
Zetterberg, P., 277
Zobiginigan, 218
Zuñi Indians
  ethnography, 139
  mana, symbolism of, 124–125
  Our Lady of Guadalupe Church, 262*f*
  Shalako celebration, 125